WORKPLACE COMMUNICATION

Workplace Communication highlights how we can build interpersonal relationships through effective communication and why this is essential to workplace wellbeing. Well-supported by contemporary, reputable empirical studies, the book also comes with exercises and open-ended questions based on the subject matter.

The book

- provides a comprehensive overview on creating an inclusive workplace and managing workplace diversity;
- covers a wide range of salient, up-to-date reputable literature on a wide range of management and business topics;
- contains practical, 'road-tested' activities to promote student reflection, experiential learning, critical thinking, research skills, and application of theory to practice and vice versa;
- examines how we communicate effectively to an increasingly diverse workforce.

Designed for a broad audience, this book will appeal to academics and students in the fields of business management and communications. It will also be a useful reference for organisational practitioners and leaders.

Joanna Crossman is Adjunct Associate Professor at the University of South Australia and Visiting Fellow at the Australian National University, College of Business and Economics, Canberra.

'*Workplace Communication* by Joanna Crossman is written in a well-organized manner: readers benefit from its rich contents, interesting examples, as well as contrasting similarities and differences. It brings together latest research findings from psychology, sociology, organizational behaviors, linguistics, and critical studies to shed insights on workplace communication patterns. It can be used as a text for upper class undergraduate program or master program of human resources management, communication, as well as organizational psychology.'

Kara Chan, *Professor of Communication Studies and Associate Dean (Teaching & Learning), School of Communication and Film, Hong Kong Baptist University*

'This book takes an innovative approach to contemporary communication challenges. It covers essential communication concepts and applies them to the context of diverse stakeholders in the workplace. Of particular interest to readers will be the chapters on intercultural and spiritual diversities. The majority of workplaces struggle with intercultural and multilingual communication and spiritual diversity can often be the elephant in the room. Dr. Crossman effectively handles these issues in the book and deftly incorporates research and practice implications for workplace communication.'

Sarbari Bordia, *Professor, Research School of Management, Australia National University, Australia*

'This book represents a timely publication as the workplace is becoming increasingly multicultural. It also provides the reader with a solid reference in Part II to intercultural theories and dimensions that are crucial for interactions and communication in the multicultural workplace.

Other chapters of this book cover additional topics with relevant theories that are focussed upon the workplace contexts such as conflict resolution, interpersonal communication, emotion at work and ethical approaches for building relationships. What is also appealing is the communication and language perspective for managing workplace diversity and conflicts and negotiation as a value-adding process.

I recommend that this book is of great relevance for both academics and practitioners to have a better understanding of communication as an important approach to not only managing organizational diversity but also contributing to a positive ambience and culture at the workplace.'

Yunxia ZHU, *Associate Professor at University of Queensland, Australia and Vice President (Chairperson) of the Asian Pacific Region of Association for Business Communication*

WORKPLACE COMMUNICATION

Promoting Workplace Wellbeing and Interpersonal Relationships in Multicultural Contexts

Joanna Crossman

Routledge
Taylor & Francis Group

LONDON AND NEW YORK

Cover image: Anastasia Benveniste

First published 2023
by Routledge
4 Park Square, Milton Park, Abingdon, Oxon OX14 4RN

and by Routledge
605 Third Avenue, New York, NY 10158

Routledge is an imprint of the Taylor & Francis Group, an informa business

British Library Cataloguing-in-Publication Data
A catalogue record for this book is available from the British Library

Library of Congress Cataloging-in-Publication Data
Names: Crossman, Joanna, author.
Title: Workplace communication : promoting workplace wellbeing and
    interpersonal relationships in multicultural contexts / Joanna Crossman.
Description: Abingdon, Oxon ; New York, NY : Routledge, 2023. |
    Includes bibliographical references and index.
Identifiers: LCCN 2022006246 (print) | LCCN 2022006247 (ebook) |
    ISBN 9780367332662 (hardback) | ISBN 9780367332679 (paperback) |
    ISBN 9780429318948 (ebook)
Subjects: LCSH: Communication in organizations. | Communication in
    management. | Intercultural communication. | Interpersonal relations. |
    Organizational behavior.
Classification: LCC HD30.3 .C76 2023 (print) | LCC HD30.3 (ebook) |
    DDC 658.4/5—dc23/eng/20220211
LC record available at https://lccn.loc.gov/2022006246
LC ebook record available at https://lccn.loc.gov/2022006247

ISBN: 978-0-367-33266-2 (hbk)
ISBN: 978-0-367-33267-9 (pbk)
ISBN: 978-0-429-31894-8 (ebk)

DOI: 10.4324/9780429318948

Typeset in Bembo
by Apex CoVantage, LLC

This book is dedicated to the ones I love: Brian, Alex, Aston, Anastasia, and Sam

CONTENTS

TABLES

INTRODUCTION TO THE BOOK

Traditionally, disciplinary scholars have separated their own focus from others in distinct terms, largely in ways that assume a honed and knowledgeable approach to understanding aspects of a particular context deeply. Despite the merits of this academic strategy, the text brings a holistic perspective to explore the meanings embedded in workplaces by drawing upon the empirical and scholarly contributions in a transdisciplinary way. That said, communication literature is a consistent thread running throughout the work, based on the well-established rationale that communicating effectively is essential to the success of organisations and the formation of positive interpersonal relationships at work. Nevertheless, a largely transdisciplinary approach is particularly valuable when investigating the interrelationship between quantitative and qualitative, the material and easily measurable, juxtaposed with the sometimes subtle but nevertheless highly influential elements of humanity: emotions, values, culture, spirituality, physical and mental health and wellbeing. The aim of this book is to intertwine all these elements in order to make sense of workplace experiences.

Although each of the chapters within this book has been written on a notionally 'stand-alone' basis, it would be remiss not to urge readers to experience it as a whole, in order to build upon and refer to earlier or subsequent chapters. This is particularly valuable since some conceptual scaffolding occurs in working through the book from beginning to end.

Please note that throughout the text, the terms *workplace* and *organisation* have been used largely interchangeably, as it is in much organisational communication literature because of the many similarities in how meanings are constructed with respect to both these contexts (Nicotera, 2019).

Most chapters contain activities designed to promote reflexivity, reflection, the application of theory to practice and vice versa, experiential learning, critical perspectives, deep learning and (re)search skills. Many of these activities have been used in my own teaching or are derived from data and participant narratives with necessary modifications. They can easily be adapted depending upon the teaching and learning context. The activities have been embedded because I hope the text will be of relevance as a text book for students in a range of disciplines (for example, communication, management, business, human resource management) at undergraduate and postgraduate levels. This is possible partly through embedding various levels of conceptual complexity to meet the needs of a wide audience. However, the book is not only a textbook. It has also been crafted as a scholarly work, drawing upon my own research and the studies of others. Some seminal works are acknowledged, but the prime focus has been to concentrate upon their relevance to workplace situations contemporaneously and to include predominantly recent contributions from researchers with expertise in a range of fields and holding a variety of perspectives.

Where possible, sources have been selected to achieve an international approach so that in some small way, a more balanced perspective can be brought to enquiry that resists the disproportionate number of empirical studies published by western and western-educated scholars. An encouraging wave of internationalisation in higher research education and publishing will hopefully create a shift from what represents a 'one-eyed' approach to (ironically) global issues, where now, more than ever, national cultures need to openly collaborate, communicate, and share perspectives for the economic, social, environmental, physical, spiritual, and mental wellbeing of all those who inhabit the planet. Global and political coalitions such as the United Nations and the Global Health Organisation are examples of how shared knowledge can transcend the interests of national cultures and stimulate our engagement with interconnectedness.

Finally, you will notice that the book has been divided into three parts. Part I is written to 'set the scene' with respect to the principles, theories, and concepts that are foundational to studies about organisations. Part II explores the implications of human diversity as applied to workplace contexts, and how under these conditions, managers and organisational members can not only bring about a sense of belonging, but also build thriving, creative, and collaborative places to work. The final part of the book takes an applied approach to communication, culture and wellbeing, brought to lines of enquiry such as negotiation, conflict, working in groups, ethics, 'dark' issues, and the role of emotions in our daily work.

Reference

Nicotera, A. (2019). *Origins and traditions of organizational communication: A comprehensive introduction to the field*. New York: Routledge.

PART I

Communication, principles, and concepts in workplace contexts

The aim of Part I is to provide an introduction to some concepts that are relevant to interpersonal relationships, communication (as an integral element to relational formation and maintenance), and wellbeing. The development of communication and language (written and spoken), communication as a discipline and its sub-disciplines (most particularly interpersonal and organisational communication) form the basis of this first part of this text. Particular attention is extended to interpersonal communication (including nonverbal communication) and organisational communication as is consistent with many other communication books. The final chapter of Part I is devoted to some basic ideas associated with wellbeing in workplace contexts and how to optimise the capacity for individuals and organisations to thrive. Although each of the chapters in Part I can be read discretely, they are designed to familiarise readers with fundamental concepts and theories as well as a vocabulary that can inform later chapters in Parts II and III and facilitate discussion.

DOI: 10.4324/9780429318948-1

1

THE NATURE AND STUDY OF COMMUNICATION AND LANGUAGE

Meanings and definitions

Few dispute that communication competence is essential to thriving in most cultures (see Larson, 2018) but communicating well is far from easy (Berger, 2016), partly because, like language and meaning, it is constantly changing (Sweet, 2014). Communication is made more challenging given a range of conditions, including the pace of social and economic change, globalisation, social media, and other technologies (Servaes, 2020). Defining communication is exacting given its nuanced, complex meanings that depend upon the disciplines, interpretations, and contexts brought to the subject matter (Berger, 2016; Dwyer, 2020; Nicotera, 2019; Simonson, Peck, Craig, & Jackson, 2012; Wybraniec-Skardowska, 2017). Varied research methodologies, ranging on a continuum from the positivist positions of the natural sciences to highly qualitative, inductive and subjectivist approaches (Rocci & Saussure, 2016), also influence how communication is defined. Nevertheless, despite these complexities, from the 1960s, schools of communication began to consolidate assumptions that helped to focus and define the discipline (Miller, 2015).

The term 'communication' derives from a Latin root word meaning 'to make known', summoning up the notion of communities connected by their communication with one another (Berger, 2016). Historically, communication has been associated with clarity and transparency or political and economic contexts such as the exchange of goods and transportation (Simonson et al., 2012). Some scholars have focused upon the purpose of communication as a means of influencing, persuading, and interacting with others and the way such interactions are largely determined by the context and culture in which they take place (Wardhaugh & Fuller, 2014).

In somewhat simple but nevertheless accessible terms, Dorochoff (2016, p. 16) defined communication as 'verbal and nonverbal language delivered either directly

DOI: 10.4324/9780429318948-2

or indirectly, that is spoken or written'. In ways that perceive communication more broadly as a construction emphasising context and social relationships, Servaes (2020, p. 5) defines communication as a 'social process constituted in a specific spatial and temporal framework [and] is the articulation of social relations amongst people'. In his view, communication is a metaphor for the very 'fabric of society' (Servaes, 2020, p. 5). Similarly, Noels, Clement, Collins, and Machintyre (2019, p. 29) construct communication in terms of its societal purpose and, emphasising its shared nature;

> communication is the means through which individuals learn and develop the shared frames of reference that form the basis of their world view and the consensual shared reality that fosters social cohesion.

Heath (2018, p. 2) highlights the role of influence as an integral concept of communication and intention, stating that;

> [c]ommunication is the means by which people (strategically and non-strategically, intentionally and unintentionally), interact with and affect/influence one another.

ACTIVITY: CRITICAL THINKING

As individuals, search for two or three other definitions of communication. Within small groups compare and contrast these definitions, identifying those themes or concepts that appear to be highlighted conceptually. Based on a number of key concepts, try to co-construct your own definitions and share them with other small groups that have undertaken the same task. Discuss any similarities and differences in your definitions.

Communication as a discipline

The study of early communication is rooted in the classical origins of ancient Greece from 466 BC–400 AD when oral communication skills, argument, and persuasion, otherwise referred to as 'rhetoric', were highly regarded and formed a key element in how Aristotle (384–322 AD), a philosopher at that time, understood democracy (Berger, 2016; Berlo, 1960; Turner & West, 2018). Greek scholars developed some of the earliest theories about which strategies in speaking and writing influence the thoughts and actions of audiences (Heath, 2018).

During 'Medieval times' in Europe through to the Renaissance period from 400–1600 AD, orality tended to be influenced by religious worldviews but from this period onwards, rhetoric increasingly favoured empirical, secular evidence to support conclusions that heralded the rise of social sciences, including communication (Turner & West, 2018). The concept of rhetoric or public speaking in communication was later to be studied in university schools of English around the turn of the twentieth century as business and other practitioners began to appreciate its importance in achieving success (Heads, 2017; Nicotera, 2019; Turner & West, 2018). As a sub-discipline of communication, rhetoric has now come to encompass speech making, presentations, and aspects of the mass media (film, books, social media, for example) that are accessed by large numbers of people (Berger, 2016). Others have explored how rhetorical approaches explain the way that persuasive communication shapes identity and identification (Scott, 2019). Rhetoric addresses the concept of audience and increasing the appeal and persuasiveness of speech in order to achieve the objectives of a speaker (Macnamara, 2015). The idea that communication is synonymous with the study of persuasion is now deemed questionable, however (Nicotera, 2019), but introductory texts of business communication continue to include a chapter on rhetoric and how to deliver effective presentations by drawing on the persuasive strategies of ethos, pathos, and logos, advocated by Aristotle. Ethos is concerned with highlighting personal character to demonstrate credibility, pathos draws upon emotional elements, and logos refers to the way logical arguments can be brought to persuade others (Berger, 2016; Gill, 2019). These principles of persuasion continue to inform how communication professionals develop organisational strategies and manage information in contexts such as advertising, marketing, public relations, and leadership (Heath, 2018). That is, when it is used to define and achieve purpose-driven outcomes and is thus inherently concerned with persuading others of a vision.

Communication models, theories, and concepts from the twentieth century

Twentieth-century ideas about communication may now seem somewhat unsophisticated but many early theories and allied models continue to be instructive today (Nicotera, 2019). Communication models and associated diagrams illustrate elements of a phenomenon and any relationships amongst them (Berger, 2016). Shannon and Weaver's mathematical one-way model, published in 1949, is known as a transmission model of communication (Dwyer, 2020). The model was developed for the Bell telephone company to help telephone engineers find efficient ways to transmit electrical signals and was depicted by a line drawn from left to right running through various boxes (Nicotera, 2019). The transmissive approach pertains to the transference of information via an input-output orientation in a process whereby a source encodes messages through a channel so that a receiver can then decode or make sense of them (Barge, 2019). A message is an idea or feeling with verbal and/or nonverbal elements, transmitted from a sender to a receiver who decodes or interprets the information in order to understand it (Dwyer, 2020). A channel refers to a medium or vehicle for conveying a message from one person to another that may be, for example, face to face, digital, or written communication (Dwyer, 2020; Rogers, 2003; Turner & West, 2018). The components of Shannon and Weaver's model included: sender (encoder), message, channel, receiver (decoder), and noise and these concepts have appeared with some modifications in many models over time.

The concept of noise

The concept of noise runs through many communication theories and is understood to be anything interfering with or distracting from the effective encoding or decoding of communication messages (see Goodwin, 2019; Hartley & Chatterton, 2015; Larson, 2018). Communication is deemed to be effective based on its level of fidelity – that is, when a message has been interpreted by a receiver as the sender intended (Berger, 2016). The concept of noise describes what happens when a message has not been received as intended. Scholars have identified a number of different kinds of noise (see, for example, Berlo, 1960; Crossman, Bordia, & Mills, 2011; De Janasz, Crossman, Campbell, & Power, 2014; Goodwin, 2019; Hartley & Chatterton, 2015; Larson, 2018; Turner & West, 2018) as exemplified in Table 1.1.

From the early 1940s, communication scholars began to criticise linear, one-directional models with a defined beginning and end that failed to take into account any interruptions or otherwise messy aspects of communication (Turner & West, 2018). Greater focus upon feedback as a verbal or nonverbal response to a message characterised this departure (Dwyer, 2020; Hartley & Chatterton, 2015). For example, shortly after the Shannon and Weaver model was published, Wilber Schramm developed a face-to-face interactional model in 1950. The model incorporated a two-way, circular, dyadic approach to communication and verbal and nonverbal feedback from sender to receiver and back to the sender. However, some

TABLE 1.1 Forms of noise

Form of noise	Illustrations
External and physical	A jackhammer being used outdoors and interfering with a conversation or a class.
Physiological.	Fatigue, a headache, hearing loss, and a consequent loss of concentration.
Semantic	Unfamiliar jargon defined as spoken or written organisational discourse that is highly technical or specialised and understood only by group members but not others, so it can serve to maintain in-groups and exclude/limit the participation of outgroups or non-users/members.
Psychological	Emotional states such as feeling overwhelmed by workplace demands, feeling irritation, bias, or prejudice towards a sender or message.

felt Schram's model still tended to focus upon the sender rather than the receiver (Nicotera, 2019; Turner & West, 2018). Criticisms of one-directional models gave rise to what came to be known as transactional communication, where messages and meanings are simultaneously exchanged and co-created through the giving and receiving of verbal and nonverbal feedback using symbols that create a shared meaning (see, Berger, 2016; Larson, 2018; Nicotera, 2019; Turner & West, 2018). Transactional models are essentially a constitutive view of communication that has provided the conceptual means for understanding many of the principles of organisational communication (Chewing, 2019; Nicotera, 2019).

Berlo (1960) also made a seminal contribution to communication in his Source, Message, Channel, Receiver (SMCR) transmission model. Berlo's model drew upon interdisciplinary perspectives and highlighted a number of contextual factors in the creation of meaning that had hitherto been largely unexplored. They included (Berlo, 1960; Dwyer, 2020):

1. the role of human relationships
2. the five senses (sight, hearing, touch, smell and taste)
3. human behaviour
4. an individual's knowledge of the subject matter
5. the social and cultural environment
6. language.

Barnlund's (1970) subsequent communication model also emphasised the co-creation of meaning (Nicotera, 2019; Turner & West, 2018) as an aspect of sense-making theory (Goodwin, 2019; Weick, 1995), generally accepted by management and organisational language scholars as the key to how individuals understand issues and events (Brown, Colville, & Pye, 2015). Thus, theories about communication from the late twentieth century became increasingly complex and holistic and included consideration of the environment (the location where it takes place, such as a sporting venue, a mosque or shopping centre), the culture, or the fields of experience of those communicating (their skills, abilities, and expertise) (see Berlo, 1960; Hartley & Chatterton, 2015; Turner & West, 2018).

The appreciation of language in creating meaning (see Berlo, 1960) and what it signals about group membership emerged from the latter half of the twentieth century and is largely sustained by scholars today (Hartley & Chatterton, 2015). Many ideas about language and communication are informed by the work of Basil Bernstein, a British sociolinguist who found that socio-economic class influences linguistic codes and how children, and indeed adults, see their place in the world (Bernstein, 1990, 2010; Berger, 2016). Bernstein differentiated between two codes: the elaborated code and the restricted/public code whereby the former is characterised by formal, rational language, complex grammatical constructions, and a wide vocabulary, more usually adopted by the well-educated, and the latter, restricted codes are tied to local social structures, the use of metaphors, and simple and short sentences (Berger, 2016; Bernstein, 2010) associated with marginalised socio-economic groups.

In concluding this section, it is worth reflecting upon the significant function of language for humans and groups. It is considered one of the most important means of initiating, synthesising, and reinforcing ways of thinking, feeling, and behaving within a social group. Quite simply, language provides its users with concepts that frame how the world is perceived and experienced (Piller, 2017). Disentangling language from human experience and thought is unimaginable.

The study of language and its development

Language is deeply rooted in cultural practices, learned generationally and developed through social interaction (Noels et al., 2019). It is difficult to find common agreement on a definition of language (Künstler, 2019) and indeed, a precise explanation of its relationship with communication beyond an assumption that one exists. The reason may lie in the variety of disciplinary lenses and contexts brought to the study of linguistics, as an enquiry into the structures and uses of human language and the relationship between the two (Finegan, Besnier, Blair, & Collins, 1992). Or it may be, as one scholar suggests (Corballis, 2011), that language is a great deal more complex than other forms of human communication. Stephens (1992) proffered that language is a means of communication that assists humans in organising and making sense of their own lives and others' and, additionally, is used to influence others through flattery, persuasion, or command, for example. Finegan et al. (1992) differentiated between three basic forms of linguistic communication. First, oral communication, which relies on the use of speech and hearing organs, and second, two kinds of visual representation, writing and signing, which many hearing- and speech-impaired people (and their friends) rely upon for communication. Language, like meaning, is constantly changing (Sweet, 2014) so exploring how language use in communication develops over time is generally well researched (Curnow, 2009) from both a synchronic and a diachronic perspective (Burridge & Stebbings, 2016). Synchronic studies consider language at a particular point in time without reference to its historical development and diachronic research focuses on the study of language over time.

Humans have reportedly been able to speak for hundreds of thousands of years (Finegan et al., 1992). Fossil evidence of humans from at least 500,000 years ago suggests that they had developed both the vocal anatomy and neurological control necessary to produce language (Wyse, 2017). Some scholars suggest that spoken language developed between 50,000 and 100,000 years ago but without tangible evidence, these assertions cannot be verified conclusively (Fromkin et al., 2012; Yule, 2017). Most scholars concur that what distinguishes humans from animals most is the complexity of human communication (Fromkin et al., 2012). Whilst it is certainly the case that the ability to produce simple vocal patterns such as grunting originates from an ancient part of the brain shared with vertebrates including fish, birds, frogs, and other mammals, it does not entirely constitute language in the way understood and enacted by humans (Yule, 2017). For example, unlike animals, humans are able to acquire language during childhood and through socialisation to refer to things in the past, for discussion, and to reflect upon language in reflexive ways (Burridge & Stebbings, 2016), meaning people are able to use language to think and talk about language itself (Yule, 2017). The ability to produce and understand grammatical sentences in a language is referred to as grammatical or linguistic competence. Gaining a level of linguistic competence involves demonstrating a mastery of phonological systems (the sounds a language has and how they are related to each other and combine to form words) and grammar (language rules) that are essential to encode or decode an infinite number of messages (Rowe & Levine, 2009; Saeed, 2016). Producing appropriate language and interpreting utterances given their cultural context is called communicative competence (Finegan et al., 1992). Communicative competence incorporates both linguistic and cultural knowledge, but unlike linguistic competence, interlocutors must be both technically correct and culturally and socially appropriate (Zhu, 2021).

Semiotics/semiology and semantics

Semiotics is a term often used interchangeably with semiology, and indeed, semiotics/semiology, and semantics are also loosely held as approximates (see Baldrick, 2015; Parikh, 2019). That said, semiotics pertains to the study of signs that communicate collectively held meanings, expressed linguistically or non-linguistically, that are influenced by culture and context (Berger, 2016; Baldrick, 2015; Burridge & Stebbings, 2016; Saeed, 2015; Stephens, 1992; Su, 2019). Thus, it is the work of a semiotician to discover the kinds of relationships that exist between a sign and the object it represents, or, to adopt Saussure's terminology, the relationship between a signifier and signified (Saeed, 2016). The term 'signifiers' basically relates to 'words', but linguists tend to adopt the term signifier because it serves as a reminder that words are only signs rather than being things themselves (Stephens, 1992).

Semiotics is founded upon the seminal work of Ferdinand de Saussure (1857–1913). Saussure was an American philosopher, who linked linguistic meaning to sign systems (Saeed, 2016). The term generally used nowadays by linguists for signed systems is discourse (Stephens, 1992). Signs are identified and created by humans, making it possible for one thing to stand for another in a process sometimes referred to as 'signification' (Saeed, 2016). Early in the twentieth century, Charles Sanders Peirce (1839–1914) identified three kinds of signs: icons, indexes, and symbols (Berger, 2016). An icon assumes a similarity between a sign and what it represents, for example a portrait and its real-life subject; an index describes a close association between a sign and what is signified, as smoke signifies fire; and finally, a symbol, as a conventional link between the sign and its signified in the way that military ranks are denoted by insignia or a state of mourning is symbolised by wearing black in some cultures (Saeed, 2016) or white in others.

While semiotics is the study of signs, semantics focuses on structures to create meaning, particularly as it pertains to linguistic expressions and the use of words and sentences (see Finegan et al., 1992; Parikh, 2019; Saeed, 2015) and the relationship among words, sentences, thoughts, and constructions of truth and reality (Pinker, 2007; Rowe & Levine, 2009; Saeed, 2016). Thinking semantically can be traced to the religious texts and traditions of Sanskrit, Greek, Hebrew, and Arabic from 3000 years ago (Parikh, 2019). Semantics also shares some similarities and differences with the linguistic fields of pragmatics and sociolinguistics. Semantics tends to explore the universal meanings of signs regardless of its users (often in texts), whereas pragmatics involves interpreting the intended meaning of linguistic utterances from the way they are used in a context or setting, taking into account the speakers involved, their backgrounds and knowledge; and sociolinguistics explores the contexts of daily life, roles, gender, the media, societal norms, policies, and laws (Ismaeel, 2021; Wardhaugh & Fuller, 2014). Similarly, linguists, especially those involved in studies about organisational ethnography, are interested in how language is used in workplaces.

ACTIVITY: RESEARCH SKILLS

Search online sources available to you for journal papers that are concerned with organisational ethnography and take note of how researchers have observed the way that language is used in an organisation and the implications and conclusions the researchers have drawn. Share your findings with other students online or in class.

Linguistic relativity

Language and culture are intertwining concepts in that language is an important sign for socialisation, playing a significant role in shaping the cultural context (Eaves & Leathers, 2018; Su, 2019). The relationship between language and culture is foundational to intracultural and intercultural communication. Theories about linguistic relativity provide insights into some challenges presented in intercultural communication because it reveals much about how languages are structured, influence worldviews, and the experiences of those who speak a language (Yule, 2017).

How people use language to describe and conceptualise colour is often cited as a way to illustrate cultural relativity under the assumption that culture profoundly influences such perceptions. In the Navaho language, for example, blue and green are represented by one word, whereas in English they are differentiated, just as Innuits have multiple words for different kinds of snow whereas, in English, there are only a few (Fromkin et al., 2012). Knowing the difference between the quality of snow could mean life or death amongst the Innuit but it may not for people living in Hong Kong or Singapore. The question is, how and to what extent these culturally based distinctions determine or influence the perceptions and thoughts of speakers (Fromkin et al., 2012).

Edward Sapir (1884–1939), a student of the German educated anthropologist, Franz Boas, was a linguist and a professor of anthropology at Yale university and with his own student, Benjamin Whorf (1897–1941), the two American researchers questioned determinist approaches to language and developed the theory of linguistic relativity based largely on Whorf's research exploring culture and language amongst the Hopi and other tribes and how these factors shape perception (Berger, 2016; Piller, 2017; Turner & West, 2018; Wardhaugh & Fuller, 2014; Yule, 2017). Sapir and Whorf's reformulation of the concept of linguistic relativity is embedded in a range of intellectual traditions and is regarded as a weak form as compared to linguistic determinism that is viewed as a strong form of linguistic relativism (Piller, 2017). Linguistic determinism suggests that society is confined by the language it adopts to the extent that it determines its culture, how people speak, perceive, and think about the world. As Rathmayr (2017) pointed out, in every language, some words are difficult to translate because certain aspects of culture are peculiar to a particular culture. However, linguistic determinism is less widely accepted than the concept of linguistic relativity in its weak form (Fromkin et al., 2012). One reason for this is that linguistic determinism is criticised on the basis that it would be almost impossible for individuals to learn multiple languages if they were constrained by their native language to the extent that they would be unable to think about something for which their language had no precise translation (Fromkin et al., 2012; Wardhaugh & Fuller, 2014).

Register, dialect, and accent

The concepts of register, dialect, and accent also affect interpersonal and team communication at work. Register, dialect, and accent are largely determined by social groups but, at the same time, an individual's way of speaking, known as an idiolect, is determined by context and community and influences communication (Fromkin et al., 2012). It is crucial to adopt an appropriate register given the context and particular conventions of the social situation, professional environment, or a recreational interest (Fromkin et al., 2012; Stephens, 1992) because not doing so can invite negative impressions (Hartley & Chatterton, 2015). For example, if an applicant being interviewed for a paralegal role in a conservative organisation remarked, 'thanks a bundle, I've had an awesome time chatting things over with you', the interview would not be likely to be followed by an offer of employment.

REGISTER ACTIVITY: EXPERIENTIAL REFLECTION AND DISCUSSION

Take a few minutes to reflect on any experiences where you witnessed an inappropriate register. Jot down some notes on the context. Address these four questions:

1. Describe the context. Where did the incident occur?
2. What was said that seemed inappropriate?
3. In what way was it inappropriate?
4. How did those present react?

Discuss with others your experience, drawing on your notes. As a group, choose one of the accounts and co-construct a written case study. Share the case study with another group.

In contrast to register, a dialect refers to a language adopted within a particular region or a social or socio-economic group (Hartley & Chatterton, 2015) that may be used to identify something about someone's ethnic, regional, social, or gender affiliations (Finegan et al., 1992).

Languages and dialects are evolving all the time (Rakic & Maass, 2019). The term 'dialect' is often associated with local, non-prestigious, powerless groups that adopt some sort of variation on a standard form of the language (Wardhaugh & Fuller, 2014). Dialects develop and are reinforced when languages in one group begin to change but nevertheless continue to be understood by others, to some extent, partly because vocabulary, syntax, and grammar remain the same (Finegan et al., 1992; Fromkin et al., 2012; Saeed, 2016).

DIALECTS ACTIVITY

Discuss any differences in dialects within your own nation. Consider the following topics:

1. Is it possible to tell where someone comes from, based on how they speak?
2. Can you make assumptions about someone's socio-economic background based on their speech?
3. How might a colleague's dialect influence the assessments of others, either positively or negatively?

Accents are adopted by those from the same geographical areas or socio-economic groups. They are similar to dialects, but the emphasis is on pronunciation or phonological differences (Fromkin et al., 2012). In a globalised world, non-native accents have become the norm and they often serve as salient cues in social perceptions in the context of workplace interactions on a daily basis (Creel, 2018; Roessel, Schoel, & Stahlberg, 2018). Depending upon the cultural context, some accents are more highly regarded than others and some organisations may consciously or unconsciously consider the accent of an applicant during the recruitment process, depending on the expectations of stakeholders (Hartley & Chatterton, 2015). In the context of non-native accents in the workplace, Roessel et al. (2018) found that they can trigger negatively biased associations on dimensions of affect (a psychological concept related to experience, feelings, emotions, and mood), trust, and competence. The implications of this finding should be a matter of concern on many levels and calls for considerable organisational attention. It certainly explains why accents can sometimes be cultivated to assume membership of a desirable cultural group or identity, perhaps to improve career prospects (Hartley & Chatterton, 2015). Stereotyping someone based on accent is, however, inadvisable because in parts of the world where a high level of socio-economic fluidity exists and where an education system is based on merit, talented individuals from unprivileged backgrounds are more frequently recruited into senior positions and perform highly successfully.

It is not the main aim of this section to document the vast field of linguistics but to explain, where relevant to the subject matter of chapters that follow, how language and communication influence workplaces and the wellbeing of those involved in them. Of course, written language, in somewhat different ways also influences and is influenced by organisational culture.

Writing and its history

Definitions of writing tend to focus upon its use of graphic signs (as images of isolated symbols), whether in the form of handwriting or in electronic forms, as visual and symbolic representations of speech that are learned over time and convey meaning (Baird, 2014; Fromkin et al., 2012; Rowe & Levine, 2009; Turner & West, 2018; Yule, 2017). In simple terms, writing can be described as any marks inscribed that have some significance (Lyons & Marquilhas, 2017) to those who interpret them. Given that writing is more resistant to change than speech (and this is why pronunciation is not always intuitively reflected by spelling), it tends to command greater trust and is therefore adopted as the main form of record keeping in most societies (Fromkin et al., 2012). For this reason alone, it has had a profound influence on civilisation.

Baird (2014) has observed that the evolution of writing tends to defy systematic analysis and, as a result, is not yet well understood and may never be so, even in cultures such as China where very old, historical records exist. Indeed, despite much scholarship, debate continues about the origin of writing and its global spread (Coulmas, 2003; Yule, 2017). Writing is thought to date as far back as 5000 years ago (Zang, 2017) with early examples found amongst native American and Australian Aboriginal communities, the Alaskan Innuits, people living on the Island of Sulaesi, the Taliu culture, the Peruvian Incas and the Yukaginaris from Siberia (Fromkin et al., 2012; Wang, 2020; Wyse, 2017). Bronze and bone inscriptions found in China dating to at least 3000 years ago are notable but may not have received the attention they deserve, particularly from western scholars more focused on the alphabetical writing system (Zang, 2017). Wang's (2020) work on the Taliu people, an ethnic Chinese minority, is illustrative of an increasing number of ethnic writing systems that have recently been discovered and researched. The Taliu writing system laid claim to the distinctive characteristics of ideographic graphs, though the language included only nouns and numerals (Wang, 2020).

Cave drawings found in Altamira, Northern Spain, France, and the Saharan desert are thought to be at least 3600 years old (Finegan et al., 1992; Fromkin et al., 2012). These drawings, known as picture-writing or pictograms, roughly approximated to cartoons or road signs and are literal, direct, recordings of events or ideas that tell a story rather than being linguistic names given to objects or representing words or sounds from a spoken language (Finegan et al., 1992; Fromkin et al., 2012; Yule, 2017). Over time, pictograms were gradually modified and became increasingly more stylised and complex and known as ideograms, meaning idea pictures or idea writing (Finegan et al., 1992; Fromkin et al., 2012). In ideographic writing, symbols represent the idea of a message as a whole rather than any specific interpretation such as an arrow sign to suggest a direction (Baird, 2014).

A form of commercial writing, cuneiform, was also established about 5000 years ago, in Sumeria, using a sharp, pointed object called a stylus to scratch into soft clay tablets (Coulmas, 2003; Finegan et al., 1992; Mautner & Rainer, 2017). The term cuneiform is derived from the Latin word 'cuneus', meaning wedge-shaped because this was the shape of the symbols used (Finegan et al., 1992; Yule, 2017). The latest cuneiform tablet dates from 75 AD and thus testifies to the longevity of this tradition (Joannes, 2017). This kind of morphographic language is known as 'logograma', where signs represent morphemes, the minimal unit of linguistic meaning that approximate to how we use, '$', '&', and'8' today (Finegan et al., 1992; Yule, 2017). As cuneiform spread throughout the Middle East, Asia Minor (comprising what is now mostly modern-day Turkey) and Mesopotamia (now part of Iraq) at the end of the 4th millennium BC, it became widely adopted throughout the region by 2000 BC, when in Assyria and Persia it evolved into a syllabic writing system where syllables began to stand for the sounds of words instead of symbols representing words (Fromkin et al., 2012; Joannes, 2017; Lyons & Marquilhas, 2017). The Egyptians also developed a writing system based on a Sumerian one but it differed in that it adopted symbols of writing that later also appeared in the Valley of the Indus (now Pakistan and India) around 2500 BC (Finegan et al., 1992).

Possibly inspired by the Mesopotamian writing system, the Chinese were beginning to use pictograms as symbols for words rather than concepts from about 2000 BC (Finegan et al., 1992). Transforming a picture into a sign, and referencing the name of an object, involves a major conceptual leap (Coulmas, 2003) not captured by pictures of events. A significant benefit of the Chinese language system is that even where communicants adopt different dialects, they are able to understand one another through the written text (Fromkin et al., 2012; Yule, 2017). The written system in China has been in continuous use for 3000 years but one difficulty for those learning the language may lie in the high number of Chinese characters – though only 2500 of them are necessary for daily communication (Yule, 2017). Similarly, Japanese Kanji has tens of thousands of logographs but only a few thousand are generally necessary (Hoover & Tunmer, 2020).

The various forms of writing as they developed in different places and over time are often broadly classified as alphabetic, syllabic, and logographic though Baird (2014, p. 6) suggests that these classifications of writing systems are both 'simplistic and contested'. Nevertheless, he concedes that alphabetic, syllabic, and logographic systems dominate almost all modern and many ancient scripts. Thus, for those who are not experts in the field, making distinctions amongst writing systems is initially useful, albeit simplistic.

In alphabetic writing systems, symbols represent phonemes as sounds (Finegan et al., 1992) in both consonants and vowels (Baird, 2014). Some debate exists about whether the alphabet emerged from logographic or pictographic scripts (Wyse, 2017), but whatever the case, these early forms of alphabet paved the way for writing in many languages including English (Wyse, 2017). However, given the focus by western academics, it is important to remember that writing is not limited to alphabetical scripts since it includes a wide variety of pictorial scripts such as Egyptian and Mayan hieroglyphic scripts or graphs from Incan cultures (Lyons & Marquilhas, 2017).

The first known alphabet made up of consonants was the Phoenician/proto-Canaanite script, adapted by the Greeks from the eighth century BC who added their own five characters to represent vowels (Finegan et al., 1992; Fromkin et al., 2012; Wyse, 2017) that over time began to be associated with the form and structure of more developed writing systems (Coulmas, 2003; Mautner & Rainer, 2017). Research also dates alphabetic writing in Egypt and from Mayan hieroglyphics scripts from between 2000 BC and 1500 BC (Lyons & Marquilhas, 2017; Wyse, 2017). Yet it was the Romans who in 600 BC developed the basis of the alphabet used in many western countries today. Some countries (Greece, Russia, the Ukraine, Bulgaria, and Serbia) use an alphabetic system that may differ from the Roman text, mostly in terms of the shape of some letters (Finegan et al., 1992). In contrast, syllabic writing, emerging from the ancient Middle East and East Asia, is based on graphs that represent syllables, consisting of a short consonant, a vowel, or a consonant vowel combination, developed from the earlier pictograms (Baird, 2014; Finegan et al., 1992). Logographic writing does not indicate pronunciation and is found in the Chinese Han system used also in Japan (Kanji) and Korea (Baird, 2014). Logographic writing symbols represent a meaningful unit within a written language such as a morpheme, or, simply put, a phrase or word (Finegan et al., 1992; Hoover & Tunmer, 2020). Cantonese and Mandarin are two examples of many Chinese languages that share the same set of Chinese characters, belonging to the logographic writing system (Ma, Wu, Sun, Cai, Fan, & Li, 2020).

A number of factors contributed to the spread of writing systems around the world. Religion and spiritual philosophies undoubtedly facilitated the acceptance of writing. For example, prior to the birth of Christ, the Chinese script was disseminated via Buddhism and Confucianism (Coulmas, 2003; Künstler, 2019). Economic relationships, trade, imperialism, and other political alliances also contributed to the widening acceptance of the written word as illustrated by the spread of soviet languages throughout Korea, Turkey, Romania, and Persia (Coulmas, 2003). Yet, for many centuries, writing was limited to a small number of scribes (Rowe & Levine, 2009). Even today, some languages do not have a written form, but of those that do, only a proportion of speakers are able to write and many millions of humans remain illiterate (Coulmas, 2003; Yule, 2017). The reason for this is multi-pronged, and in all probability, linked to economic inequality and poor access to resources in ways that inhibit the growth and potential of many.

Conclusion

This chapter has introduced some early communication theories, concepts, and terminology that remain relevant to how scholars understand and discuss communication today. A brief account of the rise of rhetoric and communication as a discipline has also been addressed. The study of language and its historical development, particularly with respect to written language, was also afforded some attention. These themes provide a wider context for appreciating language and communication as a necessary basis for engaging with concepts presented in the chapters that follow.

References

Baird, P. (2014). A brief history of documents and writing systems. In D. Doermann & K. Tombre (Eds.), *Handbook of document image processing and recognition* (pp. 3–10). London: Springer.

Baldrick, C. (2015). *The Oxford dictionary of literary terms*. Oxford: Oxford University Press.

Barge, J. (2019). A communicative approach to leadership. In A. Nicotera (Ed.), *Origins and traditions of organizational communication to the field* (pp. 326–347). New York: Routledge.

Barnlund. (1970). A transactional model of communication. In *Language Behavior* (Originally published 1970, Vol. 41, pp. 43–61). De Gruyter. https://doi.org/10.1515/9783110878752.43

Berger, A. (2016). *Messages: An introduction to communication*. Walnut Creek: Taylor and Francis.

Berlo, D. (1960). *The process of communication*. New York: Holt, Rinhart & Winston Inc.

Bernstein, B. (1990). *The structuring of pedagogic discourse*. London: Routledge.

Bernstein, B. (2010). A public language: Some sociological implications of a linguistic form. *The British Journal of Sociology, 61*(1), 53–69.

Brown, A., Colville, I., & Pye, A. (2015). Making sense of sensemaking. *Organization Studies, 36*(2), 265–277.

Burridge, K., & Stebbings, T. (2016). *For the love of language: An introduction to linguistics.* Melbourne: Cambridge University Press.

Chewing, L. (2019). Communications networks. In A. Nicotera (Ed.), *Origins and traditions of organizational communication to the field* (pp. 168–186). New York: Routledge.

Corballis, M. (2011). *The recursive mind: The origins of human language. Thought and civilization.* Princeton, NJ: Princeton University Press.

Coulmas, F. (2003). What is writing? In F. Coulmas (Ed.), *Writing systems: An introduction to their linguistic analysis* (pp. 1–17). Cambridge: Cambridge University Press.

Creel, S. (2018). Accent detection and social cognition: Evidence of protracted learning. *Developmental Science, 21*(2).

Crossman, J., Bordia, S., & Mills, C. (2011). *Business communication for the global age.* Sydney: McGraw-Hill.

Curnow, T. (2009). Communication in introductory linguistics. *Australian Journal of Linguistics, 29*(1), 27–43.

De Janasz, S., Crossman, J., Campbell, N., & Power, M. (2014). *Interpersonal skills in organisations.* Sydney: McGraw-Hill.

Dorochoff, N (2016). *Negotiation basics for cultural resource managers.* London: Routledge.

Dwyer, J. (2020). *Communication for business and the professions: Strategies and skills.* Melbourne: Pearson.

Eaves, M., & Leathers, D. (2018). *Successful nonverbal communication: Principles and applications.* Oxford: Routledge Taylor Francis Group.

Finegan, E., Besnier, N., Blair, D., & Collins, P. (1992). *Language: Its structure and use.* Sydney: Harcourt Brace Jovanovich Publishers.

Fromkin, V., Rodman, R., Hyman, N., Collins, P., Amberber, M., & Cox, F. (2012). *An introduction to language.* Melbourne: Cengage.

Gill, H. (2019). *Communication: How to connect with anyone.* Chichester: Capstone John Wiley & Sons.

Goodwin, J. M. (2019). Communication accommodation theory: Finding the right approach. In M. Brown Sr. & L. Hersey (Eds.), *Returning to interpersonal dialogue and understanding human communication in the digital age* (pp. 168–185). Hershey, PA: IGI Global.

Hartley, P., & Chatterton, P. (2015). *Business communication: Rethinking your professional practice for the post digital age.* London: Routledge.

Heads, G. (2017). *Living mindfully: Discovering authenticity through mindfulness coaching.* Oxford: Wiley Blackwell.

Heath, R. (2018). Persuasion. In R. Heath, W. Johansen, J. Falkheimer, K. Hallahan, J. Raupp, & B. Steyn (Eds.), *The international encyclopedia of strategic communication* (pp. 1–14). Hoboken, NJ: John Wiley & Sons Ltd.

Hoover, W., & Tunmer, W. (2020). *The cognitive foundations of reading and its acquisition: A framework with applications. Connecting teaching and learning.* Cham, Switzerland: Springer.

Ismaeel, M. (2021). Philosophical paradigms underlying discourse analysis: Methodological implications. In J. Crossman & S. Bordia (Eds.), *Handbook of qualitative methodologies in workplace contexts* (pp. 48–68). Cheltenham: Edward Elgar Publishing Limited.

Joannes, F. (2017). The Babylonian scribes and their libraries. In M. Lyons & R. Marguilhas (Eds.), *Approaches to the history of written culture: A world inscribed* (pp. 21–39). Cham, Switzerland: Palgrave Macmillan.

Künstler, M. (2019). *The sinitic languages: A contribution to sinological linguistics.* London: Routledge.

Larson, K. (2018). *Adaption and well-being.* London: Routledge.

Lyons, M., & Marquilhas, R. (2017). A world inscribed – introduction. In *Approaches to the history of written culture* (pp. 1–20). Cham, Switzerland: Palgrave Macmillan.

Ma, J., Wu, Y., Sun, T., Cai, L., Fan, X., & Li, X. (2020). Neural substitutes of bilingual processing in a logographic writing system: An FMRI study in Chinese Cantonese-Mandarin bilinguals. *Brain Research, 173*(8), 146794–146794.

Macnamara, J. (2015). *Organizational listening: The missing essential in public communication.* Bern, Switzerland: Peter Lang Books.

Mautner, G., & Rainer, F. (Eds.). (2017). *Handbook of business communication: Linguistic approaches.* Boston: De Gruyter Mouton.

Miller, K. (2015). *Organizational communication: Approaches and processes.* Stamford: Cengage Learning.

Nicotera, A. (2019). *Origins and traditions of organizational communication: A comprehensive introduction to the field.* New York: Routledge.

Noels, K., Clement, R., Collins, K., & Machintyre, P. (2019). Language and culture. In H. Giles, J. Harwood, J. Gasiorek, H. Pierson, J. Nussbaum, & C. Gallois (Eds.), *Language, communication and intergroup relations: A celebration of the scholarship of Howard Giles* (pp. 19–33). New York: Routledge.

Parikh, P. (2019). *Communication and content.* Berlin: Language, Science Press.

Piller, I. (2017). *Intercultural communication: A critical introduction.* Edinburgh: Edinburgh University Press.

Pinker, S. (2007). *The stuff of thought: Language as a window into human nature.* New York: Penguin Books.

Rakic, T., & Maass, A. (2019). Communicating between groups, communicating about groups. In H. Giles, J. Harwood, J. Gasiorek, H. Pierson, J. Nussbaum, & C. Gallois (Eds.), *Language, communication and intergroup relations: A celebration of the scholarship of Howard Giles* (pp. 66–97). New York: Routledge.

Rathmayr, R. (2017). On intercultural business communication: A linguistic approach. In G. Mautner & F. Rainer (Eds.), *Handbook of business communication: Linguistic approaches* (pp. 221–248). Boston: De Gruyter Mouton.

Rocci, A., & Saussure, L. (2016). *Verbal communication.* Boston: De Gruyter Mouton.

Roessel, J., Schoel, C., & Stahlberg, D. (2018). What's in an accent? General spontaneous biases against nonnative accents: An investigation with conceptual and auditory IATs. *European Journal of Social Psychology, 48*(4), 535–550.

Rogers, E. (2003). *Diffusion of innovations.* New York: Free Press.

Rowe, B., & Levine, D. (2009). *A concise introduction to linguistics.* New York: Pearson.

Saeed, J. (2015). *Semiotics.* Oxford: Wiley Blackwell.

Saeed, J. (2016). *Semantics.* Oxford: Wiley Blackwell.

Scott, C. (2019). Identity and identification. In A. Nicotera (Ed.), *Origins and traditions of organizational communication: A comprehensive introduction to the field* (pp. 207–227). New York: Routledge.

Servaes, J. (2020). *Handbook of communication for development and social change.* Singapore: Springer.

Simonson, P., Peck, J., Craig, R., & Jackson, J. (Eds.). (2012). *The handbook of communication history.* New York: Routledge.

Stephens, J. (1992). *Reading the signs: Sense and significance in written texts.* Sydney: Kangaroo Press.

Su, D. (2019). Culture is essentially meaning. In H. Giles, J. Harwood, J. Gasiorek, H. Pierson, J. Nussbaum, & C. Gallois (Eds.), *Language, communication and intergroup relations: A celebration of the scholarship of Howard Giles* (pp. 34–35). New York: Routledge,

Sweet, H. (2014). *History of language in a new English grammar: Logical and historical* (pp. 176–263). Cambridge: Cambridge University Press.

Turner, L., & West, R. (2018). *An introduction to communication*. Cambridge: Cambridge University Press.

Wang, Y. (2020). Determining the nature of Taliu script and its value for the study of early writing. *Journal of Chinese Writing Systems, 4*(2), 105–110.

Wardhaugh, R., & Fuller, J. (2014). *An introduction to sociolinguistics*. Oxford: Wiley Blackwell.

Weick, K. (1995). *Sensemaking in organizations*. Thousand Oaks: Sage.

Wybraniec-Skardowska, U. (2017). A logical conceptualization of knowledge on the notion of language communication. *Studies in Logic, Grammar and Rhetoric, 52*(1), 247–269.

Wyse, D. (2017). A history of writing. In D. Wyse (Ed.), *How writing works* (pp. 55–88). Cambridge: Cambridge University Press.

Yule, G. (2017). *The study of language*. Cambridge: Cambridge University Press.

Zang, K. (2017). Inaugural editorial: Promoting the understanding of ideographic writings. *Journal of Chinese Writing Systems, 1*(1), 3.

Zhu, Y. (2021). Using ethnography of communication in cross-cultural management and communication research. In J. Crossman & S. Bordia (Eds.), *Handbook of qualitative research methodologies in workplace contexts* (pp. 176–190). Cheltenham: Edward Elgar.

2

INTERPERSONAL COMMUNICATION

The nature of interpersonal communication

Interpersonal communication is an intrinsic aspect of organisational activities and its study is informed by a variety of disciplines (Kilduff & Rosikiewicz, 2010). As a process, interpersonal communication occurs within dyadic relationships (between two people), or amongst small groups, whether the means of communication is verbal, nonverbal, or online (Berger, 2016; Larson, 2018; Macnamara, 2015; Turner & West, 2018). It is intimately concerned with the way someone thinks, behaves, and even who they feel they are (Berger, 2016). The complexity of this form of communication is evident in its linkages to and dependence upon, a gamut of allied processes identified by Tsia (2020) as, perception, emotion, cognition, belief systems, self-image, self-awareness, personality, and attitudes. Interpersonal communication is distinguishable from intrapersonal communication that refers to internal dialogues or self-talking /writing, for example, via journal writing. As Tsia (2020) puts it, intrapersonal communication focuses on what goes on 'inside' individuals and the way in which they process, file, and generate communication messages (Tsia, 2020). Interpersonal communication is guided by a person's intrapersonal communication processes as he or she interprets the behaviour of others (Tsia, 2020).

Communication skills nourish relationships and enable their establishment, progression, and maintenance (Larson, 2018) throughout relational life stages (Turner & West, 2018) and as such, resonate with the literature on workplace wellbeing. However, interpersonal communication can also be defensive or negative, just as it can be supportive (Hartley & Chatterton, 2015). Fortunately, managers increasingly decry aggressive, defensive and deceitful communication and value those in their organisations who are relatable and sensitive to the interests of their audiences (Coffelt & Smith, 2020). So apart from being functionally and

DOI: 10.4324/9780429318948-3

technically adept within their areas of expertise, employees are now expected to be effective communicators, capable of demonstrating concern and empathy (Dwyer, 2020; Goodwin, 2019) both of which require a level of self-awareness and the ability to reflect upon the awareness of others (Costello, 2020).

Communication accommodation theory

Taking time to invest in positive interpersonal communication also facilitates the creation of shared meaning (Goodwin, 2019) and enhances relational value. Communication Accommodation Theory (CAT) (originally referred to as Speech Accommodation Theory) was put forth by Howard Giles (Zhang & Pitts, 2019), a British-American sociolinguist and communication professor. CAT has implications for fostering positive interpersonal communication. It explains how people adjust their style of speech depending upon with whom they are interacting (Harwood, Nussbaum, Pierson, Gallois, & Gasiorek, 2019). CAT is a theory that also guides how communication and language consciously and unconsciously create the maintenance and negotiation of identity in everyday interpersonal relationships (Zhang & Pitts, 2019). Thus, CAT suggests that successful communication is often determined by each party's ability to adapt, depending upon verbal/nonverbal cues, the situation and the effectiveness of strategies such as team building, discourse management, or emotional expression (Goodwin, 2019). It is a sophisticated framework that enables insight into both micro and macro levels within interpersonal and intergroup interactions, perceptually, behaviourally, and contextually (Giles, 2016; Zhang, 2019). How people make accommodations based on their interaction with others will be influenced to one extent or another by what are known as communication styles.

Communication styles

Each one of us has a distinctive way of communicating interpersonally, known as a 'communication style' or 'communicative style' (Chlopicki & Laineste, 2019). In this text, the term communication style will be adopted. Style has a more general application to linguistic choices, but the modifier 'communicative' or 'communication' is a subset of styles that focuses upon how communication is constituted and how it functions (Culpeper & Qian, 2020). The concept of communication style is more often limited to oral communication (Chlopicki & Laineste, 2019) but has its roots in earlier ideas about style explored in the discipline of linguistics where it was also applied to written contexts (Selting, 2009).

Context and who is present within that context will influence communication style (Culpeper & Qian, 2020) but it is probably more precise to note that style and context operate as part of a bi-directional process or, in other words, that they influence one another (Selting, 2009). Thus, a communication style is not fixed. It is, as Selting (2009, p. 20) pointed out, 'alterable', 'dynamic', and 'flexible' and capable of being reconstructed, depending upon how discourse is interpreted, the social interaction taking place, and relationships between or amongst those present. For this reason, it is sometimes described as an intersubjective process (see Chlopicki & Laineste, 2019). So, although a communication style is an individual approach to language, the role of context and intersubjectivity naturally give rise to thinking about the communication styles of groups (Crossman, Bordia, & Mills, 2011) and assumptions that they are culture-specific (Chlopicki & Laineste, 2019).

A communication style is actually a cluster or bundle of features that collectively and holistically refers to how language is used (Chlopicki & Laineste, 2019; Selting, 2009). It encompasses features such as turn taking, length of turns, intonation, questioning, metaphors, social actions, speech acts, and the expression of values in conversation (Chlopicki & Laineste, 2019). A number of scholars working in different fields have proposed integrated models to understand how particular sets of communication traits and behaviours form individual communicative styles (Brown, Paz-Aparicio, & Revilla, 2019). For example, De Vries, Bakker-Pieper, Konnings, and Schouten (2013), based on previous work, developed a communication styles inventory (CSI) that identified six domains: expressiveness, preciseness, verbal aggressiveness, questioningness, emotionality, and impression manipulativeness. It is their contention that individuals and groups each have a communication style that can be linked to each of these domains to a greater or lesser degree. Table 2.1 explains some communicative behaviours characterising each of these domains based on the work of De Vries et al. (2013) and Brown et al. (2019) who applied the model developed by De Vries et al. (2013) to a leadership context. As these scholars emphasise, each one of these domains is not a 'type' or a primary communication style but is measured on a scale from high to low and the unique mix of scores in combination is what constitutes a personal communication style.

ACTIVITY: REFLECTION

Discovering a personal communication style requires the use of particular tools and expertise in administering assessments. However, it is useful to reflect upon the six domains in Table 2.1 and to make a rough self-assessment about those that resonate with your own self-knowledge and those that seem to describe your communication less well. You may like to ask trusted people who know you well about those domains that seem to them to describe how you communicate. What adjustments would you consider making to your manner of communication based on your self-assessment and feedback from others? You may like to keep a journal outlining some simple changes you aim to make and your observations of how those changes affected your relationships at work or in some other organisational context.

TABLE 2.1 Communication style domains

Expressiveness	Talkative; exerts conversational dominance; humorous; informal; eloquent; finds it hard to stay silent; likes to express ideas; acts in a casual, informal way without creating unnecessary barriers; narrows the psychological distance with others; non-conflictive, conversationally adroit.
Preciseness	Adopts highly structured communication; thoughtful; communicates in a concise manner that focuses on what is relevant/pertinent; accuracy and logic in communication is valued. Thinks before speaking, choosing words carefully generally and in asking questions.
Verbal aggressiveness	Uses anger-fuelled communication; authoritative; derogatory; adopts humiliating and non-supportive approach; expects obedience; uses demanding voice tones and conveys little respect for the opinions of others.
Questioningness	A philosophical and inquisitive approach to communication where individuals encourage healthy debate, open discussion of ideas and solicit a variety of points of view. Seeks to challenge others intellectually.
Emotionality	Sentimental; elements of tension in communication; displays stress, anxiety, and defensiveness in communication; difficulty in coping with critical remarks.
Impression manipulativeness	Ingratiating; charming; inscrutable and a tendency to conceal information and true feelings in order to gain acceptance from third parties. Boasts about achievements or ideas. Communication tends to be controlling and manipulative. Communicative behaviour may be gentle, kind, polite, and courteous even with those who are disliked or in situations that are unenjoyable, if it serves personal interests.

Source: Brown et al., 2019; De Vries et al., 2013

Listening

Effective listening is an important aspect of communication (McKenna, Brown, Williams, & Lau, 2020). Research about listening is reportedly on the rise (Worthington & Worthington, 2018). This is a welcomed trend on many levels. Macnamara (2015) called for a greater focus on listening in communication studies. Other evidence also suggests listening has previously been overlooked in the literature and within organisations that fail to offer little professional training, perhaps because it is assumed that everyone knows how to listen (De Janasz, Crossman, Campbell, & Power, 2014). According to Lipetz, Kluger, and Bodie (2020), a commonly accepted definition of listening continues to elude researchers. Listening differs from hearing which is an involuntary physical processing of auditory stimuli as sound waves strike the ear drum, causing vibrations received by the brain in ways that may be heard but not necessarily attended to (De Janasz et al., 2014; Dwyer, 2020; Macnamara,

2015). Listening involves receiving, interpreting and organising messages and information so that it makes sense and an effective listener will spend about a half to two-thirds of communication time in undertaking the task (De Janasz et al., 2014).

Much of what it means to be an effective listener is achieved by adopting active listening strategies. Active listening, as the phrase suggests, simply means taking an active role in the process of listening and adopting certain practices. It is described as an interactive process where interlocutors clearly show one another that they are paying attention and wish to achieve a common understanding on matters under discussion (Chan, 2020). Effective listening can help people to connect on an interpersonal level and bring about benefits for both listeners themselves and others, but it does take patience, practice, and concentration (Gill, 2019; Lipetz et al., 2020). The literature provides many examples of how to engage in active listening in order to become a better listener (See Chan, 2020; De Janasz et al., 2014; Gill, 2019; Larson, 2018; Macnamara, 2015; Turner & West, 2018). Distilling these works and others suggests four main areas that address active listening: 1. Acknowledging the rights of others to communicate; 2. Checking interpretations; 3. Showing empathy; 4. Providing feedback. Some conceptual overlapping does occur, however, since active listening is arguably a holistic concept and therefore resists distinct classifications. The holistic nature of listening also means that people's judgements of it tend to be somewhat generalised without paying too much attention to the details of listening behaviours (Lipetz et al., 2020). The four features of active listening are explained as follows:

TABLE 2.2 The features of active listening

1.   **Acknowledging the rights of others to communicate** takes genuine and focused effort and respect and begins with consciously being attentive to a speaker and what is being said. The concept of respect in this context means putting aside personal prejudices, being open and fair without rushing to make negative judgements simply because we do not hold the same views as another. Mindful listening is an allied approach since it entails being aware of personal internal thoughts and suspending criticism.
2.   **Checking interpretations** is essential because so much can be misunderstood in human communication, partly through the tendency of noise to impede effective listening. Verifying and confirming fidelity and the intention and meaning of a speaker can be achieved by paraphrasing, summarising, or simply repeating back what you believe was said. Such a strategy characterises what is known as listening reflectively, and serves to provide a speaker with an opportunity to give more information or to rephrase their remarks if for some reason they feel their views and intentions have been misunderstood. When in doubt, a listener may also seek clarification to check their interpretation of what has been said by asking questions. Unearthing the feelings and motivations of a speaker is complex and requires care and patience. Sometimes, it requires 'reading between the lines' and pursuing intuitive thoughts about what has not been said but merely implied.
3.   **Being empathetic** in our listening requires us to engage with the feelings and perspectives that arise from someone else's experiences and circumstances and allowing one's imagination to explore what that might be like. Again, empathetic engagement is not something to which one can simply pay lip service, as with most forms of active listening, empathy requires reflection, mindfulness, and sensitivity.

4. **Providing feedback**, or 'back channelling' as it is otherwise known, can be either verbal or nonverbal. Common examples of nonverbal signals are using facial expressions, leaning forwards or backwards, or by exchanging eye glances. Providing constructive feedback may not always entail agreement but it should be expressed appropriately and concisely, especially in sensitive contexts.

As Lipetz et al. (2020, p. 71), observed, 'listening in organisations matters'. How employees, managers, and organisations listen is grounded in culture and those organisations committed to open listening cultures develop policies that embed the supporting values and principles that are espoused (see Macnamara, 2015). Values, as a concept, can be understood as internalised standards attached to constructs and phenomena in order to determine the worthiness of ideas (Larson, 2018), decisions, or behaviour. How individuals feel about money, education, or what constitutes right or wrong depends upon their values (Larson, 2018). Organisations that devote resources to training in active listening, being informed about its value in productive interpersonal and organisational communication, are likely to benefit at micro and macro functional levels.

ACTIVITY: RESEARCH, DISCUSSION, AND SYNTHESIS

Using the library sources available to you, search the literature for other sources about active listening and decide if the information you find can be classified into one of the categories in Table 2.2. Are there any concepts or ideas that may suggest that you need to add a new category? Discuss with others what you have found.

Ineffective listening behaviours

Unfortunately, some people struggle to listen effectively. Selective listening, defensive listening, interruptive listening, and pretend listening constitute some unproductive approaches. Selective listening involves focusing on limited parts of a message because of their intrinsic interest or how they resonate with personal perspectives and disregarding other information, resulting in oversights and mis-judgments (Macnamara, 2015; Turner & West, 2018). Defensive listening is held by those who tend to listen in the expectation of receiving confirmation of some hostility, a personal attack, or criticism and are simultaneously internally mounting a defense or counter attack (Macnamara, 2015; Turner & West, 2018). Interruptive listening is characterised by interrupting a speaker or 'tuning out' on what is being said, focusing, rather, upon planning a reply (Macnamara, 2015). It is best to avoid interrupting another unless absolutely necessary (De Janasz et al., 2014; Gill, 2019; Turner & West, 2018) because it tends to convey poor listening engagement and disrespect. Finally, those who feign interest in what is being said, often while planning their subsequent countering remarks are engaging in what is known as pretend listening (Macnamara, 2015). Pretend listening often results in miscommunication because so much effort is put into the act of pretending attention that important aspects of communication are overlooked. The best way to avoid ineffective listening behaviours is to reflect upon and systematically adopt the techniques used by active and effective listeners (Macnamara, 2015).

Listening styles

People vary in their listening styles that are characteristic or habitual approaches to listening (see McKenna et al., 2020) that assist them in the process of making sense of messages (Turner & West, 2018). Although listening is a universal form of communication, it is, however, understood differently depending upon the cultural context (Turner & West, 2018) and will influence listening style in some way. A variety of behaviours may suggest someone's communication style. Some may communicate in lively, spontaneous, and direct ways and others are more reserved and introverted. The nature and number of gestures adopted, soft or loud tones, and time taken in listening and talking respectively also contribute to interpretations of an individual's communication style (Gill, 2019).

Based on a review of the literature, Ramos Salazar (2017) explored the connection between likely levels of compassion/kindness for self and others and individual listening styles orientated towards people, content, logical elements, and time factors. Compassion for others was defined as the ability to recognise the suffering of others. The author found that those who have a people listening style are more likely to be capable of genuine concern and compassion for others as well as for themselves. Content-oriented listeners evaluate factual elements of messages prior to making any judgements and no correlations were found with self-compassion. Logical listeners tend to pay little attention to the emotions of others and were found to behave less compassionately towards others and themselves. Those with a time-orientated listening style tend to focus upon how much time is passing in communications rather than upon the distress of the speaker and are, thus, slightly less compassionate towards others. No correlation between this listening style and self-compassion was discovered. Depending upon the circumstances, each of these listening styles may be useful and appropriate but in situations where managers are responding to employee distress, a people-orientated listening style is most likely to convey attentive concern/compassion. Ramos Salazar's (2017) findings respond to the call from McKenna et al. (2020) for more research with respect to empathetic and engaged listening that acknowledges and responds to a speaker. Doing so is in the best interests of employee wellbeing and communication about what is happening in a given situation, more broadly.

Trust and self-disclosure

Trust has become widely researched in organisational, business, and management contexts over many decades (see Weibel et al., 2016; Six & Sorge, 2008). It has also received much attention from negotiation scholars who have recognised its role in success, particularly in integrative negotiation (Lewicki, Barry, & Saunders, 2016). In a seminal definition of trust, Six and Sorge (2008, p. 859) stated,

> Trust has been defined as a psychological state comprising the intention to accept vulnerability to the actions of another individual (a trustee), based upon the expectation that the other will perform a particular action that is important to the trustor.

The concept of vulnerability often features in definitions and explanations of trust (see Baer, Frank, & Luciano, 2021) in the acknowledgement that trusting someone comes with some risks (Kong, Dirks, & Ferrin, 2014). Kartolo and Kuo (2021) drew upon these themes in their explanation of trust as a mutual exchange based on some confidence that each party will display good intentions and not exploit any vulnerability identified in the other.

A trusting interpersonal bond reaps many positive outcomes for individuals and for organisations. People flourish in workplaces built on trust, fostered by interdependence, empathy, and mutual support (Costello, 2020). For some time, researchers have been able to link trust to multiple specific organisational benefits. The support that trust brings helps in overcoming challenges in working life and has been associated with improved job performance (Baer et al., 2021; Ferrin & Gillespie, 2010; Thomas, Zolin, & Harmen, 2009), profit margins (Fagen-Smith & Resenblum, 2013), improving organisational functions (Song, Kim, & Kolb, 2009), closer workplace relationships and fewer interpersonal conflicts (Rousseau, Sitkin, Burt, & Camerer, 1998; Grimscheid & Brockmann, 2010; Saban & Luchs, 2011; Song et al., 2009), greater satisfaction and commitment (Ferrin & Gillespie, 2010; Six & Sorge, 2008), team building (Grimscheid & Brockmann, 2010), and the development of citizenship behaviour (Ferrin & Gillespie, 2010).

When trust is lacking, however, individuals feel cautious in dealing with one another and are less likely to collaborate or exchange information (Kong et al., 2014; Lewicki et al., 2016). Both these circumstances damage communication, upon which the success of organisations rest. Given the benefits of trust relationships, it is reasonable to assume that most people would want to be trusted by their managers and employers. It would seem surprising indeed to question Goodwin's (2019, p. 180) observation that 'all leaders and all organizations need trust' and that therefore they should be 'continuously engaged in building and maintaining trust'. Yet, according to Baer et al. (2021), supervisors need to know that some employees do not welcome the extra responsibility and strain involved when they are trusted. They discovered that for employees who do not seek out a high level of trusting behaviours, being trusted can be perceived as overwhelming, and, ultimately, a failure to recognise and consider personal needs. These findings bring into question the consensus view that lower levels of trust are, in all circumstances, undesirable. Thus, trust is a matter of context and interpersonal knowledge in relationships and determines what trust means for individual interactants.

Trust relationships develop over time but it is also the case that trustworthiness is assessed via a variety of communication cues, including those that are nonverbal (Goodwin, 2019). Noise, as discussed in Chapter 1 of this book, impedes communication. Whether or not someone is trusted, and to what degree, is influenced by personal prejudices (Costello, 2020) as a form of noise that can damage interpersonal communication. Such prejudices constitute a form of emotional learning from an early age that are difficult to eschew even by adults who recognise the unfairness in holding on to them but once recognised, prejudices can be addressed in a commitment to adopting a zero tolerance for *intolerance* (Goleman, 2020).

Empirical research has demonstrated that the formulation, development, and maintenance of trust is influenced significantly by culture (Kartolo & Kuo, 2021). One empirical study by Crossman and Noma (2012), exploring trust relationships between Japanese expatriate managers and Australian supervisors working in subsidiaries of Japanese multinationals in Australia, explains how trustworthiness is signalled and perceived interculturally and can cause problems unless employees are aware of the ways in which trust is culturally constructed. An illustration of the findings relates to cultural constructions of what constitutes an excuse as opposed to an explanation, and how the differences between Japanese and Australian employees trigger assumptions about who can be trusted or not, on that basis. Kartolo and Kuo (2021) also conducted a study on intercultural trust in Taiwan and revealed how Confucianism affects how trust is understood in East Asia. Originating in China, Confucianism guides expectations about social behaviour and roles through philosophical lessons that are regarded as a practical form of ethics (Kartolo & Kuo, 2021). As one of the five virtues of Confucianism, *Xin* comes closest to being translatable as trustworthiness but it is not understood in quite the same way that it is in the West, being more tightly tied to the concepts of reliability, faithfulness, and loyalty. According to Kartolo and Kuo (2021), the western interpretation of trust has a much stronger association with morality though they acknowledge that it would be difficult to possess *Xin* and be an immoral person at the same time. The authors illustrate how it is the nature of the Confucian lens on trust that explains why Taiwan, China, and Japan as Confucian-influenced countries do not view legal contracts in business with the same level of favour as Americans, for example. *Xin* places emphasis upon verbal commitment in the context of relationships in ways that supersede the value placed in the West upon legal contracts. A perceived lack of regard for faith in someone's word and focusing only upon a contract may make it even more difficult for Taiwanese business people who have lower levels of trust compared to some other cultures to trust western outgroups (Kartolo & Kuo, 2021). Given the influence of culture and other phenomena that cause prejudice in trust contexts, self-knowledge and reflection are critical considerations in exploring any feelings of mistrust with business partners and colleagues. Reflection can also be stimulated by evidence in making decisions and one of the areas in which trust decisions are made is that of self-disclosure.

Self-disclosure

Self-disclosure is a valuable interpersonal skill that is often explored through a communication lens and refers to a willingness to share private information and inner parts of oneself (Antaki, Barnes, & Leudar, 2005; Chelune et al., 1979; Crossman, 2015; Croucher, Faulkner, & Long, 2010; Turner & West, 2018). Curiously, given its relevance to workplace environments, little has been published within management and organisation journals (Crossman, 2015). Within the literatures of psychology and psychotherapy, however, an underlying assumption prevails that self-disclosure is healthy or therapeutic whereas repressing personal feelings is not (Antaki et al., 2005).

Individuals may disclose information about personal fears, feelings, doubts (Larson, 2018) experiences, thoughts, interests, values, or, indeed, facts. Even humour can be a form of self-disclosure because sharing a joke is akin to sharing a part of oneself with another (Crossman et al., 2011). In many ways, self-disclosure involves decisions about when to speak and when not (Hartley & Chatterton, 2015). Disclosures tend to occur incrementally, over a period of time, as relationships develop, beginning with those least personal to ones that become progressively more intimate (Turner & West, 2018). Essentially, this is a process of gaining trust and explains why people tend to disclose most to those they trust and know well (Crossman et al., 2011; Crossman, 2015).

Self-disclosure can facilitate positive workplace relationships that are crucial to the wellbeing of employees (Gibson, 2018) because it has been associated with enhanced satisfaction, intrinsic motivation, and trusting relationships that, in turn, contribute to shared understandings of, for example, communication of organisational values and goal expectations (Crossman, 2015; Gibson, 2018; Wang, Zhang, Chen, & Zeng, 2018). Some of these outcomes arise because the collegial friendships at work involving self-disclosure tend to encourage motivation (Mao & An-Tien, 2012), for example, and assist in the development of social bonds especially when self-disclosure is reciprocated (Diaz-Peralta, Horenstein, & Downey, 2003). Self-disclosure is, thus, beneficial emotionally, relationally, and psychologically for the wellbeing of employees.

Scholars have also begun to consider the implications for self-disclosure in online contexts (Crossman, 2015). Melumad and Meyer (2020) found that consumers are more likely to self-disclose using a smart phone rather than on their personal computers, particularly where they believe the information is unidentifiable. Another study discovered that instant messaging via WhatsApp, as with face-to-face self-disclosure, encourages reciprocity and enhances relationships (Trepte, Masur, & Scharkow, 2018). Ho, Hancock, and Miner (2018) also explored self-disclosure using chatbot, a software application to conduct an online chat conversation via text or text to speech rather than providing contact with another person directly. Other studies have considered online self-disclosure in specific regions such as one undertaken by Wang et al. (2018) in the People's Republic of China (PRC). With respect to diversity, some scholars have focused on gender and whether women disclose more than males (see Croucher et al., 2010). Research on age and self-disclosure suggest inconclusive findings on whether some age groups self-disclose more than others (Jourard, 1971; Diaz-Peralta et al., 2003). Few studies, however, have explored self-disclosure from a cultural perspective despite evidence that culture influences when and how employees self-disclose and what is considered acceptable in Asian and western cultures (Crossman, 2015; Larson, 2018). Diversity aside, a number of factors affect decision making about self-disclosure. It is more likely to occur when people know each other well (Crossman, 2015; Derlega, Winstead, Mathews, & Braitman, 2008), are attracted to one another (Archer, 1979; Hargie, 2011), or share common interests (Derlega et al., 2008). People also tend to self-disclose when doing so will attract a positive impression and social approval (Tian, 2013) rather than stigma (Crossman, 2015). Stigma is now well researched on many levels (Zhang, Wang, Toubiana, & Greenwood, 2021) since Goffman (1959, 1963) introduced his seminal work on the topic. Few will self-disclose again after experiencing discrimination when they had done so in the past (Chelune et al., 1979; Clair, Beatty, & Maclean, 2005). Thus, decision making about whether to disclose or not involves weighing up the risks and benefits of doing so. Cross (2020) for example, suggests that those with mental ill-health are justifiably cautious about disclosure at work. Self-disclosure can be perceived as taboo, potentially misunderstood, risky (possibly motivated by malicious intent), or helpful, depending upon the organisational culture and whether it is inclusive and encourages open communication or not (Crossman, 2015; Larson, 2018).

Communication plays a significant part in how identities are constructed (Scott, 2019) and operates as a mechanism for determining relational boundaries (Mautner, 2017). Identity is a powerful aspect in everyone's life and reflected in political, religious, and other values and beliefs, cultural membership, or through online personas via social media and occupations (Larson, 2018). Decision making about whether to self-disclose at work often depends on how employees feel about where comfortable boundaries lie between the private and public self (Crossman, 2015; Derlega et al., 2008). Where there is a perceived lack of alignment between the two, individuals may feel under pressure to conceal parts of themselves in order to be acceptable to a dominant group (Clair et al., 2005), influencing the perceptions of others through impression or identity management (Turner & West, 2018) to avoid any potential stigma associated with membership of a perceived devalued identity. Some occupations are referred to as 'dirty work' because the stigmatising poor perception of the community includes telemarketing, bill collecting, real estate, and used car sales, but one study has revealed that actively trying to manage the perception of the occupation may unintentionally reinforce stigma because the self-management of stigma may convey dubious, deceptive, and possibly immoral behaviour (Mikolon, Alavi, & Reynders, 2020).

Keeping secret aspects of personal identity, however, can lead to high levels of stress because of the fear of rejection, discrimination, and loss of reputation (Crossman, 2015). Poor alignment between organisational and personal values causes chronic distress at work, the erosion of personal meaning and purpose, and poor mental and physical health through the deterioration of diet, hydration, exercise, sleep, and productivity (Brandt, 2020). When employees do decide to self-disclose, it can be interpreted as disruptive in ways that challenge an organisational culture (Gibson, 2018). Nevertheless, self-disclosure is also potentially empowering, strengthens mental health, and reduces stress arising from non-disclosure (Ho et al., 2018; Larson, 2018; Wang et al., 2018).

DISCUSSION ACTIVITY

With others, discuss whether you would disclose the following information to colleagues in the workplace:

- pregnancy
- being a recreational drug user/tobacco smoker/heavy drinker of alcohol
- a mental illness
- sexual orientation.

If you find yourself giving 'it would depend' answers, try to explicitly state what sort of factors your response would be contingent upon. For example, 'I would only disclose early pregnancy to peers I knew and trusted well'.

The topic of self-disclosure is also discussed in Chapter 8, with respect to spiritual diversity.

Nonverbal communication

Nonverbal communication refers to communication other than speech but nevertheless works to substitute, complement, reinforce, contradict, or regulate verbal communication (Frank & Solby, 2020; Givens, 2020; Larson, 2018). It involves cues such as, smiling, arm waving, and even stammering (Berger, 2016; Salem & Timmerman, 2018; Turner & West, 2018) and functions to provide information, regulate interaction, create impressions, or express emotions, for example (Eaves & Leathers, 2018). Although culture and professional context influence the interpretation of nonverbal behaviour (Eaves & Leathers, 2018), some forms are considered common or universal across cultures (Dwyer, 2020). Evidence suggests that nonverbal communication preceded linguistic expression (Givens, 2020) and as verbal communication began to develop, it became possible to convey more complex meanings (Frank & Solby, 2020). Most published work tends to focus upon verbal communication in the workplace, despite the growth of interest in nonverbal communication (Salem & Timmerman, 2018) and enquiry into proxemics, haptics, kinesics, paralinguistics, appearance, chronemics, and occlusics.

Proxemics

In the 1960s, Edward Hall, an anthropologist, pioneered proxemic research and coined the term 'proxemics' (Berger, 2016; Eaves & Leathers, 2018). Proxemics is the study of how individuals use interpersonal space and distance to influence interactions with others (Berger, 2016; De Janasz et al., 2014; Eaves & Leathers, 2018; Salem & Timmerman, 2018; Turner & West, 2018). The role of proxemics depends upon factors such as the situation, the relationship between interactants, their respective status, and culture (De Janasz et al., 2014; Hartley & Chatterton, 2015). To illustrate, Arabs and Latin Americans tend to be more comfortable in maintaining closer interpersonal distances than South Africans or the British (Hartley & Chatterton, 2015). Breaching cultural expectations about how space is used is likely to cause tension (Rowe & Levine, 2009).

Edward Hall suggested that the higher the level of relational formality, the greater the space maintained by interactants. In contrast, close friends, romantic partners, and family members, for example, tend to maintain an intimate space of about 0.45 metres, whereas most people at work generally adopt approximately a 1.2-metre space or more, depending upon the relationship, status, and the level of formality (Hartley & Chatterton, 2015; Turner & West, 2018). Territoriality is a slightly different concept from personal space in that it is concerned with spatial ownership and notions around personal territory or boundaries. Asking someone to save your space in a queue while you momentarily step away references your perceived right to that space as does hanging a jacket over the chair as a marker of ownership, or leaving personal items in an office area to define personal boundaries (Turner & West, 2018).

ACTIVITY: EXPERIENTIAL DISCUSSION

- During the Covid-19 pandemic greater social distances between people at work (usually around 1.5 metres) are now required. How do you think this state of affairs may have affected communication? If you were studying and/or working during the pandemic, was it difficult for you to maintain the required physical distance with colleagues or fellow students? Why?
- What do you think is an acceptable distance for colleagues who work together every day? Explain your response.
- It is important to pay careful attention to the nonverbal cues that co-workers communicate to avoid embarrassment, or a perceived inappropriate and unacceptable invasion of space. How do you and others seem to signal that the space between you has become uncomfortable or inappropriate?

Proxemics is also relevant to haptics because as the space around people diminishes, the likelihood is that touch will be involved at some point.

Haptics

Haptics is the study of conventions about human touch and the meaning people attribute to tactile communication (Berger, 2016; Darics & Dufrene, 2016; De Janasz et al., 2014). Touch conveys the nature of personal relationships and emotions such as aggression and affection (De Janasz et al., 2014) power, formality, and intimacy. More intimate forms of touching in professional settings are generally considered appropriate by, for example, hairdressers, doctors, or masseuses (De Janasz et al., 2014) but not generally so in other professions.

ACTIVITY: EXPERIENTIAL DISCUSSION

Discuss when the following forms of touch would be appropriate or not in a workplace or organisation with which you are familiar. Consider how national culture, organisational culture, profession, or the nature of co-worker relationships, for example, may guide your responses.

1.   A handshake
2.   A slap on the back
3.   A kiss
4.   A hug
5.   Placing a hand on a colleague's shoulder.

Kinesics

The term kinesics derives from a Greek word meaning movement. Thus, kinesics scholars explore how body movement, postures, and gestures play a part in how people communicate (Darics & Dufrene, 2016). Desmond Morris, originally an anthropologist, is a leading authority on body language who traces it to a pre-language past in human history (Anand, 2018). Cordell (2018, p. 21) defines kinesics as the 'study of physical expressions'. Eaves and Leathers (2018, p. 83), however, in their definition draw attention to the role of meaning making in this form of communication, stating, 'Kinesics is the study of observable, isolable, and meaningful movement in interpersonal communication'. However, other forms of nonverbal communication such as aspects of appearance and facial expressions fall within the broad field of kinesics.

Emotions are conveyed via body language in that anger, for example, may be accompanied by an impassive facial expression, especially when accompanied by foot tapping (Anand, 2018; Hartley & Chatterton, 2015). Other emotions such as fear, disgust, love, happiness, and sorrow can also be conveyed through kinesics and since they are linked to pre-language times in human development, the display of emotions nonverbally is largely regarded as universal (Anand, 2018) though precise expressions of emotions are influenced by culture. Paul Ekman, a Californian psychologist, produced seminal work in the 1960s on the expression of nonverbal emotions by studying facial expressions over many years, identifying eight: anger, determination, disgust, fear, neutrality, pouting, sadness, and surprise (Berger, 2016).

Gestures may be used to illustrate what is being said or may operate independently of words. Illustrators are nonverbal acts that accentuate or complement spoken words (Dwyer, 2020; Eaves & Leathers, 2018), whereas emblems such as a 'thumbs-up' gesture can be adopted independently from them and are particularly useful when extraneous noise or distance makes speech difficult (Berger, 2016). Culture tends to influence both emblems and illustrators and, indeed, some cultures use gestures more than others (Berger, 2016). Mexicans and Italians tend to use more animated gestures as compared with some Asian cultures where they may be considered rude (Turner & West, 2018). Greetings are also supported by gestures such as waving, shaking hands, nodding, or, in the Japanese culture, bowing. The conventions and nuances around bowing in Japan are complex and difficult for non-Japanese to appreciate but, generally, those of a lower status are expected to initiate the gesture and to bow more deeply than those of higher status though much depends on how formal the occasion is (Turner & West, 2018).

ACTIVITY: EXPERIENTIAL DISCUSSION

Work on your own and note down any emblems used in your own culture. Share your ideas with others and demonstrate the emblems physically. Did they come up with similar emblems and attribute the same meaning to them? If they did not, discuss possible reasons for inconsistencies in your response.

Appearance

Personal appearance affects the impressions that a communicator makes and facial appearance, according to Eaves and Leathers (2018), has a disproportionate influence upon judgements about attractiveness. Observant communicators are able to draw some conclusions about a person's appearance, identity, those things he or she values (Goodwin, 2019), and level of confidence (Heads, 2017). Uniforms, badges, or other forms of insignia can convey nonverbal messages about authority (De Janasz et al., 2014). They may command respect not simply for individuals but also for their professions and the values they embody.

ACTIVITY: REFLECTION AND DISCUSSION

Discuss with others the messages, positive, negative, or neutral, that certain professional uniforms and insignia associated with, for example, the law, healthcare, or the military convey to you. Try to reflect upon and convey why you tend to make these assumptions. In the wake of the Black Lives Matter movement, it is quite obvious, for example, how in certain communities a police uniform may well conjure feelings of fear, and in some cases revulsion. Thus, context will make a difference to assessments.

It is important to be cautious in making assumptions about others, largely because appearances can be deceptive and interpreting them is a complex process. For example, clothing may suggest something about socio-economic status, though some people understate and others overstate their status, so some care is required in analysing clothing as signals in nonverbal communication (Berger, 2016).

Appearance is a powerful form of communication that affects someone's potential to secure employment. Personal attractiveness, gender, skin, and hair (head, facial, body hair, hairstyle, colour etc.), body shape (including size and weight), tattoos, piercings, jewellery, and make-up are all signs that communicate something about a person to a perceiver, accurately or not (De Janasz et al., 2014; Goodwin, 2019; Hartley & Chatterton, 2015). Body odour also affects perceptions and decisions about how to interact with others (Eaves & Leathers, 2018). Even someone's teeth can be judged negatively if they are not white or straight (Berger, 2016). Head coverings such as turbans often communicate something about personal culture and values and under some circumstances may give rise to discrimination, conflict, or assumptions about credibility (Hartley & Chatterton, 2015). Depending upon the context, however, discrimination can be positive or negative. Those who do not conform to cultural ideals with respect to attractiveness are likely to find life hard because of the negative impact they receive and a consequent limitation of social and interpersonal rewards (Eaves & Leathers, 2018).

ACTIVITY: RESEARCH AND THEORY TO PRACTICE DISCUSSION

Form small groups. Task each member with gathering together three pictures (perhaps from magazines) of individuals beforehand. It is important that the chosen pictures are not of famous or well-known people in the community. Also avoid selecting any pictures of family members or close friends. Share the pictures with team members and ask them to make notes on any assumptions they have about persons in the photo. Each team member must then share their ideas and draw on publications about appearance as evidence to support their assessments. You may like to consider, for example:

- profession
- socio-economic status
- level of education
- personality
- trustworthiness
- interests.

The environment, artefacts, or physical objects in workspaces also communicate something about an organisational culture, nonverbally. How light, space, and colour are used, the design of furniture and where it is placed, all create impressions (De Janasz et al., 2014).

ACTIVITY: OBSERVATION AND RESEARCH

Choose to focus upon an organisation where you work, volunteer, or happen to know quite well (a university, your local dentist etc.). Discretely note down any observations of the environment in some detail and include descriptions of employees and their appearance. Consider what assumptions you would make about the organisation and its culture and write a brief report supporting your ideas, drawing upon nonverbal communication literature.

Paralinguistics

Paralinguistics and paralanguage are concerned with the study of how people speak rather than what they say with respect to nonverbal speech behaviours such as pitch, rate, volume, tone, inflection, tempo, pronunciation, disfluencies (ums and ahs), muttering, laughing, crying, groaning, pauses, or even periods of silence (Darics & Dufrene, 2016; Turner & West, 2018). Whether someone speaks softly or emphasises certain words to convey a particular meaning are other paralinguistic signals (De Janasz et al., 2014). People may draw conclusions that are sometimes negative about someone's personality based on the sound of his or her voice. Speech that does not vary in rate or pitch may be perceived as a sign of introvertism or a lack of assertion, and a nasal quality may be associated with undesirable personality characteristics (Eaves & Leathers, 2018).

As a paralinguistic feature, the many purposes of silence will usually depend upon national culture but are often practiced to acknowledge the beliefs and actions of another in an empathetic manner (Turner & West, 2018). Silence may communicate positive or negative messages (Larson, 2018) or indeed convey a neutral response. For example, it may suggest contentment (Larson, 2018), reflection (Macnamara, 2015), anger (Larson, 2018), resistance, disagreement, or exasperation (Macnamara, 2015). It may also be used, less ethically as an interview strategy to inveigle someone into revealing information they would not otherwise have shared, simply to end the discomfort that silence can sometimes bring (Macnamara, 2015). Somewhat unproductively from a communication perspective, organisations can also be silent on issues they do not wish to acknowledge (Macnamara, 2015).

DISCUSSION ACTIVITY

In small groups, experiment with expressing the following statements (or some of your own), using different paralanguage in such a way that the meaning might be interpreted differently, as a result.

1. If you really want to lead this project, you can
2. Are you asking me if I would consider giving you a pay rise?
3. . . . not now. I'm afraid I am busy all morning but may have an opening on Friday when we can meet

---

Chronemics

Chronemics is a term used to describe how people structure time and its implications for communication. Eaves and Leathers (2018, p. 352) have provided a useful, concise but sufficiently comprehensive definition of chronemics as 'the way members of a given culture define, experience, structure and use time'. The study of chronemics is brought to a variety of contexts. As the definition provided by Eaves and Leathers (2018) indicated, national culture influences whether it is acceptable or not to arrive at a meeting early, on time, or a little late, for example (De Janasz et al., 2014). Chronemic cues are also relevant to online forms of communication at work in that if a colleague does not respond to a text or email within a certain time period, it may lead to feelings of frustration and give rise to conflict with a colleague who may have quite different expectations about when it is appropriate to send a response.

The concepts of monochronic and polychronic approaches to time and how it is experienced was, according to Eaves and Leathers (2018), first coined by Hall in 1987 in the text entitled, *Hidden differences: Doing business with the Japanese*. Monochronic and polychronic time systems explain different attitudes to time where monochronic systems found in the UK, Germany, Scandinavia, Switzerland, and Australia construct time as tangible: 'found', 'saved', or 'lost', and polychronic systems favour multitasking, tolerate distraction, change, and interruptions, characterised by Arab, African, Asian, Latin American, Eastern, and Mediterranean cultural assumptions (De Janasz et al., 2014; Hall & Hall, 1990; Ting-Toomey & Oetzel, 2001). Perceptions associated with how long a decision takes are also culturally determined. Within the US, for example, quick decisions tend to convey decisiveness that is respected in that culture whereas in the Middle East, taking time to consider a decision carefully to avoid making a mistake would be better appreciated (Greenberg, 2005).

ACTIVITY: DISCUSSION

Discuss with others your personal expectations on meeting arrival times and response time for emails. Are there other examples that you can think of where time may be an issue for interpersonal communication in an organisation?

Occlusics

Occlusics relates to how the eyes are used in communication. Eaves and Leathers (2018) have drawn attention to the multiple functions of eye movements in regulating interpersonal interaction and communication (see Table 2.3) that may explain why people concentrate on the eyes more than other parts of the body.

Whether pupils dilate or contract can be revealing. Dilated pupils suggest a readiness for interpersonal communication, and positive emotions such as happiness and joy, and contracted pupils convey negative emotions, so capturing and interpreting both these physical responses constitutes a powerful resource for marketers and advertisers, for example (Eaves & Leathers, 2018). Although some consistency exists in how much eye contact individuals extend to one another, variations nevertheless occur (Crossman et al., 2011) depending upon who communicants are, the context, and the culture (Hartley & Chatterton, 2015). For example, in some cultures sustained eye contact may be considered disrespectful but not in others (Gill, 2019; Larson, 2018). Gender is also relevant to eye behaviour. Researchers make assessments of visual dominance based on the proportion of time individuals look whilst speaking and look while listening, such that communicators who exhibit high visual dominance are perceived as powerful, high-status

TABLE 2.3 Interpersonal functions of eye movements

Persuasion	Communicating emotions	Affirming power and status relationships
Playing a role in impression management	Establishing and developing intimacy	Signalling turn requesting, taking, and turn yielding in conversational management

people and, significantly, women have a lower visual dominance than men (Eaves & Leathers, 2018).

Deception and nonverbal communication

Scholars originally believed that nonverbal signals could be more reliably trusted than speech, but this perspective is now increasingly viewed as an oversimplification (Hartley & Chatterton, 2015; Turner & West, 2018). Actually, it is quite difficult to deceive others verbally or nonverbally, partly because even if someone tries to control authentic responses, nonverbal behaviours will still occur involuntarily (Hartley & Chatterton, 2015).

Nevertheless, some nonverbal behaviours are often associated with deception (see Larson, 2018):

- high pitched speech
- rapid blinking
- hand rubbing
- nose scratching
- delayed responses
- shorter, noncommittal, generalised, and evasive responses.

When verbal and nonverbal communication is consistent (e.g., both channels convey the same meaning), the message is more likely to be believed and the communication becomes more effective (Eaves & Leathers, 2018; Hartley & Chatterton, 2015). Where verbal and nonverbal cues appear to be contradictory, for example when someone indicates agreement verbally but rolls his or her eyes upward in an impatient manner, the recipient of the message will likely notice the ambiguity and decide whether to believe either the verbal or the nonverbal message and may well probe any ambiguity with a speaker to clarify the matter (De Janasz et al., 2014; Hartley & Chatterton, 2015).

Conclusion

This chapter has explained the concept of interpersonal communication and considered its implications in the workplace by focusing upon the themes of communication styles, listening, trust, self-disclosure, and nonverbal communication. It has adopted an introductory approach as a basis for scaffolding more complex conceptualisations in subsequent chapters of the book. As a construct, interpersonal communication begins with personal identity and a unique sense of self, influenced by multiple factors including culture, belief systems, and values. These factors interplay with aspects of the wider context and in the dynamic co-construction of meaning, communication with others essentially functions to create realities. Through reflection and the development of self-knowledge, it is possible to learn effective interpersonal communication strategies such as active listening that have the potential to enrich relationships.

References

Anand, R. (2018). *Happiness at work: Mindfulness, analysis and well-being.* Thousand Oaks: Sage.

Antaki, C., Barnes, R., & Leudar, I. (2005). Self-disclosure as a situated interactional practice. *The British Journal of Social Psychology, 44*(2), 181–199.

Archer, R. (1979). Role of personality and the social situation. In G. Chelune, R. Archer, C. Kleinke, L. Rosenfeld, J. Civikly, J. Herron, . . . J. Waterman (Eds.), *Self-disclosure: Origins, patterns, and implications in interpersonal relationships* (pp. 28–59). San Francisco: Jossey-Bass.

Baer, M., Frank, E., & Luciano, M. (2021). Undertrusted, overstated or just right? The fairness of (in) congruence between trust wanted and trust received. *Academy of Management, 64*(1), 180–206.

Berger, A. (2016). *Messages: An introduction to communication.* Walnut Creek: Taylor and Francis.

Brandt, M. (2020). Why focus on wellbeing? In E. Kim & B. Lindeman (Eds.), *Wellbeing* (pp. 11–19). Cham, Switzerland: Springer.

Brown, O., Paz-Aparicio, C & Revilla, A. (2019). Leader's communication style, LMX and organizational commitment. A study of employee perceptions in Peru. *Leadership and Organizational Development Journal, 40*(2), 230–258.

Chan, M. (2020). *English for business communication.* London: Routledge.

Chelune, G., Archer, R., Kleinke, C., Rosenfeld, L., Civikly, J., Herron, J., . . . Waterman, J. (1979). *Self-disclosure: Origins, patterns, and implications in interpersonal relationships.* San Francisco: Jossey-Bass.

Chlopicki, W., & Laineste, L. (2019). Communication styles: Between deliberate strategy and ambivalence. *Journal of Pragmatics, 153*, 15–19.

Clair, J., Beatty, J., & Maclean, T. (2005). Out of sight but not out of mind: Managing invisible social identities in the workplace. *Academy of Management Review, 30*(1), 78–95.

Coffelt, T., & Smith, F. (2020). Exemplary and unacceptable workplace communication skills. *Business and Professional Communication Quarterly, 83*(4), 365–384.

Cordell, A. (2018). *The negotiation handbook.* London: Routledge.

Costello, J. (2020). *Workplace wellbeing: A relational approach.* London: Routledge.

Cross, M. (2020). *Anxiety.* Sydney: Harper Collins.

Crossman, J. (2015). Being on the outer: The risks and benefits of spiritual self-disclosure in the Australian workplace. *Journal of Management & Organization, 21*(6), 772–785.

Crossman, J., Bordia, S., & Mills, C. (2011). *Business communication for the global age.* Sydney: McGraw-Hill.

Crossman, J., & Noma, H. (2012). Sunao as character: Its implications for trust and intercultural communication within subsidiaries of Japanese multinationals in Australia. *Journal of Business Ethics, 113*(3), 543–555.

Croucher, S., Faulkner, D., & Long, B. (2010). Demographic and religious differences in the dimensions of self-disclosure among Hindus and Muslims in India. *Journal of Intercultural Communication Research, 39*(1), 29–48.

Culpeper, J., & Qian, K. (2020). Communicative styles, rapport and student engagement: An online peer mentoring scheme. *Applied Linguistics, 41*(5), 756–786.

Darics, E., & Dufrene, D. (2016). *Writing online: A guide to effective digital communication at work* (1st ed.). New York: Business Expert Press.

De Janasz, S., Crossman, J., Campbell, N., & Power, M. (2014). *Interpersonal skills in organisations.* Sydney: McGraw-Hill Education.

Derlega, V., Winstead, B., Mathews, A., & Braitman, A. (2008). Why does someone reveal highly personal information? Attributions for and against self-disclosure in close relationships. *Communication Research Reports, 25*(2), 115–130.

De Vries, R., Bakker-Pieper, A., Konings, F., & Schouten, B. (2013). The communication styles inventory (CSI): A six-dimensional behaviour model of communication styles and its relation with personality. *Communication Research, 40*(4), 506–532.

Diaz-Peralta Horenstein, V., & Downey, J. (2003). A cross-cultural investigation of self-disclosure. *North American Journal of Psychology, 5*(3), 373–386.

Dwyer, J. (2020). *Communication for business and the professions: Strategies and skills.* Melbourne: Pearson.

Eaves, M., & Leathers, D. (2018). *Successful nonverbal communication: Principles and applications.* Oxford: Routledge, Taylor & Francis Group.

Fagen-Smith, B., & Resenblum, T. (2013). The value of trust: Study links. Communication, culture and employee trust with higher earnings per share. *Communication World, 30*(3), 22–24.

Ferrin, D., & Gillespie, N. (2010). Trust differences across national-societal cultures: Much to do or much ado about nothing. In M. Saunders, D. Skinner, G. Dietz, N. Gillespie, & R. Lewicki (Eds.), *Organizational trust: A cultural perspective* (pp. 42–86). New York: Cambridge University Press.

Frank, M., & Solby, A. (2020). Nonverbal communication: Evolution and today. In R. Sternberg & A. Kostic (Eds.), *Social Intelligence and nonverbal communication* (pp. 119–162). Cham, Switzerland: Palgrave Macmillan.

Gibson, K. (2018). Can I tell you something? How disruptive self-disclosure changes who 'we' are. *Academy of Management Review, 43*(4), 570–589.

Giles, H. (2016). *Communication accommodation theory: Negotiating personal relationships and social identities across cultures.* Cambridge: Cambridge University Press.

Gill, H. (2019). *Communication: How to connect with anyone.* Chichester: Capstone John Wiley & Sons Ltd.

Givens, D. (2020). Nonverbal steps to the origin of language. In R. Sternberg & A. Kostic (Eds.), *Social intelligence and nonverbal communication* (pp. 163–189). Cham, Switzerland: Palgrave Macmillan.

Goffman, E. (1959). *The presentation of self in everyday life.* New York: Anchor Books from Doubleday.

Goffman, E. (1963). *Stigma: Notes on the management of spoiled identity.* Englewood Cliffs, NJ: Prentice Hall.

Goleman, D. (2020). *Emotional intelligence: Why it can matter more than IQ.* London: Bloomsbury Publishing.

Goodwin, J. (2019). Communication accommodation theory: Finding the right approach. In M. Brown & L. Hersey (Eds.), *Returning to interpersonal dialogue and understanding human communication in the digital age* (pp. 168–186). Hershey, PA: IGA Global.

Greenberg, J. (2005). *Managing behaviour in organisations.* Upper Saddle River, NJ: Pearson.

Grimscheid, G., & Brockmann, C. (2010). Inter- and intraorganizational construction joint ventures. *Journal of Construction Engineering and Management, 136*(3), 353–360.

Hall, E., & Hall, M. (1990). *Understanding cultural differences.* Yarmouth, ME: Intercultural Press.

Hargie, O. (2011). *Skilled interpersonal communication research, theory and practice.* Hove: Routledge.

Hartley, P., & Chatterton, P. (2015). *Business communication: Rethinking your professional practice for the post digital age* (2nd ed.). New York: Routledge.

Harwood, J., Nussbaum, J., Pierson, H., Gallois, C., & Gasiorek, J. (2019). Accommodating a legend: Howard Giles and the social psychology of language and communication. In H. Giles, J. Harwood, J. Gasiorek, H. Pierson, J. Nussbaum, & C. Gallois (Eds.), *Language, communication and intergroup relations: A celebration of the scholarship of Howard Giles* (pp. 3–13). New York: Routledge.

Heads, G. (2017). *Living mindfully: Discovering authenticity through mindfulness coaching.* Oxford: Wiley Blackwell.

Ho, A., Hancock, J., & Miner, A. (2018). Psychological, relational and emotional effects of self-disclosure after conversations with a chatbot. *Journal of Communication, 68*(4), 712–733.

Jourard, S. (1971). *Self-disclosure: An experimental analysis of the transparent self.* New York: Wiley-Interscience.

Kartolo, A., & Kuo, B. (2021). Trust in the Taiwanese context. In C. Kwantes & B. Kuo (Eds.), *Trust and trustworthiness across cultures: Springer series in emerging cultural perspectives in work, organizational, and personnel studies* (pp. 53–69). Cham, Switzerland: Springer.

Kilduff, G., & Rosikiewicz, B. (2010). Challenge and threat. When interpersonal competition helps and when it harms: An integration via challenge and trust. *Academy of Management Annals, 14*(2), 908–934.

Kong, D., Dirks, K., & Ferrin, D. (2014). Interpersonal trust within negotiations: Meta-analytic evidence, critical contingencies, and directions for future research. *Academy of Management Journal, 57*(5), 1235–1255.

Larson, K. (2018). *Adaption and well-being.* London: Routledge.

Lewicki, R., Barry, B., & Saunders, D. (2016). *Essentials of negotiation* (6th ed.). New York: McGraw-Hill.

Lipetz, L., Kluger, A., & Bodie, G. (2020). Listening is listening is listening: Employees' perception of listening as a holistic phenomenon. *International Journal of Listening, 34*(2), 71–96.

Macnamara, J. (2015). *Organizational listening: The missing essential in public communication.* Bern, Switzerland: Peter Lang Books.

Mao, H. Y., & An-Tien, H. (2012). Friendship at work and error disclosure. *Business Research Quarterly, 20*(4), 213–225.

Mautner, G. (2017). Organizational discourse. In G. Mautner & F. Rainer (Eds.), *Handbook of business communication: Linguistic approaches* (pp. 609–628). Retrieved February 4, 2020, from https://ebookcentral.proquest.com

McKenna, L., Brown, T., Williams, B., & Lau, R. (2020). Empathetic and listening styles of first year undergraduate nursing students: A cross sectional study. *Journal of Professional Nursing, 36*, 611–615.

Melumad, S., & Meyer, R. (2020). Full disclosure: How smartphones enhance consumer self-disclosure. *Journal of Marketing, 84*(3), 28–45.

Mikolon, S., Alavi, S., & Reynders, A. (2020). The catch-22 of countering a moral occupational stigma in employee-customer interactions. *Academy of Management Journal.* doi:10.5465/amj.2018.1487

Ramos Salazar, L. (2017). The influence of business students' listening styles on their compassion and self-compassion. *Business and Professional Communication Quarterly, 80*(4), 426–442. doi:10.1177/2329490617712495

Rousseau, D., Sitkin, S., Burt, R., & Camerer, C. (1998). Introduction to special topic forum: Not so different after all. A cross-discipline view of trust. *Academy of Management Review, 23*(3), 393–404.

Rowe, B., & Levine, D. (2009). *A concise introduction to linguistics.* New York: Pearson.

Saban, K., & Luchs, R. (2011). The benefits of governing with a trust-central strategy. *Journal of Leadership, Accountability and Ethics, 8*(3), 43–55.

Salem, P. J., & Timmerman, C. E. (2018). Forty years of organizational communication. In P. Salem & E. Timmerman (Eds.), *Transformative practice and research in organizational communication* (pp. 1–28). Hershey, PA: IGI Global.

Scott, C. (2019). Identity and identification. In A. Nicotera (Ed.), *Origins and traditions of organizational communication: A comprehensive introduction to the field* (pp. 207–227). New York: Routledge.

Selting, M. (2009). Communicative style. In S. D'hondt, J. Ostman, & J. Verschueren (Eds.), *Pragmatics of interaction* (pp. 20–39). Amsterdam: John Benjamin's Publishing Company.

Six, F., & Sorge, A. (2008). Creating a high-trust organization: An exploration into organizational plicies that stimulate interpersonal trust building. *Journal of Management Studies, 45*(5), 857–884.

Song, J., Kim, H., & Kolb, J. (2009). The effect of learning organizational culture on the relationship between interpersonal trust and organizational commitment. *Human Resource Development Quarterly, 20*(2), 149–167.

Thomas, G., Zolin, R., & Harmen, J. (2009). The central role of communication in developing trust and its effect on employee involvement. *Journal of Business Communication, 46*(3), 287–310.

Tian, Q. (2013). Social anxiety, motivation, self-disclosure, and computer-mediated friendship: A path analysis of the social interaction in the blogosphere. *Communication Research, 40*(2), 237–260.

Ting-Toomey, S., & Oetzel, J. (2001). *Managing intercultural conflict effectively.* Thousand Oaks: Sage.

Trepte, S., Masur, P., & Scharkow, M. (2018). Mutual friends' social support and self-disclosure in face-to-face and instant messenger communication. *The Journal of Psychology, 158*(4), 430–445.

Tsia, M. (2020). The important issues for millennial workers. In *Management association, information resources editor: Five generations and only one workforce: How successful businesses are managing a multigenerational workforce* (pp. 203–232). Hershey, PA: IGI Global. doi:10.40181978-1-7998-0437-6

Turner, L., & West, R. (2018). *An introduction to communication.* Cambridge: Cambridge University Press.

Wang, G., Zhang, W., Chen, Q & Zeng, R. (2018). How is negative affect associated with life satisfaction? The moderating role of online self-disclosure in China's context. *Personality and Individual Differences, 135*, 60–66.

Weibel, A., Den Hartog, D., Gillespie, N., Searle, R., Six, F., & Skinner, D. (2016). How do controls impact employee trust in the employer? *Human Resource Management, 55*(3), 437–462.

Worthington, D., & Worthington, G. (2018). Defining listening: A historical theoretical and pragmatic assessment. In D. Worthington & G. Bodie (Eds.), *The sourcebook of listening research* (pp. 3–19). New York: John Wiley & Sons Ltd.

Zhang, R., Wang, M., Toubiana, M., & Greenwood, R. (2021). Stigma beyond levels: Advancing research on stigmatization. *Academy of Management Annals, 15*(1), 188–222.

Zhang, Y. (2019). Intergenerational harmonies and tensions. In H. Giles, J. Harwood, J. Gasiorek, H. Pierson, J. Nussbaum, & C. Gallois (Eds.), *Language, communication and intergroup relations: A celebration of the scholarship of Howard Giles* (pp. 167–168). New York: Routledge.

Zhang, Y., & Pitts, M. (2019). Interpersonal accommodation. In H. Giles, J. Harwood, J. Gasiorek, H. Pierson, J. Nussbaum, & C. Gallois (Eds.), *Language, communication and intergroup relations: A celebration of the scholarship of Howard Giles* (pp. 192–216). New York: Routledge.

3

ORGANISATIONAL COMMUNICATION

Conceptualising organisational communication and allied lines of enquiry

Organisational communication has been defined as 'the study of how, in a complex, system-orientated environment people send and receive information within the organization and the effect it has on organizational structure' (Bell & Martin, 2017, p. 6). The explanation is serviceable but other concepts need to be considered in order to capture what Mills (2011) describes as the complicated, dynamic dialectic of communication and organising. Communication creates a context for organising, constitutes the means by which it is achieved, and is also a consequence of organising in terms of how people experience and make sense of their roles (Mills, 2011). Within organisations, communication guides relationships horizontally and vertically and forms responses to initiatives. It can be viewed through a departmental, professional, or institutional lens and mediated through a range of communication channels (meetings, the intranet, online newsletters, emails, and via training badges, for example). Communication facilitates organising through the coordination of human activities to accomplish tasks, share networks, control, and manage (Brown, Paz-Aparicio, & Revilla, 2018; Chewing, 2019) and is fundamental to the way society functions (Sias & Shin, 2019a). Indeed, it is hardly possible to imagine that organisations could function or even exist without some form of communication (Methot, Rosado-Solomon, Downes, & Gabriel, 2020). Research assumes that organisations and communication are co-dependent in the creation of meaning (Methot et al., 2020) and that communication, culture, and relationships in organisations constitute cogent forces in developing, maintaining, changing, and even, ultimately, destroying organisations (Nicotera, 2019). Who has power in organisations is central to communication and how it is theorised because both communication and power constitute the organisational process

DOI: 10.4324/9780429318948-4

(Zoller & Ban, 2019). Communication is relevant to almost all organisational activities including embedded cultural knowledge, ethical codes, principles, procedures, and rules, many of which are expressed and codified in documents and databases (Dwyer, 2020; Hartley & Chatterton, 2015).

The intertwining connection amongst organisational behaviour, management, and communication theory is evident in the publication of communication research in business and management journals. An increasing emphasis upon communication was heralded by the shift from focusing upon efficiency measures favoured by classical management theorists, the subsequent emergence of Abraham Maslow's theory of the hierarchy of human needs and motivation, and, perhaps even more significant, the development of a human relations perspective (Miller, 2015). This perspective was based on the seminal work of Elton Mayo and his team at Harvard during the 1920/30s centred on research conducted at an electrical plant in Hawthorn, Illinois, revealing that the task environment (such as whether social and emotional needs are met) influences efficiency and performance as well as worker satisfaction (Miller, 2015). Thus, a shift from focusing almost exclusively upon financial priorities to an approach that balanced them with social and psychological phenomena formed the basis of the human relations perspective (Miller, 2015). From the 1980s increasing attention has been brought to culture, rituals, ceremonies, norms, metaphors, and humour (Zoller & Ban, 2019). All these issues lend themselves well to scholarly interest in workplace wellbeing and communication because they tend to focus upon human experiences and emotions at a deeper level and consider the implications of these matters in organisational practice. Communication researchers often probe these issues by paying attention to narratives, otherwise known as telling stories about personal experiences in specific contexts (Stephens, 1992). Recent literature has also paid more attention to occupational relationships and communication internally and externally with stakeholders. For example, Badham (2020) has framed communication with stakeholders in terms of organisational stakeholder love (OSL). He maintains that organisational strategic communication has hitherto regarded stakeholders in ways that treat them essentially as a means to an end, understood to be a one-way and asymmetrical communication model and advocates for two-way approaches to these relationships. Essentially this and other scholarship dating back to the 1980s entertains the ways in which analysis of healthy personal relationships may inform relationships with customers, suppliers, and even competitors (Badham, 2020). From a wellbeing perspective, these emerging ideas are highly relevant.

Business and management disciplines have long since acknowledged that communication is an essential element of organisational success (Nicotera, 2019; Turner & West, 2018) yet reportedly many managers and employees have poor communication skills (Ramos Salazar, 2017). Both these realities may account, at least in part, for the rise of organisational communication research over many decades with a well-defined disciplinary focus (Miller, 2015). The term 'organisational communication' is now commonly used having superseded 'industrial communication' from about the 1970s (Salem & Timmerman, 2018), presumably as the terminology expresses a broader line of enquiry. Highly regarded publications such as, the *Journal of Business Communication, Management Communication Quarterly, Journal of Applied Communication Research,* and *Business Communication Quarterly* have done much to establish the status of organisational communication as a study (Salem & Timmerman, 2018). However, variances occur depending upon disciplinary strands such as management or psychology and research approaches (e.g., positivism, post-positivism, critical perspectives and interpretivism that acknowledges subjective perspectives and inductive reasoning) (Nicotera, 2019).

Academic literature about organisational communication, including this text, often refers to the concepts of organisational culture and climate. Although these ideas have much in common, Costello (2020) distinguishes between the two, maintaining that 'climate' was used from the 1960s and focused primarily upon analysing policies, practices, and procedures. Bell and Martin (2017, p. 16) have described organisational climate as 'the environmental quality' experienced by employees. A positive and supportive climate, they maintain, is largely achieved when organisational leaders are open to a varied ideas and input in decision-making processes and demonstrate trust and a non-judgemental approach.

The study of organisational culture, Costello (2020) suggests, emerged after the concept of climate and may in fact be made up of multiple, cultural subgroups that exist concurrently and may be described as villages or tribes. Although such tribes exist, organisational culture can also be conceptualised as the aggregate of every employee in an organisation (Emery, 2019). The literature (see Bell & Martin, 2017; Costello, 2020; Emery, 2019; Harrington, 2018; Ruhl & Sub, 2020) suggests that the concept of organisational culture includes the following:

1. It relates to complex, intangible, and multiple phenomena, entrenched assumptions, powerful ingrained values that tend to be non-negotiable, and shared perceptions that may not be consciously held.
2. Cultures have their own identities that distinguish one organisation from others in terms of purpose, strategy, and how objectives are achieved through employee engagement.
3. Culture is learned through social interaction often in teams and language expressed through stories and metaphors, for example.
4. Cultures are influenced by experiences relating to mistakes made or external circumstances.
5. Cultures are shaped by behaviours, beliefs, attitudes, rituals, norms, history, expectations, and even the physical environment.
6. Organisational culture is influenced by national culture.

Much research work has also distinguished between formal and informal communication. Simply put, formal communication focuses upon organisational roles and informal communication pertains to all other non-role related communication (Salem & Timmerman, 2018). Informal communication also tends to involve phatic elements. Phatic communication is derived from the Greek word meaning 'to speak' (Porter, 2017) and refers to ubiquitous, normative, short, or relatively inconsequential conversations or 'small talk' that assist in establishing contact or socialising, rather than sharing information that is core to task completion (Methot et al., 2020).

Small talk is also useful in settings where a manager may address an issue with a subordinate without assuming an authoritative approach and, likewise, a subordinate may use small talk to express concern or disagreement with a management decision in a less confrontational, indirect way (Chan, 2020). Studies in phatic communication may also explore digital and social media settings as well as intercultural ones (Porter, 2017). Although phatic communication can be distracting, it should not be underestimated or necessarily suppressed, given its organisational benefits, including (Methot et al., 2020):

- the improvement of employee mood
- the creation of positive emotions and climates at work
- deeper feelings of belonging
- the demonstration of organisational citizenship behaviours (OCB)
- the enhancement of general wellbeing.

Thus, social and relational factors seem to influence communication and establish meaning in the working lives of employees (Sias & Shin, 2019a). Formal and informal communication may also be tied to location in that conversations in a lavatory are likely to be rather different from those in the board room. Some areas or spatial configurations such as photocopying and coffee making areas facilitate informal communication rather more than others (Hartley & Chatterton, 2015).

An area of scholarship that provides systematic insights into interpersonal and organisational communication is communication networks. Simply put, networking pertains to the creation of a system or information chain by encouraging and building professional relationships (De Janasz, Crossman, Campbell, & Power, 2014). Given the value of such relationships in developing careers and organisations, it is surprising that business schools reportedly allocate little attention in the curriculum to networking (Pasmore & Woodman, 2017). However, significant work has also been undertaken in the area of communication networks that explore who works with whom, to what degree and in what way (Dwyer, 2020). Networks connect people, providing opportunities to organise and communicate, and has been largely facilitated as a study by the emergence of technologies such as email and social media (Stephens & Kee, 2020). Networks occur among people, organisations, websites (through hyperlink analysis), supply chains, or neighbourhoods and are the patterns of communication sometimes referred to as 'ties' (usually amongst individuals referred to as 'nodes') that may be strong or weak, formal or informal, providing contexts for probing power, influence, and access to resources (Chewing, 2019).

ACTIVITY: DISCUSSION

Discuss with others any potential disadvantages of small talk in organisational communication. Should it be encouraged or discouraged? Explain your response based on personal reading about phatic communication.

ACTIVITY: RESEARCH AND SYNTHESIS

Search available library resources to find out more about weak and strong network ties. Make notes on factors that characterise a network as either weak or strong. Remember to record the references you use. In class, form small groups and pool what you discovered before presenting your conclusions to the rest of the class. If you have access to the reference used in this section (Chewing, 2019), you will find out more details on strong and weak network ties, but other resources will also be of value.

Language and organisations

Language plays a central role in global and international business, but scholars have recently observed that the nature and impact of language in these contexts is under-explored (Darics & Dufrene, 2016; Zhu, 2021). This is surprising given that interdisciplinary research findings on organisational/institutional/professional discourse (Mautner & Rainer, 2017) reveal many ways in which language is integral to organisational success. For instance, as a result of organisational discourse studies, managers appear to be increasingly conscious of the benefits of communicating information in ways that resonate with a specified target audience (Goodwin, 2019), internal or external to the organisation. It is also now clear that how senior managers communicate verbally or in writing affects investor attitudes and, ultimately, stock price (Guo, Sengul, & Yu, 2020). Where high uncertainty exists about a company's earnings, investor perceptions are more likely to be positive when discourse is credible, simple, comprehensible, and contains 'fresh' content (Guo et al., 2020).

Organisational culture and expectations will determine to a large extent the attention and response that is given to language issues and shape communicative interaction (Crossman, Bordia, & Mills, 2011; Larson, 2018). In those organisations where a high level of linguistic diversity exists, one might expect to see considerations of language being embedded into both decision making and policy development (see Lesk, Lavric, & Stegu, 2017). The wisdom of integrating language into approaches about practices and procedures cannot be overlooked. One reason why is that bilingual or multicultural speakers align or distance themselves from other colleagues or groups simply by choosing one language (or specific distinctive jargon) over another, and in so doing, adopt a personal, professional, and group identity (Mautner & Rainer, 2017). Such identifications have a powerful effect on how organisations operate and their success.

The insights and meaning of metaphors and tropes is an area of organisational discourse that has attracted much attention. Metaphors provide assistance in comprehending abstract concepts such as power, organisational culture, hierarchies, identities, conflicts, and relationships that would otherwise be difficult to understand (Jameson, 2019; Rakic & Maass, 2019). Qualitative organisational communication researchers have been trained to pay careful attention to metaphors in participant data for this reason. Mautner (2017) provides an interesting illustration of how metaphors are indicative of culture in alluding to the way an organisation may refer to itself as 'a family' in order to communicate that employee bonds and relational closeness are valued, but at the same time when an organisation fails to operate in ways consistent with the metaphor, employees may begin adopting the counter references of a 'dysfunctional family'. Misalignments like this between organisational language and actions can cause problems. This is no doubt why Heads (2017) calls for authentic/honest speech in organisations in the expression of ideas, whether positive or negative. A simple search online can identify many organisational communication studies that analyse metaphors. Dulek (2015) is one example of such a work in the context of organisational change.

As indicated in Chapter 2 with respect to self-disclosure, it is clear that identity work is carried out through language (Mautner, 2017). Individual identities are intertwined with the organisations that employ them through a process of identification (Toubiana, 2019). Identities are social constructions of reality interpreted through language in both personal and organisational communication that employees will often seek to manage, particularly where some resistance to an organisational identity becomes apparent (Scott, 2019) such as when unwelcomed changes are introduced.

Organisational change and communication

As Neenan and Dryden (2020, p. 171) observed, '[n]othing is constant. Change occurs whether you welcome it or fight against it'. The inevitability of change in organisations thus invites opportunities to take a strategic approach in how that process can be managed effectively and creatively for the benefit of all stakeholders. Enquiry and discussion about organisational change has occurred amongst academics and business practitioners since the middle of the last century (Smith, Skinner, & Read, 2020). A rich and multidisciplinary scholarship now exists, and within this community a rising interest has become evident in discovering more about how communication plays a part in the process, particularly with reference to stakeholder perspectives, organisational outcomes, individuals, and behaviours (Lewis, 2020).

At a simplistic level, the notion of change refers to the alteration or modification of a procedure, a capacity, or a policy, for example, that is substituted by some kind of alternative (Smith et al., 2020). Change is a perceived departure from the expected (Noels, Clement, Collins, & Machintyre, 2019) or the *status quo*. Lewis (2020, p. 406) defined the term organisational change as a process 'involved in introducing new ideas into practice'. As Cameron and Green (2015) have suggested, change is a learning experience. Learning facilitates the transition and adjustment necessary to move from one state of affairs to another. Although some conservative religious, educational, government, and bureaucratic institutions tend to change slowly because ways of doing things are so entrenched (Driskill & Laird, 2011; Graetz, Rimmer, Smith, & Lawrence, 2011; Holbeche, 2006), organisations are generally considered to be rapidly changing in complex ways, largely due to globalisation and advancements in digital communication (see Barratt-Pugh, Bahn, & Gakere, 2013). Goodwin (2019) has identified some characterising conditions in the twenty-first century that have influenced the nature of organisational communication and change:

- The transition from prioritising face to face interaction to communication via the Internet.
- A shift from globalisation to multipolarity as a lens for diversity that gathers up economic, geographic, cultural, and political considerations.
- A retreat, to some extent, from the unquestioned dominance of the US-led economy in the face of global expansion and influence of the PRC.
- The normalisation of higher levels of uncertainty.
- Growing concern about data privacy.
- Intensified calls for inclusion.

Change is triggered when organisational stakeholders begin to observe internal or external environmental issues, communicate them, and make a case for change (Lewis, 2019). Shifts in the environment that herald change may seem obvious or subtle and examples include: technological innovation, financial necessity, market variation, competitive pressure, or political policies (Smith et al., 2020). Whatever the trigger, as Laurie (2019) points out, change is essential for organisations to remain relevant, competitive, and responsive to environmental conditions, bring about cultural transformation, introduce innovative technologies that meet market needs, and to address issues such as injustice and poor practice. With respect to remaining responsive to environmental conditions, a world beset by the Covid-19 pandemic has necessitated change for many organisations and businesses because their very survival depended upon their capacity to pivot. That is, to adopt flexible and creative ways to respond to quickly changing circumstances. Although some scholars have observed that most change initiatives fail, others regard this contention as myth (Smollan & Morrison, 2019) and suggest that a large proportion are, in fact, successful (Allen, Jimmieson, Bordia, & Irmer, 2007; Lewis, 2019) – provided, of course, they are able to adapt to market needs.

Since communication is a crucial factor in the success of organisational and cultural change (Campbell, Carmichael, & Naidoo, 2015; Dulek, 2015; Palmer, Dunford, & Akin, 2009; Holbeche, 2006; Hughes, 2010), it behoves managers to plan the communication of change carefully in order to minimise the disruption to daily routines (Lewis, 2019). How disruptive a change is will largely depend upon how different the new reality is from an existing culture, values, beliefs, norms, behaviours, and assumptions (Noels et al., 2019). However, it is worth remembering that even prior to the initiation of change, organisations are rarely completely stable at any time because they are constantly, if sometimes imperceptibly, changing in one way or another (Laurie, 2019; Van de ven & Sun, 2011). As Gasiorek (2019) observed, the only constant is change itself and on an individual level, people continually make adjustments to their behaviour depending upon situations as they arise. Indeed, advances in neuroplasticity reveal that the brain is highly malleable, demonstrating that humans are in fact entirely capable of adapting to change (Emery, 2019).

Change communication may be formal or informal. Formal change communication is often captured in making official announcements. These may be to provide updates, such as instructions about timing, progress reports, or to invite feedback, whereas informal change communication tends to refer to occasions when employees feel they can share personal stories about their change experience that are 'off the record'/confidential and unofficial (Lewis, 2019). Another key distinction to be made about change is whether it is planned or unplanned. Achieving goals, making progress, and, indeed, avoiding crises are considered vital to organisations and generally involve some level of strategising with respect to planned changes (Graetz et al., 2011; Lewis, 2019). Unplanned changes may be more challenging because they usually relate to the unexpected and where a response is required much more quickly. Examples might lie in the outbreak of a pandemic or political unrest in an area that disrupts crucial supply lines. However, although the distinction between planned and unplanned changes is broadly useful, it is nevertheless questionable given that all change is arguably embedded in the surrounding environment and the multiplicity of shifts that influence organisations (see Lewis, 2020).

Change models

Models to help practitioners plan for change and its communication have been available since the middle of the twentieth century. Each of the models are influenced by disciplinary approaches and paradigmatic frameworks – in other words, an established, accepted disciplinary perspective (Smith et al., 2020). There isn't necessarily an ideal model because as Smith et al. (2020) suggest, how effective a model is will depend upon the circumstances and, indeed, some models seem to work better in one kind of organisation than another. In this text, it is not intended to provide a detailed exposition of change models but rather to acknowledge that they can be useful to practitioners in suggesting principles and strategies to consider in devising change plans.

Earlier models of organisational change tended to be linear, depicting steps, stages, and phases that assumed a relatively smooth transition from the identification of new ideas through to implementation (that is, where innovative ideas are applied or put to practical use) and become routinised (see Laurie, 2019). Lewis (2020, p. 408) also characterises these earlier models as ones that typically emphasised 'stability-change-restabilization', based on the assumption that organisations follow set patterns in how new ideas are surfaced, embraced, introduced, and, finally, if they are not rejected, become routinised.

Kurt Lewin's seminal action research change model has influenced the change and development field since its formulation in the late 1940s and is characterised as a *from-to* approach in planned change in that it moved organisations from a less to a more productive state (Pasmore & Woodman, 2017). Lewin's model is regarded as one of the least complex but has been criticised because it assumes that organisations are generally stable (Smith et al., 2020). He identified three phases: 1. unfreezing, 2. Changing, and 3. refreezing in what amounted to a blueprint for planned change. Unfreezing involves thoroughly preparing for change by analysing problems and gathering data through interviews, observation, and questionnaires (Waddell, Creed, & Cummings, 2019) and asking questions about what is happening in an organisation. This step usually involves some dismantling of those forces that maintain an organisation's behaviour as it exists (Waddell et al., 2019; Schermerhorn, Hunt, & Osborn, 1997).

The second phase is essentially focused on implementation. As Lewis (2020) and Smith et al. (2020) indicate, it is a period mostly related to communication and persuading others of the benefits of a particular change (Lewis, 2020). During this period, it is crucial to remind employees of the rationale for change and any benefits, in order to facilitate acceptance (Smith et al., 2020). Thus, changing refers to the phase of identifying the best people to implement a change, communicating information, addressing the tasks involved and any structural and technological issues (Schermerhorn et al., 1997). This period of implementation is costly, time consuming, and invariably psychologically challenging (Waddell et al., 2019). Refreezing entails reinforcing the new organisational culture, policies, structures, and norms, bringing about stabilisation and institutionalisation, providing additional support where necessary, and evaluating feedback on the change process (Schermerhorn et al., 1997; Waddell et al., 2019). The importance of monitoring the effectiveness of an implemented change and making any necessary adjustments continues to be emphasised in contemporary change practices (see Laurie, 2019; Waddell et al., 2019).

Lewin's model for change continues to be taught in business schools and is referred to in texts like this one. However, Pasmore and Woodman (2017) find the endurance of the model surprising, especially since Lewin's work was focused upon group-level changes in performance rather than being applied to the context of large and complex organisations, as it clearly has been. One explanation for the durability of this early theory and others like it may lie, quite simply, in their inherent accessible and concrete nature (Kang et al., 2020).

Another example of an early, somewhat linear change model was devised by Rogers in the first edition of his work in 1962. His book, entitled *The diffusion of innovations*, addressed the issue of how, why, and at what rate new ideas spread largely in the organisational context. Rogers, Professor of Communication, defined diffusion as a special type of communication that is concerned with new ideas and innovation via particular channels, over time, among members of a social system (Rogers, 2003). He emphasised five key stages in communicating change: 1. Agenda setting that relates to the process of determining what an organisation (or system) will address first, next, and so on. Agenda setting occurs at the point an organisational problem is identified, creating a perceived need for an innovation. 2. Matching, the next stage refers to the matching of the problem with the innovation. In a sense, this means that a certain idea or innovation is identified as a viable way to address an issue. 3. Redefining/restructuring is the stage at which the imported innovation begins to become more familiar. It is slowly reinvented to accommodate the organisational context more closely. 4. Clarifying occurs as the innovation is adopted more widely in an organisation and becomes gradually clearer to organisational members. 5. Routinising is the final stage of Rogers' model and relates to the point at which an innovation becomes embedded into the organisation's regular activities and is increasingly accepted, though Rogers warns that this stage should not be regarded as simple or straightforward.

Kotter's change model for change management continues to be widely adopted by organisations, especially in administrative and technological contexts (Kang et al., 2020). Although not generally considered to be highly complex, it does contain more stages than the Lewin model and has been criticised for the rigidity of its approach especially with respect to an insistence that each step is followed on the basis that any omissions are likely to cause the failure of the entire change process (Smith et al., 2020).

Kotter (1996) developed an eight-stage process of creating major change. They are: 1. Establishing a sense of urgency; 2. Creating a guiding coalition (that is, by putting together a group with enough power to lead the change and getting the group to work together like a team); 3. Developing a vision and strategy: Creating a vision to help direct and change effort and developing strategies for achieving that vision; 4. Communicating the change vision by using every vehicle possible to constantly communicate the new vision and strategies; 5. Empowering broad-based action such as getting rid of obstacles, changing systems, or structures that undermine the change vision. Obstacles may prove to be certain individuals, entrenched traditions, or alternative ideas (Smith et al., 2020), 6. Generating short-term wins. This stage is one that pays particular attention to motivating stakeholders, perhaps by rewarding individuals as significant milestones are reached (see Smith et al., 2020); 7. Consolidating gains and producing more change (using increased credibility to change all systems, structures, and policies that don't fit together and work with the transformation, and hiring, promoting, and developing those who can implement the change vision; 8. Anchoring new approaches in the culture by, for example, improving performance and hiring strong, effective leadership and management who, in turn, are able to articulate the connection between new behaviours and organisational success. Kotter's model of iterative cycles of change involved considerable participation and collaboration amongst organisational members, development practitioners, or change agents (Waddell et al., 2019).

Understanding these longstanding models of organisational change and the role of communication within them has been valuably informed by the distinction of four 'mental' (p. 59) models of organisational change: teleological, life cycle, dialectics, and evolution (Van de Ven & Sun, 2011). Van de Ven and Sun (2011) explained these mental models as follows: Teleology refers to a planned change model that approaches change through a repetitive sequence of goal formulation, implementation, evaluation, and modification, based on what has been learned or intended by stakeholders in a social construction of a desired end state. Life-cycle models regulate changes through a process, sequence of steps, or stages of development. In this, the lifecycle model as a metaphor emanates from a biological philosophy. The assumption of this philosophy is that organisations are living organisms that evolve through a kind of lifecycle of developmental stages from 'birth' (start-up) to 'death' (divestment) (Smith et al., 2020, p. 66). Dialectics refers to conflictive change arising from confrontation and resulting in the synthesis of opposing interests and evolution to competitive change that arises from variation, selection, and retention decisions among competing units (Van de Ven & Sun, 2011). Also, emerging from the biological philosophy is a change theory based on organisational ecology. Similar to the lifecycle model, organisational ecologists consider how growth, transformation and failure occur. Organisational ecologists, consistent with Darwin's theory of human evolution, believe that organisations are struggling to survive by adapting in an environment of competing forces and these notions have underpinned new ways of understanding organisational change (Smith et al., 2020).

Van de Ven and Sun (2011) argued that although it is natural to want to explain and control organisational change, it is not always possible because organisations do not necessarily change in a manner that is consistent with a particular conceptual model and when this happens, breakdowns or problems arise. The idea that organisational change can be managed simply by implementing the right intervention is patently inadequate (from the perspective of organisational ecologists) because if change was so straightforward then the reported high rates of failure in change management would largely become a phenomenon of the past (Smith et al., 2020). This criticism of traditional models of organisational change – as though the process has a distinct beginning, middle and end that fails to capture the unpredictable, complex, and ambiguous nature of the world – is one also expressed in the work of Emery (2019). The mental models of teleology, lifecycle, dialectical, and evolution allow organisations to adopt a contingency approach to implementation whereby a model or some sort of hybrid can be adopted as best fits a given situation (Van de Ven & Sun, 2011). In other words, a change model is not forced but can be modified depending upon the circumstances or nature of the organisation.

Kotter's (1996) change model is best described as teleological since it is characterised as pre-planned, top-down, and linear with a vision that is expected to be determined at the outset (Kang et al., 2020). As Lewis (2020) has observed, shifting perspectives in change communication reflects a questioning of top-down approaches, embedded in Kotter's ideas. A change process is unlikely to be successful if it is brought to some presumed dysfunction at a point in time that requires control and stabilisation because the perspective fails to take continuity into account; that is, where all things are constantly in a state of change and change processes are a work in progress (see Smith et al., 2020). In some respects, the shift in perspectives on change management are from a mindset that preferences stability, control, and inevitable stagnation, to one that acknowledges opportunities for creativity that comes with the messy ambiguities and contradictions of real life despite, in extreme circumstances, the allied potential for disruption and crisis (see Smith et al., 2020).

Another departure from earlier approaches to change communication is the emergence of the positive change model. Waddell et al. (2019) describe this trend as one that is based on the assumption that change should be driven by the existing strengths of an organisation in an effort to make it even better. As these authors point out, such an approach differs markedly from Lewin's action research process that focused upon organisational problems and deficits. The positive model also places much more emphasis upon participant involvement rather than change communication consultants (Waddell et al., 2019). The model progresses through a number of stages from the initiation of an enquiry amongst organisational members and encouraging them to share their stories about best practices and successful changes in the past, largely through interviews. Thematic analysis of the data occurs and gives rise to the development of a change vision and its subsequent design and delivery (Waddell et al., 2019).

Increasingly apparent is that organisations are moving in a different direction with respect to how they wish to function and how they wish to approach change. This shift is characterised in a progressive rejection of earlier *from-to* approaches to change, to those that better reflect today's dynamic, flexible, learning organisations that are unprepared to accept bounded and static conceptions of either themselves or their plans for the future (see Pasmore & Woodman, 2017). Intrinsically, contemporary approaches to change question misguided confidence in simplistic, unidimensional, reducible, step by step processes, choreographed by leadership that invariably fail (Smith et al., 2020).

Rational philosophies of change were rooted in the work of Frederick Taylor at the turn of the twentieth century who believed that the scientific management of organisations as closed systems controlled entirely by appointed leaders was the way to drive efficiency (Smith et al., 2020). Albeit prescriptive, and teleological (focused on the desired outcome), this change philosophy dominated management strategy until at least the 1990s, but contemporaneously, as discussed, recognition of flexible and iterative approaches to change management are now receiving much attention (Smith et al., 2020).

Change agents

Change agents have a formal role in transforming an idea about a change into practice and for this reason they may also be referred to as implementers (see Lewis, 2019). These individuals have crucial responsibility in diagnosing, managing, problem solving, and interpreting behavioural patterns during the change process (Harrington, 2018; Van de Ven & Sun, 2011). Those appointed as change agents may be internal or external to an organisation or a combination of the two, but external change agents are likely to be consultants with experience and qualifications in behavioural science techniques in contexts of change (Waddell et al., 2019). In the context of internal recruitment to the role, human resource departments tend to focus on managers as change implementers (Barratt-Pugh et al., 2013) though immediate supervisors who tend to be more highly trusted by workers than managers are also viable candidates since they may well be able to bring about two-way effective communication between management and workers (Allen et al., 2007). However, change agents do not necessarily have to be selected from those in either of these roles, partly because there are other criteria to be considered. Change agents need to have a high level of persuasive negotiation skills and persistence because managing change in organisations is often a complex, difficult, poorly supported, and protracted process (Barratt-Pugh et al., 2013; Laurie, 2019). As a communicator, an implementer is called upon to address a range of audiences such as employees, clients, and partners about how the change will work, how stakeholders will need to engage with it, how problems will be addressed, and how progress evaluations will drive any necessary adjustments along the way (Lewis, 2020).

Since key messages can be misinterpreted when communicated via a single channel, these individuals also need to have insight, expertise, and knowledge of a wide variety of strategies, channels, and delivery methods to be brought to the task (Hughes, 2010; Waddell et al., 2019). A simple example of such knowledge would be in deciding to use a face-to-face medium of communication, despite it being time consuming because of its effectiveness in non-routine or difficult situations or where miscommunication has arisen. Change agents are conscious, too, that whatever the medium of communication, transparency and concise, clear messages (see Allen et al., 2007; Palmer et al., 2009) are essential so that they can be grasped by most employees. Choosing a change agent is also likely to involve consideration of his or her age, education, or socio-economic status since these factors will affect the perceptions of stakeholders, not only about the change agent but also about any proposed change itself (Allen et al., 2007; Palmer et al., 2009).

Many scholars (see Driskill & Laird, 2011; Graetz et al., 2011; Holbeche, 2006; Klein, 1996; Laurie, 2019; Lewis, 2019; Neill, Men, & Yue, 2019; Palmer et al., 2009; Schermerhorn et al., 1997) have provided broad direction on those features that should characterise an effective communication plan. Organisations are exhorted to communicate the vision for change, making clear whether a change is surface (evolutionary and building on existing practices) or deep/extensive in nature, involving a merger or some kind of significant restructuring. Early presentation of a rationale is considered essential, in order to engage stakeholders on an intellectual level. The literature advises that employees need to be informed about every stage in the process with any confusion along the way being clarified and addressed. Some attention is also brought to the idea of tailoring change communication to particular audiences (generational cohorts, for example) and varying the media used to convey information, presumably to take into consideration individual learning styles and to maintain interest in the subject. Fostering open, positive communication that welcomes feedback and participation is also thought to empower stakeholders in the decision-making process and is likely to be more successful than coercion managed through rewards or punishments because compliance tends to last only as long as the rewards and punishments prevail.

Historically, much of the scholarship on change communications has focused upon the strategies and decisions made by change agents in introducing change, addressing resistance, encouraging cooperation, and implementing new policies, technologies, and practices (Lewis, 2020). However, Lewis (2020) notes this state of affairs is beginning to be countered by an interest in how stakeholders communicate with one another, influence how change initiatives are framed, tell their own stories of organisational change, and create meaning. In many ways, this shift reflects a call for a more democratic, bottom-up, and holographic approach to the change process. As Van de ven and Sun (2011) observed, much of the literature has been replete with the expectation that the role of change agents is primarily to ensure individuals conform to a vision and model of change rather more than it should.

Change resistance and its management

Resistance refers to a refusal to accept or comply with something (Waddell et al., 2019). Given that resistance to change is a complex construct, it is unsurprising that scholarly opinion appears to be divided on whether resistance is inherently positive or negative or serves to help or hinder change (Waddell et al., 2019). Whatever the case, resistance is often provided as a rationale for the failure of change management initiatives (see Clancy, 2018; Waddell et al., 2019) and, thus, it is imperative that change agents and leaders are briefed and aware of various schools of thought with respect to resistance, what drives it, and how best to communicate with those who experience it.

Waddell et al. (2019) outline three paradigms or perspectives on resistance: the mechanistic, the social, and the conversational. A mechanistic view assumes that change is a natural and normal phenomenon that cannot occur without some form of resistance, simply as evidence that something is occurring. A social view rejects some longstanding assumptions about resistance. Notably that

- it is exceptional and only happens in response to change
- it is implicitly detrimental whereas change is viewed as inherently beneficial
- resistance lies elsewhere, amongst a discrete group of troublesome employees.

The third, conversational view of resistance maintains that conversations are speech acts that occur through varied simultaneous and sequential conversations within groups or networks rather than as a single language about a change that everyone has access to.

Some employees may be reluctant to openly disclose their resistance to change in organisational cultures that seek to silence and punish objection, or where workers feel promotion prospects are likely to be damaged (Allen et al., 2007). Such a climate is more likely to be found where management approach change from a behavioural perspective, assuming that a combination of rewards and punishments is the most effective strategy for motivating individuals to comply with a change initiative (Cameron & Green, 2015). It is these kinds of organisational cultures that are most vulnerable to compromising ethical codes of practice in ways that can be insidious but not necessarily obvious. Ethical behaviour in organisational change is characterised by openness, constructive criticism, clear communication, and maintaining workplace respect (Waddell et al., 2019). In planning for change, devising ethical codes or principles of conduct should represent an early priority in the process.

Change alters things in the workplace; how we function, what is valued. Since people strive to experience a harmonious world of thought where cognitions are aligned rather than contradicting one another (Lauer, 2021), it is clear that change can present some complex, psychological challenges. The underlying reasons for resistance to organisational change may not always be apparent. Discovering what lies beneath the surface requires patient and active listening as communication devices and acknowledging them should form a part of any organisational communication plan. Resistance is much more complex than assuming employees are simply governed by pay and benefits (Waddell et al., 2019), or are otherwise too lazy to make the necessary adjustments. Resistance may reside within individuals who tend to develop habitual, ingrained ways of behaving when adjusting to change (Driskill & Laird, 2011). Attitudes to change are also influenced by personal roles, age, seniority, values, background, and trust in leadership (Heim & Sardar-Drenda, 2020). Some employees fear the process takes them out of their comfort zone, requires more effort, has the potential to remove existing benefits, or may cause displacement of some kind (Smith et al., 2020). Sometimes people perceive change as a threat (Emery, 2019) but organisational change communication can be framed in ways that helps them to feel safe. Resistance may also relate to how the change has been communicated and managed, or the nature of the change per se. How managers listen to employee feedback and address narratives relating to employee voice and justice issues will certainly have implications for the success of organisational changes (Jameson, 2019).

ACTIVITY: CRITICAL DISCUSSION

Forms of resistance, based on the literature (see for example, Allen et al., 2007; Clancy, 2018; Laurie, 2019; Schermerhorn et al., 1997; Waddell et al., 2019), have been set out in Table 3.1. Discuss with others which of the forms of change resistance listed next appear to be driven by the individual, the way the change was communicated, or the nature of the change itself.

TABLE 3.1 Sources of resistance to change

Feeling a loss of control or a loss of something valuable that requires protection	Cognitive rigidity (dogmatism and closed-mindedness)	Poor psychological resilience
Having to admit past practices were less than desirable	A reluctance to spend additional time learning new practices or to giving up old habits	Low levels of preference for stimulation and novelty
Loss of status, security or power	A reaction to too much organisational change	Fear of the unknown
Insufficient information	Seeing no reason for change	Feeling the change will bring more problems than it resolves
Disruption of routines	Feelings of insecurity	Uncertainty about any changes in how people are rewarded and developed

TABLE 3.2 Some emotions associated with workplace change

anger	depression	grief	sadness
apathy	enthusiasm	loss	shock
cynicism	envy	resistance	anxiety
denial	fear	rivalry	hostility

Emotional responses

Change can be challenging and uncomfortable, psychologically and emotionally (Holbeche, 2006). When employee confidence, sense of control, comfort, or personal competence are compromised by change, lower stability and productivity, higher stress, anxiety, fatigue, and conflict are common outcomes (Noels et al., 2019). However, personal responses differ and may evoke one or more of the following emotions and states to one degree or another (see Campbell et al., 2015; Driskill & Laird, 2011; French, 2001; Schermerhorn et al., 1997; Waddell et al., 2019);

How managers and change agents can approach employee feedback and resistance

Early on in communications about change, inviting employee feedback, even negative feedback, is essential. Employees undergo a period of reflection and sensemaking before they decide whether to support or resist a change (Laurie, 2019) and this period therefore represents a moment of opportunity for those planning change. Inviting participation and involvement in the planning of change is one trusted strategy for overcoming resistance and can provide a wide range of information and ideas contributing to informed innovative approaches (see Allen et al., 2007; Palmer et al., 2009; Waddell et al., 2019).

Facing resistance can be confronting and sometimes frustrating for those who believe that a change is essential to the future success of an organisation. A defensive response to negative feedback or resistance however is largely unhelpful. Resistance is not the same thing as wrongdoing. As Clancy (2018) suggests, managers would be well advised to invest sufficient time and resources into exploring both the facts and the feelings surrounding what exactly resistance communicates as a symptom, rather than as a problem. When approached with curiosity and compassion, resistance can generate productive critical discussion and inform decision making about how resources are invested into the change process at team meetings (Clancy, 2018). Organisational listening can result in management and change leaders recognising a need for greater clarity in organisational communication. Clarifying is beneficial since, as Heim and Sordai-Drenda (2020) suggest, employees tend to respond better to proposed changes when they understand them or when they make sense logically, and explanatory updates about the purpose of a change can improve employee readiness, perhaps particularly for older and more experienced staff members. Countering rumours with transparent and trustworthy communication helps to reduce anxiety and encourages participation and involvement and the effective implementation of organisational change (Barratt-Pugh et al., 2013; Waddell et al., 2019). Managers and change leaders can help to reassure employees in positive ways by providing empathy and support (Waddell et al., 2019). Indeed, from a wellbeing perspective, all those involved in organisational change adapt better when they engage in mindful practice, feel they are accepted and that their perspectives are met with compassion, kindness (Heads, 2017), and respect.

ACTIVITY: EXPERIENTIAL REFLECTION AND DISCUSSION

Consider the models and perspectives raised in this section about change communication. Focusing on any organisational changes with which you are familiar, discuss with others those ideas or strategies that you believe were brought to the change process and those that were not (and perhaps should have been). Assess the strengths and weaknesses of the change you observed and any consequences of how the change was managed.

ACTIVITY: REFLECTION

Expressing how we feel about change can be a useful tool for reflecting upon personal attitudes. Focus upon a specific change that you have recently experienced in an organisational setting (a workplace, somewhere where you volunteer, or your university). Draw a picture to express your personal, change experience. Use colour if you wish. Share your picture with others and ask them to interpret it and what it seems to suggest about your experience of the change. Your facilitator may like to summarise some of the emotions about change that are revealed as a group. It is not important how well you draw, and the exercise does not require qualifications and experience as a psychologist. The point of interpreting someone's picture is to probe and discuss emotions around change sensitively.

ACTIVITY: EXPERIENTIAL REFLECTION AND RESEARCH

Focus upon an organisational communication concerning a recent organisational change. What channel was adopted to communicate the message (presentation, email, meeting, social media, text, letter. . .)? Was it appropriate? Who communicated the change? Was it appropriate for the audience? Did it include all the people it needed to? Did the communication address emotions, values, beliefs, and other individual factors? In terms of noise, did anything interfere with the clear communication of the message? How could the change communication have been improved? Write an evidence-based report linking your ideas to relevant sources.

Online communication

Online/digital and social networking sites (SNS) are forms of communication in organisations that are ubiquitous and bring significant improvements in terms of reduced transaction and coordination costs, meeting operational efficiencies, organisational goals, productivity objectives, knowledge transfer, faster communication, and employment engagement (see Baker & Sangiamchit, 2019; Ceci & Masciarelli, 2020; Darics & Dufrene, 2016; Dwyer, 2020). Communication researchers have also begun to turn their attention to how relational communication differs depending upon whether it is conducted in a face-to-face medium or online and via social media (Turner & West, 2018). The dynamic space of online communication provides opportunities to be creative, to transcend the impracticalities of distance and travel, making the cultivation of international relationships more possible than they have ever been. The previous section made clear that technology is now an important driver of change so it is vital that organisational change communication is sufficiently sophisticated, effective, and nimble to capitalise upon the potential that technology offers.

Email communication and its challenges

The impact of email communication is immeasurable and, by now, something of a cliché. Email now commands a legal status and is routinely accepted in developing, maintaining, and even terminating relationships in the workplace (Beer, 2017; Turner & West, 2018). Despite the widespread uptake of email communication by organisations, it does need to be managed at a strategic level and employees should be aware of the challenges it can present and how they can be mitigated. The relationship between written, face to face and email forms of communication is complex, not least because email messages often contain inter-textual references to face-to-face meetings and telephone calls, for example (Beer, 2017). Another challenge is that emails may invite miscommunication because when people do not have all the information they need (e.g., warmth, humour, and humanity are harder to communicate in emails), recipients tend to fill in the blanks using their own imagination (Costello, 2020). Although emails are generally considered less formal than other forms of written communication, it is context that determines how formal or informal a message should be, but whatever the level of formality, emails should be well edited and grammatically correct, because errors can introduce noise into the communication, creating misunderstandings and a poor impression of the sender (Beer, 2017). However, in a study of 169 business people who were asked to comment on three versions of emails with different kinds of errors or characteristics, it was found that although participants made some allowances for grammatical errors, inappropriate tone or failure to meet expectations of politeness was far more bothersome than grammatical errors (Wolfe, Shanmugaraj, & Sipe, 2016). So, it is the relational aspects of this form of communication that seems to be most significant.

As a channel of communication, email can be harmful when improperly managed. Employees may become stressed and overwhelmed by the number of emails they receive or when colleagues engage in political grandstanding by including unnecessary recipients (Beer, 2017; Porter, 2017). Setting expectations on appropriate periods for responding to email communication can also help in dispelling assumptions that the instantaneous nature of email communication should be matched with an instantaneous response. Clear policies on expected codes of conduct based on informed input from legal and human resource professionals is one way to counter the negative impact of these kinds of issues and others related to data security and protection against system hackers with state-of-the art anti-virus software (Beer, 2017; Dwyer, 2020).

Decisions about the best communication channel to use, depend upon the purpose and context. For example, email has the disadvantage of not being synchronous, so delays in communication can give rise to misunderstandings that do not occur to the same extent in face-to-face communication, partly because the sender of a message has the flexibility to alter how the communication progresses almost instantaneously, depending upon the verbal or nonverbal cues received (see

Goodwin, 2019). Nevertheless, it is the asynchronous nature of email communication that allows for some flexibility and convenience in terms of crafting a considered response (Stephens & Kee, 2020).

Some online mediums convey content best while others, such as texting, are preferable when establishing phatic communication (Berger, 2016), discussed earlier in this chapter, as a means of maintaining social interaction and bonding. Porter (2017) calls for greater attention to phatic discourse in professional communication, especially in intercultural contexts and when using social media, virtual teamwork situations such as blogging, and user help settings. As Porter (2017) suggested, employees often violate principles of phatic communication in emails, especially when stressed and rushing responses, forgetting to say, 'please' and 'thank you', adopting an inappropriate tone, expressing anger, and ranting. The emergence of emoticons in email can be useful but still do not convey the emotional subtleties of face-to-face communication (Beer, 2017). However, emoticons did give rise to the creation of emojis, cartoon-like pictures that can be inserted into text, GIFs, and memes, all of which can be used on social media, in texts, and emails to express an understanding, concept, or idea amongst online users (Corey & Grace, 2019). So, despite the constraints of email communication and other forms of online communication, innovations are continually being developed to overcome them.

Social media

The use of social media in organisations also invites layers of complexity for policy makers given its role in communication with both specific stakeholders and mass audiences as part of brand development, fostered by specialists in public relations and marketing teams (Chewing, 2019) who generally understand the importance of constantly learning in the area of social media in order to meet and exceed organisational goals. For example, one Hong Kong study explored how cyber-balkanization may occur where likeminded groups, communities, and individuals ignore or express dislike for non-members – in other words a bias exists where people expose themselves to online information that reinforces their own perspectives (Chan, Siu-Lun Cow, & Fu, 2019). Marketing teams will need to be aware of this tendency towards the segregation of the Internet into smaller communities to the extent that any contradictory views are rejected when planning marketing strategies using social media. Social media presents a new set of realities in organisational, political, and social settings with implications for discourse, values, and paradigms. Jones (2020) suggests that liberal democracy is now compromised by an existential crisis that has been displaced by emotive and poorly informed online-driven populism creating a post-truth era where 'facts' are invented or the obvious is denied, in ways that run counter to the principles of enlightenment. The whole paradigm of empiricism seems to be under siege by the emergence of social media and its beguiling and powerful nature has implications for society, organisations, how we educate, establish reality, and the trust we place in certain forms of information.

Artificial intelligence

One of the most recent areas of interest in the study of online and organisational communication concerns artificial information, robots, and virtual reality that simulate human intelligence in interactions with people (Gilikson & Woolley, 2020; Stephens & Kee, 2020). Studied for more than 50 years, artificial intelligence (AI) prioritises human social intelligence as an important aspect of functioning, but the development of algorithms that enable a robot to process and synthesise human behaviour so that it is able to provide a real-time response is far from easy (Kappas, Stower, & Vanman, 2020). An example of simple AI would be chatbots. Customers now routinely engage with chatbots that are able to screen and provide pre-scripted answers prior to being transferred to a human employee (Stephens & Kee, 2020). Thus, chatbots simulate interactive human conversation using pre-calculated auditory or text-based signals (Dwyer, 2020). However, a real challenge for both designers and organisations in using AI communication is establishing user trust in physical robots, virtual agents, or chatbots (Gilikson & Woolley, 2020).

ACTIVITY: DISCUSSION

Discuss with others a recent experience engaging with a chatbot and any observations or feelings you had about the process. Are there any changes you feel need to be made in order to improve the quality of the communication?

Conclusion

This chapter has discussed the dynamic interrelationship between communication and organisations and the study of organisational communication. It provides an introduction to lines of enquiry such as informal and formal communication, communication networks, and online communication but focuses primarily on the contexts of change communication and how language plays a role in organisations. Organisational communication encompasses a wide range of scholarly lines of enquiry. The aim of this chapter has been to highlight some of the areas that prepare readers to understand and build upon concepts presented in the remaining chapters in this text rather than providing an in-depth summary of the many aspects of organisational communication that are presented in sources dedicated to this subject matter.

References

Allen, J., Jimmieson, N., Bordia, P., & Irmer, B. (2007). Uncertainty during organizational change: Managing perceptions through communication. *Journal of Change Management,* 7(2), 187–210.

Badham, M. (2020). Love wins: A love lens approach to cultivation of organization – stakeholder relationships. In A. T. Verčič, R. Tench, & S. Einwiller (Eds.), *Joy: Advances in public relations and communication management* (Vol. 5, pp. 3–20). Bingley: Emerald Publishing Limited. doi:10.1108/S2398-391420200000005003

Baker, W., & Sangiamchit, C. (2019). Transcultural communication: Language communication and culture through English as a lingua franca in a social networking community. *Language and Intercultural Communication, 19*(6), 471–487.

Barratt-Pugh, L., Bahn, S., & Gakere, E. (2013). Managers as change agents: Implications for human resource managers engaging with culture change. *Journal of Organizational Change Management, 26*(4), 748–764.

Beer, A. (2017). From business letters to email and mobile communication. In G. Mautner & F. Rainer (Eds.), *Handbook of business communication: Linguistic approaches* (pp. 153–175). Berlin: De Gruyter.

Bell, R., & Martin, J. (2017). *Managerial communication for organizational development*. New York: Business Expert Press.

Berger, A. (2016). *Messages: An introduction to communication*. Walnut Creek: Taylor and Francis.

Brown, O., Paz-Aparicio, C., & Revilla, A. (2018). Leader's communication style, LMX and organizational commitment: A study of employee perceptions in Peru. *Leadership & Organization Development Journal, 40*(2), 230–258.

Campbell, K., Carmichael, P., & Naidoo, J. (2015). Responding to hostility: Evidence-based guidance for communication during planned organizational change. *Business and Professional Communication Quarterly, 78*(2), 197–214.

Cameron, E., & Green, M. (2015). *Making sense of change management: A complete guide to the models, tools and techniques of organizational change*. London: Kogan Page.

Ceci, F., & Masciarelli, F. (2020). *Cultural proximity and organization: Managing diversity and innovation*. New York: Routledge.

Chan, C., Siu-Lun Chow, C., & Fu, K. (2019). Echoslamming: How incivility interacts with cyberbalkanization on the social media in Hong Kong. *Asian Journal of Communication, 29*(4), 307–327.

Chan, M. (2020). *English for business communication*. London: Routledge.

Chewing, L. (2019). Communications networks. In A. Nicotera (Ed.), *Origins and traditions of organizational communication to the field* (pp. 168–186). New York: Routledge.

Clancy, A. (2018). Manage resistance to change. *Manage and Lead, 50*(1), 81–82.

Corey, S., & Grace, M. (2019). *Generation Z: A century in the making*. Oxford: Routledge.

Costello, J. (2020). *Workplace wellbeing: A relational approach*. London: Routledge.

Crossman, J., Bordia, S., & Mills, C. (2011). *Business communication for the global age*. Sydney: McGraw-Hill.

Darics, E., & Dufrene, D. (2016). *Writing online: A guide to effective digital communication at work*. New York: Business Expert Press.

De Janasz, S., Crossman, J., Campbell, N., & Power, M. (2014). *Interpersonal skills in organisations*. Sydney: McGraw-Hill Education.

Driskill, G., & Laird, B. (2011). *Organizational cultures in action: A cultural analysis workbook*. London: Sage.

Dulek, R. (2015). Instituting cultural change at a major organization: A case study. *Business and Professional Communication Quarterly, 78*(2), 231–243.

Dwyer, J. (2020). *Communication for business and the professions: Strategies and skills*. Melbourne: Pearson.

Emery, J. (2019). *Leading for organizational change: Building purpose, motivation and belonging*. Chichester: John Wiley & Sons Ltd.

French, R. (2001). Negative capability: Managing the confusing uncertainties of change. *Journal of Organizational Change Management, 14*(5), 480–492.

Gasiorek, J. (2019). Interpersonal accommodation. In H. Giles, J. Harwood, J. Gasiorek, H. Pierson, J. Nussbaum, & C. Gallois (Eds.), *Language, communication and intergroup relations: A celebration of the scholarship of Howard Giles* (pp. 192–216). New York: Routledge.

Gilikson, E., & Woolley, A. (2020). Human trust in artificial intelligence: Review of empirical research. *Academy of Management Annals, 14*(2), 627–660.

Goodwin, J. M. (2019). Communication accommodation theory: Finding the right approach. In M. Brown Sr. & L. Hersey (Eds.), *Returning to interpersonal dialogue and understanding human communication in the digital age* (pp. 168–185). Hershey, PA: IGI Global.

Guo, W., Sengul, M., & Yu, T. (2020). The impact of executive verbal communication on the convergence of investors opinions. *Academy of Management Journal, 64.* doi:10.5465/amj.2019.0711

Graetz, F., Rimmer, M., Smith, A., & Lawrence, A. (2011). *Managing organisational change.* Milton: Wiley.

Harrington, H. (2018). *Innovative change management.* Milton: ICM Productivity Press.

Hartley, P., & Chatterton, P. (2015). *Business communication: Rethinking your professional practice for the post digital age.* New York: Routledge.

Heads, G. (2017). *Living mindfully: Discovering authenticity through mindfulness coaching.* Oxford: Wiley Blackwell.

Heim, I., & Sardar-Drenda, N. (2020). Assessment of employees' attitudes toward ongoing organizational transformations. *Journal of Organizational Change Management, 34*(2), 327–349.

Holbeche, L. (2006). *Understanding change: Theory implementation and success.* Burlingham, MA: Elsevier.

Hughes, M. (2010). *Managing change: A critical perspective.* London: Chartered Institute of Personnel and Development.

Jameson, J. (2019). Conflict. In A. Nicotera (Ed.), *Origins and traditions of organizational communication to the field* (pp. 307–326). New York: Routledge.

Jones, B. (2020). *What is to be done? Political engagement and saving the planet.* Victoria, Australia: Scribe.

Kang, S., Chen, Y., Svihla, V., Gallup, A., Ferris, K., & Datye, K. (2020). Guiding change in higher education: An emergent, iterative application of Kotter's change model. *Studies in Higher Education,* 1–20. doi:10.1080103075079.2020

Kappas, A., Stower, R., & Vanman, E. (2020). Communicating with robots: What we do wrong and what we do right in artificial social intelligence and what we need to do better. In R. Sternberg & A. Kostic (Eds.), *Social intelligence and nonverbal communication* (pp. 233–254). New York: Palgrave Macmillan.

Klein, S. (1996). A management communication strategy for change. *Journal of Organizational Change Management, 9*(2), 32–46.

Kotter, J. (1996). *Leading change: The leadership challenge.* San Francisco: Harvard Business Review Press.

Larson, K. (2018). *Adaption and well-being.* London: Routledge.

Lauer, T. (2021). *Change management: Fundamentals and success factors.* Berlin and Heidelberg: Springer.

Laurie, L. (2019). Organizational change. In A. Nicotera (Ed.), *Origins and traditions of organizational communication: A comprehensive introduction to the field* (pp. 406–423). New York: Routledge.

Lesk, S., Lavric, E, & Stegu, M. (2017). Multilingualism in business: Language policies and practices. In G. Mautner & F. Rainer (Eds.), *Handbook of business communication: Linguistic approaches* (pp. 269–319). Berlin and Boston: De Gruyter. doi:10.1515/9781614514862

Lewis, L. (2019). *Organizational change: Creating change through strategic communication*. Malden, MA: Wiley Blackwell.

Lewis, L. (2020). Organizational change. In A. Micotera (Ed.), *Origins and traditions of organizational communication: A comprehensive introduction to the field* (pp. 406–424). New York: Routledge.

Mautner, G. (2017). Organizational discourse. In G. Mautner & F. Rainer (Eds.), *Handbook of business communication: Linguistic approaches* (pp. 609–628). Berlin: De Gruyter.

Mautner, G., & Rainer, F. (Eds.). (2017). *Handbook of business communication: Linguistic approaches*. Retrieved February 4, 2020, from https://ebookcentral.proquest.com

Methot, J., Rosado-Solomon, E., Downes, P., & Gabriel, A. (2020). Office chit-chat as a social ritual: The uplifting yet distracting effects of daily small talk at work. *Academy of Management Journal*. doi:10.5465/amj.2018.1474

Miller, K. (2015). *Organizational communication: Approaches and processes*. Stamford, CT: Cengage Learning.

Mills, C. (2011). Grappling with the dark side of organisations. *Australian Journal of Communication, 38*(1), 1–19.

Neenan, M., & Dryden, W. (2020). *Cognitive behavioural coaching: A guide to problem-solving and personal development*. Oxford: Taylor & Francis Group.

Neill, M., Men, L., & Yue, C. (2019). How communication climate and organizational identification impact change, communication climate and organizational identification, impact change. *Corporate Communications: An International Journal, 25*(2), 281–298.

Nicotera, A. (2019). *Origins and traditions of organizational communication: A comprehensive introduction to the field*. New York: Routledge.

Noels, K., Clement, R., Collins, K., & Machintyre, P. (2019). Language and culture. In H. Giles, J. Harwood, J. Gasiorek, H. Pierson, J. Nussbaum, & C. Gallois (Eds.), *Language, communication and intergroup relations: A celebration of the scholarship of Howard Giles* (pp. 19–33). New York: Routledge.

Palmer, I., Dunford, R., & Akin, G. (2009). *Managing organizational change: A multiple perspectives approach*. Sydney: McGraw-Hill.

Pasmore, W., & Woodman, R. (2017). The future of research and practice in organizational change and development. In *Research in organizational change and development* (Vol. 25, pp. 1–32). Bingley: Emerald Publishing Limited. doi:10.1108/50897-3016201

Porter, J. (2017). Professional communication as phatic: From classical eunoia to personal artificial intelligence. *Business and Professional Quarterly, 80*(2), 174–193.

Rakic, T., & Maass, A. (2019). Communicating between groups, communicating about groups. In H. Giles, J. Harwood, J. Gasiorek, H. Pierson, J. Nussbaum, & C. Gallois (Eds.), *Language, communication and intergroup relations: A celebration of the scholarship of Howard Giles* (pp. 66–97). New York: Routledge.

Ramos Salazar, L. (2017). The influence of business students' listening styles on their compassion and self-compassion. *Business and Professional Communication Quarterly, 80*(4), 426–442.

Rogers, E. (2003). *Diffusion of innovations*. New York: Free Press.

Ruhl, S., & Sub, S. (2020). Presenteeism & absenteeism at work – an analysis of archetypes of sickness attendance cultures. *Journal of Business and Psychology, 35*, 241–255.

Salem, P. J., & Timmerman, C. E. (2018). Forty years of organizational communication. In P. Salem & E. Timmerman (Eds.), *Transformative practice and research in organizational communication* (pp. 1–28). Hershey, PA: IGI Global. doi:10.4018/978-1-5225-2823-4.ch001

Schermerhorn, J., Hunt, J., & Osborn, R. (1997). *Organizational behaviour*. New York: John Wiley & Sons Ltd.

Scott, C. (2019). Identity and identification. In A. Nicotera (Ed.), *Origins and traditions of organizational communication: A comprehensive introduction to the field* (pp. 207–227). New York: Routledge.

Sias, P., & Shin, Y. (2019a). Socialization. In A. Nicotera (Ed.), *Origins and traditions of organizational communication to the field* (pp. 149–167). New York: Routledge.

Smith, A., Skinner, J., & Read, D. (2020). *Philosophies of organizational change: Perspectives, models and theories for managing change*. Cheltenham: Edward Elgar Publishing.

Smollan, R., & Morrison, R. (2019). Office design and organizational change: The influence of communication and organizational culture. *Journal of Organizational Change Management*, *32*(4), 426–440.

Stephens, J. (1992). *Reading the signs: Sense and significance in written texts*. Sydney: Kangaroo Press.

Stephens, K., & Kee, K. (2020). Technology and organizational communication. In A. Nicotera (Ed.), *Origins and traditions of organizational communication: A comprehensive introduction to the field* (pp. 370–389). New York: Routledge.

Toubiana, M. (2019). Once I orange always in orange? Identity paralysis and the enduring influence of institutions on identity. *Academy of Management Journal*, *63*(6), 1739–1774.

Turner, L., & West, R. (2018). *An introduction to communication*. Cambridge: Cambridge University Press.

Van de ven, A., & Sun, K. (2011). Breakdowns in implementing models of organization change. *Academy of Management Perspectives*, *25*(3), 58–74.

Waddell, D., Creed, A., & Cummings, T. (2019). *Organisational change*. Melbourne: Cengage.

Wolfe, J., Shanmugaraj, N., & Sipe, J. (2016). Grammatical versus pragmatic error: Employer perceptions of the non-native and native English speakers. *Business and Professional Communication Quarterly*, *79*(4), 397–415.

Zhu, Y. (2021). Using ethnography of communication in cross-cultural management and communication research. In J. Crossman & S. Bordia (Eds.), *Handbook of qualitative research methodologies in workplace context* (pp. 176–190). Cheltenham: Edward Elgar.

Zoller, H., & Ban, Z. (2019). Chapter 12, power and resistance. In A. Nicotera (Ed.), *Origins and traditions of organizational communication: A comprehensive introduction to the field* (pp. 228–249). New York: Routledge.

4

WELLBEING IN WORKPLACE CONTEXTS

The concept of wellbeing

A somewhat pessimistic perspective expressed by Anand (2018) is that contemporary 24/7 lifestyles, exacerbated by smartphones, leaves many feeling that they pass through life without necessarily enjoying it. It doesn't have to be this way, but in all likelihood it is, for many. The surge of exposure in the literature to scholarly works about wellbeing (Anand, 2018) is perhaps not surprising given that people spend a lot of time at work and, logically, the workplace has a considerable influence on personal wellbeing (Cross, 2020). The holistic and expanded understanding of wellbeing in the workplace is of interest to researchers and practitioners from a variety of disciplines (see Scaria, Brandt, Kim, & Lindeman, 2020), making it more difficult to reach consensus with respect to defining the concept, or even deciding on the spelling of the term and whether or not it should be hyphenated (Leiter & Cooper, 2017). In this text, the unhyphenated version 'wellbeing' is adopted. Constructions of wellbeing vary. Anand (2018) tends to use the concepts of wellbeing and happiness interchangeably, reflecting the perspectives of Martin Setigman, the father of the positive psychology movement. In this chapter, wellbeing is constructed in much broader terms and with more varied applications, but the study of happiness is nevertheless addressed later in the text in the context of emotions.

Wellbeing is often regarded as a contemporary phenomenon, but in fact evidence suggests that it was referred to in the works of Plato, Socrates, Epicurus, and Aristotle (Scaria et al., 2020). The term (like wellness) was also used in the seventeenth century but fell out of favour until at least the 1960s when it was adopted in medical/health contexts, suggesting an absence of disease (Pradarelli, Shimizu, & Smink, 2020; Scaria et al., 2020). Today, however, the concept of wellbeing addresses mental, physical, and indeed spiritual health and tends to be approached from a holistic perspective and in a positive and proactive manner

DOI: 10.4324/9780429318948-5

(see Leiter & Cooper, 2017). Despite a holistic appreciation of wellbeing, psychologists, at least, tend to differentiate between wellbeing perspectives that are either grounded in clinical psychology focused on healing the sick and positive psychology, founded in the seminal works of Martin Setigman, that targets 'normal' people who wish to enhance the quality of their lives (Anand, 2018). As Anand (2018) suggests, the concept of wellbeing is also often presented in terms of the absence of negative states where individuals are not bullied, ignored, or overwhelmed at work and do not lead monotonous lives, feel anxious about the future, or experience undue regret about the past. This chapter tends to adopt this lens as a rationale for paying attention to the issue, but at the same time, acknowledges the counterpart of this perspective and the wonderful gifts at all levels in addressing wellbeing in the workplace.

Employers and governments who previously interpreted wellbeing rather more narrowly, in terms of preventing workplace injuries and physical safety, for example, are now beginning to appreciate the broader applications of wellbeing (see Leiter & Cooper, 2017; Costello, 2020) and its benefits. Organisational benefits in paying focused attention to wellbeing include improved productivity, positive financial returns, fewer compensation claims, lower absenteeism and presenteeism (when people go to work ill but are unproductive), and higher levels of performance (Cross, 2020). In a departure from traditional perspectives on priorities, employee performance and wellbeing are now regarded as important as organisational outcomes (Pawar, 2020).

Stress and burnout

Stress may lie within or beyond individuals or reflect an interplay between the two (Anand, 2018) but wherever it originates, according to Maravelas (2020), depression, interpersonal hostility, and stress are becoming more common. Some level of stress is normal, sometimes positive, and may keep life interesting but at some point, it can become detrimental to wellbeing and, indeed, shorten lives because disease is associated with stress that in turn is linked to controllable factors such as poor diet and inadequate exercise (Larson, 2018). Too much workload stress can ultimately lead to burnout. Burnout is a metaphor to describe a sense of depersonalisation, emotional exhaustion, cynicism, low energy, frustration, diminished sense of personal accomplishment, feelings of failure, inadequacy, compassion fatigue (particularly in professions like nursing and emergency work where people witness trauma regularly), disengagement from work, deterioration in effectiveness (Tracy & Redden, 2019), and failure to achieve goals (Larson, 2018). By way of an example, one Chinese study revealed how nurses suffering from fatigue, high turnover, and burnout give rise to concerns about wellbeing (Li, Feng, Wang, Geng, & Chang, 2021). A gamut of literature testifies to global concerns about burnout at work.

Establishing the causes of stress, its consequences, and how it can be remedied is a complex matter (Larson, 2018). The consequences are felt personally, but also negatively impact organisations, as workplace satisfaction and morale diminish, and absenteeism, turnover, and sick leave increase (Huhtala, Feldt, Lamsa, Mauno, & Kinnunen, 2011; Larson, 2018; Miller, 2015). Workplace stress and burnout may also be triggered by a variety of personal and organisational factors. On a personal level, the realities of divorce, pregnancy, moving house, or looming retirement can have an affect (Miller, 2015). Organisational factors associated with stress and burnout include (Larson, 2018; Leong & Crossman, 2009; Miller, 2015; Shahnawaz & Baig, 2018):

TABLE 4.1 Triggers of stress and burnout

Role ambiguity	Workload	Inadequate resourcing
'Dead-end' positions providing little satisfaction	Adjusting to change over which individuals feel they have little control	Transitioning from training roles to professional ones

Stress and burnout manifest in different ways. Addictive behaviours such as excessive drinking, drug use (Crossman, Bordia, & Mills, 2011), and tobacco smoking are self-destructive, escapist strategies to self-medicate, but in reality, they often result in increasing levels of psychological and physical dependency, diminishing functionality at work, sometimes rendering individuals unemployable and inevitably placing additional pressures upon loved ones (Larson, 2018). Stress is not always created by psychological issues, however. It may be triggered by physical conditions such as minor headaches, common colds, allergies, asthma, colitis, fatigue, high blood pressure, and rapid heart rates, for example (Larson, 2018).

Stress and burnout are relatively common in organisations. Responsible leaders consider how best to support employees experiencing these conditions. When supervisors invest time and express genuine concern into providing emotional support to employees, it can make a significant difference in reducing stress (Jia, Cheng, & Hale, 2017). Creating a culture of fairness has also been associated with employee psychological wellbeing (Costello, 2020). Organisations cannot assume that it is the sole responsibility of individual employees to overcome the debilitating consequences of workplace stress by investing their salaries into meditation, spa weekends, seeing counsellors, or reviewing their consumption of alcohol and recreational drugs. As information is received about employees feeling they have little to no control over expected outcomes and are experiencing emotional exhaustion and high levels of stress, it should also be a signal to management to scrutinise what is happening, and to prioritise the investigation of workloads (Larson, 2018). Organisational listening is a proactive strategy that can be brought to bear in order to gain feedback on the functioning of the organisation as a whole, and on employee wellbeing. This can be achieved by routinely organising focus groups, individual interviews, or by conducting surveys (Maravelas, 2020) in order to drive any necessary change.

The entire responsibility for managing employee wellbeing is not only a matter for organisations, however, because, as Costello (2020) remarked, wellbeing is a complex physiological, social, and political phenomenon. As such, it requires all stakeholders to become engaged in the space and to become informed in their decision making, aware of the holistic nature of work-life matters. Raising awareness about ageing, grief, sadness, insomnia, addictive behaviours, and other markers of ill-health associated with stress and depression could and should become an integral component of training programmes as part of occupational health and safety initiatives. Insomnia, for example, affects most people at some point in their lives. Insufficient sleep from stress may create many perceptual distortions and can lead to a gamut of serious problems for wellbeing. They include oversensitivity, imagining threats that do not exist in reality, chronic inflammation associated with heart disease, diabetes, and the decline of cognitive functioning (Larson, 2018). It may help to offer those who suffer from insomnia, flexible working hours so that they can adjust their engagement to times during the day when they feel most alert. Such arrangements may improve performance as a consequence of reducing the anxiety individuals feel about being at work on time and being able to cope.

It will be apparent in reading through the previous chapters of this text that the relational context for communication between and amongst colleagues is paramount. As Sias and Shin (2020, p. 187) recently remarked, 'workplace relationships are central to organisational processes'. Developing supportive relationships and communicating care for one another should be an ongoing priority and not simply a response in moments of challenge or crisis because relationships and interpersonal communication are built over time. In circumstances where organisational cultures create competitive, pressured environments and where individuals feel there is not enough time in the day to undertake professional and personal activities, stress is a common phenomenon for which employers need to accept some responsibility. Workaholism is one response by employees to circumstances such as this (Larson, 2018). In the short term, it may seem like a sensible strategy but in the long term has negative consequences for both employee and organisational wellbeing and needs to be addressed by clear communication about expectations of workload that are mindful of employee health. It may be that creative responses to meeting financial goals with smart deployment of resources would be able to achieve organisational goals in ways that reduce stress on workers. Overworking employees should not be the default position in meeting goals.

Supporting employees who suffer from depression, panic disorders, anxiety, and PTSD may come in the form of offering no-cost counselling services that are nevertheless transparently confidential. Cognitive behavioural therapy (CBT) is a counselling technique that has reportedly led to much success in these circumstances (Neenan & Dryden, 2020). Counselling can be useful in addressing workplace issues that improve employee wellbeing, in part because of the use of highly effective communication tools including probing questions about emotional issues, listening skills, and developing trust and patience, and, indeed, a counsellor knowing when someone simply needs to express their feelings under stress and seek another perspective (De Janasz et al., 2014). It is inadvisable for line managers to undertake the task of counselling not only because it would patently constitute a conflict of interest but also because counselling professionals are experienced and qualified in an area that demands a high level of expertise. Managers may, however, suggest a referral to counselling services and many organisations provide employment assistance and wellness programmes that can arrange for appropriate support for a range of issues including mental ill-health, substance abuse, family and financial matters (De Janasz et al., 2014), and other symptoms associated with stress and burnout at work. Counselling staff, organisations, and employees should all be clear, however, that they understand the role confidentiality plays in these arrangements. Accessing such services may also involve the development of a safe, personal proposal to be negotiated with management about possible adjustments, perhaps on a temporary level, with respect to roles and responsibilities or flexible work conditions. Although managers are not counsellors, they do have a role in supporting and attending to subordinates who are distressed in other ways. Active listening can be therapeutic and help someone feel less isolated when they experience difficulties in coping, sadness, upset, and depression and even if this aspect of interpersonal communication does not immediately resolve a central issue, it can help to reveal underlying aspects of a problem, soothe distress, and initiate productive conversations (Gill, 2019; Macnamara, 2015).

Supporting colleagues is part and parcel of creating an organisational culture that prioritises wellbeing. Maravelas (2020) has much to say about how creating supportive cultures where compassion, kindness, and connectedness in workplace relationships can be achieved in practical, everyday ways by sharing emotions, expressing a genuine interest in someone's wellbeing, and mirroring the behaviour of others. When these behaviours are present in interpersonal communications, on a physical level the biochemical response will be to produce dopamine, oxytocin, and serotonin that boost energy, drive, and concentration as well as feelings of bonding and stabilising mood in ways that can help to diminish the effects of depression (Maravelas, 2020). Both individuals and organisations can also bring about positive biochemical changes by making healthy choices and decisions with respect to diet, exercise, and engaging in spiritual practices (Anand, 2018). At the organisational level, lunchtime business meetings may replace platters of pizza and burgers for example with fresh fruit, vegetables, and other healthy options. Some organisations offer weekly yoga classes and in my own practice I have instituted 'walk talks' when meeting in groups of up to three people. Not only do people enjoy getting out in the fresh air and exercising, one of the unexpected outcomes was that individuals tend to adopt more open, informal communication and are highly creative once they move out of offices. Some spiritual practices are also associated with wellbeing with applications in the workplace. Anand (2018), for example, refers to prayer and reports that the rhythmic elements of prayer actually produce oxytocin and intensify social bonding (and one assumes interpersonal communication). More attention will be given to spiritual practice and wellbeing in Chapter 8 of this book.

Mental health in workplace contexts

Mental ill-health manifested in conditions such as anxiety, post-traumatic stress disorder, and depression compromise wellbeing, create much distress, and make it difficult to function and meet everyday demands at work (Costello, 2020; Scaria et al., 2020). Depression is a complex condition that varies in intensity. It has been described as a sense of loss, affecting self-esteem, possibly accompanied by self-blame and feeling sorry for oneself over misfortunes and unwanted life changes and crises in contexts such as personal relationships, issues at work, religious faith, or sexual matters (Neenan & Dryden, 2020). Depression, severe enough to require treatment, affects about 10–12 per cent of employees at any one time and its effects are compounded by correlated physical conditions such as compromised immune systems and heart problems (Maravelas, 2020; Neenan & Dryden, 2020). Those who suffer from chronic anxiety often experience physical symptoms such as asthma, arthritis, headaches, peptic ulcers, and heart disease and emotional ones, including sadness (Goleman, 2020). In quantitative terms, fatigue, loss of focus, and irritability associated with mental ill-health is reportedly equivalent to losing five hours per week at work (Maravelas, 2020). Severe, chronic, psychological (as well as physical) distress raises qualitative and ethical issues for organisations that may run counter to quantitative, profit-orientated considerations (see Brandt, 2020). However, organisational narratives are increasingly demonstrating an acknowledgement of the importance of balancing the wellbeing of the workforce and financial success – indeed the former may well be a key force in enhancing the latter.

Some other normal, inevitable life changes such as grief and ageing influence how employees feel and perform at work, sometimes giving rise to more serious health conditions such as depression and anxiety. Grief resulting from bereavement is an understandable condition that most employees will experience at some point, especially when they approach middle age and parents begin to pass away (Larson, 2018). The sense of anxiety and trauma when a source of support and advice disappears can be debilitating (Worden, 2018). Sometimes well-respected and liked colleagues also pass away and organisations need to address how to acknowledge grief amongst staff and celebrate the life of someone who is well known to them. Feeling and expressing empathy and compassion for colleagues who are grieving can help them through the process of coping. Empathy is not always as forthcoming as one might assume. Psychologists have discovered that although from infancy babies are able to feel sympathetic to the distress of those around them, they soon become aware that the misery of another is separate from their own experience (Goleman, 2020). When this happens, empathy becomes less acute. Nevertheless, it is important to develop levels of personal empathy for others through active listening and being conscious that each person experiences grief differently (Larson, 2018). Gaining knowledge and insights into the nature of grief will help in developing empathy for colleagues who experience it and working out ways to assist them.

Grief is not only experienced during bereavement but may also be associated with the loss of resources, personal faith (Huron, 2018), or the end of important relationships. Grief may stimulate surges in motivation to fulfil personal and organisational goals and a sense of emancipation or relief when someone has endured a long period of illness (Huron, 2018; Worden, 2018) but also comes with a number of negative symptoms/challenges about which colleagues and managers should be aware, bearing in mind that individuals are most unlikely to experience all these states, at least at the same time. They include (Huron, 2018; Larson, 2018; Worden, 2018):

TABLE 4.2 Symptoms of grief

Emotional symptoms of grief

Sadness	Weeping	Anger
Blame	Guilt	Self-reproach
Anxiety	Insecurity	Panic
Depression	An obsessive focus upon the deceased	Loneliness
Fatigue	Shock and disbelief	Yearning
Numbness that may be perceived as a lack of feeling	Relief (especially in cases of a lengthy illness)	Absent mindedness
Social withdrawal		

Physical symptoms of grief

Tightness of chest	Oversensitivity to noise	Depersonalisation
Shortness of breath	Muscle weakness	Low energy
Dry mouth	Sleep disturbance	Eating problems
Restlessness	Hyperactivity	

How individual employees respond to getting older varies and how cultures view that process will also impact on the experience of ageing colleagues. In some countries, it is accepted that an ageing workforce brings with it many opportunities for both organisations and individuals to thrive. That said, the realities of health conditions that come with age and an increasing awareness of mortality can add to worry and stress (see Larson, 2018). Concerns about ageing are not only a matter of concern for those colleagues in the final phase of their working lives. Even middle-aged employees can become conscious about their physical appearance in terms of their weight, wrinkles, or greying hair (Larson, 2018) especially in organisational cultures where youth is revered rather more than maturity. As employees advance through certain life stages, they may also become preoccupied with changing family relationships as children become increasingly independent and parents require greater support (Larson, 2018).

Other lines of enquiry brought to the study of workplace wellbeing

The applications and implications of wellbeing at work and ways to improve it are evident in the many varied lines of enquiry brought to its study, such as attendance at work, the physical environment, resilience, mindfulness, personality, gender, and gratitude.

One line of enquiry of relevance to wellbeing at work focuses on attendance behaviour which considers the implications of both absenteeism and presenteeism. The concept of presenteeism pertains to employees who continue to work despite feeling unwell (Ruhl & Sub, 2020). Typical symptoms include tiredness, severe headaches, and neck and back pain (Costello, 2020). More than 15 per cent of employees engage in presenteeism, possibly because they are comforted by relationships with colleagues who are coping well or because they enjoy the structure work nevertheless brings to their day (Costello, 2020). These explanations for presenteeism arguably illustrate the relational nature of wellbeing and the value of interconnectedness (see Crossman, 2018). They also have implications for wellbeing in terms of social interaction and membership in groups and communities in that it is very difficult to thrive independently of them (Costello, 2020). However, presenteeism may also be attributable to aspects of a negative culture where employees feel under pressure to achieve certain outcomes that outweigh the symptoms of ill-health. Rather than benefiting organisations, however, when people work whilst ill, the organisation is negatively impacted from an economic point of view, and if the illness is contagious, the cost of course will be compounded (Ruhl & Sub, 2020).

ACTIVITY: DISCUSSION, REFLECTION, AND SYNTHESIS

Choose one of the following activities:

1. Before class, search your library resources to discover what you can about presenteeism and any factors that may influence presenteeism from an individual perspective. For example, during outbreaks of COVID-19, some people with mild symptoms still went to work because they were paid on contracts and relied on the money. Make notes on what you find, remembering to include references for the sources you cite. In class, pool your findings with others in small groups and prepare a poster presentation to share with other groups. Note differences and similarities in information, theories, concepts, and perspectives amongst these group findings.
2. Based on what you have discovered, consider and discuss whether you as an individual would go to work when unwell. What factors would you take into account in making your decision?
3. In a small group, co-construct an entry on presenteeism as a subsection of a wellbeing policy. Define the concept and based on evidence, make clear statements on employee rights and responsibilities and the expectations of the workplace. Keep the entry to no more than 500 words.

Some scholars are pursuing the influence of the physical workplace environment and its relation to wellbeing. For example, the biophilia hypothesis that humans have an innate desire to connect with the environment has arguably helped to increase awareness amongst employers of the importance of incorporating nature into professional spaces (Klotz & Bolino, 2020). Doing so communicates to employees, clients, and other stakeholders what is valued in the organisational culture; namely, the environment in a broad sense and the wellbeing of those who engage with the organisation. Resilience is another line of enquiry emerging from wellbeing literature concerned with the process of successful adaptation despite the challenges of past trauma, threat, adversity and tragedy, conditioning or present circumstances (see Heads, 2017). Being healthy, happy, and perhaps prosperous can assist in being resilient and in responding to stress at work (Scaria et al., 2020).

Mindfulness is often associated with wellbeing. It has its roots in Hindu and Buddhist practice but contemporaneously is regarded as secular and compatible with most religious beliefs (Owens & Daul-Elhindi, 2020). The practice originated about 2500 years ago and continues to be popular throughout India, Thailand, China, and Korea and, indeed, now has a certain cache in a variety of professions in the West (Zhuo, 2020). Mindfulness focuses upon appreciating the present moment rather than reflecting on the past or the future and at the same time being aware of a broader perspective (Ramos Salazar, 2017; Turner & West, 2018). For example, someone who is seriously ill may come to accept the condition and find themselves able to resist identifying with that illness to the extent that it diminishes his or her emotional wellbeing (Ramos Salazar, 2017). The daily practice of mindfulness enables awareness about personal thoughts, emotions, sensations, or feelings in a non-judgemental, focused way and can be transformational, transcending space and time in order to overcome habitual thinking, revealing other possibilities and fostering intuition in making decisions (Heads, 2017).

Not everyone responds to stressful events in the same way and thus individual differences in diverse workplaces will influence wellbeing in varied and nuanced ways. Some work suggests that Type A personalities may respond to stress by exhibiting impatience and hostility to others while Type B personalities reportedly tend to adopt a more easy-going and relaxed approach, mindful of maintaining relationships at home and in the workplace (Larson, 2018). Gender may also moderate responses to stress in that men tend to withdraw socially and seek responses independently and females are more likely to seek social support and solutions from trusted others when stressed (Larson, 2018). In addition, for males, a deterioration of their wellbeing as a result of changing workplace conditions may be made more complex given that workplace identity is much more closely tied to self-concept (Larson, 2018). Another study conducted by Anthony and Sheldon (2019) also provides insights into some differences in how males and females respond to interpersonal conflicts at work with respect to forgiveness. Largely overlooked in the literature, forgiveness has an important function with implications for wellbeing in that it is linked to mental and physical health and helps to maintain relationships over time (Anthony & Sheldon, 2019). The authors reveal that females become more distressed when trusted female co-workers disclose personal information to others whereas males are less likely to forgive colleagues at work when they feel someone has encroached upon other close relationships. If breaches of trust are overcome, men are more likely to communicate forgiveness by minimising the significance of an incident that caused conflict (Anthony & Sheldon, 2019).

Gratitude

The twenty-first century has witnessed a growing number of studies about gratitude, undertaken particularly by positive psychology scholars (Sun, Sun, Jiang, Jia, & Li, 2020). According to the literature, gratitude is an affective trait or an emotional state, akin to thankfulness and appreciation when someone is favoured in some way by another (Sun et al., 2020). Its effects are sufficiently impactful to manifest neurologically (Macfarlane, 2020). Feeling and expressing gratitude is generally regarded as a worthy characteristic amongst most people and appears to transcend culture (Manela cited in Macfarlane, 2020). Gratitude is largely presented in the literature as a positive construct giving rise to prosocial outcomes that highlight altruism and helping behaviours and also benefits individuals intrapersonally and interpersonally in the form of higher levels of satisfaction and closer social bonds (Gulliford, Morgan, Hemming, & Abbott, 2019). These bonds are no doubt strengthened through gratitude because they are tied to notions of reciprocity and trust because when individuals receive gratitude, they are more likely to carry out similar desirable behaviours that are appreciated and thus reinforced (Macfarlane, 2020). In this way, expressing gratitude by acknowledging co-worker contributions can also assist in developing team relational bonds (Macfarlane, 2020).

The implications of gratitude for wellbeing are well documented (see Anand, 2018). One recent study of Chinese adolescents, for example, examined the relationship between anxiety, depression, and gratitude, finding significant correlations amongst gratitude and its positive effects upon both depression and anxiety (Sun et al., 2020). The authors of the study concluded that practicing gratitude may serve as an effective way to protect individuals from psychological problems like anxiety and depression and may also assist in interventions aimed at reducing the effects of these conditions. Some authors have considered ways to encourage feelings of gratitude, given its benefits. Anand (2018), for example, has noted how keeping a gratitude journal, recollecting at least three things daily for which someone is grateful, can contribute to wellbeing.

As discussed, gratitude is generally considered as a positive phenomenon. However, critical perspectives have also been brought to this line of enquiry. Gulliford et al. (2019) have pointed out that gratitude may have a 'dark side' if it becomes part of a manipulative and self-serving strategy in the process of impression management with ingratiation as its tool. The potential for these unpleasant tactics to be employed certainly exists and being able to interpret when they are at play in interpersonal communication requires a level of sensitive perception. However, the benefits of gratitude personally and for others in general terms are not obviated by the possibility that some colleagues do not always behave as well as they might.

ACTIVITY: BRAINSTORMING, CREATIVITY, AND INNOVATION

In small groups consider practical ways that individuals and organisations can demonstrate gratitude to colleagues and even departments. For example, one might leave a small note of thanks for some assistance on a co-worker's desk for them to find later.

ACTIVITY: RESEARCH AND DISCUSSION

The Organisation for Economic Cooperation and Development (OECD) draws upon international statistical data to provide an independent analysis of economic and wellbeing factors in order to inform policies and decision making. Their aim is to foster prosperity and equality in accessing opportunities for the wellbeing of all.

Using the link underneath, research one particular country noting the data provided. Prepare notes on those areas of economic and wellbeing strength and areas which require further development. How does your chosen country compare with others in the same region and internationally? Working in small groups, interview others on their own findings and answer questions/share what you have discovered. What criteria were used to assess wellbeing? How was economic information related to wellbeing data, in your view?

www.oecdbetterlifeindex.org/about/better-life-initiative/

Conclusion

This chapter has explored the conceptual nature of wellbeing and a number of lines of enquiry related to it, based on contemporary literature. Emotional and physical aspects of the construct were considered and the implications for individuals and organisations when wellbeing is compromised. Practical examples of how wellbeing can be supported and enhanced are also provided. The chapter has contributed some foundational concepts that serve as scaffolding for appreciating, at a deeper level, the relationship between wellbeing and communication in a variety of organisational contexts approached in the remainder of the book.

References

Anand, R. (2018). *Happiness at work: Mindfulness, analysis and well-being*. Thousand Oaks: Sage.

Anthony, M., & Sheldon, P. (2019). Is the friendship worth keeping: Gender differences in communicating forgiveness in friendships. *Communication Quarterly, 67*(3), 291–311.

Brandt, M. (2020). Why focus on wellbeing? In E. Kim & B. Lindeman (Eds.), *Wellbeing* (pp. 11–19). Cham, Switzerland: Springer.

Costello, J. (2020). *Workplace wellbeing: A relational approach*. London: Routledge.

Cross, M. (2020). *Anxiety*. Auckland: Harper Collins.

Crossman, J. (2018). Celebrating interconnectedness as a spiritual paradigm for teaching learning and internationalization of higher education. In S. Dhiman, G. Roberts, & J. Crossman (Eds.), *The Palgrave handbook of workplace spirituality and fulfillment* (pp. 1013–1031). Cham, Switzerland: Palgrave Macmillan.

Crossman, J., Bordia, S., & Mills, C. (2011). *Business communication for the global age*. Sydney: McGraw-Hill.

De Janasz, S., Crossman, J., Campbell, N., & Power, M. (2014). *Interpersonal skills in organisations*. Sydney: McGraw-Hill Education.

Gill, H. (2019). *Communication: How to connect with anyone*. Chichester: Capstone John Wiley & Sons.

Goleman, D. (2020). *Emotional intelligence: Why it can matter more than IQ*. London: Bloomsbury Publishing.

Gulliford, L., Morgan, B., Hemming, E., & Abbott, J. (2019). Gratitude, self-monitoring and social intelligence: A prosocial relationship? *Current Psychology, 38*(4), 1021–1032.

Heads, G. (2017). *Living mindfully: Discovering authenticity through mindfulness coaching*. Oxford: Wiley Blackwell.

Huhtala, M., Feldt, T., Lamsa, A., Mauno, S., & Kinnunen, U. (2011). Does the ethical culture of organisations promote managers' occupational well-being? Investing indirect links via ethical strain. *Journal of Business Ethics, 101*(2), 231–247.

Huron, D. (2018). On the functions of sadness and grief. In H. Lench (Ed.), *The functions of emotions* (pp. 59–91). Cham, Switzerland: Springer.

Jia, M., Cheng, J., & Hale, C. (2017). Workplace emotion and communication supervision nonverbal immediacy: Employees' emotion experience and communication motives. *Management Communication Quarterly, 31*(1), 69–87.

Klotz, A., & Bolino, M. (2020). Bringing the great outdoors into the workplace: The energizing effect of biophilic work design. *The Academy of Management Review, 46*(2), 231–251.

Larson, K. (2018). *Adaption and well-being*. London: Routledge.

Leiter, P., & Cooper, C. (2017). The state of the art of workplace wellbeing. In C. Cooper & M. Leiter (Eds.), *The Routledge companion to wellbeing at work* (pp. 1–10). Oxfordshire: Taylor & Francis Group.

Leong, Y., & Crossman, J. (2009). What nursing managers need to know: Role transition for newly qualified nurses in Singapore. *Singapore Nursing Journal, 36*(2), 28–35.

Li, X., Feng, X., Wang, L., Geng, X., & Chang, H. (2021). Relationship between emotional intelligence and job well-being in Chinese registered nurses: Mediating effect of communicating satisfaction. *Nursing Open, 8*(4), 1778–1787.

Macfarlane, J. (2020). Positive psychology: Gratitude and its role within mental health nursing. *British Journal of Mental Health Nursing, 9*(1), 19–30.

Macnamara, J. (2015). *Organizational listening: The missing essential in public communication*. Bern, Switzerland: Peter Lang Books.

Maravelas, A. (2020). *Creating a drama-free workplace: The insider's guide to managing conflict, incivility and mistrust*. Newbury Port, MA: Career Press.

Miller, K. (2015). *Organizational communication: Approaches and processes* (7th ed.). Stamford, CT: Cengage Learning.

Neenan, M., & Dryden, W. (2020). *Cognitive behavioural coaching: A guide to problem-solving and personal development*. Oxford: Taylor & Francis Group.

Owens, T., & Daul-Elhindi, C. (2020). *The 360 librarian: A framework for integrating mindfulness, emotional intelligence and critical reflection in the workplace*. Chicago: Association of College and Research Libraries.

Pawar, B. (2020). *Well-being, leadership justice support and workplace spirituality*. New York: Routledge, Taylor & Francis Group.

Pradarelli, J., Shimizu, N., & Smink, D. (2020). Important terms in wellbeing. In E. Kim & B. Lindeman (Eds.), *Wellbeing* (pp. 23–30). Cham, Switzerland: Springer.

Ramos Salazar, L. (2017). The influence of business students' listening styles on their compassion and self-compassion. *Business and Professional Communication Quarterly, 80*(4), 426–442.

Ruhl, S., & Sub, S. (2020). Presenteeism & absenteeism at work – an analysis of archetypes of sickness attendance cultures. *Journal of Business and Psychology, 35*(2), 241–255.

Scaria, D., Brandt, M., Kim, E., & Lindeman, B. (2020). What is wellbeing? In E. Kim & B. Lindeman (Eds.), *Wellbeing* (pp. 3–11). Cham, Switzerland: Springer.

Shahnawaz, M., & Baig, M. (2018). Impact of job demands-resources model on burnout and employee's well-being: Evidence from the pharmaceutical organizations of Karachi. *Indian Institute of Management, 30*(2), 119–133.

Sias, P., & Shin, Y. (2020). Workplace relationships. In A. Nicotera (Ed.), *Origins and traditions of organizational communication: A comprehensive introduction to the field* (pp. 187–206). New York: Routledge.

Sun, P., Sun, Y., Jiang, H., Jia, R., & Li, Z. (2020). Gratitude as a protective factor against anxiety and depression among Chinese adolescents: The mediating role of coping flexibility. *Asian Journal of Social Psychology, 23*(4), 447–456.

Tracy, S., & Redden, S. (2019). The structuration of emotion. In A. Nicotera (Eds.), *Origins and traditions of organizational communication: A comprehensive introduction to the field* (pp. 348–369). New York: Routledge.

Turner, L., & West, R. (2018). *An introduction to communication*. Cambridge: Cambridge University Press.

Worden, J. (2018). *Grief counselling and grief therapy: A handbook for the mental health practitioner*. New York: Springer.

Zhuo, M. (2020). Learning from the 'right' ground of mindfulness: Some insights for the 'good' interculturalist. *Language and Intercultural Communication, 20*(1), 50–61.

PART II

Diversity, inclusion, and belonging

Diversity has become a paradigm – a lens through which we are able to see the world and one most organisations are employing in the development of policies and practices. The term and concept of managing diversity arose in the United States during the 1980s in response to demographic changes affecting the workforce but exactly how diversity is managed elsewhere in the world will depend upon specific national contexts, social perspectives, and relevant aspects of employment legislation (Strachan, French, & Burgess, 2010). Generally, however, the beneficial contribution of a diverse workforce reflecting a range of abilities, genders, cultures, ages and ethnicities, for example, are now increasingly acknowledged (see Miller, 2015). Scholars of organisational communication have contributed extensively to literature examining the implications of diversity in shaping workplace experiences (McDonald, 2019). One of the outcomes of this kind of research has led to many organisations insisting upon the adoption of inclusive language, and effective communicators know how powerful this kind of discourse is as a way of facilitating a culture with one voice and shared goals (Goodwin, 2019). Shifts in discourse are pushing back to counter inequitable, prejudicial practices.

Bhabha's (2011) work is seminal in exploring the meaning of being recognised as an individual who has particular social and institutional conditions of alterity, the state of being different or 'other'. He suggests that diversity is best understood as paradoxical communities in which people work alongside one another at the intersections of beliefs, ideas, and identities. He deems it paradoxical because of the multiple identifications that can co-exist, making it possible for an individual to be simultaneously the 'same and other', 'indigenous and foreign', 'citizen and alien', rendering the assumptions about the rights of individuals both complex and ambiguous (Bhabha, 2011). Developing the metaphor of paradoxical communities as a woven fabric, he points out that it can be resilient, or its threads torn apart at times when religious, racial, and ethnic conflicts arise. Bhabha (2011) insists

DOI: 10.4324/9780429318948-6

that multicultural and transnational organisations need to recognise the rights of minorities and intersubjective expressions as an ethical requirement underpinning respect and dignity.

Managing diversity in equitable ways requires some attention to the intertwining constructs of organisational discourse and culture. Employees are socialised into workplaces in powerful ways so how diversity is valued (or not) is learned through organisational discourse/communication (Ladegaard & Jenks, 2015). Adding to complexity, the multiple discourses of class, gender, race, and other forms of human diversity are not only to be considered singly or individually, but also in how they overlap with one another and this line of enquiry is referred to as intersectionality (Zoller & Ban, 2019). Intersectionality explores how, for example, gender, race, age, and socio-economic background may interact as factors of diversity and the implications of that interaction. To illustrate, professionals with certain disabilities, as described, often suffer at work as a result of prejudice but the problem is compounded when someone with a disability is also female or more mature than colleagues (see Sharma & Mann, 2020).

Part II reveals in different ways how discrimination can manifest in the workplace – a topic further pursued in Part III. Discrimination is characterised by language and behaviour that is exclusionary, abusive, demeaning, and harmful, contributing to negative stereotypes often in ways that are homophobic, racist, or sexist in nature (Turner & West, 2018). Homophobic language, for example, demeans gays and lesbians, bi-phobic and trans-phobic language degrades transgender, and bisexual people and sexist language demeans or excludes one sex, for example, by using the generic use of 'he' (Turner & West, 2018). The consequences of discrimination and prejudice are manifold, not least in the impact they have upon employee mental and physical wellbeing. Discrimination is also associated with demotivation, reduced productivity, absenteeism, and increased turnover (Sharma & Mann, 2020). Some forms of discrimination are less direct. For example, organisations may advertise employment vacancies listing amongst criteria that applicants should be clean shaven, thereby precluding applications from members of particular religions (Sharma & Mann, 2020). According to Zhang (2021), much of the empirical work about workplace discrimination appears to have been generated in the West but much less is known about its incidence and associated health problems in contemporary China. Opportunities to share findings from around the world have the potential to inform this line of enquiry.

Anxiety, stress, post-traumatic stress disorder, low morale, burnout, and violence appear to prevail amongst marginalised and vulnerable groups and communities based on gender, sexuality, colour, socio-economic status, citizenship status, (dis) abilitiy, spiritual beliefs and age, for example (Cross, 2020; Dwyer, 2020; McDonald, 2019). One form of discriminatory behaviour is harassment, defined as disrespectful and threatening behaviour involving racial or sexist comments and degrading slurs or jokes (Sharma & Mann, 2020). Harassment contributes to psychological and physical health issues that harm workers and organisations. Organisations that tolerate discriminatory behaviour miss the opportunity to take full advantage of the benefits that workplace diversity presents (Sharma & Mann, 2020).

Social inequality and exclusion can pervade organisational practices with varying levels of subtlety and include the contexts of hiring, role allocations, promotions, fringe benefits, access to training, authority allocation, and compensation whereby certain individuals can be relegated to less well-paid positions and others to more lucrative ones (Amis, Mair, & Munir, 2020; Sharma & Mann, 2020). In Australia, for example, Indigenous people continue to be one of the most disadvantaged groups in the labour force, reflected in low rates of remuneration, participation, and employment (Strachan et al., 2010). Despite claims of meritocracy and neutrality, homophily (where people associate with and favour those most similar to themselves) prevails in recruiting through informal (often personal) networks in contexts including western business schools (Amis et al., 2020; Lawrence & Shah, 2020). Human resource departments have a clear role in managing equitable processes.

How actively CEOs and HR managers are committed to equitable practices in diversity management in their words and actions will influence whether employees merely survive or thrive (Ng & Sears, 2018). Leadership plays a very important role in strengthening the management of organisational diversity (Sharma & Mann, 2020). Strategies and policies must clearly state that discriminatory behaviour is considered unacceptable in documents and in other forms of communication (Sharma & Mann, 2020). The encouragement to seek out common ground in cultural perspectives, values, and beliefs, emphasising 'we' more than 'I' and sacrificing personal desires and political gains, for example, are critical to effective communication (Goodwin, 2019). Effective communication thus not only involves communicating clearly *about* diversity but also entrenching discourse co-constructed *from* diverse perspectives and representations.

The tendency for humans to define and differentiate themselves from others is rooted in the psychological need to experience a sense of belonging (Coleman, 2021; Kim, 2017) and workplaces are no exception to this general statement. The title of Part II includes the concept of belonging because it is integral to the notion of diversity and indeed inclusivity. It is difficult to imagine how an employee may feel they belong to an organisation and identify with it, if they are excluded from opportunities to contribute in meaningful ways or where their contribution remains unacknowledged. Even where an employee is included in activities appropriately, it may not be sufficient to experience a sense of belonging because belonging is a state of *feeling* included. The extent to which employees feel a sense of belonging in an organisation is not a state of affairs that is limited to that particular environment but rather reflects broader societal forces – not least in education at all levels. Slee (2019), for example explores how children with disabilities may not feel a sense of belonging at school, despite rhetoric about inclusion that focuses upon getting the communication right and often. Intentions, he suggests, fail to turn intentions into realities on a day-to-day level.

Belonging means feeling that our true selves can, for the most part, be brought to the workplace. Inclusion is more often associated with strategic decision making in how organisations hire, for example and make decisions that reflect a commitment to diversity. Yet, unless employees feel they belong, something is missing. A slippage exists between organisational aims to reflect diversity in decision making and whether employees actually feel they belong without having to make considerable efforts to conceal parts of themselves. This distinction explains the difference between inclusion and belonging despite their obvious conceptual interconnection.

In introducing Part II, I have necessarily discussed the concepts embedded in its title (diversity, inclusion and belonging) at some length because the inherent perspectives underscore discussions in the chapters that follow, addressing communication in the contexts of culture, gender, generation and spiritual diversity.

References

Amis, J, Mair, J., & Munir, K. (2020). The organizational reproduction of inequality. *Academy of Management Annals, 14*(1), 195–230.

Bhabha, H. (2011). *Our neighbours, ourselves*. Boston: De Gruyter.

Coleman, R. (Ed.). (2021). *Belonging through a psychoanalytic lens*. London: Routledge.

Cross, M. (2020). *Anxiety*. Auckland: Harper Collins.

Crossman, J. (2008). A different way: Student perspectives on international and cultural learning. *Employment Relations Record, 8*(2), 34–45.

Dwyer, J. (2020). *Communication for business and the professions: Strategies and skills*. Melbourne: Pearson.

Goodwin, J. M. (2019). Communication accommodation theory: Finding the right approach. In M. Brown Sr. & L. Hersey (Eds.), *Returning to interpersonal dialogue and understanding human communication in the digital age* (pp. 168–185). Hershey, PA: IGI Global.

Kim, Y. Y. (2017). Identity and intercultural communication. In *The international encyclopedia of intercultural communication* (pp. 1–9). New York: John Wiley & Sons Ltd. doi:10.1002/9781118783665.ieicc0002

Ladegaard, H., & Jenks, C. (2015). Language and intercultural communication in the workplace: Critical approaches to theory and practice. *Language and Intercultural Communication, 15*(1), 1–12.

Lawrence, B., & Shah, N. (2020). Homophily: Measures and meaning. *Academy of Management Annals*, in-Press. doi:10.5465/annals.2018.01477

McDonald, J. (2019). Difference and intersectionality. In A. Nicotera (Ed.), *Origins and traditions of organizational communication: A comprehensive introduction to the field* (pp. 270–287). New York: Routledge.

Miller, K. (2015). *Organizational communication: Approaches and processes*. Stamford, CT: Cengage Learning.

Ng, E., & Sears, G. (2018). Walking the talk on diversity: CEO beliefs, moral values, and the implementation of workplace diversity practices. *Journal of Business Ethics, 164*(4), 437–450.

Sharma, S., & Mann, N. (2020). Workplace discrimination: The most critical issue in managing diversity. In *Management association, information resources editor. Five generations and only one workforce: How successful Businesses are managing a multigenerational workforce* (pp. 1–19). Hershey, PA: IGI Global.

Slee, R. (2019). Belonging in an age of exclusion. *International Journal of Inclusive Education, 23*(9), 909–922.

Strachan, G., French, E., & Burgess, J. (2010). *Managing diversity in Australia: Theory and practice.* Sydney: McGraw-Hill.

Turner, L., & West, R. (2018). *An introduction to communication.* Cambridge: Cambridge University Press.

Zhang, H. (2021). Workplace victimization and discrimination in China: A nationwide survey. *Journal of Interpersonal Violence, 36*(1–2), 957–975.

Zoller, H., & Ban, Z. (2019). Power and resistance. In A. Nicotera (Ed.), *Origins and traditions of organizational communication: A comprehensive introduction to the field* (pp. 228–249). New York: Routledge.

5

CULTURE AND INTERCULTURAL COMMUNICATION

Globalisation

Globalisation has facilitated shifts in rethinking how to address diversity given its defining impact upon societies, organisations, and the interaction amongst members of cultures and nations around the world (Maddux, Lu, Affinito, & Galinsky, 2020). The construct of globalisation, however, remains both complex and contested (Hirst & Thompson, 2019). Competing narratives about globalisation and de-globalisation reflect perspectives about cultural proximity in organisations with some advocating that cultural similarity makes for better communication and interaction and others pointing out unwanted consequences (Ceci & Masciarelli, 2020), such as groupthink, that does little to invite innovative ideas.

Many definitions of globalisation exist and one of them, suggested by Ietto-Gilles (2019, p. 155), is as follows:

> globalisation is both a process of a geographical/spatial outreach and of an increased degree of interconnectedness and interdependence between people, groups and institutions based in different countries of the world.

Similarly, Hirst and Thompson (2019), maintain that globalisation involves intense international connectedness that facilitates trade flows, investment, and communication between and amongst nations. While the terms globalisation and internationalisation are sometimes used interchangeably, Marginson (2000) distinguished between the two in positing that internationalisation is concerned with the intensification of relationships amongst national cultures, whereas globalisation tends to emphasise world systems. Many forces for change in recent decades

DOI: 10.4324/9780429318948-7

have facilitated globalisation. They include (see Bhabha, 2011; Hirst & Thompson, 2019; Ietto-Gilles, 2019; Miller, 2015; Noma & Crossman, 2012):

1. faster, cheaper travel and transportation via jet aircraft, capable of travelling long distances
2. better communication and technology as a result of the emergence of the Internet, satellites, and fibre optics
3. the outsourcing of manufacturing and service centres
4. government and organisational cooperation to improve security and to counter terrorist attacks
5. increased global investment
6. cross-border trade, international relationships with suppliers, investors and clients
7. migration.

Cultural engagement has occurred for thousands of years in a waxing and waning fashion yet the recent focus in the literature upon the rise of globalisation in the late twentieth and twenty-first century mistakenly suggests that globalisation is a 'new' phenomenon or that it is somehow more intensive now than ever before. Yet, as Hirst and Thompson (2019) point out, during the period from 1850–1940, increased manufacturing gave rise to intense trading, labour migration, and global capital that, all things considered, suggest a similar or greater scale of globalisation than we see today.

Globalisation does have a dark underbelly, however, when one considers issues such as people trafficking (see Chapter 13 on Dark Issues) and, indeed, some aspects of migration. As Bhabha (2011) suggests, the notion of a borderless, global world that references the migration of refugees and nomads neglects to acknowledge that many of them seek asylum, a home, a nationality, an education, and the ability to claim economic or cultural rights through citizenship – all aspects of status that elude so many of them for long periods of time. He thus calls for the redistribution of resources based on a transnational moral economy to enable those marginalised.

The phenomenon of 'cultural cringe' is another less than desirable outcome of imperialism, as one form of globalisation historically. 'Cultural cringe' refers to a kind of cultural memory following periods of imperialism (Yadong & Bates, 2020) where people revere the achievements of powerful national cultures while diminishing their own cultural contributions in a kind of out-culture favouritism or preference (Ji & Bates, 2020). The notion of cultural cringe has been attributed to Phillips (1950) who tried to explain an apparent tendency amongst Australians to view their own achievements with less respect than they did those of the British. Today, the concept is beginning to attract some attention in intercultural and international communication studies (Ji & Bates, 2020). By way of example, Yadong and Bates (2020) identified cultural cringe arising from colonisation and western imperialism in the areas of Shanghai, Guangzhou, Qindao, Hong Kong, and Macao.

Despite some of the disagreeable elements of globalisation, some scholars have offered counterbalancing benefits. To illustrate, Miller (2015) has suggested that it has resulted in a greater protection of worker rights internationally. Also, Maddux et al. (2020) argue that globalisation has

1. enabled collaboration on shared challenges such as climate change, race relations, or pandemics
2. led to profound multicultural experiences giving rise to psychological outcomes such as improved intrapersonal cognition, the broadening of personal attitudes and behaviours, and enhanced interpersonal relationships, that in turn benefit organisations
3. created confidence in multicultural partnerships and their perpetuation as experience of them grows
4. enhanced performance through the multicultural experience with influential members who have successfully been able to lower operating costs by exercising culturally collective creative approaches.

The pace of globalisation for some decades has not been lost on university business schools that have recognised their role in developing graduates with the relevant knowledge and expertise to function as leaders in complex cultural contexts in response to rising demand from organisational recruiters (Crossman, 2008, 2009, 2010; Noma & Crossman, 2012). Specifically, a cultural context is understood as the 'circumstances that form the setting for an event, statement or idea and in terms of which it can be fully understood' (Waddell, Creed, & Cummings, 2019, p. 116). Clearly, the knowledge and cultural sensitivity leaders need to appreciate contexts beyond those in which they are familiar and conditioned to operate is a skill that takes time to acquire and a level of expertise few reach successfully in complex, intercultural. and organisational relationships. Scholars of international and cultural leadership (ICL) from the 1990s onwards increasingly called for greater engagement in this space to understand the personal and organisational implications of developing strategies for leadership in one cultural context that would not necessarily be effective in another (see Bjerke, 1999; Crossman, 2009; Gardner, 1990; Tjosvold & Leung, 2003). Within the discipline of communication, some have criticised the dominance of western perspectives upon curricula internationally, considered 'too white', and focusing almost exclusively upon the contexts and priorities of liberal democracies and 'the global north' (Wasserman, 2020). One way to address these concerns is to encourage business schools to design programmes based on experiential forms of intercultural learning such as online student collaborations internationally to develop intercultural teamwork and decision making (see Crossman, 2008, 2011). Also, some business journals such as the *Journal of International Education in Business* have ensured that their brief and scope address international rather than simply western perspectives and worldviews that often appear to prevail, even in cases where research is undertaken in non-western cultural contexts.

Much of the discussion about globalisation and internationalisation until quite recently, has tended to be tied to the concepts of the nation state and national culture (culture defined by geographical, hard borders). The relevance of these concepts was called into question with the emergence of the idea of a global culture that transcended both time and place (Ladegaard & Jenks, 2015). Yet, a global culture cannot be guaranteed indefinitely and it may be naïve to assume its existence as an all-encompassing, consistent view of culture. Relationships change. The PRC, for example, shifted towards greater globalisation following economic reforms and an open market policy over the last half century but more recently shows some signs of rising nationalism that may temper some of these trends (Yadong & Bates, 2020). As Hirst and Thompson (2019, p. 16) remarked,

> although we have had a long period of growing international interconnectedness there is no reason to assume that such processes will continue indefinitely or that they have an inherent dynamic that prevails over countervailing forces.

Nation states may become overwhelmed by pressures brought about by climate change and migration patterns with consequent rises in tariffs designed to protect national industries and greater significance placed on state borders (Hirst & Thompson, 2019). Trends like these will inevitably influence how societies and organisations think about diversity.

Culture

It is unsurprising that workplaces pay attention to culture given its ubiquitous influence. Culture goes deep and affects communication, sometimes subtly but nevertheless, profoundly (Lu, 2018). It affects how people display trust, their moral flexibility, and leadership and communication competence (Maddux et al., 2020). Organisations thrive when they capitalise upon cultural mixes amongst employees or international partners. Relationships and decision-making processes are improved when cultural awareness informs interpersonal and organisational communication (Dwyer, 2020). Organisations also perform better financially and in terms of managing staff, developing marketing strategies for local and international markets and meeting diverse customer needs (see Crossman, 2008; Crossman, Bordia, & Mills, 2011). The obvious motivation for scholars to discover as much as possible about the nature of culture in organisations and how it operates is clear. Nevertheless, as Triandis implied in his foreword to the GLOBE study, cultural research is not for the fainthearted (see House, Hanges, Javidan, Dorfma, & Gupta, 2004). Perhaps one reason for this is the complex, intertwining way that culture operates with almost all other concepts about self and social behaviour. For example, interpersonal communication is both influenced by and forms its basis on culture, and so the relationship between the two is reciprocal (Noels, Clement, Collins, & Machintyre, 2019).

An online search for definitions of culture will likely reveal a large number that vary by virtue of discipline or a particular empirical approach, and for this reason a single, conclusive definition is unlikely to be identified (House et al., 2004; Minkov, 2013). Workplaces inevitably function at the interface between language, culture, and communication, and their interdependence as both concepts and disciplines means that each of these phenomena are rarely understood in isolation of the others (see Crossman et al., 2011; Servaes, 2020). So although definitions of culture are influenced by disciplines, the holistic nature of culture as a concept suggests that it is unlikely to be successfully explained without an interdisciplinary approach or an acknowledgement of varied perspectives, even in studies that are highly focused upon, for example, linguistic research questions.

Piller (2017) asserts that the concept of culture is constructed by actors who reproduce social categories and boundaries that help humans to understand the reasons, forms, and consequences at play in intercultural communication. Hofstede and Bond (1988) emphasised group membership in their definition of culture where members of one group are distinguished from another whether on a national or corporate level. These lenses construct a comparative (and perhaps polarising) view of national cultures embodying a '*we* are like this and *they* are like that' way of thinking. Indeed, few scholars subscribe to the idea of universal cultural laws (Fukuyama, 1995), and in the last quarter-century since Fukuyama's observation, little evidence disputes his claim. Yet the concept of culture is patently more nuanced than binary thinking would suggest. As Lewicki, Barry, and Saunders (2016) pointed out, countries may lay claim to more than a single culture and, indeed, cultures do transcend national borders.

Other themes emerging from definitions are consistently identifiable. The idea that culture is constructed through shared meanings emerged primarily from the work of Clifford Geetz, an American anthropologist (Minkov, 2013), and is now espoused quite widely. Based on the literature (see Hofstede & Bond, 1988; House et al., 2004; Kim, 2017; Lewicki et al., 2016; Low, 2020; Minkov, 2013; Palazzo, 2019; Pierson, 2019; Roy, 2020; Ting-Toomey & Oetzel, 2001; Servaes, 2020; Su, 2019; Turner & West, 2018; Yule, 2017), culture can be constructed as,

> a deeply rooted, enduring (yet modifiable) and socially acquired way of making sense of the world as a shared system of meanings. Membership in a culture is manifested and referenced in behaviour and concepts such as,

- identity
- values, beliefs, attitudes, spirituality
- norms
- traditions
- ideas, assumptions, ideologies
- symbols, concepts
- collective procedures and practices
- sharing rituals

- jargon – words or phrases familiar to some but not others
- ceremonies
- myths, stories and legends
- language
- race and ethnicity.

Defining a *specific* culture, however, for example the culture of Singapore or West Malaysia, is challenging. One reason for this may be that cultures are not fixed but constantly changing, dynamic, unpredictable, and fluid (Turner & West, 2018).

ACTIVITY: RESEARCH

Locate at least three definitions of culture from library sources (remembering to reference them appropriately). What themes are identifiable in those definitions? Are they included in the list provided or could they be added to expand the list?

ACTIVITY: REFLECTION AND DISCUSSION

Reflect upon the culture with which you most closely associate. Try to encapsulate what characterises that culture, making some notes as you develop ideas. Share your ideas with others who have chosen the same or a different culture and discuss how your perceptions and experiences are similar or different. Try to account for these differences. Co-construct a brief description of one of these cultures.

Scholars have often drawn upon metaphors to explain, illustrate, and illuminate complex ideas. Ting-Toomey and Oetzel (2001) did so in exploring the notion of culture in comparing it to an iceberg where some layers of culture might be considered as accessible and obvious to a traveller (e.g. likened to the part of an iceberg one can identify above water), whereas beliefs and values would be more difficult to identify because they are not necessarily explicit in observable behaviours.

ACTIVITY: EXPERIENTIAL REFLECTION

Discuss with others a country you have visited for a period of time. What things did you instantly notice that were different from your own cultural experience? What did you later learn about the cultural norms that were less obvious?

Appreciating less obvious aspects of culture take time. The process of cultural adaptation and adjustment when someone relocates from one culture to another is known as acculturation (Dwyer, 2020) or enculturation. Enculturation involves learning about practices, customs, values, and patterns of cultural interaction (Turner & West, 2018) and can be challenging, exciting, and sometimes humiliating. For example, a young western teacher may not immediately realise that the decision on how appropriate it is to wear a sarong to go shopping in a local kampung in East Malaysia is based upon a whole gamut of considerations concerned with age, status, the activity in hand, and the function and location in which an activity takes place. Ignorance of culture can lead to trouble with the law in unexpected ways; the expatriate child, for example, who throws a date at another in the Middle East without knowing that a trifle in his own culture is unlawful in the one in which he finds himself.

Cultural beliefs run deep in human cognition, perceptions, and how people construct their realities, and so ideas that challenge such beliefs and introduce unacceptable levels of doubt and uncertainty are likely to meet with resistance (Marsella, 2005; Nicholson & Wong, 2001). This may account for what is known as ethnocentrism, a term derived from the Greek words, 'ethnos' (nation) and 'Kentron' (centre). Ethnocentrism is the unfavourable evaluation of the behaviour of others based on personal cultural standards assumed to be superior (see Dwyer, 2020; Ting-Toomey & Oetzel, 2001; Turner & West, 2018). Similarly, stereotyping is the process of adopting a somewhat fixed impression of a group of people and communicating with an individual in ways that assume that he or she automatically represents that group without considering individual differences (Turner & West, 2018). Thus, stereotyping is a form of cultural generalisation and may be negative or indeed positive. For example, one might hear that people from Hong Kong are hardworking without appreciating exceptions. Whether a stereotype is positive or negative, it has the potential to cause serious problems that impede communication (Larson, 2018) but which can also, as Miller (2015) has pointed out, become misleading, dangerous, and cause systematic barriers to the wellbeing and success of others. Prejudice and discrimination are often fuelled by stereotyping (Larson, 2018) whether it is based on culture, colour, gender, or a religious group, for example. Unfortunately, stereotypes are highly resistant to change (Lewicki et al., 2016).

Cultural intelligence

For several decades, scholars have been exploring the factors contributing to intercultural competence and, subsequently, cultural intelligence (known as CQ) (Liao & Thomas, 2020; Mayer, 2020). The relevance of CQ to organisational activity in a globalising world is now widely appreciated and documented (Alon, Boulanger, Meyers, & Taras, 2016).

CQ is a relatively new field in psychology but has been applied to a variety of other disciplinary contexts such as management and education (Serdari, 2020; Servaes, 2020). According to Liao and Thomas (2020), despite a plethora of models available that purport to explain the skills and abilities of intercultural effectiveness, not all have been subjected to the highest levels of empirical rigour.

The concept of CQ emerged from the theory of multiple intelligences, put forth by American psychologist Howard Gardner, who rejected the idea of a single general intelligence (IQ) that focused upon literacy and numeracy was limited to western educational models (Ang et al., 2007; Serdari, 2020). Gardner first published his theory of multiple intelligences in 1983 and defined seven of them: verbal-linguistic, logical mathematical, visual-spatial, musical, kinesthetic, interpersonal, and intrapersonal (Gardner, 2011). According to Serdari (2020), the visual-spatial, musical, and kinesthetic intelligences are probably those most relevant to CQ.

However, it is Early and Ang who are credited with developing the multidimensional construct of CQ in 2003, describing it as an individual's capacity to function and manage in culturally diverse situations (Ang et al., 2007). The Early and Ang construct consisted of four elements of CQ: 1. metacognitive, 2. cognitive, 3. motivational, and 4. behavioural (Early & Ang, 2003). Caputo, Oluremi, Amoo, and Menke (2019) describe these elements based on their reading of Early and Ang's work as follows:

The elements in Table 5.1 provide some insight into the kinds of abilities that a person with a high CQ is likely to possess and demonstrate. Drawing on the literature, Serdari (2020) also observes the capacity to suspend judgement as an element of CQ because doing so ensures that sufficient time to reflect and act upon the cultural context is available and can inform any necessary adjustments to modes of speech, gestures, and facial expressions. As Alon et al. (2016) concede, CQ has many overlapping dimensions, including an ability for cross cultural adaptation, emotional intelligence, and cognitive capacities. They also note that CQ correlates with conscientiousness, agreeableness, extraversion, and having a bicultural upbringing and multiple cultural identities.

TABLE 5.1 Elements of cultural intelligence

Metacognitive CQ	The conscious awareness of cultural interactions and the ability to identify the thoughts of others and one's own in order to develop an appropriate strategy.
Cognitive CQ	Knowledge of the norms, values and beliefs of a particular cultural group and appreciating their importance and implications for social interaction across cultures including business situations.
Motivational CQ	Individual interest and willingness to learn about cultural differences. Motivation may be intrinsic as a result of the personal pleasure of participating in a culturally diverse situation or extrinsic motivation where tangible benefits of culturally diverse experiences are available. Also, self-efficacy can be enhanced when personal confidence is boosted through successful cross-cultural encounters.
Behavioural CQ	The ability to choose appropriate verbal and physical actions to accomplish goals when interacting with people from different cultures.

Source: Early and Ang, cited in Caputo et al., 2019

Shortly after Early and Ang's work was published in 2003, Ang et al. (2007), in a Singapore/US study, added greater precision to the CQ construct by testing the relationships between the four CQ dimensions introduced by Early and Ang in 2003 (metacognitive, cognitive, motivational, and behavioural) and three intercultural effectiveness outcomes (cultural judgement, decision making, cultural adaptation, and task performance). They found that 'metacognitive CQ and cognitive CQ predicted cultural judgement and decision making; motivational CQ and behavioural CQ predicted cultural adaptation; and metacognitive CQ and behavioural CQ predicted task performance' (Ang et al., 2007, p. 335). The researchers concluded that these expanded and nuanced understandings of CQ would be highly relevant to organisational practices such as recruitment, preparation for expatriate roles, global leadership, cross-cultural negotiations, training, and ultimately developing a culturally intelligent workforce. Other researchers have also noted culturally diverse contexts where development in cultural awareness is regarded as positive and beneficial, if not essential. For example, intercultural negotiation (Caputo et al., 2019), global virtual teams (Shalik, Makhecha, & Gouda, 2020), expatriatism (Ren, Yunlu, Shaffer, & Fodchuk, 2021), graduate employability (Crossman & Clarke, 2010), organisational behaviour and culture (Kubicek, Bhanugopan, & O'Neill, 2019), and knowledge sharing and innovation (Berraies, 2020).

The good news is that CQ can be developed through training and awareness programmes that offer experiential learning experiences (Shalik et al., 2020). However, although CQ is generally associated with positive aspects of individual capabilities, a dark side, or in other words, a negative dimension of the construct, also exists in that those with high CQ, while excelling in, for example, customer relationship performance, may simultaneously use their capabilities to engage in unethical and opportunistic practices (Lorenz, Ramsey, Andzulis, & Franke, 2020). It is for each of us to be mindful of right action when ethical dilemmas in intercultural situations arise.

Intercultural communication

As Lu (2018, p. 1) points out, 'Culture affects communication in subtle and profound ways' and the study of intercultural communication is part of discovering more about the relationship between the two. Although the term 'intercultural communication' is now in common usage, Piller (2017) suggests that it is interpreted in disparate and sometimes incompatible ways. Nevertheless, many organisational scholars would arguably accept Tomasell's (2020) explanation of intercultural communication as a concept that focuses upon how goals can be achieved when members of diverse cultures collaborate, in contrast to cross-cultural communication that tends to be more concerned with typical styles of communication in some national cultures and how they differ from others. Intercultural communication has a greater sense of synergy than cross-cultural communication because the whole (the co-created space) is quite a different reality from its parts (the cultural interactants as individuals). Such a perspective owes much to

Homi Bhabha, the post-colonial critic who drew attention to the metaphor of the 'third space', generally adopted in many disciplines including intercultural communication (Xiaowei & Pilcher, 2019). The construct of the third space challenges how self is understood when engaging with historic, cultural, linguistic experiences and liminal contexts signified through intersubjective dialogue amongst interlocutory agents who assume identities that are contingent and open ended (Bhabha, 2011).

The study of intercultural communication is continually evolving, reflecting changing relationships and priorities globally. In a review of the literature, Baker and Sangiamchit (2019) concluded that applied linguistics and intercultural communication research is currently undergoing something of a 'trans-turn', manifested in lines of enquiry about trans-languaging, trans-modality, trans-nationalism, and transcultural communication, whereby the trans- prefix emphasises a dynamic perspective on contexts as interactants communicate *through* borders, thus transcending and blurring them.

The intensification of multidisciplinary enquiry into intercultural communication during the twentieth century is attributed to a variety of conditions. The Second World War, for example, highlighted the need for a greater understanding of cross-cultural and intercultural communication in the context of diplomacy and peace movements that became consolidated from the 1960s (Tomasell, 2020), culminating in widespread multiculturalism that Piller (2017) argued contributed to the development of intercultural communication studies. International tourism and the emergence of global economies no doubt also played some part in the recognition that intercultural communication was intrinsic to the success of these trends (Crossman et al., 2011). Also, the development of intercultural communication as a line of enquiry was facilitated by business communities who were becoming aware that ineffective and poorly managed intercultural communication comes at a high cost (see Beamer, 1995). Today, intercultural (business) communication in culturally diverse organisations is now very much a common business practice where expertise is expected (Broome et al., 2019; Rathmayr, 2017).

Academics, too, are increasingly working together interculturally and learning from one another (see Crossman, Lui, & Tang, 2008). In an interconnected world, scholarly reflexivity has informed how ideas are constructed, based on the multiple cultural identities of academics whose lives have been forged through intercultural communication. A case in point is the work of Zhuo (2020) who brought both his Chinese and English life experiences to enrich the epistemological basis of his own scholarship about how Buddhist mindfulness can be useful in developing ethical insights. Since the seminal work of Tajfel and Turner (1986) on social identity, extensive work has been undertaken in this line of enquiry in the disciplines of psychology, communication, and other social sciences (Kim, 2017). The application of theories about multiple identities to the context of interculturality has largely found acceptance and support (see Kim, 2017).

The idea of multiple cultural identities also takes into account the concept of co-cultures. Until quite recently, the concept of 'subculture' was adopted in cultural studies to describe those whose views or experiences that differed in some sort of defining way from the norm in an otherwise shared culture (Turner & West, 2018). For example, one might think of artists, criminal gangs, religious groups, or skateboarding enthusiasts as subcultural groups. However, the term subculture has attracted some criticism on the basis that it tends to assume the existence of a dominant voice in diverse and complex societies whereas its replacement, 'co-culture', is considered more relevant to the assumption that communities co-exist (Turner & West, 2018) and are viewed through a less hierarchical perspective. The concept of interculturality has clearly broadened in its scope amongst scholars more recently. As Kim (2017, p. 2) remarked, '[a]ny interpersonal encounter is considered intercultural whenever the interactants differ or perceive themselves to be different from each other'. In essence, what occurs is an ongoing process of identity development through personal experiences and interactions with social groups and other individuals (Kim, 2017).

Salient cultural theories impacting on relationships and communication in the workplace

A large body of literature based on cultural theories and topologies informs ideas essentially about who people are, depending upon culturally influential learning and experiences throughout their lives. Some of these seminal theories have been resistant to criticisms over time and continue to be widely accepted. The contribution they make, at the very least, is to assist individuals and groups to be reflective about why they think, feel, and behave as they do and the meanings they create in communication and in building relationships with others. The aim in this section is to provide an accessible overview of theories that a reader may wish to follow up with other sources for a deeper appreciation of them.

High and low context cultures

Edward Hall (1976, 1981) is credited with the development of a prevailing theory of high and low context cultures. Hall's experience of living in Asia and training business professionals about cross-cultural communication formed the basis of his cultural observations. His approach included ritual, nonverbal, less rational aspects of cultural expression, such as gesture, proxemics, emotions, tone of voice, time, and facial expression in a departure from more mechanistic communication theories of his day (Tomasell, 2020). The following explanation of high and low context cultures is presented in an attenuated form, based on a range of sources including Hall (1976, 81), Rathmayr (2017), Roy (2020), and Triandis (1995). Although ideas associated with high and low cultures are depicted in a somewhat polarised manner for the reader's convenience in Table 5.2, they are, in fact, far more nuanced and range on a continuum.

TABLE 5.2 Broad characteristics of high and low context cultures

High context cultures (e.g. India, China, South Korea, Vietnam, Arabic cultures, Japan)	Low context cultures (e.g. Switzerland, Germany, US, Canada, UK & Australia)
Relates to homogenous cultures.	Relates to heterogeneous/diverse cultures.
A focus on interpreting implicit cultural cues and establishing meaning from context enabled through homogenous cultures where information is understood intuitively, making it difficult for outsiders to understand meaning/communicate.	Explicit, direct, expression of ideas verbally and in writing. Communication is more accessible to a wider community.
Reliance on nonverbal and subtle body language and in-group communication.	Emphasis on verbal and written communication.
Long-term relationships are valued.	Respect for rules more than relationships.
Avoidance of unpleasant or embarrassing communication that may lead to prevarication.	Prevarication is not encouraged. Timely and verbalised communication is valued but may be interpreted as 'talking down' by those from high context cultures.

ACTIVITY: REFLECTION AND RESEARCH

Consider the descriptions of high and low context culture and search, using the library resources available to you on this topic, to gain further insights. Write a few paragraphs explaining in what ways you identify with high or low context cultures and provide illustrations from the literature that resonate with your own experience.

Analogue and digital mindsets

Studies about analogue and digital mindsets emerged from growing interest in East/West communication and have helped managers to appreciate and foster creative and holistic approaches (Noma & Crossman, 2012). Analogue and digital mindsets are equally important conceptions that co-exist in complementary ways, whereby analogue representations tend to be holistic, intuitive, and continuous and digital ones tend to be complex, analytical, abstract, and focused on accuracy (Noma & Crossman, 2012). Although analogue mindsets are associated with eastern national cultures such as Korea and Japan and digital ones with western cultures, globalisation has meant that such associations are less bipolar than they might have been in the past (Noma & Crossman, 2012).

Hiyashi (1994) explored multinational corporations for two decades and considered analogue and digital mindsets reflected the differences between O (organic) type organisations and M (mechanistic) type organisations. Specifically, organic organisations are influenced by analogue perspectives, favouring indirect and tacit communication generally adopted in high context cultures and M-type organisations tend to focus on digital information, characteristic of low context cultures that preference explicit, verbal information (Hiyashi, 1994; see Hall, 1976; 1983).

ACTIVITY: DISCUSSION

In small and preferably intercultural groups, discuss the following proposition:

> Your cousin asks for a position advertised in your company. He communicates well with others around him. You know he works hard, is adaptable, and gets things done. He has never let you down in family matters. He has recently lost his job and meets some of the required criteria but not all. Some other applicants are better qualified but unknown to you. Would you hire him? Explain your answer.

Universalist and particularist cultures

The international manager often faces dilemmas arising from the tension that can exist between universal truth and a particular or local circumstance (see Trompenaars, 1996). Universalist cultures, common in protestant countries, tend to respect rules that represent a strong moral reference, even when friends are involved. They prefer to adopt strategic approaches and like to have detailed, drafted contracts whereas in particularist cultures, it is generally accepted that certain circumstances or relationships (family, friends) are more important than rules in employment contexts (Trompenaars, 1996).

Monochronic and polychronic cultures

Cultures may also be described as being largely monochronic or polychronic. The UK, Germany, Scandanavia, Switzerland, and Australia are examples of monochronic cultures. Those who come from monochronic cultures tend to conceive time as tangible and sequential and prefer to complete one task before beginning another (Ceci & Masciarelli, 2020). Time is referred to as a countable resource to be found, lost, or saved (Hall, 1990; Ting-Toomey & Oetzel, 2001). Individuals from polychronic cultures are more likely to undertake multiple tasks simultaneously and, unlike those raised in monochronic cultures, are comfortable being interrupted in their work and changing plans (Ceci & Masciarelli, 2020; Hall,

1990; Ting-Toomey & Oetzel, 2001). Many polychronic cultures are found in Arabia, Africa, Asia, Latin America, Eastern Europe, and the Mediterranean (Hall, 1990; Ting-Toomey & Oetzel, 2001).

Hofstede's work on cultural dimensions

The seminal work of Geert Hofstede, an eminent Dutch anthropologist in the 1980s, intensified interest in how culture is relevant to business and management disciplines and practice (Ceci & Masciarelli, 2020). Hofstede (2001) developed a theory based on cultural dimensions that explained the influence of a society's culture upon behaviour and values. His works are now the most highly cited in his field (Palazzo, 2019). Using factor analysis, Hofstede analysed an international survey of IBM employee values between 1967 and 1973 and, based on his findings, originally proposed four dimensions addressing cultural values: individualism-collectivism, power distance, masculinity-femininity, and uncertainty avoidance, with the fifth and sixth dimensions of long-term orientation and indulgence versus self-restraint being added later (see Hofstede & Bond, 2016). Hofstede's work is praised for the contribution it has made to the understanding of national culture and intercultural communication (Palazzo, 2019), the impact it has had on both the corporate world and academia, and the rigorous approach taken in collecting data (Roy, 2020).

Despite global accolades over decades, Hofstede's dimensions attracted some criticisms. Amongst them are a failure to acknowledge globalised, borderless, and online intercultural communication and the attention brought to emerging ideas about multiple cultural identities as a counter to the tendency for Hofstede's work to generalise cultural characteristics (Fang, 2010; Fisher, Doughty, & Mussayeva, 2008; Metcalf, Bird, Peterson, Shankarmahesh, & Lituchy, 2007). Also, Hofstede's theories were questioned on the basis that they tended to suggest that cultural and national borders were one and the same thing, that data collected from one company could reflect an entire group of cultures, and that he identified too few dimensions to reflect the complexity of cultures (Palazzo, 2019; Roy, 2020). Relatedly, Hofstede's work has also been attacked for apparently assuming that the domestic populations of countries are generally homogenous (Palazzo, 2019; Roy, 2020). Such criticisms of essentialist approaches and the conflation of individual behaviour being linked to national cultures persist and represent an increasing shift away from considering communication as a phenomenon that occurs in-between cultures (Baker & Sangiamchit, 2019). Essentialist approaches are a particular challenge for multinational and other organisations with a multicultural and international staff because it is difficult to consider the extent to which a particular norm can be isolated and addressed as a valid cultural consensus (Bulow & Kumar, 2011). Another criticism of Hofstede's work is that the survey method he adopted tends to be vulnerable to social desirability bias (Palazzo, 2019; Roy, 2020). Social desirability bias refers to the tendency of participants to select responses to surveys about potentially sensitive issues concerned with personal attributes in socially acceptable ways rather than expressing a truthful account of their thoughts, ideas, or feelings that may be less acceptable (Meisters, Hoffman, & Musch, 2020). In addition, the survey method cannot measure or determine cultural discrepancies or analyse subjective and sensitive matters well (Palazzo, 2019; Roy, 2020).

Based on a range of publications including the work of Hofstede himself (Dubrin, Dalglish, & Miller, 2006; Hofstede, 2001; Hofstede & Bond, 1984; Hynes, 2008; Koeszegi, 2004; Larson, 2018; Lewicki et al., 2007; Palazzo, 2019; Ting-Toomey & Oetzel, 2001; Velo, 2012; Volkema & Fleck, 2012), the following notes provide a relatively crude, explanatory snapshot of his cultural dimensions. Although the ideas are compared in a somewhat polarised fashion, it should be remembered that Hofstede's dimensions were intended to be viewed as relative concepts on a conceptual continuum. This perspective is particularly important when considering that cultural differences and values are not fixed but constantly changing given the influence of the global village that tends to blur cultural assumptions (Larson, 2018). So, for example, while the national cultures noted in the next section as collectivist are rather less so in India, Iran, and Arab countries, they nevertheless cannot be described as individualist (Fang, 2010). The other thing to consider in the simplified presentation of Hofstede's dimensions in the tables that follow, is that they should not be taken as a basis for stereotyping individuals or indeed organisations.

As you read through the descriptions of cultural dimensions, some concepts appear to be consistently relevant. For example, Confucianism is referred to in individualism and collectivism and long- and short-term orientation. In a work by Hofstede and Bond (1988) an account of the principles of Confucius and its cultural implications for many parts of Asia is provided. Confucius (originally named Kong Fu Ze) was a senior civil servant in China about 500 BC who was renowned for his wisdom and teaching, particularly in the area of practical ethics rather than any religious content (Hofstede & Bond, 1988). Confucianism has continued to define the character of Chinese social relations for more than two and a half millennia (Fukuyama, 1995). Confucian rules or principles frame the obligations people have to society in complementary, albeit unequal ways and are rewarded in fulfilment of those obligations with a level of protection (Hofstede & Bond, 1988). The Confucian family serves as a prototype for organisations such that membership and allegiance are prioritised and everyone's face is maintained. The authors identify Confucian virtues such as seeking out learning and development, working hard, parsimony and moderation (as conspicuous consumption is taboo), patience, perseverance, and remaining calm. In their 1988 work, Hofstede and Bond also refer to Herman Kahn's coining of the concept of neo-Confucianism, referring to East Asian countries that have been influenced by the teachings of Confucius, providing them with a competitive business advantage on the global stage.

Individualism and Collectivism (IND/COLL)

The characteristics of individualism and collectivism are presented in the simplified version that follows, drawing on the works of many (see Brown, Paz-Aparicio, & Revilla, 2018; Dubrin et al., 2006; Gill, 2019; Hofstede & Bond, 1988; 2016;

Lewicki et al., 2007; Noels et al., 2019; Palazzo, 2019; Ting-Toomey & Oetzel, 2001; Triandis, 1995; Waddell et al., 2019). Although collectivism and individualism are one of the dimensions adopted by Hofstede, they are derived from and similar to those arising from the work of Triandis (1995). The terms individualism and collectivism are far from new, dating back to English political and philosophical discourse in the eighteenth and nineteenth centuries, although the meaning of individualism equated more closely to notions of liberalism and individual freedom (Triandis, 1995). Today, individualism is concerned with situations where people are expected to take care of themselves and immediate family thus maintaining loose ties (Hofstede & Bond, 1988, 2016). Collectivist societies are usually influenced by Confucianism and focus on belonging to strong, cohesive in-groups, extended families, or collectives (that should not be confused with any political meaning) and take care of people in exchange for loyalty (Hofstede & Bond, 1988, 2016). An extension of this collectivist world view is found in guanxi, a relational code found in Chinese society that refers to personal and social relationships that govern the reciprocal exchange of favours (Tsia, 2020) and make establishing and maintaining relationships and networks a priority (Low, 2020).

The IND/COLL dimension is captured in many ways on a continuum (see Fang, 2010) of attention based on self-concepts dependent upon a range from 'I' to 'We' perspectives (Hofstede & Bond, 2016). Understanding the notion of the dimension as a continuum is important. One reason for this, as Triandis (1995) pointed out, is that individuals (like societies) have elements that are both individualist (idiocentric) and collectivist (allocentric) in different combinations.

Triandis (1995) connected individualism and collectivism to the influence of two specific syndromes: cultural tightness versus simplicity, in that individualism is associated with looseness and cultural complexity and collectivism is associated with tightness and cultural simplicity. Tightness refers to the extent to which members of a culture that are usually isolated from others over time (e.g. Japan, though it is becoming looser with time) form a consensus of what constitutes appropriate action and expect people to conform if they do not wish to suffer the negative consequences of doing otherwise (Triandis, 1995). In loose, heterogeneous societies (e.g. New Zealand), people are rewarded for independent decisions. Tight and loose cultures, like individualism and collectivism, are not binary but range on a continuum so tightness or looseness may be characteristic across some situations but not all (Triandis, 1995). That is, a culture may be tight from a social and political perspective and considered loose from an economic or religious one. Thus, in describing cultures as tight or loose, it is acknowledged that these characteristics are applicable in many but not all situations (Triandis, 1995).

High and low power distance (PD)

PD 'is the degree to which members of an organisation or society expect and agree that power should be stratified and concentrated at the higher levels

TABLE 5.3 Individualism and collectivism

Individualism (commonly associated with the national cultures of the France, Germany, Norway, UK, US, Australia, New Zealand, and Canada, for example)	**Collectivism** (commonly associated with the national cultures of Africa (south of the Sahara), Arab countries, Eastern Europe, Indonesia, Korea, Pakistan, China, Korea, Japan, Peru, Philippines, Taiwan and Singapore, and Guatemala, for example)
Society is organised around individuals, comfortable working on their own, focused on individuals and immediate families. 'I' orientated communication.	Society is organised upon the needs of wider groups, thus socially orientated, familiarity, and 'We' orientated.
Emphasis on individual identity and rights.	Emphasis on group obligations, harmony, interdependence, conflict avoidance, hierarchy.
Loose bonds where individuals take care of themselves and immediate family.	Membership in solid in-groups such as tribes, clans, and extended families emphasised that look after one in return for obedience.
Personal distinctions and achievement are highly respected.	Influenced by Confucianism and group achievements.
Self-assertion and self-orientation are accepted.	Self-enhancement tends to be shunned.
Contracts are highly respected.	Relationships respected.
Focus on goals.	Focus on developing relationships.
The construction of individual identity.	Contrast and deviation to be avoided.
Communication tends to be direct, analytical, explicit with the intention of maximising clarity, even at the expense of relationships. The focus is upon verbal messages that emphasise content.	Communication is holistic, indirect and dependent upon hints out of concern for the feelings of others. Meaning and communication are embedded in the context (tone of voice, occlusics, proximity, gestures, posture etc.).
Flatter organisational structures.	Submission and humility expected from subordinates.

of an organisation' (House et al., 2004, p. 12). Culture, whether national or organisational, influences the forms of power that are viewed as legitimate or illegitimate, how individuals use and respond to influence in ways that often create inequalities, and the degree to which 'power over' or power with' orientations are dominant (Lewicki et al., 2016). The broad characterisations of high/ lower power distance (PD) are drawn from the following works (Altschul, 2007; Brown et al., 2018; Hofstede, 2001; Hofstede & Bond, 1988, 2016; House et al., 2004; Lewicki et al., 2016; Palazzo, 2019; Thomas & Inkson, 2004; Waddell et al., 2019):

TABLE 5.4 High and low power distance

High power distance (Asia, East Europe, Malaysia, Japan, Spain, Brazil, Peru, Indonesia, and South Africa)	Low power distance (Australia, Germany, Ireland, Israel, Scandanavia, The Netherlands, and the United States)
Differences and inequalities expected and accepted.	Differences and inequalities viewed as distasteful.
Power tends to be centralised.	Power tends to be decentralised and advisory.
Employees may experience concern and anxiety.	Employees tend to experience few concerns and experience less anxiety.
'Power over' approaches tend to be dominant.	'Power with' approaches tend to be dominant.

TABLE 5.5 Masculinity and femininity

Masculinity (characterised by, for example, Japan, Italy, the US, and China)	Femininity (for example Norway, Netherlands, Sweden, and Costa Rica)
Assertiveness and strength are respected. Task orientation versus person orientation. Materialism, prosperity, and acquisitiveness.	Focus upon quality of life. Helping/ nurturing/caring behaviours, sympathy and support for the weak. Emphasis on friendships and relationships. Serenity, wellbeing, security, non-materialist values.
Motivated by power, achievement, success, competition, work, career, aiming to be the best, assertion.	Not achieving 'success' is accepted. Consultation is encouraged.
Sharp distinctions between gender roles.	Less rigid gender roles and a tendency to solve problems in an indirect and subtle way.
Higher job stress.	Stress acknowledged with strategies to address it and provide support.

Masculinity and femininity (MAS/FEM)

The information on masculine and feminine cultures are based on the following sources (see; Griffin & Pustay, 2005; Hofstede & Bond, 1988, 2016; Jian, Pettey, Rudd, & Lawson, 2007; Palazzo, 2019; Paramasivam, 2007; Tomasell, 2020). It is important to note that the dimension of masculinity-femininity is applied on a societal rather than personal level (Palazzo, 2019). Masculinity relates to societies where success and money are highly esteemed and associated with societal values in contrast to feminine societies where caring for others and respecting quality of life are two highly regarded values (Hofstede & Bond, 2016).

TABLE 5.6 High and low uncertainty avoidance

High uncertainty avoidance (Israel, Austria, Japan, Italy, France, Greece, Germany, and Korea)	Low uncertainty avoidance (USA, Denmark, UK, Singapore, Hong Kong, and Malaysia)
High discomfort with ambiguity/uncertainty. Anxious in dealing with uncontrolled, surprising, unusual events.	Feeling comfortable with uncertain situations and risk taking.
Tends to save money for unknown future events to preserve security.	Tends to spend money on immediate needs.
Prefers unambiguous and strictly applied rules and guidelines. Likes to have details addressed.	Prefers fewer rules and subtlety and tends to approach uncontrolled, surprising, unusual events with relative calm. Tolerance for high levels of flexibility in procedures.
Cautious about accepting diverse perspectives.	Open-minded, accepting of diverse perspectives, tolerant.

High/low uncertainty avoidance (UA)

Some examples of resources that address uncertainty avoidance and upon which the information that follows is based include Hofstede (2001), Hofstede and Bond (2016), House et al. (2004), Lewicki et al. (2007), and Palazzo (2019). UA is concerned with the extent to which people are prepared to accept a lack of structure to their lives, feel threatened by ambiguous situations, and the institutions and beliefs they create to avoid uncertainty or vagueness (Hofstede & Bond, 2016; Palazzo, 2019).

Short-term orientation (STO) and long-term orientation (LTO)

The dimension of long-term and short-term orientation was the fifth dimension added to Hofstede's theory (Minkov & Hofstede, 2012) that originated from Bond's Chinese value system, emphasising the role of Confucian values in LTO (see Hofstede & Bond, 1988). The dimension highlighted the attention societies and organisations place upon the future, the present, or the past (Palazzo, 2019) in approaching issues and making decisions. For example, one recent study (Lin, Shi, Prescott, & Yang, 2019) conducted in China's pharmaceutical industry analysed questionnaire data gathered from 750 firms, and found that temporal orientation affects strategic decision making amongst top managers and that LTO positively affects the comprehensiveness, speed, and creativity of decision-making processes that are moderated by industrial contexts. The notations in Table 5.7 are based on sources from the literature (see Guo, Liu, Li, & Qiao, 2018; Lin et al., 2019; Palazzo, 2019).

TABLE 5.7 Short-/long-term orientation

Short-term orientation (Australia, US, Latin America)	Long-term orientation (Many Asian countries, Eastern and Central Europe)
Influenced by consideration of the present or reflection upon the past.	Learns from the past but focuses upon future possibilities.
Meeting short-term deadlines take priority.	Long-term goals are more likely to be prioritised.
Tends to seek immediate satisfaction of needs and desires.	Emphasises virtues associated with future rewards such as; parsimony and perseverance.
	Thus, prepared to delay gratification of social success, material benefits and emotions to prepare for the future.
Tends to be less concerned with shame and face.	Sensitive to feelings of shame, protecting face.
May be satisfied with cultivating short-term business relationships and goals.	Focuses on long-term relationships with stakeholders.
Tends to promote fewer initiatives.	Cultivates entrepreneurial activity.
Respects traditional practices.	Able to adapt, open to change and values innovation.

Indulgence and restraint orientation (IVR)

The sixth dimension (and probably least explored in the literature) that Hofstede added in 2010 addressed the tendency of societies to be more or less sympathetic to indulgence or restraint. This dimension related to the desire for satisfaction and pleasure as opposed to controlling human needs (Palazzo, 2019). The indulgence versus restraint dimension largely originated from the World Values Survey and has some links with long-/short-term orientation and, for example the World Giving Index (WGI) which is a measure of prosocial behaviour such as donating, volunteering and being ready to help others one knows less well (Guo et al., 2018). Some of these prosocial behaviours are also identified in organisational spiritual identities (OSI) in work on spiritual diversity (Crossman, 2016) referred to in Chapter 8.

Table 5.8 on indulgent vs. restrained societal approaches is informed by the following sources: Gallego-Alvarez & Pucheta-Martinez, 2020; Guo et al., 2018; Hofstede, Hofstede, & Minkov, 2010; Palazzo, 2019.

The GLOBE study

The GLOBE study (Global Leadership and Organizational Behaviour Effectiveness) (House et al., 2004) was based on Hofstede's work but aimed to extend it (Ceci & Masciarelli, 2020). The study was ambitious. It took more than a decade to complete with data collected from 17,000 managers, 951 organisations and in 62 countries via questionnaires, interviews, focus group discussions, and the content

TABLE 5.8 Indulgence and restraint orientation

Indulgent societies (South and North America, Western Europe, Sub-Saharan Africa)	Restrained societies (Eastern Europe, Asia, Middle East)
Freedom of expression/speech is valued.	Expressing feelings and ideas may be limited or considered unwise.
Focus on positive feelings.	Some caution about expressing feelings positive or otherwise.
Accepts the gratification of human needs.	The gratification of pleasure is sometimes controlled or withheld.
Permissive in relation to the need to enjoy life and experience fun through recreation and leisure, spending money, consumerism and sexuality.	Strict social norms tend to constrain desires for material acquisitions, spending money, and relaxation.

analysis of printed media (House et al., 2004). Robert House and his team developed nine attributes or dimensions of cultures and global leader behaviours: 1. Future orientation, 2. Gender egalitarianism, 3. Assertiveness, 4. Humane orientation, 5. In-group collectivism, 6. Institutional collectivism, 7. Performance orientation, 8. Power concentration v de-centralisation (frequently referred to as PD in cross-cultural literature), 9. Uncertainty avoidance (House et al., 2004). These dimensions were selected on the basis of a review of the literature relevant to the measurement of culture in previous large sample studies and cultural theory at that time (Ceci & Masciarelli, 2020). While the concepts of collectivism, uncertainty avoidance, and power distance, for example, have been explained previously in the discussion of Hofstede's work, gender egalitarianism, assertiveness, future orientation, and performance orientation constituted if not a departure from Hofstede's dimensions, then a reinterpretation of them.

ACTIVITY: COMPARING AND CONTRASTING

Read the definitions of gender egalitarianism, assertiveness, future orientation and performance orientation that follow. Refer to other theories and models of cultural values presented in this chapter or in other literature available to you. Consider which of those ideas resonate with the dimensions defined by House et al. (2004, p. 12):

1. Gender egalitarianism is, 'the degree to which an organization or a society minimises gender role differences while promoting gender equality'.
2. Assertiveness pertained to the extent to which 'individuals in organizations or societies are assertive, confrontational and aggressive in social relationships'.

3. 'Future orientation is the degree to which individuals in organizations or societies engage in future-orientated behaviours such as planning, investing in the future, and delaying the individual or collective gratification'.

4. 'Performance orientation is the degree to which an organization encourages and rewards group members for performance improvement and excellence' and is distinguished from human orientation as the extent to which individuals in organizations or societies nurture and reward people for fairness, altruism, friendliness, generosity, and being caring and kind to others (House et al., 2004).

More recently, other studies have sought to quantify cultural differences and similarities. Mahdavi, Fatehi-Rad, and Graham (2020), for instance, in their analysis of data from 20 cultural groups theorised that people from similar national cultures would find it easier to negotiate with one another. They devised numerical cultural profiles based on measures such as language, nonverbal behaviour, values and decision-making processes, for example, and calculated correlation coefficients of paired national cultures. Thus, the higher the correlation coefficient, the greater the cultural similarity was assumed to be and the smoother the process of negotiation. Taiwan and Guangzhou (r=94) and Spain and the Czech Republic (r=92) attracted high scores and the authors concluded that culture would be less likely to impede negotiations. Examples of lower scores suggesting cultural dissimilarity were found in pairing Norway with the Philippines (r=16) and the USA and Japan (r=1). Mahdavi et al. (2020) also noted that regions within national cultures varied in similarity, in that, for example, two mainland Chinese regions were found to be more similar (r=79) than two Canadian regions (r=65). Although the authors offered some well-established practical ideas for bridging challenges in intercultural communication such as asking more questions, paying attention to nonverbal communication and using translators, they did not appear to consider, in depth, the influence of other factors in negotiations such as financial limitations that make for a more nuanced appreciation of intercultural negotiations. Some other cultural implications in negotiation contexts are considered in Chapter 9 of this text.

Conclusion

This chapter has selected some key theories and perspectives that inform intercultural communication. Contributions to this field, over time, are extensive and difficult to capture in a concise form. An increasingly culturally diverse world and workplaces necessitate, however, taking the time to understand the implications of culture in our communications and relationships. Learning about culture requires continual and active attention and reflection in order to make decisions about appropriate, sensitive, and effective ways of interacting with others and seeking out opportunities for belonging and growth through exposure to unfamiliar perspectives.

References

Alon, I., Boulanger, M., Meyers, J., & Taras, V. (2016). The development and validation of the business cultural intelligence quotient. *Cross Cultural & Strategic Management, 23*(1), 78–100.

Altschul, C. (2007). Internal coordination in complex trade negotiations. *International Negotiation, 12*, 315–331.

Ang, S., Van Dyne, L., Koh, C., Ng, K., Templer, K., Tay, C., & Chandrasekar, A. (2007). Cultural intelligence: Its measurement and effects on cultural judgment and decision making, cultural adaptation and task performance. *Management and Organization Review, 3*(3), 335–371.

Baker, W., & Sangiamchit, C. (2019). Transcultural communication: Language communication and culture through English as a lingua franca in a social networking community. *Language and Intercultural Communication, 19*(6), 471–487.

Beamer, L. (1995). A schemata model for intercultural encounters and case study: The emperor and the envoy. *Journal of Business Communication, 32*(2), 141–161.

Berraies, S. (2020). Effect of middle managers' cultural intelligence on firms' innovation performance. *Personnel Review, 49*(4), 1015–1038.

Bhabha, H. K. (2011). *Our neighbours, ourselves.* Berlin and Boston: De Gruyter. doi:10.1515/9783110262445

Bjerke, N. (1999). *Business leadership and culture: National management styles in the global economy.* Cheltenham: Edward Elgar.

Broome, B., Derk, I., Razzante, R., Steiner, E., Taylor, J., & Zamora, A. (2019). Building an inclusive climate for intercultural dialogue: A participant generated framework. *Negotiation and Conflict Management Research, 12*(3), 234–255.

Brown, O., Paz-Aparicio, C., & Revilla, A. (2018). Leader's communication style, LMX and organizational commitment: A study of employee perceptions in Peru. *Leadership & Organization Development Journal, 40*(2), 230–258.

Bulow, A., & Kumar, R. (2011). Culture and negotiation. *International Negotiation, 16*, 349–359.

Caputo, A., Oluremi, A., Amoo, N., & Menke, C. (2019). The relationship between cultural values, cultural intelligence and negotiation styles. *Journal of Business Research, 99*, 23–36.

Ceci, F., & Masciarelli, F. (2020). *Cultural proximity and organization: Managing diversity and innovation.* New York: Routledge.

Crossman, J. (2008). A different way: Student perspectives on international and cultural learning. *Employment Relations Record, 8*(2), 34–45.

Crossman, J. (2009). Academic perspectives on developing international and cultural leadership through experiential learning. *International Journal of Business Research, 9*(4), 223–234.

Crossman, J. (2010). Act them into a new way of thinking: Multiple stakeholder perspectives on developing international and cultural leadership (ICL) through experiential learning. *The International Journal of Management Education, 9*(1), 33–42.

Crossman, J. (2011). Experiential learning about intercultural communication through intercultural communication, internationalising a business communication curriculum. *Journal of Intercultural Communication, 25*, 1–6.

Crossman, J. (2016). Alignment and misalignment in personal and organizational spiritual identities. *Identity: An International Journal of Theory and Research, 16*(3), 154–168.

Crossman, J., Bordia, S., & Mills, C. (2011). *Business communication for the global age.* Sydney: McGraw-Hill.

Crossman, J., & Clarke, M. (2010). International experience and graduate employability: Stakeholder perceptions on the connection. *Higher Education, 59*(5), 599–613.

Crossman, J., Lui, J., & Tang, J. (2008). Sharing spaces: Perceptions of university teaching and learning in China and Australia and their relation to western educational literature. *TESOL in Context: Teaching English to Speakers of other Languages, 17*(2), 21–29.

Dubrin, A, Dalglish, C., & Miller, P. (2006). *Leadership*. New York: Wiley.

Dwyer, J. (2020). *Communication for business and the professions: Strategies and skills.* Retrieved from http://ebookcentral.proquest.com

Early, P., & Ang, S. (2003). *Cultural intelligence: Individual interactions across cultures.* Stanford, CA: Stanford Business Books.

Fang, T. (2010). Asian management research needs more self-confidence: Reflection on Hofstede (2007) and beyond. *Asia Pacific Journal of Management, 27*(1), 155–170.

Fisher, C., Doughty, D., & Mussayeva, S. (2008). Learning and tensions in managerial intercultural encounters: A dialectical interpretation. *Management Learning, 39*(3), 311–327.

Fukuyama, F. (1995). *Trust: The social virtues and the creation of prosperity.* London: Penguin.

Gallego-Alvarez, I., & Pucheta-Martinez, M. (2020). Hofstede's cultural dimensions and R&D intensity as an innovation strategy: A view from different institutional contexts. *Eurasian Business Review.* doi:10.1007/s40821-020-00168-4

Gardner, H. (2011). *Frames of mind: The theory of multiple intelligences.* New York: Basic Books.

Gardner, J. (1990). *On leadership.* New York: The Free Press.

Gill, H. (2019). *Communication: How to connect with anyone.* Chichester: Capstone John Wiley & Sons.

Griffin, R. W., & Pustay, M. (2005). *International business: A managerial perspective.* Upper Saddle River, NJ: Pearson Prentice Hall.

Guo, Q., Liu, Z., Li, X., & Qiao, X. (2018). Indulgence and long term orientation influences prosocial behavior at national level. *Frontiers in Psychology, 9*, 1798. doi:10.3389/fpsyg.2018.0798

Hall, E. (1952/1990). *The silent language.* New York: Doubleday.

Hall, E. (1976). *Beyond culture.* Garden City, NY: Doubleday.

Hall, E. (1981). *Beyond culture.* New York: Anchor Books.

Hall, E. (1983). *The dance of life.* New York: Doubleday.

Hirst, P., & Thompson, G. (2019). The future of globalization In J. Michie (Ed.), *The handbook of globalisation* (pp. 16–31). Cheltenham: Edward Elgar Publishing.

Hiyashi, K. (1994). *Ibunka interface keiei [Intercultural interface management].* Tokyo: Nihon Keizai Shimbun Sha.

Hofstede, G. (2001). *Culture's consequences.* Thousand Oaks: Sage.

Hofstede, G., & Bond, M. (1984). The need for synergy among cross-cultural studies. *Journal of Cross-Cultural Psychology, 15*(4), 417–433.

Hofstede, G., & Bond, M. (1988). The Confucius connection: From cultural roots to economic growth. *Organizational Dynamics, 16*(4), 5–21.

Hofstede, G., & Bond, M. (2016). Hofstede's cultural dimensions. *Journal of Cross-Cultural Psychology, 15*(4), 417–433.

Hofstede, G., Hofstede, G. J., & Minkov, M. (2010). *Cultures and organizations: Software of the mind.* New York: McGraw-Hill.

House, R., Hanges, P., Javidan, M., Dorfma, P., & Gupta, V. (Eds.). (2004). *Culture, leadership and organizations: The globe study of 62 societies.* Thousand Oaks: Sage.

Hynes, G. (2008). *Managerial communication strategies and application.* New York: McGraw-Hill Irwin.

Ietto-Gilles, G. (2019). The role of transnational corporations in the globalization process. In J. Michie (Ed.), *The handbook of globalisation* (pp. 155–164). Cheltenham: Edward Elgar Publishing.

Ji, Y., & Bates, B. (2020). Measuring intercultural/international outgroup favoritism: Comparing two measures of cultural cringe. *Asian Journal of Communication, 30*(2), 141–154.

Jian, G., Pettey, G., Rudd, J., & Lawson, D. (2007). Masculinity/femininity and compliance-gaining in business negotiations: A cross-cultural comparison. *Journal of the Northwest Communication Association, 36*, 93–110.

Kim, Y. Y. (2017). Identity and intercultural communication. In *The international encyclopedia of intercultural communication* (pp. 1–9). New York: John Wiley & Sons Ltd. doi:10.1002/9781118783665.ieicc0002

Koeszegi, S. (2004). Trust-building strategies in inter-organizational negotiations. *Journal of Managerial Psychology, 19*(6), 640–660.

Kubicek, A., Bhanugopan, R., & O'Neill, G. (2019). How does cultural intelligence affect organizational culture, ambiguity and overload? *The International Journal of Human Resource Management, 30*(7), 1059–1083.

Ladegaard, H., & Jenks, C. (2015). Language and intercultural communication in the workplace: Critical approaches to theory and practice. *Language and Intercultural Communication, 15*(1), 1–12.

Larson, K. (2018). *Adaption and well-being.* London: Routledge.

Lewicki, R., Barry, B., & Saunders, D. (2007). *Essentials of negotiation.* Sydney: McGraw-Hill.

Lewicki, R., Barry, B., & Saunders, D. (2016). *Essentials of negotiation.* New York: McGraw-Hill.

Liao, Y., & Thomas, D. (2020). *Cultural intelligence in the world of work: Past, present and future.* Cham, Switzerland: Springer.

Lin, Y., Shi, W., Prescott, J., & Yang, H. (2019). In the eye of the beholder: Top managers' long-term orientation, industry context and decision-making processes. *Journal of Management, 45*(8), 3114–3145.

Lorenz, M. P., Ramsey, J. R., Andzulis, J. 'Mick', & Franke, G. R. (2020). The dark side of cultural intelligence: Exploring its impact on opportunism, ethical relativism, and customer relationship performance. *Business Ethics Quarterly, 30*(4), 552–590.

Low, K. (2020). *Successfully negotiating in Asia.* Cham, Switzerland: Springer.

Lu, P. (2018). When different 'codes' meet: Communication styles and conflict in intercultural academic meetings. *Language and Communication, 61*, 1–14.

Maddux, W., Lu, J., Affinito, S., & Galinsky, A. (2020). Multicultural experiences: A systematic review and new theoretical framework. *Academy of Management Annals.* doi:10.5465/annals.2019.0138

Mahdavi, M., Fatehi-Rad, N., & Graham, J. (2020). Planting orange trees in twenty cultures: The practices of international negotiations. *Negotiation Journal, 36*(4), 421–440.

Marginson, S. (2000). Rethinking academic work in the global era. *Journal of Higher Education Policy and Management, 22*(1), 23–35.

Marsella, A. (2005). Culture and conflict: Understanding, negotiating, and reconciling conflicting constructions of reality. *International Journal of Intercultural Relations, 29*(6), 651–673.

Mayer, C. (2020). *Intercultural mediation and conflict management training: A guide for professionals and academics.* Cham, Switzerland: Springer.

Meisters, J., Hoffmann, A., & Musch, J. (2020). Controlling social desirability bias: An experimental investigation of the extended crosswise modes. *PLoS One, 15*(12). doi:10.1371/journal.pone.0243384

Metcalf, L., Bird, A., Peterson, M, Shankarmahesh, M & Lituchy, T. (2007). Cultural influences in negotiations: A four country comparative analysis. *International Journal of Cross-Cultural Management, 7*(2), 147–168.

Miller, K. (2015). *Organizational communication: Approaches and processes.* Stamford, CT: Cengage Learning.

Minkov, M. (2013). The concept of culture. In *Cross-cultural analysis: The science and art of comparing the world's modern societies and their cultures* (pp. 9–18). Thousand Oaks: Sage.

Minkov, M., & Hofstede, G. (2012). Hofstede's fifth dimension: New evidence from the world values survey. *Journal of Cross-Cultural Psychology, 43*(1), 3–14.

Nicholson, J., & Wong, Y. (2001). Culturally based differences in work beliefs. *Management Research News, 24*(5), 1–10.

Noels, K., Clement, R., Collins, K., & Machintyre, P. (2019). Language and culture. In H. Giles, J. Harwood, J. Gasiorek, H. Pierson, J. Nussbaum, & C. Gallois (Eds.), *Language, communication and intergroup relations: A celebration of the scholarship of Howard Giles* (pp. 19–33). New York: Routledge.

Noma, H., & Crossman, J. (2012). Analogue and digital mindsets: Some implications for intercultural communication between western and eastern organisations. *Asian Academy of Management, 17*(1), 115–129.

Palazzo, M. (2019). *Mapping the field: Cultural dimensions explored by Hofstede*. Hershey, PA: IGI Global.

Paramasivam, S. (2007). Managing disagreement while managing not to disagree: Polite disagreement in negotiation discourse. *Journal of Interpersonal Communication Research, 36*(2), 91–116.

Phillips, A. (1950). The cultural cringe. *Meanjin, 9*(4), 299–302.

Pierson, H. (2019). Language and culture. In H. Giles, J. Harwood, J. Gasiorek, H. Pierson, J. Nussbaum, & C. Gallois (Eds.), *Language, communication and intergroup relations: A celebration of the scholarship of Howard Giles* (pp. 17–19). New York: Routledge.

Piller, I. (2017). *Intercultural communication: A critical introduction*. Edinburgh University Press. Edinburgh.

Rathmayr, R. (2017). On intercultural business communication: A linguistic approach. In G. Mautner & F. Rainer (Eds.), *Handbook of business communication: Linguistic approaches* (pp. 221–248). Boston: De Gruyter.

Ren, H., Yunlu, D., Shaffer, M., & Fodchuk, K. (2021). Thriving and retention of expatriates: Cultural intelligence and organizational embeddedness in puts. *International Journal of Cross Cultural Management, 21*(2), 203–226.

Roy, D. (2020). Formulation of Hofstede's global cultural dimension index (HGCDI): A cross-country study. *Journal of Transnational Management, 25*(3), 195–224.

Serdari, T. (2020). A close look at cultural intelligence. In T. Serdari (Ed.), *Rethinking luxury fashion: The role of cultural intelligence in creative strategy* (pp. 95–109). Cham, Switzerland: Springer.

Servaes, J. (2020). *Handbook of communication for development and social change*. Singapore: Springer.

Shalik, F., Makhecha, U., & Gouda, S. (2020). Work and non-work identities in global virtual teams: Role of cultural intelligence in employee engagement. *International Journal of Manpower, 42*(1), 51–78.

Su, D. (2019). Culture is essentially meaning. In H. Giles, J. Harwood, J. Gasiorek, H. Pierson, J. Nussbaum, & C. Gallois (Eds.), *Language, communication and intergroup relations: A celebration of the scholarship of Howard Giles* (pp. 34–35). New York: Routledge.

Tajfel, H., & Turner, J. (1986). The social identity theory of intergroup behaviour. In S. Worchel & W. Austin (Eds.), *Psychology of intergroup relations* (pp. 7–24). Chicago, IL: Nelson-Hall.

Thomas, D., & Inkson, K. (2004). *Cultural intelligence: People skills for global business*. San Francisco: Berrett-Koehler Publishers Inc.

Ting-Toomey, S., & Oetzel, J. (2001). *Managing intercultural conflict effectively*. Thousand Oaks: Sage.

Tjosvold, D., & Leung, K. (2003). Cross cultural foundations: Traditions for managing in a global world. In D. Tjosvold & L. Kwok (Eds.), *Cross cultural management foundations and future*. Hampshire: Ashgate.

Tomasell, K. (2020). Intercultural communication: A Southern view on the way ahead: Culture, terrorism and spirituality. *Annals of the International Communication Association*, *44*(1), 19–33.

Triandis, H. (1995). *Individualism and collectivism*. Oxford: Westview Press.

Trompenaars, F. (1996). Resolving international conflict: Culture and business strategy. *Business Strategy Review*, *7*(3), 51–68.

Tsia, M. (2020). The important issues for millennial workers. In *Management association, information resources editor: Five generations and only one workforce: How successful Businesses are managing a multigenerational workforce* (pp. 203–232). Hershey, PA: IGI Global. doi:10.40181978-1-7998-0437-6

Turner, L., & West, R. (2018). *An introduction to communication*. Cambridge: Cambridge University Press.

Velo, V. (2012). *Cross-cultural management*. New York: Businessexpert Press.

Volkema, R., & Fleck, D. (2012). Understanding propensity to initiate negotiations. *International Journal of Conflict Management*, *23*(3), 266–289.

Waddell, D., Creed, A., & Cummings, T. (2019). *Organisational change*. Melbourne: Cengage.

Wasserman, H. (2020). Moving from diversity to transformation in communication scholarship. *Annals of the International Communication Association*, *44*(1), 1–3.

Xiaowei, V., & Pilcher, N. (2019). Revisiting the 'third space'. *Language and Intercultural Communication*, *19*(1), 1–8.

Yadong, J., & Bates, B. (2020). Measuring intercultural/international outgroup favouritism: Comparing two measures of cultural cringe. *Asian Journal of Communication*, *30*(2), 141–154.

Yule, G. (2017). *The study of language*. Cambridge: Cambridge University Press.

Zhuo, M. (2020). Learning from the 'right' ground of mindfulness: Some insights for the 'good' interculturalist. *Language and Intercultural communication*, *20*(1), 50–61.

6

GENDER AND COMMUNICATION

The concept of gender

Paradoxically, gender has been referred to as an important social category that helps people to understand and differentiate one another, yet defining the concept is far from straightforward (Chin, 2018). One reason for some ambiguity is the dynamic nature of gendered communication reflecting simultaneous shifting of societal norms in which gendered interactions take place (Gamble & Gamble, 2021). Gender plays a major part in the communicative process and human relationships (Gamble & Gamble, 2021) and arguably, since the 1990s, has been explored more than any other form of difference (Crossman, Bordia, & Mills, 2011; McDonald, 2019). Many studies have focused upon the implications of gender and communication in workplace contexts (Turner & West, 2018) as female participation in the workforce has increased (Menz, 2017). The direction and focus of these investigations, however, have become more inclusive conceptually rather than simply being restricted to female and male behaviour and discourse.

Some scholars suggest that gender differences are, at least, partially hardwired (Larson, 2018). Others espouse a socialisation model of gender purporting that men and women learn primarily through communication with, and exposure to, various agents of socialisation such as parents, peers, and the mass media (Hibbard & Buhrmester, 2010; Moschis, 2007). Social class, race, and ethnicity, too, influence how people are gendered and such is the complexity of these permutations that multiple ways and forms of gendering exist (Gamble & Gamble, 2021). So powerful is socialisation that by the time children are three years old they are already preferencing communication with those of the same gender (Yule, 2017).

Gender and sex are regarded as related but nevertheless separate concepts that unfortunately are too often conflated in organisational communication studies literature (Scott, Stretyick, & Bochantin, 2020). How sex and gender are understood

DOI: 10.4324/9780429318948-8

and differentiated has recently brought greater clarity in understanding complex interpersonal workplace relationships and communication. In many cultures and historically, perceptions of sex categories have tended to be binary, focusing on males and females. Exceptions do exist however in some pre-colonial and Indigenous cultures. Sex was associated with biological characteristics largely innate, assigned at birth by assessments of genitalia, genetics, chromosomes, and hormones but contemporaneously, sex and gender categories tend to be considered as more fluid concepts, that are culturally, discursively, and societally constructed and learned (see Buzzanell, 2019; Gamble & Gamble, 2021; Hollander and Renfrow, 2011; Kendall & Tannen, 2015; Larson, 2018; Wardhaugh & Fuller, 2015). Certainly, many people feel at odds with the sex to which they have been assigned (Berenbaum, Blakemore, & Beltz, 2011; Schilt & Westbrook, 2009) and one reason for this may be because gender is intertwined and intersected with identity (an individual's perception and subjective experience of gender) in powerful ways (Fisher & Ryan, 2021; Gamble & Gamble, 2021). Feeling that physical aspects of oneself are not aligned with personal identifications with a particular gender can lead to a level of psychological distress when social and cultural expectations make it difficult for people to interact with others as their authentic selves. Gender expression, or the way individuals communicate their own unique gender to others (Gamble & Gamble, 2021), is related to self-disclosure, how safe someone feels in self-disclosing and whether feelings of belonging in the workspace are experienced – remembering that belonging is dimensional and has many forms and degrees of connectedness rather than being a static concept (Yörükoğlu, 2020). Indeed, not feeling one belongs in a workplace is not limited to gender issues but may also be linked to other factors. For example, in organisations where few spaces for socialisation exist, where occasions of personal celebration like birthdays are ignored or where workers are hired on short-term contracts rather than continuing positions, employees may well not feel they belong (Franklin et al., 2019).

Those who tend to resist rigid role categorisations, identifying with both masculine and feminine genders, are referred to as psychologically androgynous, a term derived from the Greek words 'andros' meaning man and 'gyne' meaning woman (Gamble & Gamble, 2021; Schilt & Westbrook, 2009). An androgynous female, for example, may communicate with emotionality and be forceful in doing so, or an androgynous male may be both highly competitive and deferential (Gamble & Gamble, 2021). However, as perceptions of gender become more fluid and less prescriptive in societies, both these scenarios may arise for individuals who do not necessarily regard themselves, nor are regarded by others, as androgynous.

People born with the biological attributes of one sex category, but who identify very strongly with another, are referred to as being transgender, but how individuals feel comfortable in expressing their gender may vary. Some may do so through cross-dressing (Gamble & Gamble, 2021). Others choose to transition physically from one sex category to another when biological attributes of a sex category are inconsistent with their gender, or in cases where someone is intersex (born with ambiguous biological characteristics of both sexes) (Larson, 2018; Wardhaugh &

Fuller, 2015). Whatever the personal circumstances of a person who is making some sort of transition with respect to their gender, the social implications of that journey can be challenging. Challenging because it will inevitably involve making adjustments with respect to relationships, communication patterns, voice and body that will take time (Gamble & Gamble, 2021). The support of colleagues in safe, inclusive working environments during this period is essential in terms of wellbeing and, ultimately, performance. Understanding the terminology and concepts that surround gender informs employees and helps to create organisational cultures that cultivate belonging. Sensitivity to shifts in discourse also flag inclusion (or exclusion). For example, the term 'cisgender', describing those whose gender matches their physical sex category (Kendall & Tannen, 2015; Wardhaugh & Fuller, 2015), and references to being a *cis*man or a *cis*woman (Gamble & Gamble, 2021) send a message that the binary default of being understood as male or female is becoming an anachronism. Cisgender, signals that the alignment of sex and gender is not conceptualised as a norm, against which all other gender options are aberrations. It is one form of gender amongst a range of other possibilities.

As understandings about gender become more sophisticated, it is also acknowledged that females can no longer be regarded as a homogenous group, being, for example, racially and socio-economically differentiated (Vokić, Obadić, & Ćorić, 2019; Jansen & Terblanche, 2021), as indeed are men. As discussed, how gender is conceptualised and constructed is continually changing. Gamble and Gamble (2021) point out that men tend to assume more relational roles in the form of caregiving, being home orientated and sensitive to the ideas of others than previous male generations did, just as women participate more in the working environment today and undertake task-related roles, more than those of previous generations (Gamble & Gamble, 2021).

Equity and gender

Perspectives about sex, gender, and feminisms have been debated politically, domestically, and in workplaces, especially through the lens of equity and the material consequences for those who both conform to, and violate sex-role expectations (Buzzanell, 2019). The consequences, in relational terms, may sometimes be subtle but no less cogent. For example, those who conform to socially constructed gender roles are perceived as more likeable and superior communicators when compared to those who do not (Gamble & Gamble, 2021). Obviously, such perceptions will have implications relationally and for career progression.

Much of this section is concerned with sexism, described by Gamble and Gamble (2021) as the attribution of characteristics based on sex (or gender) in ways that are often discriminatory, inappropriate, or unjust. Terminologically, and by way of definition, however, *sexism* does not encompass all genders and neither does this way of conceptualising it, entirely (hence my own insertion in brackets). Gay, lesbian, and transgender people also face prejudice, particularly in contexts where there are fixed expectations about how someone is supposed to behave. When individuals are perceived to breach gender expectations, they may be highly criticised for feminine conversational styles, for example even when empirical evidence reveals that most people are actually unable to distinguish the speech style of a cisgender person from someone who is not, though women who adopt masculine speech patterns are tolerated somewhat more than males who adopt a feminine speech style (Gamble & Gamble, 2021).

The imbalanced representation of men and women in senior positions and the significant difference in how male counterparts are perceived not only reflect a failure to identify an individual's talents but also indicate systematic discrimination and barriers to the lives of working women (Miller, 2015; Perriton, 2009; Shubhra, 2006). Women continue to lag behind men in terms of career advancement and remuneration though the situation may be somewhat less dire with respect to women who are highly educated (Timberlake, 2005; Vokić et al., 2019). Unfortunately, early research findings from studies conducted during the global COVID-19 pandemic suggest that this chain of events in health has not only impeded progress in gender equality but exacerbated gender inequalities on multiple levels, including financial instability and gendered divisions of labour (Fisher & Ryan, 2021). Prejudicial assumptions are made by male managers even when evidence suggests otherwise. To illustrate, one research study suggested that managers continued to assume that females experience family work conflict, even when they don't (Hoobler, Wayne, & Lemmon, 2009). What they do want, apparently, as working parents (as do their partners), is for greater flexibility in working hours in order to achieve a healthy work/home balance (Miller, 2015).

Buzzanell (2019) posits that feminist theories have altered societal attitudes dramatically over decades but much work clearly needs to be undertaken in order to counter prejudice and to overcome what is metaphorically known as the *glass ceiling*, referring to the apparent invisibility of barriers to female promotion (Hoobler et al., 2009) that patently continue to exist such that women are arguably the largest marginalised social group worldwide (Rakic & Maass, 2019). One area where marginalisation can be addressed is by focusing upon women in leadership positions. Female representation in corporate governance across Europe, the United States, and Japan was recently studied by Binder, Morehead, Niculina, Schipani, and Averianova (2019). The authors identified a number of initiatives in all three targeted areas such as the adoption of board quotas and in Japan, the passing of an Act on Promotion of Women s Participation and Advancement in the Workplace in order to advance the reaching of targets for promoting women. Despite these efforts and the fact that data were analysed from developed countries, Binder et al. (2019) concluded that progress on equal opportunity and advancement for women remains slow though Europe appears to be making better progress than the other locations studied. Similarly, another study undertaken in Taiwan, as a developed country, noted that high female workforce participation rates are no guarantee of being treated equally with male counterparts in terms of pay (Chin, 2018). What is required in developed (and indeed developing) countries is for organisations to appreciate that women have the capacity to add value in their contribution to social as well as financial progress and international businesses, particularly, should take greater initiative in challenging the status quo (Binder et al., 2019).

The workplace is not the only context where segregation and inequality can arise however. They are also observable in homes, educational systems, and in society and will no doubt continue to be so as long as these ideas persist in the minds of both males and females around the globe who self-segregate (Vokić et al., 2019). The notion of males and females being better suited to quite different roles in their families and society that spill over into workplace roles, relationships, and communication is captured in the gender essentialism hypothesis. The gender essentialism hypothesis maintains that males and females have fundamental, innate, biological differences in both skills and aptitudes such that women are stereotypically directed towards emotionally rich, caring, and nurturing roles and men are assumed to be emotionally stable, logical, analytical, and generally better suited to positions of authority (Vokić et al., 2019). However, from the 1970s essentialist biological determination of male and female behaviour was increasingly questioned (Kendall & Tannen, 2015). Managers who subscribe to essentialist perspectives of women being more interpersonally orientated, for example, contributes to the belief that men are more productive and better suited to senior and well remunerated roles; a prejudice that consigns women to comparatively lower paid positions with fewer opportunities for promotion (Vokić et al., 2019). Expensive childcare, few affirmative action initiatives in the form of quotas, too few female role models, and too few gender-awareness training and leadership programmes compound the challenges faced by women (Vokić et al., 2019). Addressing gender inequality will have most impact if it is encouraged and reinforced by initiatives at micro and macro levels. State-level antidiscrimination legislation, cheaper quality childcare, radical *implementation* of gender equality policies and men and women sharing a more equal distribution of unpaid, domestic workload are some of the ways in which this might make a difference (Chin, 2018; Vokić et al., 2019). Also, increasing participation rates of women in the workplace (albeit often in part-time positions) (Vokić et al., 2019, p. 18) may empower them as major stakeholders in the labour force, capable of negotiating greater equality.

Language can be used to subjugate particular genders and when entrenched in discourse over long periods can often go unacknowledged. This idea is allied to a performative perspective that speech and language change the world (Bucholtz, 2014). One example is how, until the 1980s, the widespread use of the so-called generic 'he' and use of 'man' in words like 'mankind', 'spokesman' and 'chairman' in the English language were understood to include females in an implicit perpetuation of a heterosexual lens (Wardhaugh & Fuller, 2015) and embedded sexism. These terms might be replaced by 'humanity', chairperson, spokesperson, for example (see Gamble & Gamble, 2021). In efforts to correct the practice, some opted to use the default of she/her but doing so simply replicates the lack of inclusivity in using 'he' generically. Others revert to adopting the plural form that does not discriminate among genders. Others still now use Ze/Hi to counter patriarchy (Gamble & Gamble, 2021). Fortunately, workplaces, universities, and publishing houses now insist that non-sexist language is required and called-out when it arises. Changing deeply embedded assumptions in the workplace are challenging, however. Men have historically dominated institutional life and masculine forms of communication are standard in most work environments and feminine styles not just perceived as just different, but as inferior (Kelan & Jones, 2010). The term *linguistic violence* is used to describe how powerful and powerless speech can be adopted in organisations whereby powerful speech is directed at marginalised groups on the basis of their sexual orientation or gender identity (Kalbfleisch & Herold, 2005). Organisations need to be vigilant in identifying linguistic violence in communication and not only through instituting the relevant policies and procedures but by calling out linguistic violence as it happens. Doing so sometimes takes courage, especially where a power differential exists between the target of linguistic violence or the witness and an employee in a senior or line management position. A lot of slippage exists between policy and implementation on a day-to-day level.

One theory about male/female inequality in workplaces is that female communication networks are often narrower than their male counterparts who thus have access to more skills and knowledge (Timberlake, 2005; Vokić et al., 2019). One area where networking for women has proven an encouraging phenomenon, however, is in the rise of networked feminism, via social media that has called into question entrenched political, economic, societal, and cultural discrimination. For instance, hashtag feminisms are influenced by many social movements that document and make possible virtual spaces for gender and justice stakeholder groups such as the 'MeToo' movement and the 'Times Up' campaign that encourage women to confront sexual harassment and assault at work to counter the implicit assumption that female accomplishments are non-normative (Buzzanell, 2019). Scott et al. (2020) have also noted that the #MeToo social movement has intensified attention to hegemonic masculinity that critical and postmodern gender scholars have identified in empirical studies undertaken in organisations over some decades.

A reluctance to subscribe to essentialism in the context of gender and the workplace may well be tempered by the logical assumption that all 'men do not benefit from gender privilege and not all women are disadvantaged similarly' (Gamble & Gamble, 2021, p. 19) but the literature on gender in the workplace would be better captured in the statement that males have largely benefited from privileges and women, amongst other genders, have largely been disadvantaged in workplace contexts. According to Bucholtz (2014), for radical feminists, the root cause of social inequality is gender inequality, brought about through the patriarchal, systematic, and structural subordination of women rather than necessarily being focused on any male individual's abuse of power. She argues however that all men do benefit in innumerable ways from these systems of oppression whether they do so intentionally or not, and even if they are sympathetic to feminist aims.

Men are not immune to vulnerability however. A recent quantitative study undertaken in Australia found how men are more likely to experience periods of loneliness as a direct outcome of not feeling that they belong (see Franklin et al., 2019). Thus, to observe empirical findings that a particular gender or genders face significant challenges is not an automatic and concurrent assumption that others do not. Gender and gendered communication in workplace settings can be a complex matter that some liberal feminists approach by downplaying the differences between men and women as a means to achieve gender equality (Bucholtz, 2014). Radical cultural feminism, however, elevates the practices of women above those of men and generally adopt the perspective that they are superior cognitively and affectively and look for a female-led society as a reality preferable to male domination (Bucholtz, 2014).

For many years, how males experience gender has been largely ignored in radical feminist literature but more recently, masculine studies are increasingly undertaken not simply to explore gender inequality but as a research aim in its own right (Bucholtz, 2014). These directions will no doubt illuminate what we understand about gender in organisations and society. Nevertheless, the cost of stifling opportunities for women to contribute and ignoring the talents of half the population in most nations is socially, morally, and economically myopic. By the same token, for individuals, having the courage to reject the limitations of socially constructed norms of gender and gendered behaviour can present a wealth of possibilities and choices that would not otherwise be possible. The transition to authenticity, in terms of gender, is a gift individuals can give to themselves and in the revelation of becoming all they can be, becomes a gift to others.

Communication behaviours in males and females

Feminist linguistic theories have successfully raised considerable awareness about the concerns women have about the role language plays in gender inequality, and over time, approaches have become more inclusive as critical feminists also explore race, colonialism, and masculinity (Bucholtz, 2014). From a disciplinary perspective, discourse and gender have also been pursued by scholars, often in interdisciplinary studies amongst linguists, anthropologists, social psychologists, education, communication, and literature experts (Kendall & Tannen, 2015). Language, communication, and gender are tightly tied. Sex-role stereotyping and gender greatly impact female-male interaction verbally and nonverbally, in terms of grammar and speech style, in powerful ways (Eaves & Leathers, 2018; Rakic & Maass, 2019). At the same time, gendered discourse is also influenced by the cultures in which individuals live (Kendall & Tannen, 2015). Research has provided insights into how males and females communicate and behave respectively, and according to some scholars these apparent differences explain why misunderstandings may occur between them (Keener, Strough, & DiDonato, 2012; Kostelnik, Gregory, & Soderman, 2011).

Nevertheless, the statements that follow reflect a distillation of gender literature that should be viewed as tendencies and generalisations on a continuum that will vary, depending upon the context and the extent to which new social constructions and identities that run counter to traditional roles and conformance to established gender stereotypes are embraced (see Yule, 2017). Table 6.1 reflects some of

TABLE 6.1 Broad representations of gendered communication and behaviours

Male behaviour and communication	Female behaviour and communication
Comfortable socialising in large groups.	Comfortable socialising in small groups.
Competitive, adversarial, attention commanding, and hierarchical.	Favour cooperation and collaboration and more likely to compromise than males, gentle speech.
Tends to control/dominate discussions.	
Problem-solving and task-orientated communication	Prepared to share credit for success.
	Uses warm, friendly speech.
	More inclined to be submissive, unobtrusive, and deferential in communication.
Takes longer turns in speaking.	Sensitive to turn taking.
Back-channelling (showing what has been said has been understood) is less frequent.	Back-channelling in the form of responses such as 'really?' or 'hmmm' more frequent.
Males adopt more abstract forms of speech.	Females use more concrete language.
Less prepared to acknowledge and communicate vulnerability, loneliness and sadness.	More comfortable with open communication and to share feelings of vulnerability.
Ask questions but with a with a tendency to do so in order to gain advantage.	Seek clarification by asking questions and happy to build on the ideas of others.
Drawn to logicality in speech.	More inclined to express feelings and emotions.
Speech is concise and straightforward.	Speech tends to be more expansive.
Changes topics frequently.	Changes topics more gradually than men.
Not necessarily engaging with the ideas of others as a listener.	Tends to listen attentively and actively.
Interrupts females frequently even when they are in senior positions.	Responsive to the ideas of others and prepared to build on them.
	Less likely to interrupt.
Communication patterns less orientated to relational goals.	More likely to use communication to form connections, closeness and intimacy.
Prone to using 'I' statements that leave the female listener feeling largely ignored.	Empathises more in conversations.
	Conscious of saving the face of others.
	Uses inclusive, other-directed communication, balancing personal needs with those of others in priorities.
	Relationally oriented.

the empirical literature and reviews, focusing on language and gender in cross-sex interaction (see Barker & Zifcak, 1999; Carli, 2007; Gamble & Gamble, 2021; Hibbard & Buhrmester, 2010; Huang, Joshi, Wakslak, & Wu, 2020; Keener et al., 2012; Kelan & Jones, 2010; Kostelnik et al., 2011; Larson, 2018; Moschis, 2007; Tannen, 2002; Turner & West, 2018; Yule, 2017). The point of presenting this information is to inform personal reflection on gendered communication rather that to encourage and reinforce gender essentialism. As Gamble and Gamble (2021) observe, women are no more alike than are all men.

The communication patterns amongst females displayed in Table 6.1 do tend to reinforce inequality and submissiveness more often associated with subordinate roles in the workplace. However, some forms of female communication such as openness, being other directed, and warm may be less pronounced when women rise to senior positions (Carli, 2007; Faes, Swinnen, & Snellinx, 2014; Kelan & Jones, 2010; Tannen, 2002).

Females are less likely to communicate personal achievements believing they will not be liked if they do so (Kelan & Jones, 2010; Tannen, 2002) and indeed, perhaps they are right to remain reserved in displaying confidence, pride, and empowerment to the same degree as their male counterparts (in the expectation that male communication behaviours will help them to progress their careers), because such behaviour invariably invites censure and their abilities are judged much more harshly (see Carli, 2007). Thus, it would seem that adopting male communication patterns may not serve women well. Rather, what is required may be to recognise that both male and female approaches to communication can both have their place, depending upon the context and provided that workplaces acknowledge this and do not reward male modes of communication more highly than female approaches to communication.

As communications in the workplace are increasingly undertaken remotely and online, scholars have explored the implications of these mediums in cross-gender situations. Kendall and Tannen (2015) in their review of the literature have concluded that many of the features of discourse and gender-related speech patterns identified between males and females by scholars do not appear to differ markedly when communication takes place online. Similarly, Gamble and Gamble (2021), also drawing upon the literature, suggest that people communicating with avatars online believing they know their genders tend to communicate with the avatars in the way they would towards people of those genders in a face-to-face context. What this may mean is that inequalities perpetuated in face-to-face cross-gender situations are consistently perpetuated across mediums of communication. Thus, technological innovation does not necessarily translate to new patterns of gendered communication.

Conclusion

This chapter has explored the concept of gender and associated terminology, focusing primarily on the implications for interpersonal communication and relationships in the workplace, belonging, and the empirical evidence of gender inequality from a number of perspectives. It has celebrated the richness of humanity in the multiplicity of genders in a departure from historical binary constructions that have limited individuals and, in consequence, organisations.

References

Barker, R., & Zifcak, L. (1999). Communication and gender in workplace 2000, creating a contextually based integrated paradigm. *Journal of Technical Writing & Communication*, *29*(4), 335–347.

Berenbaum, S., Blakemore, J., & Beltz, A. (2011). A role for biology in gender-related behavior. *Sex Roles*, *64*(11–12), 804–825.

Binder, B., Morehead, T., Niculina, N., Schipani, C., & Averianova, I. (2019). The plight of women in positions of corporate leadership in the United States, the European union, and Japan: Differing laws and cultures, similar issues. *Michigan Journal of Gender & Law, 26*(2), 279–340.

Bucholtz, M. (2014). The feminist foundation of language, gender, and sexuality research. In S. Ehrlich, M. Meyerhoff, & J. Holmes (Eds.), *The handbook of language, gender, and sexuality* (pp. 23–48). Chichester: John Wiley & Sons Ltd.

Buzzanell, P. (2019). Gender and feminist theory. In A. Nicotera (Ed.), *Origins and traditions of organizational communication: A comprehensive introduction to the field* (pp. 250–269). New York: Routledge.

Carli, L. (2007). Gender issues in workplace groups: Effects of gender and communication style on social influence. In M. Barrett & M. Davidson (Eds.), *Gender and communication at work: Gender and organizational theory series* (pp. 69–83). Aldershot: Ashgate.

Chin, T. F. (2018). *Everyday gender at work in Taiwan*. Singapore: Springer.

Crossman, J., Bordia, S., & Mills, C. (2011). *Business communication of the global age*. Sydney: McGraw-Hill.

Eaves, M., & Leathers, D. (2018). *Successful nonverbal communication: Principles and applications*. Florence: Routledge. doi:10.4324/9781315542317

Faes, W., Swinnen, G., & Snellinx, R. (2014). Gender influences on purchasing negotiation objectives, outcomes and communication patterns. *Journal of Purchasing & Supply Management, 16*(2), 88–98.

Fisher, A., & Ryan, M. (2021). Gender inequalities during covid-19. *Group Processes & Intergroup Relations, 24*(2), 237–245.

Franklin, A., Neves, B., Hookway, N., Patulny, R., Tranter, B., & Jaworski, K. (2019). Towards an understanding of loneliness among Australian men: Gender cultures, embodied expression and the social bases of belonging. *Journal of Sociology, 55*(1), 124–143.

Gamble, T., & Gamble, M. (2021). *The gender communication connection*. New York: Routledge, Taylor Francis.

Hibbard, D., & Buhrmester, D. (2010). Competitiveness, gender, and adjustment among adolescents. *Sex Roles, 63*(5), 412–424.

Hollander, J., & Renfrow, D. (2011). *Gendered situations, gendered selves: A gender lens on social psychology*. Lanham, MD: Rowman & Littlefield Publishers.

Hoobler, J., Wayne, S., & Lemmon, G. (2009). Bosses' perceptions of family work conflict and women's promotability: Glass ceiling effects. *Academy of Management Journal, 52*(5), 939–957.

Huang, L., Joshi, P., Wakslak, C., & Wu, A. (2020, April 14). Sizing up entrepreneurial potential: Gender differences in communication and investor perceptions of long-term growth and scalability. *Academy of Management Journal*, 1–56. doi:10.5465/amj.2018./417

Jansen, G., & Terblanche, N. (2021). The spill-over effects of postgraduate coaching studies in the resilience of women on triple roles. *Coaching: An International Journal of Theory, Research and Practice, 14*(1), 78–91.

Kalbfleisch, P., & Herold, A. (2005). *Sex, power and communication*. Paper presented at the annual convention of the International Communication Association, New York.

Keener, E., Strough, J., & DiDonato, L. (2012). Gender differences and similarities in strategies for managing conflict with friends and romantic partners. *Sex Roles, 67*(1–2), 11–15.

Kelan, E., & Jones, R. (2010). Gender and the MBA. *Academy of Management Learning & Education, 9*(1), 26–43.

Kendall, S., & Tannen, D. (2015). Discourse and gender. In D. Tannen, H. Hamilton, & D. Schiffrin (Eds.), *The handbook of discourse analysis* (pp. 639–661). Oxford: Wiley Blackwell.

Kostelnik, M., Gregory, K., & Soderman, A. (2011). *Guiding children's social development and learning*. Belmont, CA: Wadsworth.

Larson, K. (2018). *Adaption and well-being*. London: Routledge.

McDonald, J. (2019). Difference and intersectionality. In A. Nicotera (Ed.), *Origins and traditions of organizational communication: A comprehensive introduction to the field* (pp. 270–287). New York: Routledge.

Menz, F. (2017). Business meetings. In G. Mautner & F. Rainer (Eds.), *Handbook of business communication: Linguistic approaches*. Berlin: De Gruyter.

Miller, K. (2015). *Organizational communication: Approaches and processes*. Stamford, CT: Cengage Learning.

Moschis, G. (2007). Life course perspective on consumer behavior. *Journal of the Academy of Marketing Science, 35*(2), 295–307.

Perriton, L. (2009). 'We don't want complaining women!': A critical analysis of business case for diversity. *Management Communication Quarterly, 23*(2), 218–243.

Rakic, T., & Maass, A. (2019). Communicating between groups, communicating about groups. In H. Giles, J. Harwood, J. Gasiorek, H. Pierson, J. Nussbaum, & C. Gallois (Eds.), *Language, communication and intergroup relations: A celebration of the scholarship of Howard Giles* (pp. 66–97). New York: Routledge.

Schilt, K & Westbrook, L. (2009). Doing gender, doing heteronormativity: 'Gender normals,' transgender people, and the social maintenance of heterosexuality. *Gender & Society, 23*(4), 440–464.

Scott, C., Stretyick, A., & Bochantin, J. (2020). Organizational discourse and sexuality in male-dominated organizational settings. In M. Goins, J. McAlister, & B. Alexander (Eds.), *The Routledge handbook of gender and communication* (pp. 365–388). Oxford: Routledge.

Shubhra, G. (2006). Achieving inter-gender communication effectiveness in organizations. *Vision: The Journal of Business Perspective, 10*(2), 11–19.

Tannen, D. (2002). *I only say this because I love you: How the way we talk can make or break family relationships throughout our lives*. London: Virago.

Timberlake, S. (2005). Social capital and gender in the workplace. *Journal of Management Development, 24*(1), 34–44.

Turner, L., & West, R. (2018). *An introduction to communication*. Cambridge: Cambridge University Press.

Vokić, N., Obadić, A., & Ćorić, D. (2019). *Gender equality in the workplace: Macro and micro perspectives on the status of highly educated women*. Cham, Switzerland: Palgrave Macmillan.

Wardhaugh, R., & Fuller, J. (2015). *An introduction to sociolinguistics*. Chichester: John Wiley & Sons Ltd.

Yörükoğlu, I. (2020). *Acts of belonging in modern societies sexuality, immigration, citizenship* (1st ed.). Cham, Switzerland: Springer International Publishing, Imprint in Palgrave Macmillan. https://doi.org/10.1007/978-3-030-45172-1

Yule, G. (2017). *The study of language*. Cambridge: Cambridge University Press.

7
INTERGENERATIONAL COMMUNICATION

Key concepts of intergenerational research

'Intergenerational communication refers to interactions in the workplace among employees who are members of different generational cohorts' (Way & Medved, 2017, p. 1). Nor, Arokiasamy, and Balaraman (2019) maintain that generational diversity is as significant to organisations as cultural differences and the considerable interest in the subject matter in the last 30 years would suggest that they are not alone in their assessment. Part of the relevance of this line of enquiry is that it would be difficult to find an organisation of any size that did not have employees of different generations represented. As Hummert (2019) observed, communication is almost always intergenerational.

The origins of ideas about intergenerational communication in the workplace are usually credited to the work of Karl Mannheim who published his theories in the mid-twentieth century. Karl Mannheim, a German sociologist, purported that generational cohorts could be profiled in terms of identities, based on the periods in which individuals are born and the political, historical, and social events they experience at formative times in their lives (see Espinoza, Ukleja, & Rusch, 2010; Gentina, 2020; Joshi, Dencker, Franz, & Martocchio, 2010). Generally, salient occurrences noted in the literature are social movements, the behaviour of key members of society, economic events, and major conflicts that have had a significant impact upon not only a particular generation but society as a whole (Corey & Grace, 2019; Nor et al., 2019). The complexity of intergenerational communication as a line of enquiry has attracted multidisciplinary and interdisciplinary studies pursuing a range of analytical approaches and topics (Gentina, 2020; Law, Young, & Almeida, 2019).

Two factors have influenced an interest in intergenerational communication in the workplace. First, people are tending to live longer and second, as a result, some

DOI: 10.4324/9780429318948-9

governments have increased the age when funded retirement is accessible (Management Association, Information Resources Editor, 2020; McElfresh & Stark, 2019; Parmar, 2020). Individuals are remaining in the workforce longer and organisations are facing the challenges and opportunities of engaging a workforce that may span up to five generations whereby people will have different motivations, career expectations, and communication styles (Management Association, Information Resources Editor, 2020; McElfresh & Stark, 2019; Way & Medved, 2017). Age arguably impacts communication in organisations more profoundly than ethnicity and gender and when managed appropriately, draws upon a range of experiences, perspectives, and social networks that can enhance performance, teamwork, creativity and innovation (Kearney, Gebert, & Voelpel, 2009; Management Association, Information Resources Editor, 2020). Organisational costs become apparent when managers lack awareness of intergenerational communication and its significance (Way & Medved, 2017). That said, research has yet to fully explore factors other than age in intergenerational communication such as marginalised groups and gender and the role it plays in organisational inclusion (Law et al., 2019).

Unfortunately, each generational group tends to hold stereotypical views about the others and when misinformation is added into the mix, tensions and conflict can arise (Bowman & Mulvenon, 2020; Law et al., 2019) from associated discrimination, communication problems, and negative climates (Crossman, 2010; Johnson, Indik, & Rawlins, 2009). To temper some of these conflicts, it is essential that organisations promote effective communication by providing development opportunities about generational communication styles, respecting those differences (Bowman & Mulvenon, 2020) and capitalising upon them. However, more recent research suggests that prior studies have overstated the differences between younger generations and older workers with respect to work values and beliefs about gender and indeed that older and younger cohorts may be highly similar (Way & Medved, 2017). In the same vein, Woodward and Vongswasdi (2017), who investigated the business communication practices of managers and global leaders, found that any distinguishing characteristics (particularly in terms of technological preferences and use) amongst generations, were far more nuanced than earlier studies suggested. Such criticisms expressed particularly in most recent studies appear to persist and in reading the descriptions of generational characteristics that follow in this section on intergenerational communication, it is important to keep them in mind. As Law et al. (2019) note, despite the continued growth of intergenerational studies, compelling questions remain unanswered or unsatisfactorily so, about individual and social identity across the lifespan.

The very nature of ascribing certain values and approaches to generational cohorts also invites criticisms of generalisations in the literature when, clearly, many individuals do not fit into stereotypes (Strachan, French, & Burgess, 2010). Despite the volume of work, little data appears to support the notion that generational cohorts actually exist in terms of distinct employment attitudes or expectations, prompting calls for higher quality empirical research in the area (Law et al., 2019; Treuren & Anderson, 2010). Maturational Theory (Espinoza et al., 2010) reflecting a belief that people change, mature, and develop their values, attitudes, and preferences as they age may also account for perceptions of differences amongst generations rather than sole attention being paid to environmental influences.

ACTIVITY: REFLECTION AND DISCUSSION

Identify and discuss significant political, historical, and social events that have occurred during your own lifetime that you believe influenced your generation as you were growing up. Take into account that adolescence and young adulthood is a period when most individuals are susceptible to influence (Espinoza et al., 2010). Discuss with others how you feel these events have shaped your values, work ethic, attitudes about work and authority. Compare your answers and note any differences in your responses that may be based on individual differences such as age or culture, for example.

Some evidence from the literature cited by Crossman (2010) suggests that generational cohorts influence emotional responses to situations, perspectives about the attention each generational group pays to phenomena; their values, professional aspirations, ethics and attitudes about authority. Despite the belief that cultural context also appears to play a significant part in the experiences and shaping of generational cohorts (Corey & Grace, 2019), most studies have been undertaken in the West and therefore fail to capture cultural phenomena relevant to other parts of the world. However, some excellent Asian studies (see Gentina, 2020; Yang, Wang, & Hwang, 2020) are enriching insights into how culture may moderate generalising about a particular cohort. Fein, Tziner, and Vasiliu's (2010) research on leadership and generational cohorts in Romania has also been useful in comparing leadership styles before and after the fall of communism.

Generational cohorts

Drawing on the literature from the twenty-first century, seven generational cohorts can be identified:

- GI Generation (born from 1901–1924) (the oldest living generation)
- Veterans/Matures/Traditionalists/Silents (born before 1946)
- Baby boomers (1946–1964)
- Generation X (1965–1981)
- Generation Y/Millennials/Nexters/Net Generation (1982–2000)
- Generation Z/iGen/Digital Natives/Post-Millennials (1995–2010)
- Generation Alpha (2011–2026).

The time span and dates ascribed to each generation vary in the literature so need to be applied with some flexibility, amounting to a few years either side of the dates provided. Typically, the span of each cohort is about 15 years. The oldest and youngest members of a generation (known as 'cuspers') may differ somewhat, having more in common at times, with the two adjacent generations and parental generations can obviously influence perspectives to some extent – a reminder that in every study there are outliers who do not conform to emergent research themes (Corey & Grace, 2019). In the descriptions of the generational cohorts that follow, the GI Generation has not been discussed, largely because they are unlikely to be employed. Nevertheless, they will have influenced the generation that followed them in some way.

Veterans/Matures/Traditionalists/Silents (born 1925–1945) (Adams & Galanes, 2009; Bowman & Mulvenon, 2020; Corey & Grace, 2019; Crossman, 2010).

Veterans were influenced by hardships endured during the Great Depression in the West, and the Second World War and are characterised as dedicated, diligent, obedient, loyal, self-sacrificing, persevering, conservative and fiscally prudent, cautious workers (Anderson et al., 2021; Bowman & Mulvenon, 2020; Corey & Grace, 2019). This generation felt if they worked hard and sacrificed, they would be comfortable and able to buy a family home and a car and to raise their families on one wage (Bowman & Mulvenon, 2020). Veterans conform and are accepting of institutional authority (Corey & Grace, 2019), hierarchies and a top-down management approach, albeit during a period when labour unions were rising to power. Veterans adopt a formal and detailed communication style and although they engage online, they tend to prefer face-to-face and other written forms of communication (Adams & Galanes, 2009; Crossman, 2010).

Veterans are characterised as reliable and dependable, placing work before their personal lives and focusing upon the common good; at the same time, they appreciate acknowledgement of their efforts through plaques and signed pictures with dignitaries, for example (Adams & Galanes, 2009; Sherman, 2006). Veterans are cautious about spending money and tend to save rather than drawing on credit (Adams & Galanes, 2009; Sherman, 2006). Some scholars have suggested that this cohort is more honest and trustworthy than those of other generational groups but these assumptions are now widely refuted given a lack of empirical evidence (Posthuma & Campion, 2009). Common and inaccurate stereotypes about older workers include the belief that they are poor performers, less motivated, resistant to change and learning new things (Posthuma & Campion, 2009). For this reason, older people may be uncertain and somewhat anxious about how to respond to the negative perceptions of younger people directed towards them (Law et al., 2019).

Baby Boomers (BB) (born 1945–1965) (see Anderson et al., 2021; Bowman & Mulvenon, 2020; Corey & Grace, 2019; Edwards & Robinson, 2020; Oh, Dinitto, & Powers, 2020).

Baby Boomers were born following the Second World War during a healthy and relatively stable period, socially and economically, when individuality and creativity were valued (Adams & Galanes, 2009; Bowman & Mulvenon, 2020;

Crossman, 2010). In many ways, they appear to be quite different from the Veteran generation who grew up in politically and economically unstable times (Anderson et al., 2021). They are named Baby Boomers because birth rates during this period were high (booming). Their perspectives are shaped by events such as the Vietnam War, the Cuban missile crisis, Woodstock (a music festival), the Beetles (iconic performers), the Cold War, President Kennedy's assassination in the US, and landing on the moon (Bowman & Mulvenon, 2020; Corey & Grace, 2019). Some scholars have suggested that the influence of civil rights activism is associated with some evidence that Baby Boomers are inclined to distrust authority, challenge traditional ways of doing things, and adopt open and optimistic approaches that leave them feeling empowered (Adams & Galanes, 2009; Bowman & Mulvenon, 2020; Crossman, 2010). Baby Boomers have also been regarded as the creators of a counter culture in their canvassing for social, political, and economic rights through student activism, their opposition to the conscription of their generation to fight in the Vietnam War, and the way in which they embraced the Hippie movement and the 'flower children' who advocated for 'free love' (Corey & Grace, 2019, p. 6) and peace in the world.

Baby Boomers are also reportedly loyal, capable of multitasking, collegial and like to be consulted, which may mean that they appear idealistic and self-centred (Adams & Galanes, 2009; Bowman & Mulvenon, 2020; Crossman, 2010). According to some reports, they are hard workers who prioritise professional life at the expense of their personal lives as do Veterans, and expect others to share these perspectives (Adams & Galanes, 2009; Bowman & Mulvenon, 2020; Crossman, 2010). They are also purported to be ambitious, competitive, and with a tendency to micro-manage (Lowe, Levitt, & Wilson, 2008). In terms of interpersonal communication, Baby Boomers are reportedly quite formal but nevertheless personable, generally preferring face-to-face forms of communication (Reynolds, Campbell, Bush, & Geist, 2008). Baby Boomers are also motivated by recognition through newsletter entries, awards, and designated parking spaces, for example. They have also been described as being more productive than younger colleagues, absent less often, and more compliant with health and safety in the workplace (see Johnson et al., 2009).

Those over 55 are now making retirement decisions and many are choosing second and encore careers, to upskill, and continue to have a significant impact on the economy (Edwards & Robinson, 2020; Oh et al., 2020). The motivation to continue working, at least for some, may be related to the loss of retirement savings in the stock market crash of 2008 (Bowman & Mulvenon, 2020). In the context of the People's Republic of China, Chen (2016) has also noted that the disproportionately large Baby Boomer cohort is now approaching retirement and may be experiencing difficulty in relinquishing their decision-making power and autonomy. As they leave the workplace, their long-term experience will no doubt prove highly useful in mentoring relationships with younger cohorts as part of organisational succession planning.

Generation X (GX) (born 1965–1981) (see Anderson et al., 2021; Bowman & Mulvenon, 2020; Corey & Grace, 2019).

Generation X represents a smaller cohort than Baby Boomers but as Baby Boomers are now retiring, many of this generation are now in senior positions and attention has turned to how Generation X communicate in workplace settings (Adams & Galanes, 2009; Anderson et al., 2021; Crossman, 2010; Reynolds et al., 2008). Destabilising events that reportedly influenced the perspectives of GXers include the AIDS crisis, corporate downsizing and the Gulf War (Anderson et al., 2021; Bowman & Mulvenon, 2020). Some more positive experiences included *Sesame Street* (a programme for children known for the development of values), the end of the Cold War, and the fall of the Berlin Wall (Anderson et al., 2021; Bowman & Mulvenon, 2020; Corey & Grace, 2019).

Studies suggest that GX are independent, autonomous, adaptable, self-reliant thinkers who dislike being micro managed and enjoy freedom (Adams & Galanes, 2009; Anderson et al., 2021; Corey & Grace, 2019; Crossman, 2010; Reynolds et al., 2008). In broad terms, the literature paints GX as pessimistic, negative, irreverent, sceptical, and unmotivated. These characteristics may be related to a reputed suspicion of authority, political and economic promises, and an aversion to hierarchical organisational structures (Anderson et al., 2021; Bowman & Mulvenon, 2020) that resonate with some of the literature on Baby Boomers. Since they are less likely to conform to hierarchy and organisational rules than previous generational cohorts (Adams & Galanes, 2009; Crossman, 2010) this may account for some evidence that GXers need to respect a manager/supervisor rather than relying on authority alone (Strachan et al., 2010).

Assumptions about independence may emanate from research suggesting that working parents were not always available to supervise and the rising divorce rates accompanied by single parenting may also have led to the need for children to develop greater independence than in previous generations when one parent was more likely to have been at home after school (Adams & Galanes, 2009; Anderson et al., 2021; Crossman, 2010; Reynolds et al., 2008). Bowman and Mulvenon (2020) suggest that GXers tend to be economically conservative given instability, double-digit inflation, and the experience of parental stress during times of high unemployment. High unemployment may also have given rise to some distrust of large organisations. Generation X are computer literate and comfortable with technology, having grown up with the beginning of the information age and the emergence of computer games – experiences that may account for their apparent expectation of instant and satisfying responses to their needs compared to previous generations (Adams & Galanes, 2009; Bowman & Mulvenon, 2020; Crossman, 2010; Reynolds et al., 2008). Also, Generation X reportedly give greater consideration to work/life balance and many prefer flexible working hours over promotion, subscribing to the view that spending more time at work does not necessarily equate to higher productivity (Corey & Grace, 2019; Mayer, 2006).

Generation X favour direct communication more than Baby Boomers and Traditionalists/Veterans (Adams & Galanes, 2009; Crossman, 2010; Reynolds et al., 2008). However, they are not insensitive to the perspectives of others in diverse workplace environments. Indeed, one advantage that this generation may have in a period of intense globalisation is their acceptance of social and workplace diversity over uniformity, their tolerance of varied viewpoints and change in the workplace (Adams & Galanes, 2009; Anderson et al., 2021; Crossman, 2010; Reynolds et al., 2008). They are also flexible multi-taskers who easily change jobs and don't expect loyalty from organisations (Bowman & Mulvenon, 2020; Gibson, 2009; Strachan et al., 2010). Gibson (2009) suggested that Generation X like to progress quite quickly in their careers and stay current in order to ensure they remain employable. They may be impeded in these aspirations, however, given that some researchers have concluded that they lack social skills (see Lowe et al., 2008). Finally, Generation X are predominantly motivated by cash bonuses, tangible rewards, paid time off, and innovative projects but at the same time they also value intellectually and spiritually nourishing environments.

Generation Y (GY) /Millennials/digital natives (born 1982–2000) (see Anderson et al., 2021; Bowman & Mulvenon, 2020; Corey & Grace, 2019; Nor et al., 2019; Way & Medved, 2017).

The bulk of intergenerational communication research focuses on GY employee values, their attitudes towards older colleagues, mentoring preferences, and information and technology use (Way & Medved, 2017). Although raised in a somewhat turbulent time, characterised by global terrorism, global warming, violent mass shootings in US schools, and access to illegal drugs, GY has been attentively nurtured by 'helicopter' parents who raised them with tight, structured schedules of extracurricular activities that may account for some reports that this generation lack well-developed coping skills or the same level of independence as previous cohorts (Anderson et al., 2021; Bowman & Mulvenon, 2020; Corey & Grace, 2019; Sherman, 2006; Way & Medved, 2017).

An asset that GY employees bring to the workplace that they share with GX is that they are reportedly comfortable and tolerant when communicating in diverse workplaces (see Jenkins, 2008; Sherman, 2006; Skiba, 2005). Given the increasing diversity of organisations, their clients, and stakeholders, the readiness of GYs to accept differences in the backgrounds and perspectives of others is essential for effective collaboration in sharing a common purpose and achieving goals.

GY also tend to be differentiated from other cohorts in the literature because they are highly savvy technologically (Nor et al., 2019), having had maximum exposure to technology, growing up in households centred around computers, smart phones, social media such as Snapchat, Facebook, Spotify, and information technologies. However, this level of exposure may also mean that their desire to be entertained and stimulated may be relatively demanding, suggesting a high level of self-interest and entitlement but also an entrepreneurial, socially connected, and innovative predilection (Bowman & Mulvenon, 2020; Corey & Grace, 2019; Way & Medved, 2017). Their competence with technology explains why they are also known as 'digital natives' (Way & Medved, 2017) but, from another perspective, based on the literature, this strength means they are also somewhat dependent on media and Internet for information (Nor et al., 2019) so any cyberattacks on the Internet may prove both highly stressful and challenging.

Strachan et al. (2010) noted that GYs were less motivated by security than previous generations and tended to consider making employment changes about every two years. However, a decade and more has passed since their observation, so it is possible that GYs who may well now be young parents have a rather different perspective on mobility. As each cohort ages, some adjustments may well be made by virtue of experience, maturity, and responsibility. For this reason, up-to-date research is crucial to this field of study. However, employers may need to take into account some of those experiences GYs are looking for if they are to retain them. Retaining GYs depends upon understanding their need for stimulation, often through ongoing professional development and receiving timely and constructive feedback (Way & Medved, 2017). They enjoy learning experientially rather than having to read a great deal (Adams & Galanes, 2009; Crossman, 2010; Hartman & Cambridge, 2011) and particularly value training in technical skills (Bowman & Mulvenon, 2020). Since GYs are more interested in results than process (Bowman & Mulvenon, 2020), it may be important to plan training where the benefits are immediately accessible and relevant.

A desire to be respected, trusted, and given responsibility, regardless of their age and relative inexperience, is also apparent (Adams & Galanes, 2009; Bowman & Mulvenon, 2020; Crossman, 2010; Way & Medved, 2017). GYs seek out positive communication and a sense of rapport in the working environment (Strachan et al., 2010; Way & Medved, 2017), complementing their optimistic, energetic, action-orientated, creative, and innovative approach to work (Adams & Galanes, 2009; Bowman & Mulvenon, 2020; Crossman, 2010; Nor et al., 2019) and perhaps these desires explain their interest in entrepreneurial pursuits (Way & Medved, 2017).

Like GX, Generation Y are deemed somewhat cynical but balance idealism with pragmatism reflected in the expectation that they will be well paid (see Nor et al., 2019; Sampath, 2007). Whether pragmatic or venal, GYs are less accommodating when it comes to their attitude towards unpaid overtime compared to other generations (Busch, Venkitachalam, & Richards, 2008) which may not be welcomed by supervisors who are Baby Boomers and Veterans. At the same time, balancing work time with their personal lives is a priority. For this reason, a fulfilling career where they can thrive and accomplish their goals also needs to be accompanied by a flexible work schedule (Bowman & Mulvenon, 2020; Way & Medved, 2017). Nor et al. (2019), in their Malaysian study, also suggest that based on their review of the literature, GY have high expectations in terms of their work-life experience and actively search for a career that is meaningful, interesting, challenging, rewarding, and satisfying. Such expectations have implications for an organisation's ability to recruit and retain GYs and human resource managers, mentors, and line managers will need to be mindful of what motivates this cohort.

It became apparent, early on in the twenty-first century, that organisations would need to plan how they would communicate with GY if they were to retain them (Reynolds et al., 2008). A potential point of conflict between Traditionalists and Baby Boomers in communicating with GYs is that while the older generations may be more accustomed to a formal style, GYs tend to be more casual and colloquial in expressing themselves so even when older generations have strong technological skills, they may experience difficulty in understanding and communicating with GYs (Bowman & Mulvenon, 2020). This may be particularly difficult for Baby Boomers who value personal status and may not appreciate the directness and informality of GY communication (Way & Medved, 2017). At the same time, GYs can find the communication of older cohorts negative and underaccommodative (Law et al., 2019). It is essential to pay attention to these issues because when managers do not adjust communication styles to accommodate those of younger, talented employees, they will find other employers who do (Way & Medved, 2017).

Being promoted regularly may also tempt talented GYs to stay longer in an organisation (see Sampath, 2007). A capacity to pursue opportunities for social connection through networking and developing relationship capital either virtually or on a face-to-face basis (Adams & Galanes, 2009; Clarke, 2007; Crossman, 2010) may assist this cohort in achieving the promotions they want to keep them interested in staying. Unfortunately, the desire for speedy promotion (Bowman & Mulvenon, 2020) may have contributed to a reputation for being 'me' orientated, entitled, and desirous of rewards before they are necessarily earned (Strachan et al., 2010; Way & Medved, 2017). However, whatever the benefits and the challenges of this generation, their impact on the workplace is rapidly growing as Traditionalists and Baby Boomers retire (Bowman & Mulvenon, 2020).

Generation Z (GZ) (born from 1995) (Anderson et al., 2021; Corey & Grace, 2019; Gentina, 2020).

Since GZ has only very recently joined the workforce, it may be some time before researchers will be able to assess their impact in the workplace (Corey & Grace, 2019). Some work is beginning to emerge, however, linking events that occurred during the formative years of this cohort and consequent characterising generational profiles. Significant events since 1995 include 9/11, terrorist attacks, racial inequality and the rise of the Black Lives Matter movement in the West, continued gender and pay inequality, climate change, and the 2008 economic depression. GZ is reportedly keenly aware of and anxious about global problems, safety, and financial conservatism with a focus on security and achieving financial goals for the future (Anderson et al., 2021; Corey & Grace, 2019; Gentina, 2020). Concerns about finances, however, are not predominantly related to a desire for acquiring material goods (Gentina, 2020), indeed from a values perspective, this generation places great store by wanting to contribute to society in positive ways (Pasmore & Woodman, 2017). They do so through philanthropy and spending their money only at businesses that align with their values and are committed to social change and making a difference in their communities and the world (Corey & Grace, 2019).

In the context of Asia, Gentina (2020) identified sufficient variation amongst those of this generation to advise usage of the plural form (GZs). Within China, some of the prevailing characterisations of GZs' formative years include continued and longstanding social stratification, higher levels of materialism in an expanding economy, the growth of digitisation, a de-emphasis on the extended family, and exposure to educational and employment opportunities nationally and internationally, made possible by the government reforms of 1978 and an open-door policy (Yang et al., 2020).

According to Gentina's (2020, p. 3) Asian study of GZs, like GY, they are 'digital natives' who have abandoned computers for mobile devices, spending, in South Korea, at least five hours a day on smart phones from the age of 10. This generation has a voice and huge potential for making an impact, not least because they represent up to 20 per cent of China's population (Yang et al., 2020). As digital influencers, they are highly skilled with respect to social media, and enthusiastic about continuing to expand their knowledge of new technologies. Technical multitasking switching from task to task and app to app constitutes the norm for this generation (Corey & Grace, 2019; Yang et al., 2020).

Personal growth is very important to GZs (Pasmore & Woodman, 2017). In terms of professional development, they appear to be motivated by the receipt of credit badges achieved through online, self-paced, game-like experiences providing instant feedback at all levels of achievement rather than receiving public recognition, social acceptance, experiencing competition, or feeling the need to return favours (Corey & Grace, 2019). This last characteristic may have implications in terms of guanxi in China and traditional expectations of how relationships work and may cause some tension with older generations.

This generation value their anonymity (Corey & Grace, 2019) and are masters of creating their own multiple personal and social identities, making full use of profile pictures and avatars as often as one might change hairstyles or clothing (Gentina, 2020). They are careful, however, to differentiate between using social media and Instagram accounts in private modes with close friends and more professional forms of communication (Corey & Grace, 2019). They are clearly open to social interaction, collaboration, and sharing ideas, particularly through online communication (Gentina, 2020). Such openness to connecting with others in person or online may not be apparent to other generations, however, who note and may be irritated by GZs who use their phones during religious services, sharing family meals (Corey & Grace, 2019) in a lecture, or during a meeting. Some interpersonal conflict across generations may also occur at work because although GZ are digitally adept, they are unenthusiastic about writing emails or making phone calls, both of which are common means of communication (Corey & Grace, 2019). Not engaging in these practices or a reluctance to communicate by email in a timely fashion can cause colleagues frustration and give rise to further miscommunication, but a reported high level of emotional and social intelligence (Corey & Grace, 2019) should serve this cohort well in cultivating positive interpersonal relationships.

GZs in the PRC are less wedded to the concept of the iron rice bowl, a metaphor that relates to guaranteed job security and the attractions of a steady income and benefits (Yang et al., 2020). This is a generation of creative individuals who generally embrace freelancing and solopreneurship without the commitment of long-term contracts (Corey & Grace, 2019) so they are not afraid to break with traditional forms of working. GZs are conscious of the importance of work/life balance (and indeed in balancing real and virtual lives) as part of a general prioritisation of physical health and wellbeing through exercise and a clean diet (Corey & Grace, 2019). Although they seek a sense of purpose in their work, Yang et al. (2020) has also found that GZs in the PRC appear to be quite resistant to working overtime and may also question authority and organisational rules if they perceive them to be unfair. The authors also observe that the cohort is less intimidated by powerful leaders or hierarchical organisational structures and tend to respect those in leadership positions only if they meet other criteria beyond status, such as being charming rather than dictatorial and holding egalitarian attitudes (Yang et al., 2020). Breaking with long-held and Confucian traditions about relationships in this respect will likely be difficult to navigate in the workplace and it is not hard to see how the potential for conflict with older generations might arise. Pasmore and Woodman (2017) made similar assumptions in contexts other than Asia, suggesting that GZs did not want to work in jobs they did not enjoy simply to survive and actively sought out organisations that provided opportunities for freedom of expression.

Another intergenerational communication study of young Japanese and Thai adults exploring respectful communication was conducted by Ota, McCann, and Honeycuff (2012). These researchers found that both cultural groups of young people communicated with greater respect, politeness, and deference in interacting with older people. They also found that older Thai participants tended to use more respectful communication towards younger generations than the Japanese which may explain why some young Japanese participants tended to avoid communication with middle-aged adults. These findings resonate with an observation made by Strachan et al. (2010) more than a decade ago, expressing concern that younger workers are more likely to be bullied as a result of their limited working experience. Bullying is not synonymous with disrespectful communication but the two are related and this is one area where further research could be enlightening. In addition, the study by Ota et al. (2012) highlights that the nature of intergenerational communication varies from culture to culture. In multinational companies, high levels of cultural awareness in intergenerational communication contexts will be necessary to avoid tensions. Such organisations will need to send clear messages about their expectations with regard to respectful communication intergenerationally – as they will with regard to other forms of diversity in the workforce.

ACTIVITY: DISCUSSION AND SYNTHESIS

Having carefully read the characterisations of each generational cohort and made notes on other sources available to you, in groups, discuss any ways you think each cohort may find synergies or points of tension with others? What implications might exist in the workplace in terms of interpersonal communication?

ACTIVITY: APPLICATION AND SYNTHESIS

Using the information based on the literature cited in this chapter and other sources available to you, create an 'at a glance' representation (a table, for example) of characteristics associated with each generational cohort in a way that enables others to quickly grasp some of the potential synergies and differences in behaviour attitudes and communication patterns.

ACTIVITY: DESIGN

Design a programme that could be used by a human resource department to develop intergenerational communication between any two cohorts. Prepare a simple written report and present your ideas to others, seeking their feedback.

Conclusion

This chapter has explained the concept of generational cohorts and its implications for communication in the workplace as a diversity issue. The literature cited tends to support the view put forth by Nussbaum (2019) that intergenerational relationships and communication can be both complex and frustrating. Nevertheless, investing in intergenerational communication is essential for optimal performance in organisations. The literature suggests both synergies and potential points of tension between or amongst generational cohorts influence communication patterns and ultimately workplace relationships. Organisations that appreciate the contribution of generational cohort theories, their potential, and impact will take a strategic approach through professional development. The chapter has noted some research about how certain generational cohorts prefer to learn, so in developing organisations about intergenerational communication, human resource professionals will need to take these preferred ways of learning into account. An experiential approach to assisting learning about effective intergenerational communication may be to partner individuals from relevant generations that appear to have particular difficulties in communicating. In a reciprocal mentoring relationship participants could assist a counterpart in the process by providing personal insights and working through any challenges and teasing out differences between individuals on a generational basis and those that may be related to other factors such as personality, gender, culture, or spirituality.

References

Adams, K., & Galanes, G. (2009). *Communicating in groups: Applications and skill*. New York: McGraw-Hill.

Anderson, K., Ohme, J., Bjarnoe, C., Bordacconi, M., Alboek, E., & Vreese, C. (2021). *Generational gaps in political media use and civic engagement*. London: Routledge.

Bowman, S., & Mulvenon, S. (2020). Effective management of generational dynamics in the workplace. In *Management association, information resources editor: Five generations and only one workforce: How successful businesses are managing a multigenerational workforce* (pp. 76–92). Hershey, PA: IGI Global. doi:10.40181978-1-7998-0437-6

Busch, P., Venkitachalam, K., & Richards, D. (2008). Generational differences in soft knowledge situations: Status, need for recognition, workplace commitment and idealism. *Knowledge and Process Management, 15*(1), 45–58.

Chen, L. (2016). *Evolving eldercare in contemporary China*. New York: Palgrave Macmillan.

Clarke, A. (2007). The new reality: Using benefits to attract and retain talent. *Employment Relations Today, 34*(3), 47–53.

Corey, S., & Grace, M. (2019). *Generation Z: A century in the making*. Oxford: Routledge.

Crossman, J. (2010). Act them into a new way of thinking: Multiple stakeholder perspectives on developing international and cultural leadership (ICL) through experiential learning. *The International Journal of Management Education, 9*(1), 33–42.

Edwards, M., & Robinson, P. (2020). Baby boomers and online learning: Exploring experiences in the higher education landscape. In *Management association, information resources editor: Five generations and only one workforce: How successful Businesses are managing a multigenerational workforce* (pp. 48–74). Hershey, PA: IGI Global 2020. doi:10.40181978-1-7998-0437-6

Espinoza, C., Ukleja, M., & Rusch, C. (2010). *Managing the millennials: Discover the core competences for managing today's workforce*. Hoboken, NJ: John Wiley & Sons Ltd.

Fein, E., Tziner, A., & Vasiliu, C. (2010). Age cohort effects, gender, and Romanian leadership preferences. *Journal of Management Development, 29*(4), 364–376.

Gentina, E. (2020). Generation Z in Asia: A research agenda. In E. Gentina & E. Parry (Eds.), *The new generation Z in Asia: Dynamic differences, digitization* (pp. 3–23). Bingley: Emerald Publishing.

Gibson, S. (2009). Enhancing intergenerational communication in the classroom: Recommendations for successful teacher-student relationships. *Nursing Education Perspectives, 30*(1), 37–39.

Hartman, J., & Cambridge, J. (2011). Optimising millennials communication styles. *Business Communication Quarterly, 74*(1), 22–44.

Hummert, M. (2019). Intergenerational communication. In H. Giles, J. Harwood, J. Gasiorek, H. Pierson, J. Nussbaum, & C. Gallois (Eds.), *Language, communication and intergroup relations: A celebration of the scholarship of Howard Giles* (pp. 130–161). New York: Routledge.

Jenkins, J. (2008). Strategies for managing talent in a multigenerational workforce. *Employment Relations Today, 34*(4), 19–26.

Johnson, P., Indik, J., & Rawlins, C. (2009). 'Will you still love me when I'm 64?' The boomers at work. *Journal of Organizational Culture, Communications and Conflict, 13*(1), 101–107.

Joshi, A., Dencker, J., Franz, G., & Martocchio, J. (2010). Unpacking generational identities in organisations. *Academy of Management Review, 35*(3), 392–414.

Kearney, E., Gebert, D., & Voelpel, S. (2009). When and how diversity benefits teams: The importance of team members need for cognition. *Academy of Management Journal, 52*(3), 581–598.

Law, J., Young, T., & Almeida, J. (2019). Intergenerational communication – an interdisciplinary mapping review of research between 1996 and 2017. *Journal of Intergenerational Relationships*, *17*(3), 287–310.

Lowe, D., Levitt, K., & Wilson, T. (2008). Solutions for retaining generation Y employees in the workplace. *The Business Renaissance Quarterly: Enhancing the Quality of Life at Work*, *3*(3), 3–58.

Management Association, Information Resources Editor. (2020). *Five generations and only one workforce: How successful businesses are managing a multigenerational workforce*. Hershey, PA: IGI Global. doi:10.40181978-1-7998-0437-6

Mayer, D. (2006). The changing face of the Australian teaching profession: New generations and new ways of working and learning. *Asia-Pacific Journal of Teacher Education*, *34*(1), 57–71.

McElfresh, J., & Stark, R. (2019). Communicating across age lines: A perspective on the state of intergenerational communication. *Journal of Hospital Librarianship*, *19*(1), 1–11.

Nor, N., Arokiasamy, L., & Balaraman, R. (2019). The influence of Internet of things on employee's engagement among generation Y at the workplace, an empirical study. *Global Business and Management Research: An International Journal*, *11*(1), 419–427.

Nussbaum, J. (2019). Intergenerational relations. In H. Giles, J. Harwood, J. Gasiorek, H. Pierson, J. Nussbaum, & C. Gallois (Eds.), *Language, communication and intergroup relations: A celebration of the scholarship of Howard Giles* (pp. 129–129). New York: Routledge.

Oh, S., DiNitto, D., & Powers, D. (2020). A longitudinal evaluation of government sponsored job skills training and basic employment services among US baby boomers with economic disadvantages. *Evaluation and Program Planning*, *82*, 1–10.

Ota, H., McCann, R., & Honeycuff, J. (2012). Inter-Asian variability in intergenerational communication. *Human Communication Research*, *38*(2), 172–198.

Parmar, S. (2020). Women, ageism and sexism: Changing paradigms. In *Management association, information resources editor: Five generations and only one workforce: How successful businesses are managing a multigenerational workforce* (pp. 19–30). Hershey, PA: IGI Global. doi:10.40181978-1-7998-0437-6

Pasmore, W., & Woodman, R. (2017). The future of research and practice in organizational change and development. In *Research in organizational change and development* (Vol. 25, pp. 1–32). Bingley: Emerald Publishing Limited. doi:10.1108/50897-3016201

Posthuma, R., & Campion, M. (2009). Age stereotypes in the workplace: Common stereotypes, moderators, and future research directions. *Journal of Management*, *35*(1), 158–188.

Reynolds, L., Campbell Bush, E., & Geist, R. (2008). The gen Y imperative. *Communication World*, *25*(2), 19–22.

Sampath, R. (2007). Generation Y to require new recruiting strategies, organization reshaping. *Natural Gas & Electricity*, *24*(4), 21–27.

Sherman, R. (2006). Leading a multigenerational nursing workforce: Issues, challenges and strategies. *Online Journal of Issues in Nursing*, *11*(2), 13.

Skiba, D. J. (2005). The millennials: Have they arrived at your school of nursing? *Nursing Education Perspectives*, *26*(6), 370–371.

Strachan, G., French, E., & Burgess, J. (2010.). *Managing diversity in Australia: Theory and practice*. Sydney: McGraw-Hill.

Treuren, G., & Anderson, K. (2010). The employment expectations of different age cohorts: Is generation Y really that different? *Australian Journal of Career Development*, *19*(2), 49–61.

Way, A., & Medved, C. (2017). Intergenerational communication in the workplace. In *The intergenerational encyclopedia of organizational communication* (pp. 1–9). New York: John Wiley & Sons Ltd. doi:10.1002/9781118955567.wbieoc116

Woodward, I., & Vongswasdi, P. (2017). More that unites than divides: Intergenerational communication preferences in the workplace. *Communication Research and Practice*, *3*(4), 358–385.

Yang, Z., Wang, Y., & Hwang, J. (2020). Generation Z in China: Implications for global brands. In E. Gentina & E. Parry (Eds.), *The new generation Z in Asia: Dynamic differences, digitization* (pp. 23–37). Bingley: Emerald Publishing.

8

SPIRITUAL DIVERSITY

Rising interest in workplace spirituality in popular and scholarly media

Spiritual diversity (SD) stems from the broader line of enquiry known as workplace spirituality but is also highly relevant to diversity management studies. Olalere (2018) has bemoaned the lack of a consistently supported definition of workplace spirituality but in essence, workplace spirituality is concerned with employee experiences at work and the fulfilment of their spiritual needs (Pawar, 2019). Others have referred to a search for meaning and purpose in the performance of work, a quest that dates back to antiquity (see Olufemi-Ayoola & Ogunyemi, 2018).

Spiritual issues in otherwise secular workplaces attracted increasing interest from about the 1990s amongst scholars, managers, and other practitioners (Crossman, 2015b; Gupta & Mikkilineni, 2018; Wang, Wang, & Sun, 2020), coinciding with what has been described as a 'spiritual awakening' in American workplaces and a dramatic rise in publications in the area, reportedly, as a reaction to perceived corporate greed in the previous decade (Garcia-Zamor & Haensel, 2018, p. 926). At about the same time, Americans were also paying greater attention to personal forms of spirituality inspired by Eastern spiritual traditions such as Zen Buddhism, yoga, and meditation (Neal, 2018). Additionally, popular literature and the media were beginning to emphasise spiritual values. Bookshops in international airports routinely carried stock relating to spiritual issues in business including the highly successful work of Stephen Covey (2013), *7 habits of highly effective people* (earlier editions published in both 1989 and 2004) and Deepak Chopra (2007). The Oprah Winfrey show from the mid-1990s also focused on themes of mindfulness and spirituality and contributed to the show host's popularity in the States and around the world. From early on in the twenty-first century, millions of dollars were invested into professional development on workplace spirituality in the US, particularly

DOI: 10.4324/9780429318948-10

at senior levels (see Cavanagh & Bandsuch, 2002; McKew, 2002; Pinto & Pinto, 2010; Thompson, 2000). A cursory review of the reference list for this chapter is only a modest insight into the number of studies about workplace spirituality published in Asia, and many in the People's Republic of China. Aburdene's (2005) vision of workplace spirituality as a megatrend has come to fruition as one of the fastest growing areas in publishing at the time of writing.

Much research attention has been brought to the identification of outcomes in spiritually driven organisations and, with time, studies have tended to become more rigorous from an empirical perspective (see Neal, 2018). Research findings suggest that spiritually rich workplaces and spiritual leadership correlate with positive outcomes for individuals and organisations alike. Findings of studies in Asia and in the West reveal that the fulfillment of spiritual needs influences performance, employee innovation, job satisfaction, affective commitment, financial success, social responsibility, experiencing a sense of meaning at work, employee helping behaviours, and wellbeing (Fry & Nisiewicz, 2013; Pawar, 2019; Zou et al., 2020; Wang et al., 2020; Zhang & Yang, 2021).

These feelings of wellbeing may emanate from reports that spiritual belief brings with it a sense of personal security, gratitude, and calm (Anand, 2018), reducing anxiety and uncertainty about the future (Sarkar & Garg, 2020). Gupta and Mikkilineni (2018, p. 691) suggest attending to spirituality at work contributes to strong organisational identification, engagement, and productivity. Spiritual perspectives also appear to be a predictor of nonviolence in workplaces, partly attributable to individual spiritual practices such as yoga, mindfulness, and meditation that are associated with empathy, listening, creating meaning in communications, and compassion (Sarkar & Garg, 2020). For this reason, Sarker and Garge (2020) urge managers including human resource managers, leaders, and other workplace professionals to facilitate spirituality in the workplace through these practices. Pandey and Navare's (2018) chapter in *The Palgrave handbook of workplace spirituality and fulfilment*, provides some useful insights into both yoga and mindfulness. Yoga, they suggest, is a spiritual process that has been explored from social and physiological perspectives, relevant to workplace spirituality. The topic of mindfulness has already been addressed in the concluding chapter of Part I of this book, but by way of a reminder, it is a practice rooted in the long history of Buddhism and the search for enlightenment that, according to Pandey and Navare (2018), has been pursued through the research disciplines of science (medicine, psychology, neuroscience) and business as well as being applied to practical contexts. Within medicine, earlier studies about spirituality tended to focus upon end of life care but, increasingly, holistic approaches are brought to patient care more widely (Pinto & Pinto, 2010). It is now well established that mindfulness helps to reduce workplace stress and is particularly useful in that it can be learned quite quickly by most people, and its effects enhanced further through regular practice (Ohu, Laguda, & Ogunyemi, 2018).

One reason for the interest in workplace spirituality is an acknowledgement that it is difficult for people to separate aspects of their personal lives, beliefs, and identities that are important to them, from their professional identities. It calls for more holistic approaches to matters concerned with mind, body and spirit (Crossman, 2018a). Also, many are questioning the assumption that spirituality, the arts, and qualitative perspectives are the polar opposite of rationality, science, logic, and quantitative perspectives that have dominated the workplace since what western scholars refer to as the 'Enlightenment' period in the eighteenth century. Enlightenment prompted what is referred to as the 'Cartesian split', in an acknowledgement of the work of Descartes. Essentially, the notion of the Cartesian split relates to the separation of matters of state, emphasising empirical constructions of rationality from religious worldviews (Crossman, 2018a). Those who study workplace spirituality today however, 'acknowledge and celebrate subjective perspectives hitherto relegated by the dominance of so-called objective ways of understanding the world' (Crossman, 2018a, p. 1015).

As Meyer-Galow (2018) observes, scientists investigating quantum physics now recognise that interconnectedness, creativity, nonduality, and nonlinearity are crucial to understanding what was thought to be a purely scientific phenomenon (Meyer-Galow, 2018). Thus, the idea that one can entirely separate the professional from the personal and the spiritual; the qualitative from the quantitative, for example, is now regarded by many as a simplistic interpretation of individuals and how they work. A more holistic approach to the care of mind, body, emotions, and spirit is now being brought to the analysis of how individuals work (see Neal, 2018). Human beings have needs beyond self-interest, the physical or the material that are sometimes described as the transcendent, a spiritual term pertaining to the experience of one's higher self (Pawar, 2019).

The study of spiritual diversity raises questions for managers who may need assistance, including legal advice, in their decision making with respect to a wide range of spiritual matters. For example (Crossman, 2015b, 2015c, 2016):

- the display of religious and/or spiritual artefacts at work (jewellery, crucifixes)
- providing accommodations related to appropriate times and places for prayer
- special diets
- celebrations and how they are described (Christmas party or end of year social celebration)
- inclusivity and nurturing self-disclosure.

Defining spirituality and marking out the conceptual terrain

As Callahan remarked, '[s]triving for a universal definition of spirituality may be futile' (Callahan, 2017, p. 54). Nevertheless, in this text and in others, I define spirituality as a non-partisan, inclusive, eclectic, dynamic, and trans-religious phenomenon pertaining to individual constructions of meaning, values, and beliefs as compared to religion that relates to a collective, institutionalised expression of belief and faith, often expressed through rituals and sacred contexts (see Crossman,

2003, 2015b, 2015c). The assumption embedded in this definition is that religion and spirituality are related but being spiritual does not necessarily suggest that an individual is religious, but that religion is one expression of spirituality that will have some sort of influence depending upon the person (Crossman, 2015a, 2015b; Fairholm, 2015). Other literature arising from a variety of disciplines has also described spirituality as a transcendent connection emanating from within one's self or beyond self, from the environment, other people or a divine power, for example (Callahan, 2017).

Spirituality is commonly regarded as an individual construction (see Hodge, 2020). Each individual has a personal, unique experience of spirituality that can be highly eclectic because people may be inspired by more than one religion or from non-religious experiences, such as feeling a connection with the earth and a commitment to stewardship in caring for the planet (Crossman, 2015c). Others may combine New Age perspectives with practices such as yoga and mindfulness and also identify with a particular religion. One Australian study found that individual spiritual perspectives and experiences are not fixed since individuals may change their spiritual views and practices over time, in dynamic ways (Crossman, 2015c). However, research undertaken in other cultures, where greater consistency exists in spiritual beliefs within populations may not reap the same results. That said, our world appears to be increasingly characterised by diverse cultural and spiritual perspectives (Nelson-Becker & Moeke-Maxwell, 2020).

Spirituality in the workplace may be associated with values such as tolerance, honesty, respect, courage, caring, empathy, and connectedness (Crossman, 2015c) so there are strong overlaps between workplace spirituality and business and virtue ethics. Sarkar and Garg (2020) found that constructions of spirituality also tend to refer to leading a meaningful life, transcendence, faith, practising spirituality, and a connection with others and a higher power. I (Crossman, 2018a, p. 1014) suggest that connectedness/interconnectedness are synonymous terms rooted in Buddhist, Ubuntu and Islamic values and to be understood as, 'a state of being, an experience and at the same time . . . useful as a way of seeing the world, paradigmatically'. Like Sarkar and Garg (2020), I view interconnectedness in my reading of workplace spirituality literature in multiple ways; connectedness to a workplace, a spiritual being, certain values, and a sense of a higher meaning and purpose in life. Such is the accepted import of connectedness that it is reportedly consistently measured across most workplace spirituality scales (Gupta & Mikkilineni, 2018).

Organisational spiritual identity (OSI)

Organisations vary in their approaches to spiritual diversity. OSI is a phenomenon that can be audited, evaluated, and influenced at all levels with the intention of bringing benefits to its members (Crossman, 2018b). OSI is a way of framing the interrelationship of spirituality in the workplace and personal identities with implications for congruency and fit (Crossman, 2018b). I (Crossman, 2016) argued that the phenomenon of OSI was communicated through spiritual signifiers in multiple ways such as:

- shared values
- practices
- discourse
- nonverbal artefacts
- written documents
- policies
- contributions to specified charities.

Related to the idea of organisations choosing to support charities, Larson's work (2018) also provided examples of how some organisations demonstrate acknowledgement of the value of creating spiritual meaning in workplace cultures by supporting employees who volunteer for community work, for example, by providing paid time off or flexible working hours to support such activities.

Even consciously adopting a spiritually inclusive or spiritually 'neutral' approach is, in a sense, a reflection of an OSI. However, one danger I (Crossman, 2016) identified in my research was that when personal and organisational spiritual identities were misaligned, the potential for conflict and dilemmas to arise intensified. For this reason, it is important to draw upon strategies for onboarding and professional development that can serve as powerful means of communicating something of an OSI to employees. Taking opportunities like this for building inclusive cultures and communicating expectations can be highly valuable. Creating trust environments where individuals are able to share their beliefs and learn from one another may be helpful in team building where members are highly diverse. Reflecting upon any alignment and misalignment between personal spiritual identity (PSI) and OSI will be of value for both employees and managers (Crossman, 2016). However, managing spiritual diversity should not be mistaken for organisations high-jacking workplace spirituality principles by demanding spiritual allegiance and developing cultures founded upon favouritism, coercion, zealotry, and the marginalisation of staff who do not tightly conform, not least because such actions ultimately have a negative impact on organisational goals (Fernando & Jackson, 2006; Crossman, 2007).

The basic principles of self-disclosure have been addressed Part I of this text but some attention is given here to the specific implications for spiritual self-disclosure, especially in workplaces where employees are recruited from a cross-section of cultures, ages, genders, abilities, and spiritual orientations, for example. The long-standing separation of professional and personal experiences, values, and beliefs which has hitherto existed in secular organisations may explain why many employees prefer not to disclose parts of their spiritual selves (Crossman, Bordia, & Mills, 2011). Indeed, spiritual self-disclosure has largely been perceived as taboo (see Tisdell, 2001). It can also be potentially stigmatising, marginalising, and 'risky', inviting property damage, resignations, abusive emails, dismissal, co-worker aggression, shunning, repugnance, ridicule, and hostile humour, especially in workplace cultures where rejection and hurt prevail despite the potential of legal disputes in cases of discrimination (Crossman, 2015a). To illustrate, some evidence suggests that in the US, a number of people practicing particular religions are frequent victims of hate crimes (Hodge, 2020) and discrimination and it seems likely that other national cultures will be exposed to spiritual intolerance in one form or another, in broader society and at work. Spiritual discrimination does not occur in a vacuum (Hodge, 2020). What happens in workplaces will reflect elements of wider society. At work, spiritual discrimination may be expressed in the form of negative microaggressive communication (Hodge, 2020), some forms more subtle than others.

It is useful to proffer a definition here of stigma as 'a symbol of disrepute, dishonour or admonishment assigned to a person's character' (Sharma & Mann, 2020, p. 9). The risks of self-disclosure may intensify for evangelists though other forms of spirituality such as meditation, yoga, and mindfulness appear to be more broadly accepted in secular contexts and thus may be disclosed without much risk, at least in countries such as Australia (Crossman, 2015a). Individuals may be well advised to undertake an assessment of the risks before disclosing their spirituality unless they work in spiritually safe, inclusive organisations (Crossman, 2016). That said, spiritual self-disclosure is likely to be influenced by culture and thus how and under what circumstances it takes place will vary from country to country (Crossman, 2015a).

ACTIVITY: SELF-REFLECTION

Reflect upon the following question and discuss your ideas with others, if you are comfortable doing so. Remember, there are no right or wrong answers to this question.

Would you self-disclose your spiritual beliefs to others at work or your educational institution? Why?/Why not?

Spiritual leadership

One line of enquiry in the discipline of workplace spirituality is spiritual leadership. Without appropriate leadership it would be difficult to realise the benefits of addressing spirituality and spiritual diversity in the workplace. Leadership is addressed in Part III of this text but some remarks on spiritual leadership are highly relevant to this particular chapter. Table 8.1 describes the key behaviours of spiritual leadership, drawn from the literature (see Chang, Xiaoxiao, & Wu, 2021; Fairholm, 2015; Fry & Nisiewicz, 2013; Fry, Vitucci, & Cedillo, 2005; Wang et al., 2020). Spiritual leaders:

The behaviours of spiritual leaders are driven through personal attributes that might also be regarded as a way of seeing the world; a lens that is closely interwoven with personal character. Demonstrating hope and faith (see Fry & Nisiewicz, 2013;

TABLE 8.1 Behaviours associated with spiritual leadership

nurture the spiritual lives of self and others through practices such as; spending time in nature, meditation, observing religious traditions, prayer, yoga, and writing a journal.	have an ability to identify the needs of both leaders and followers so they feel understood.	inspire and encourage others in ways that support a sense of calling, purpose, meaning, and making a difference.
model and create environments that prioritise ethical practices.	create corporate cultures based on altruistic love.	maintain relational harmony and trust even when members do not agree.
consider themselves in service to organisational members and stakeholders.	are concerned for the wellbeing of others from a holistic perspective.	show care and appreciation for self and others.
nurture a sense of membership in the workplace as a community.	motivate and inspire others.	create and communicate a vision for the organisation.
builds close relationships with others.	establish value congruence at all levels of the organisation.	empower individuals, teams and the organisation as a whole.

Wang et al., 2020), a strong sense of personal values and communicating authenticity (see Fairholm, 2015) are some examples of these attributes.

One of the advantages of spiritual leadership is that it can be applied to almost any organisational context and culture or indeed to any individual employee. Fry and Nisiewicz (2013) maintain that spiritual leadership is applicable, regardless of spiritual or religious beliefs and indeed to those who are agnostic or atheist and simply have no confidence in traditional forms of leadership and are looking for a more sustainable approach for the benefit of all. Indeed, an assumption now widely exists that some knowledge of spiritual leadership is essential for leaders of all kinds of organisations today (see Fairholm, 2015; Fry & Nisiewicz, 2013) and can transform them in ways that impact processes, structures, co-worker attitudes, and behaviour in ways that cultivate a genuine concern for the wellbeing of others (Fairholm, 2015).

Spiritual leadership resonates with other theories on leadership such as transformational, environmental (Crossman, 2010) and authentic leadership that occurs, according to Leroy, Anseel, Gardner, and Sels (2015, p. 1677), 'when individuals enact their true selves in their role as a leaders'. Published work about authentic leadership tends to adopt either an intrinsic or an extrinsic focus. Intrinsic studies explore the personal orientations of leaders in reflecting upon who they are as individuals, what is important to them and any development required and extrinsic studies adopt an intellectual approach to the development of authenticity and understanding both personal role expectations and those expectations of whom they lead in order to work out how best to fulfil them (Ulrich, 2020).

However, it is arguably servant leadership that appears to share most of the defining features of spiritual leadership. Robert Greenleaf's work in the 1970s on servant leadership is regarded as a seminal work that laid the foundations of workplace spirituality as a movement (Neal, 2018). Although there is no operational or conceptual definition of servant leadership, it is associated with the attributes of; altruism, a capacity to heal, egalitarianism, serving others, facilitating the growth and success of others and *agapao* (meaning to dearly love in Greek) (Roberts, 2014). Roberts (2014) also alludes to the notion of stewardship as a related, foundational element of servant leadership. Stewardship, he suggests, involves the accomplishment of an organisation's mission, inspiring others with vision and creating a sense of community. These achievements are undertaken by virtuous means reflecting a character that embraces integrity, morality, empathy, humility, trust, hope, courage, forgiveness. Roberts, an eminent professor in his field, also draws attention to compelling evidence that servant leadership has a favourable influence upon employee attitudes towards work, work behaviours, performance, and other outcomes that enhance quality of life in the workplace (Roberts, 2014).

Spiritual intelligence (SI)

By the beginning of the twenty-first century, much work had already been published about spiritually intelligent leadership (Pinto & Pinto, 2010) and how spiritual leaders foster spiritual intelligence in organisational communities (Fairholm, 2015), particularly where high levels of diversity exist. Spiritual intelligence however is not a construct that is limited to spiritual leaders and can be cultivated and developed by most people, over time (Vasconcelos, 2020).

Roberts and Hess-Hernandez (2018, p. 427) maintain that those with spiritual intelligence:

- have a capacity for mindfulness
- have an awareness of the inner self
- are orientated towards community
- feel a sense of purpose
- foster harmony
- seek meaning from work
- experience a sense of spiritual transcendence
- focus on interpersonal relationships.

Based on an extensive literature review, Vasconcelos (2020) identified moral courage, altruism, hope, optimism, cooperation, an organisational justice mindset and listening to be present in constructions of SI. It is with little surprise perhaps that these themes resonate with those characterising spiritual leadership in salient publications in the last two decades – if one accepts the assumption that spiritual leaders are spiritually intelligent. Similarly, SI is also associated with positive outcomes for individuals and, ultimately, organisations that call to mind those identified in workplace spirituality literature. A case in point is one scholarly work focused on medical contexts, suggesting that SI is correlated with lower levels of burnout, resilience, and a sense of wellbeing (Pinto & Pinto, 2010). Although spiritual leadership and intelligence appear to be tightly aligned conceptually, some variations emerge across cultures with respect to how SI attributes appear to manifest. For example, Feng, Xue-Yuan, and Li (2019) found, in comparing western constructions of SI with those in China, that although there are many similarities in attributes, some differences do exist, particularly in that Chinese samples indicate that greater emphasis is placed upon meaning as an attribute of SI than in the West.

Despite the apparent interest in spiritual intelligence, it remains a somewhat contested field. Indeed, one Polish study found no evidence to support the validity of any factors associated with SI in their self-report inventory, making measurement of SI highly problematic – an outcome, the authors maintain, that suggests the need for caution and robust research if this seemingly promising line of enquiry is to be pursued further with any confidence (Atroszko, Skrzypińska, & Balcerowska, 2021).

Approaches organisations can take to implementing spiritual initiatives in the workplace

As discussed, consciously or unconsciously, organisations communicate something of their spiritual identity (OSI) through spiritual indicators. Spiritual leadership involves taking a proactive approach to developing an OSI by paying attention to spiritual indicators. Indicators might include donating a percentage of profits to charity, giving employees paid time to engage in community projects that help the vulnerable in society in some way, or looking after the environment. OSI may be communicated by artefacts on display, the language adopted, levels of spiritual self-disclosure, professional development on matters related to spiritual diversity, or respecting the need for accommodations that facilitate spiritual needs (prayer rooms, for example). It may mean creating a spiritual place of peace for all employees who may engage in mindfulness, yoga classes, listen to music, or participate in religious services. Some organisations recruit chaplains or spiritual counsellors.

In consideration of the benefits of spiritual approaches to work and organisations, organisations may like to consider taking steps to enrich the spiritual experience of their members whatever their personal spiritual orientations or beliefs, religious and otherwise. They may wish to enhance understandings about spiritual diversity and communicate expectations of behaviours and values. Whatever the motivations for leading change in OSI, the following observations may be useful and are based upon my own research and the work I have cited in those publications listed among references. Chapter 3 provides some information about organisational change theories and the variety of perspectives that can potentially be brought to the process of facilitating the creation of a vision for workplace spirituality and implementing the process.

Become informed

Being informed is a non-negotiable activity in developing a vision and a strategy for workplace spirituality. Understandings can be gained by reading empirical and scholarly work, inviting and including expert academics in workplace discussions or, indeed, inviting members of other organisations who have travelled the same path to share their experiences. Funding employee attendance at workplace spirituality conferences, distributing case studies, or engaging in blogs would also be useful for stimulating ideas. Organisations may also seek out influencers in this area who contribute TED Talks on the subject. These kinds of activities will assist those who may be asked to present a proposal to management suggesting how to go about the change, how it can be resourced, communicated, and implemented in a sustainable and inclusive way. Some consideration will need to be brought to the appointment or recognition of a spiritual leader as well as prospective spiritual followers to champion the initiative. Human resource managers will be able to communicate any legal implications for managing spiritual diversity in the organisation at the local level and, possibly, any laws internationally that may be relevant to organisational partners and stakeholders.

Identify and empower champions

Identify a diverse team to guide the process and be responsible for communicating and reporting on progress to all levels of the organisation. Fostering spiritual diversity comes with creating diverse teams and sends the message that all perspectives are respected and acknowledged. Such is the basis for embedding spiritually safe environments where people are able to express their beliefs and ideas in order to drive innovation and change. Ensure any internal champions have sufficient time allocated to their tasks and access to necessary resources in order to achieve the vision of a spiritual leader and the organisation. The appointment of an external facilitator with expertise in the field could be a critical decision in driving the change process. Spiritual leaders and followers, as champions, will need to demonstrate authenticity and integrity – especially in the sense of aligning personal behaviour with words in order to inspire and communicate confidence, hope, faith in the process, and, ultimately, a shared sense of what successfully achieving the spiritual vision will look like.

Conduct an organisational spiritual audit as a basis for planning the future and crystallising the vision

It is possible to conduct an audit of spiritual and nonspiritual organisational signifiers of spiritual identity (OSI) (Crossman, 2018b). This step involves making an assessment of activities, processes, structures, and aspects of culture that indicate some acknowledgement of spirituality or the potential for a spiritually driven approach. It is concerned with discovering what is currently happening in the workplace. This can be done through interviews, surveys, document analysis of policies, procedures, written communications, and so on, that are available. Examine any spiritual elements in mission statements and where they are realised and aligned in organisational practices (or not). Consider using observation, common in organisational ethnography, as a data collection tool because people express spirituality through artefacts on their person and in their working spaces (tattoos, jewellery, positive words on plaques, for example). The findings and recommendations arising from the audit will need to be submitted to those with the power and insight to ask the right questions, provide feedback, approve, support, resource recommendations, or, indeed, request major revisions.

Not all recommended or agreed initiatives need to be implemented simultaneously. It is possible that one initiative will be sufficient to assess or ignite interest without leaving employees feeling overwhelmed. Setting aside a space for spiritual activities may be a useful starting point or designing a professional development component on spiritual diversity. If the implementation of one or two initiatives proves successful, changes to the OSI may arise organically. While implementing changes is necessary in strategic approaches to developing a vision for the OSI, voluntary rather than compulsory participation is advised. People need time to process the implications of initiatives for their own spiritual orientation or PSI. As I have argued in this chapter and elsewhere, PSI is often eclectic and dynamic. People will find different meanings in different activities at different times in their careers. When they do engage in initiatives they will be investing in the development of their spiritual intelligence.

Monitor progress

Following the implementation of any new initiative to meet the spiritual needs of people at work and the development of spiritual intelligence, it will be important to monitor how effective those initiatives are by gathering further data (Sarkar & Garg, 2020). The change process with respect to an OSI is more likely to prove successful when conducted in an iterative and circular manner. It should be regarded as an ongoing activity with periodic assessment, reflection, and relevant interventions and modifications in order to continually inform the process rather than being regarded as a discrete project to be proposed, implemented, and achieved in a linear way.

Conclusion

This chapter is intended to provide those with little experience of workplace spirituality to appreciate some key concepts and become informed about this line of enquiry. It has presented some evidence of the benefits for individuals and organisations alike in adopting spiritual approaches to a variety of secular workplace contexts. The chapter considers workplace spirituality in relation to spiritual diversity, employee wellbeing, and, ultimately, organisational performance – as Fry and

Nisiewicz (2013) would say, it addresses the concept of the triple bottom line. The chapter draws on the literature to explain the notion of spiritual leadership and spiritual intelligence and concludes with some practical, non-prescriptive ideas about how organisations might approach the embedding of spiritual initiatives in order to reap the benefits that workplace spirituality offers. It advocates for the recognition of spiritual diversity, the cultivation of a sense of belonging that comes through shared values, the creation of spiritually safe workplaces, and the encouragement of all to find meaning and purpose in their lives, personally and professionally.

ACTIVITY: CRITICAL REFLECTION, CREATIVITY, AND ROLE PLAY

In small groups discuss your responses to the following questions. Remember to be respectful and sensitive to the spiritual beliefs of others participating in the activity. All of the scenarios are based on some real-life cases that emerged from empirical data.

1. Some organisations in the world do not allow staff to wear jewellery or have other religious artefacts in workspaces because they are concerned that the display or nonverbal communication of personal, spiritual beliefs may be confronting or send messages to those with different beliefs that they may not belong. Other organisations encourage such personal displays because the organisational culture is aligned with those spiritual beliefs and some secular (non-religious) organisations neither support nor discourage the display of spiritual or religious artefacts.

   Role play as a small group of managers who have to decide on how the organisation will address this issue. It may help to select an organisation you all know well before making your decision because the context or the culture of an organisation is likely to make a difference to your response.

2. Organise individuals into three small groups. One group has to argue in defense of a prayer room for those members of staff who would like to pray and/or believe they are obligated to pray during the working day. The other group must offer counterarguments to this position. Finally, a third group, role playing as managers, agree on a decision that would be acceptable to both groups, showing sensitivity to diversity and maintaining a spirit of inclusiveness.

3. You work in a multinational retail company in your own country. You are aware that many of your colleagues have different spiritual beliefs and some have no interest in religious or spiritual matters. The staff all get on

quite well and work as an effective team. Your manager says she wants to reward you for a year of hard work by hosting a 'Christmas' party. Some people have complained about the party being described in this way as they are not Christians and none of their own religious festivals are celebrated in the organisation. As a small group of staff, prepare a case to be put to the manager and a solution to the problem. Appoint an individual or individuals to role play as a general manager and a human resources manager. Come to an agreement that is acceptable to you all.

4. You are a manager in a large freight company. One of your supervisors comes to you for advice. Clients who come to the warehouse and some staff have made complaints about a hardworking member of staff, Lee, who is efficient and congenial. The problem is that Lee intersperses much of his discourse with exclamations such as 'Praise the Lord!' and 'Halleluiah'. What advice would you give your supervisor about how to approach the issue? Provide a rationale for the advice you give and those things you believe should be considered in making a decision.

References

Aburdene, P. (2005). *Megatrends 2010: The rise of conscious capitalism*. Charlottesville: Hampton Roads Publishing.

Anand, R. (2018). *Happiness at work: Mindfulness, analysis and well-being*. Thousand Oaks: Sage.

Atroszko, P. A., Skrzypińska, K., & Balcerowska, J. M. (2021). Is there a general factor of spiritual intelligence? Factorial validity of the Polish adaptation of spiritual intelligence self-report inventory. *Journal of Religion and Health, 60*(5), 3591–3605.

Callahan, A. (2017). *Spiritual diversity: In spirituality and hospice social work*. New York: Columbia University Press.

Cavanagh, G., & Bandsuch, M. (2002). Virtue as a benchmark for spirituality in business. *Journal of Business Ethics, 38*(1–2), 109–117.

Chang, P., Xiaoxiao, G., & Wu, T. (2021). Sense calling, job crafting, spiritual leadership and work meaningfulness: A moderated mediation model. *Leadership & Organization Development Journal, 42*(5), 690–704.

Chopra, D. (2007). *Buddha: A story of enlightenment*. New York: First HarperLuxe.

Covey, S. (2013). *The 7 habits of highly effective people: Powerful lessons in personal change*. New York: Rosetta Books.

Crossman, J. (2003). Secular spiritual development in Education from international and global perspectives. *Oxford Review of Education, 29*(4), 503–520.

Crossman, J. (2007). The spirit of business: Spiritualising otherwise secular work and learning contexts. *International Employment Relations Review, 13*(2), 1–11.

Crossman, J. (2010). Conceptualising spiritual leadership in secular organizational contexts and its relation to transformational, servant and environmental leadership. *Leadership & Organization Development Journal, 31*(7), 596–608.

Crossman, J. (2015a). Being on the outer: The risks and benefits of spiritual self-disclosure in the Australian workplace. *Journal of Management & Organization, 21*(6), 772–785.

Crossman, J. (2015b). Manager perspectives on embedding spirituality into the business curriculum: Bridging the gap. *Thunderbird International Business Review, 57*(5), 367–378.

Crossman, J. (2015c). Eclecticism and commonality in employee constructions of spirituality. *Journal of Management, Spirituality and Religion, 12*(1), 59–77.

Crossman, J. (2016). Alignment and misalignment in personal and organizational spiritual identities. *Identity: An International Journal of Theory and Research, 16*(3), 154–168.

Crossman, J. (2018a). Celebrating interconnectedness as a spiritual paradigm for teaching, learning and the internationalization of higher education. In S. Dhiman, G. Roberts, & J. Crossman (Eds.), *The Palgrave handbook of workplace spirituality and fulfilment* (pp. 1014–1031). Cham, Switzerland: Palgrave Macmillan.

Crossman, J. (2018b). Internal auditing of organisational spiritual identity (OSI). In S. Dhiman, G. Roberts, & J. Crossman (Eds.), *The Palgrave handbook of workplace spirituality and fulfilment* (pp. 833–856). Cham, Switzerland: Palgrave Macmillan.

Crossman, J., Bordia, S., & Mills, C. (2011). *Business communication for the global age.* Sydney: McGraw-Hill.

Fairholm, G. (2015). *Overcoming workplace pathologies: Principles of spirit-based leadership.* Cham, Switzerland: Springer.

Feng, M., Xue-Yuan, X., & Li, J. (2019). Spiritual intelligence scale-Chinese form: Construction and initial validation. *Current Psychology, 38*(5), 1318–1327.

Fernando, M., & Jackson, B. (2006). The influence of religion-based workplace spirituality on business leaders' decision-making: An interfaith study. *Journal of Management and Organisation, 12*(1), 23–39.

Fry, L., & Nisiewicz, M. (2013). *Maximising the triple bottom line through spiritual leadership.* Stanford: Stanford University Press.

Fry, L., Vitucci, S., & Cedillo, M. (2005). Spiritual leadership and army transformation: Theory, measurement and establishing a baseline. *The Leadership Quarterly, 16*(5), 835–862.

Garcia-Zamor, J., & Haensel, K. (2018). Spirituality's relationship with ethics and religion and its role in the workplace. In S. Dhiman, G. Roberts, & J. Crossman (Eds.), *The Palgrave handbook of workplace spirituality and fulfilment* (pp. 925–941). Cham, Switzerland: Palgrave Macmillan.

Gupta, M., & Mikkilineni, S. (2018). Spirituality and employee engagement at work. In S. Dhiman, G. Roberts, & J. Crossman (Eds.), *The Palgrave handbook of workplace spirituality and fulfilment* (pp. 682–695). Cham, Switzerland: Palgrave Macmillan.

Hodge, D. (2020). Spiritual microaggressions: Understanding the subtle messages that foster religious discrimination. *Journal of Ethnic and Cultural Diversity in Social Work, 29*(6), 473–489.

Larson, K. (2018). *Adaption and well-being.* London: Routledge.

Leroy, H., Anseel, F., Gardner, W., & Sels, L. (2015). Authentic leadership, authentic followership, basic need satisfaction, and work role performance: A cross-level study. *Journal of Management, 41*(6), 1677–1697.

McKew, M. (2002, February 12). Lunch with Maxine McKew. *The Bulletin, 42.*

Meyer-Galow, E. (2018). *Business ethics 3.0: The integral ethics from the perspective of a CEO.* Boston: De Gruyter.

Neal, J. (2018). Overview of workplace spirituality research. In S. Dhiman, G. Roberts, & J. Crossman (Eds.), *The Palgrave handbook of workplace spirituality and fulfilment* (pp. 4–57). Cham, Switzerland: Palgrave Macmillan.

Nelson-Becker, H., & Moeke-Maxwell, T. (2020). Spiritual diversity, spiritual assessment, and Māori end-of-life perspectives: Attaining Ka Ea. *Religions, 11*(10), 536.

Ohu, E., Laguda, E., & Ogunyemi, K. (2018). Mindfulness and stress reduction: Managing workplace stress. In S. Dhiman, G. Roberts, & J. Crossman (Eds.), *The Palgrave handbook of workplace spirituality and fulfilment* (pp. 238–267). Cham, Switzerland: Palgrave Macmillan.

Olalere, A. (2018). Workplace spirituality and creativity. In S. Dhiman, G. Roberts, & J. Crossman (Eds.), *The Palgrave handbook of workplace spirituality and fulfilment* (pp. 989–1010). Cham, Switzerland: Palgrave Macmillan.

Olufemi-Ayoola, F., & Ogunyemi, K. (2018). Genesis and growth of workplace spirituality. In S. Dhiman, G. Roberts, & J. Crossman (Eds.), *The Palgrave handbook of workplace spirituality and fulfilment* (pp. 901–922). Cham, Switzerland: Palgrave Macmillan.

Pandey, A., & Navare, A. (2018). Paths of yoga: Perspective for workplace spirituality. In S. Dhiman, G. Roberts, & J. Crossman (Eds.), *The Palgrave handbook of workplace spirituality and fulfilment* (pp. 101–126). Cham, Switzerland: Palgrave Macmillan.

Pawar, B. (2019). *Employee performance and well-being: Leadership, justice, support and workplace spirituality*. London: Routledge.

Pinto, C., & Pinto, S. (2010). From spiritual intelligence to spiritual care: A transformative approach to holistic practice. *Nurse Education in Practice, 47*, 102823–102823.

Roberts, G. (2014). *Servant leader human resource management: A moral and spiritual perspective*. New York: Palgrave Macmillan.

Roberts, G., & Hess-Hernandez, D. (2018). Christian workplace spiritual intelligence: A preliminary analysis. In S. Dhiman, G. Roberts, & J. Crossman (Eds.), *The Palgrave handbook of workplace spirituality and fulfilment* (pp. 424–447). Cham, Switzerland: Palgrave Macmillan.

Sarkar, A., & Garg, N. (2020). Peaceful workplace only a myth? *The international Journal of Conflict Management, 31*(5), 709–728.

Sharma, S., & Mann, N. (2020). Workplace discrimination: The most critical issue in managing diversity In *Management association, information resources editor: Five generations and only one workforce: How successful businesses are managing a multigenerational workforce* (pp. 1–19). Hershey, PA: IGI Global. doi:10.40181978-1-7998-0437-6

Thompson, W. D. (2000). Can you train people to be spiritual? *Training and Development, 54*(12), 18.

Tisdell, E. (2001). *Exploring spirituality and culture in adult and higher education*. San Francisco: Jossey-Bass.

Ulrich, T. (2020). *Spiritual leadership: A guide to focus, awareness and mindfulness*. Cham, Switzerland: Springer.

Vasconcelos, A. (2020). Spiritual intelligence: A theoretical synthesis and work-life potential linkages. *International Journal of Organizational Analysis (2005), 28*(1), 109–134.

Wang, L., Wang, H., & Sun, Y. (2020). How spiritual leadership contributes to followers' helping behaviour. *Social Behavior and Personality, 48*(11), 1–12.

Zhang, Y., & Yang, F. (2021). How and when spiritual leadership enhances employee innovative behavior. *Personnel Review, 50*(2), 596–609. doi:10.1108/PR-07-2019-0346

Zou, W., Zeng, Y., Peng, Q., Xin, Y., Chen, J., & Houghton, J. D. (2020). The influence of spiritual leadership on the subjective well-being of Chinese registered nurses. *Journal of Nursing Management, 28*(6), 1432–1442.

PART III

Communication contexts and applications

Part III of this text takes an applied approach to some of the theories presented in earlier chapters and considers them in terms of specific workplace contexts and topics. It also introduces additional theories relevant to these contexts. *Communication contexts and applications* also draws on topics that pervade everyday aspects of organisational life with implications for individuals and groups. It includes chapters on negotiation and managing conflict, working in groups, developing others for growth, ethical approaches to communication and relationships, dark organisational issues and finally emotions at work.

The chapter dedicated to negotiation and managing conflict receives more attention than the others, largely because negotiation is a form of conflict and thus rather difficult to also disentangle conceptually into two discrete chapters. Although the length of chapters is otherwise fairly well balanced, the length of any chapter does not reflect a perceived value attributed to the contribution of a particular subject matter. Such is the complexity of humanity, society, and organisations that, in reality, all these chapters are interrelated and inform one another.

Exposure to Parts I and II in the book will enrich personal responses and engagement with many of the activities in Part III. Like the preceding chapters, Part III does not claim to provide an in-depth analysis of all research or even a comprehensive assessment of research undertaken in a certain area over a period of time. It largely provides snapshots of current and emerging lines of enquiry with some discussion of any relevant historical roots that have informed contemporaneous perspectives. It should provide insights to stimulate practitioners, leaders, and managers at different points in their careers and their responsibilities in supporting the growth of themselves and others with a particular emphasis on ethical practice and wellbeing.

DOI: 10.4324/9780429318948-11

9

NEGOTIATING AND MANAGING CONFLICT

Key concepts and terms in negotiation

Scholars of management and organisational behaviour have been applying themselves to the context of negotiation for more than half a century, emphasising the implications and relevance for practitioners (Brett & Thompson, 2016). Multi-and transdisciplinary approaches have been applied, especially in the research fields of economics, psychology, politics, sociology, anthropology, science, and communication (Brett & Thompson, 2016; Gardani, 2017). Arguably, the study of negotiation seems most appropriate through the lens of communication because it is inconceivable that negotiation can occur without some form of communication (Cahn & Abigail, 2007; Dorochoff, 2016; Hynes, 2008). Thus, communication has a crucial influence upon the negotiation process (Tsia, 2020). When communication is poor, negotiations often become protracted, costly, and require renegotiations resulting from a breakdown of interpersonal and organisational relationships (Schoop, Kohne, & Ostertag, 2010).

Negotiation is an everyday occurrence and a communication skill that can be learned though some people have traits that will enhance or indeed hinder their ability to negotiate (Weiss & Ury, 2020). It is intimately applied, ultimately, to improve or create the life personally envisioned (Low, 2020). The value of individuals developing negotiation skills can hardly be underestimated given their influence in determining the outcome of interviews, applications for promotion, and discussions about salary and, particularly so for women, in the light of compelling research findings that they are disadvantaged relative to men in negotiating remuneration (Bowles, Thomason, & Bear, 2019). Some research suggests bringing tailored professional development, relevant to female negotiators, would be more effective than the gender-blind approach to negotiation training and notions of best practice (Kulik, Sinha, & Olekalns, 2020). Another motivation for improving

DOI: 10.4324/9780429318948-12

negotiation skills may lie in the rise of employees who negotiate 'i-deals' or individualised work arrangements with their employers, a process requiring a high level of skill in the negotiation (Simosi, Rousseau, & Weingart, 2021, p. 186) that many do not possess.

Negotiating avoids the need to engage in aggression, end a relationship, capitulate, or undergo the costs of litigation and when successful, can ease emotional tensions so that all concerned are able to move forward with a sense of confidence and accomplishment in addressing future issues, so the benefits become compounded (Cahn & Abigail, 2007; De Janasz, Crossman, Campbell, & Powers, 2014; Hynes, 2008; Lewicki, Barry, & Saunders, 2016). According to Lewicki et al. (2016), negotiations generally take place for one of three, main reasons: they may be to form an agreement on how to allocate a resource such as time, money, or land; they may be held to create or innovate in ways that could not be achieved independently (see also Schoop, 2021); and they may be conducted to solve a problem or resolve a dispute.

However, there are times when it is unwise to negotiate. Negotiations are best avoided when (Baber & Fletcher-Chen, 2020; Lewicki et al., 2016):

1. poorly prepared
2. insufficient time for effective negotiation is available
3. participants are not motivated and do not seem to be concerned about the outcome one way or another
4. a perception exists that a counterpart cannot be trusted
5. a counterpart appears to be making unethical demands
6. the negotiation is more likely to be successful at a later stage
7. the costs are too high.

Definitions of negotiation

In the following activity about definitions, some concepts emerge consistently and need to be understood in order to appreciate how various scholars construct negotiation. For example, the term 'party' appears in most definitions of negotiation and applies to a person or group that has some common interests, though they do not all necessarily hold the same views, beliefs, values, or preferences (Thompson, 2009). In a negotiation, parties will have both some shared and some opposing interests (De Janasz et al., 2014).

ACTIVITY: CRITICAL ANALYSIS

A number of definitions exist for negotiation. Consider the following examples and note any shared or distinctive concepts among them. For example, the notion of negotiation as a process and that it involves more than one party appears to be a consistent theme. Find two more definitions in the resources available to you, and compare them with those provided.

Please note that some of the definitions presented are direct quotations and others have been slightly altered whilst retaining meaning.

> 'Business negotiation is the solution to reach an agreement or to solve the disagreement. It is also a process of exchanging, discussing and even arguing about an issue' (Zhang, 2013, pp. 50–56).
>
> Negotiation is an interactive process in which 2 or more parties seek to find common ground on an issue or dispute of mutual interest to reach a mutually acceptable agreement (Dwyer, 2020).
>
> Negotiation is 'a process where interested parties resolve disputes, agree upon causes of action, bargain for individual or collective advantage and or attempt to craft outcomes which serve their mutual interest' (Samina & Vinita, 2010, p. 26).
>
> 'Negotiation is a social interaction between two (or more) parties who provide arguments in an attempt to influence the other to accept their view regarding the value of a negotiated object' (Maaravi, Ganzach, & Pazy, 2011, p. 245).
>
> Negotiation is essentially a form of interpersonal communication. Both verbal and nonverbal expressions in communication processes are crucial to the success of negotiation and the resolution of any conflict (Lewicki et al., 2016).
>
> Negotiation is a process in which two or more people or groups share their concerns and interests to reach an agreement of mutual benefit (Fisher, Ury, & Patton, 1991).

Distinguishing interests and positions

Interests are rooted in basic human needs, desires, and fears to be addressed. Interests may relate to the need for security (financial or otherwise), the experience of belonging, recognition, and having some sort of control in life's decisions. Interests represent the underlying motivations of a negotiator and can be intrinsic or instrumental. That is, a desired salary may be motivated by a need for self-worth (intrinsic) or enable the purchase of someone's first home (instrumental) (Lewicki, Barry, & Saunders, 2007). In contrast, a negotiator's position is concerned with an action such as a demand or a proposal. It may involve proposing to work more hours, for example, but an instrumental interest in this case may be that increased hours would enable a party to be able to afford a rent increase.

Distributive and integrative approaches

The literature on negotiation generally distinguishes between two types of approaches or strategies: a distributive/instrumental/competitive/position-based/ zero-sum/win–lose approach and an integrative/principled/win–win, mutual gains/expressive/interest-based, collaborative approach (see Cordell, 2018). Nevertheless, the observation of Kong, Dirks, and Ferrin (2014), that negotiations are rarely either integrative or distributive strategies but more often a combination of the two, is notable. Cordell (2018, p. 3), for example, also notes the rise of a third kind of negotiation referred to as a 'win/perceived win' approach that is gaining attention amongst both academics and practitioners who perceive it to be 'a pragmatic, commercially astute alternative'. Ultimately, selecting an appropriate strategy will depend upon personal preference, the situation, and how highly the relationship is valued in the long term (De Janasz et al., 2014).

A distributive bargaining strategy assumes a fixed amount of resources to be divided up and a win-lose outcome and is often prompted when, for whatever reason, a party believes it essential to gain a certain proportion of limited resources available (Baber & Fletcher-Chen, 2020) that may include not having much time (Lewicki et al., 2016). It is also a strategy where each party is attempting to gain a larger share of a pie in an adversarial relationship. The pie metaphor, referring to all the resources, of whatever nature that are under discussion, is frequently adopted in negotiation literature. A distributive approach tends to be associated with a high level of competition, coercion, a focus on differences, power plays a resistance to concessions, negative emotions, conflict, instrumentalism, and a tendency to demonstrate a greater concern for self than others (Cordell, 2018; Crossman, Bordia, & Mills, 2011; De Janasz et al., 2014; Lewicki et al., 2016). Of the four basic strategies used by negotiators: 1. Avoidance, 2. Accommodation, 3. Competition, and 4. Collaboration – a competitive or even a competitive and accommodating approach is most often adopted in distributive negotiations resulting in a win-lose situation (Dorochoff, 2016).

The aim is often to achieve immediate and short-term goals with little energy being invested into sustaining long-term relationships (De Janasz et al., 2014). Distributive approaches are often characterised by making extreme offers, a resistance to sharing information, not reciprocating concessions, exploiting power advantages, and self-protective behaviours (Kong et al., 2014). Distributive approaches are more likely to involve dubious ethical tactics that may include (Cahn & Abigail, 2007; Hynes, 2008; Lewicki et al., 2016):

- playing *good cop/bad cop*, to increase receptivity to the friendlier party
- agreeing to points initially but returning to them later so that the other party feels they have invested too much at a late stage to quibble
- making early concessions over minor issues to heighten a sense of obligation later in the process when a more significant concession is required
- providing so much information that a party will feel overloaded and pay less attention to details that may be important.

Integrative negotiation as a concept coined in the seminal text, *Getting to Yes* by Fisher et al. (1988; Fisher, Ury, & Patton, 2011), offered an alternative to viewing negotiation as a confrontational struggle. Integrative negotiation is also known as *expressive negotiation* because it does recognise the emotions of parties, the relationship between them, and the importance of soft (communication) skills (Altschul, 2007; Raj, 2008; Royce, 2005). However, although rationalist outcomes are not the main consideration in an integrative negotiation, they are unlikely to be entirely absent from consideration. According to Baber and Fletcher-Chen (2020), it is most useful in complex situations where multiple issues that may well be connected need to be addressed and where capitalising on any opportunities for creating value is a prime concern.

Parties are willing to engage in an integrative approach when they believe they have common interests and potential exists for all concerned to achieve their main objectives and find a solution through collaboration – an approach that is most likely to result in a win-win outcome (Cordell, 2018; Dorochoff, 2016). The focus is upon establishing commonalities, making the space for action, acknowledging varied perspectives to build trust, problem solving, exchanging ideas and information, adding value, and devising creative alternative solutions so that more resources can be made available or existing ones can be more effectively coordinated and shared (Cordell, 2018; Goodwin, 2019; Lewicki et al., 2016; Mayer, 2020). From the perspective of a mediator and an advocate of integrative negotiation, Mayer (2020) notes that the focus of discussion should be directed towards interests rather than positions.

Essentially, an integrative negotiation involves 1. Identifying and defining the problem, 2. Establishing needs and interests, 3. Generating alternative solutions to the problem, and 4. Evaluating the identified alternatives before selecting one or more that both parties agree upon (Lewicki et al., 2016). The tendency for integrative negotiators to develop long-term relationships assists in unpacking sensitive situations, differentiating between needs and interests and arriving at mutually beneficial solutions (Weiss & Ury, 2020). The open exchange of ideas, information, and interests in a respectful and trust-filled environment is a part of this relationship building. Mayer, Davis, and Schoorman's (1995) definition of trust as the willingness to accept others' vulnerabilities given positive expectations of their conduct, is longstanding and highly cited. The level of trust negotiators share, however, will ultimately depend upon each party's chronic disposition towards trust (governed by personality differences that influence some individuals to be more trusting than others), the historical aspects of the relationship between them, and situational factors (how much time they have been able to spend on communicating with one another) (Lewicki et al., 2016). Trust is no guarantee of success, but it does facilitate the process through, for example, effective communication and self-disclosure (Cahn & Abigail, 2007; Hynes, 2008; Lewicki et al., 2016).

As Broome et al. (2019) point out, developing an inclusive environment particularly for intercultural dialogue requires empathy, openness, listening skills, and for participants to examine personal prejudices and biases. It is essential to remain open to the perspectives of a counterpart and to develop some awareness of any personal cognitive biases that may exist and serve to block communication and relationship development. A cognitive bias refers to some kind of influence over how someone thinks that has the potential to give rise to perceptual errors and poor decision making (Baber & Fletcher-Chen, 2020). Some examples of cognitive bias include (Baber & Fletcher-Chen, 2020):

- confirming/expectation bias where data are interpreted based on what is expected
- emotional bias when feelings of loathing or sympathy may impact negatively on sound decision making
- prejudice where information received is improperly processed because of existing negative ideas about a counterpart.

ACTIVITY: REFLECTION

Reflect on a recent negotiation. Consider those aspects that appeared to suggest an integrative approach and those that may have suggested a distributive one. Did one approach dominate, or would you describe the negotiation as a combination of the two? Provide a rationale to support your conclusions.

Stages in negotiation

Negotiations move through phases as they progress, but perhaps the most important is preparation (Wach, 2012) because it can take up to 80 per cent of the total time invested in a negotiation (Thompson, 2009) given the many issues to be considered. Being prepared also has the psychological benefit of leaving a negotiator feeling confident and informed about the interests of all parties and possible strategic options should the negotiation take an unexpected direction (Weiss & Ury, 2020). Crucially, the pre-negotiation phase is also a period when a clear vision of the desired goal or outcome, known as a target point, is developed but not yet shared with a counterpart (Thompson, 2009). At the same time, a resistance point is identified. A resistance point refers to the point at which a negotiator considers it in his or her best interests to proceed or not. The range between what deal would be acceptable and the resistance point provides an indication of how much flexibility a negotiator has (De Janasz et al., 2014). Cordell (2018, p. 39) refers to this range as a ZOPA (the 'zone of possible agreement' where targets for a negotiation are set as well as any minimum 'fall-back' positions). The preparation period also provides an opportunity for the allied concepts of the best and worst alternative to a negotiated agreement of all parties. A BATNA (best alternative to a negotiated agreement) empowers a negotiator because it means that he or she has other options and is in a position to cease negotiating if an offer is insufficiently attractive compared to others that are available. If the BATNA appears to be likely, then there would be little motivation to negotiate, and if the worst alternative negotiated agreement (WATNA) seems likely, there is a compelling rationale for negotiation and careful crafting of strategies (Lewicki et al., 2016; Fisher et al., 1988). Making the decision on whether to proceed with a negotiation requires careful considera-tion of the BATNA and WATNA (Baber & Fletcher-Chen, 2020).

Gathering intelligence about another party during the preparation stage is criti-cal to successful communication (Dorochoff, 2016). Depending upon the context, it may involve finding out about another company's products or services (Low, 2020) or other details that provide some insight into their goals, initial position, or how they may respond to some kind of an offer (Dorochoff, 2016). The time spent in considering what negotiation counterparts wish to achieve and why, the tactics they are likely to adopt and their strengths and weaknesses in relation to one's own (De Janasz et al., 2014) cannot be underestimated. It is also important at this junc-ture to consider any potential legal and financial implications, who will be negoti-ating for the other party, their place in the organisation, and how empowered they are likely to be in terms of making decisions (Cahn & Abigail, 2007; Hynes, 2008; Lewicki et al., 2007). This kind of information may be particularly important in intercultural negotiations at the corporate level. Armed with information, role playing a negotiation with others to develop persuasive arguments, and indeed counter arguments, can be a powerful form of preparation.

The preparation phase of a negotiation is also a time to consider the advantages and disadvantages of certain venues for the negotiation and whether it should be held in one's own organisation or office, in the organisation or office of the other party, or in some other neutral location. Holding a negotiation on familiar home ground means being able to decide who sits where, when breaks are held and assures access to internal resources and experts (Eunson, 2007). However, a nego-tiation held in the organisation or office of another party means that it is easier to discover more about them, by observing their environment and to leave, if and when desirable, but the lack of familiarity may also give rise to more stress and trav-elling may incur some costs (Eunson, 2007). So, given the risks and benefits of the first two options, parties may prefer to choose a neutral location (Eunson, 2007).

The period prior to the actual negotiation where parties meet is often referred to as the pre-negotiation stage. An essential task is for parties to collaborate on any ground rules including acceptable behaviours, such as remaining respectful, estab-lishing a mutual intolerance for verbal or physical aggression, or any other standards that need to be upheld (De Janasz et al., 2014; Malone, 2017). Negotiation leaders will no doubt actively contribute at this stage in stating expectations. During the actual negotiation phase, those expectations will require some follow-through and modelling such that leaders should avoid using aggressive communication them-selves, or allowing destructive negotiation techniques such as ridiculing, ambig-uous or inappropriate questioning, flattery, or feigned helplessness, for example (Malone, 2017). Parties may also agree to set a date for the negotiation, an agenda of the issues to be discussed and in what order, and identify a neutral, respected facilitator, acceptable to all concerned, if necessary (Malone, 2017).

When the actual negotiation takes place, parties will present carefully prepared and persuasive arguments while simultaneously trying to establish a counterpart's position (Chan, 2020). Information and statistical reports and data may well be exchanged. Negotiators are well served by being competent in statistics and should insist on high quality data (clearly explained and non-aggregated) and an in-depth (Baber & Fletcher-Chen, 2020). In an integrative negotiation, all concerned should be operating creatively and constructively to bring about a mutually acceptable solution and ways to 'expand the pie' in order to achieve that (Chan, 2020; De Janasz et al., 2014). Relationship building not only occurs prior to negotiation or in social activities but can be developed 'at the table' by using nonverbal signals of being positively disposed to counterparts in culturally acceptable ways, listening carefully to build empathy, asking questions, sharing information, and/or reciprocating when others do the same (Baber and Fletcher-Chen, 2020).

An opening offer is normally made quite soon in the negotiation stage and is invariably rejected and met with a counter offer (Lewicki et al., 2016). Such offers and counter offers give rise to concessions or trade-offs. A concession is an effective means of encouraging cooperation by granting something valued without necessarily asking anything in return and is an effective way to encourage cooperative behaviour (Cahn & Abigail, 2007). A trade-off is a useful strategy adopted when certain aspects of a negotiation cannot be agreed upon, but where some other benefit is suggested instead. If the price of a product cannot be negotiated down, for example, free delivery or an extended guarantee may be possible. Negotiators may also draw on a strategy known as making mutual adjustments. An example of a mutual adjustment would be a situation where someone is offered a job interstate and does not find the offer particularly attractive. Employers may make an adjustment to the original offer by offering generous relocation allowances, paying for rental accommodation, and a hire vehicle for a period. Any offers are generally made with care during this phase of the negotiating process because any initial offer tends to influence counter offers such that the higher the initial offer, the higher the counter offer (Maaravi et al., 2011). It is only in the final phase of the negotiation that parties begin to draw conclusions, discuss any concessions, and outline agreements (Chan, 2020).

Post negotiation, it is useful to summarise and paraphrase the meaning of what has been heard and share these perspectives with a counterpart and to seek clarification where any disparity in perspectives arise (Malone, 2017). This process of reflection and discussion is one that elicits responses from both parties and may include feelings as well as content (Malone, 2017).

Third parties in negotiation

Sometimes, negotiators recruit an experienced third party to facilitate the process. Doing so is particularly useful when individuals or groups have been unable to address an issue independently (Miller, 2015). Third parties are valuable contributors to the conflict resolution process. They are able to provide assistance in analysing conflicts from multiple perspectives and are often highly effective communicators (Jameson, 2019). Third party involvement in negotiations may refer to mediation, conciliation, or arbitration.

Mediation is a form of managing conflict which will be addressed in more detail, later in this chapter, but it is useful to provide a brief explanation of it here as it pertains to negotiation. Drawing on the support of a neutral third party has a long history. Mediation has been practiced for centuries in ancient China, Japan, and Sub-Saharan Africa where mediators are viewed as consultants on matters of moral and social values and norms (Mayer, 2020). In the PRC, mediation continues to be encouraged today through the people's conciliation committees (Proksch, 2016). Reports suggest that 90 per cent of approximately eight million cases in the PRC are resolved with the assistance of mediators and this may be one reason why, despite having a population five times larger, the total number of lawyers in the PRC amounts to only 5 per cent of the number engaged in that profession in the US (Mayer, 2020). The expertise derived from these Chinese traditions for conflict resolution has spread around the world and indeed Chinese immigrants are credited with establishing the first US mediation centres (Proksch, 2016).

In workplace contexts, a mediator, is usually paid but nevertheless maintains a neutral role based on their experience and training (Baber & Fletcher-Chen, 2020). Membership in professional associations that set out ethical guidelines generally provides confidence about a mediator's adherence to them (Mayer, 2020) and membership should therefore be checked prior to any appointment. The role of the mediator does not include being empowered to impose an outcome. Of most relevance in this text is in-company mediation, conducted within organisations. In-company mediation may be undertaken by suitably qualified and experienced internal or external mediators (Proksch, 2016). Proksch (2016) describes the characteristics of the mediation process in detail but broadly they entail a preliminary stage of preparation, defining parameters, identifying the main issues, actual discussion of the conflict, agreement, and a post-mediation phase to assess the effectiveness of the process. Mayer (2020) provides some detail to these stages in the process. He maintains that during the preliminary phase of the mediation, participants are welcomed, and the procedure is explained, drawing attention to any opportunities and limitations before expectations and objectives are discussed, hopefully in a growing environment of trust. Ideally, the mediator should not have any vested personal interests but if there are any, they should be declared in order to establish confidence in the transparency of the process.

The mediator will work to clarify some of the background information to the conflict and any feelings involved as well the interests and positions of parties. In discussing the conflict itself, participants are encouraged to provide an account from their own perspective, but urged to accept personal responsibility in what has occurred. Participant accounts are directed to the mediator who is engaged in active listening and asking pertinent questions using neutral discourse, in order to gain necessary insights into the process (Mayer, 2020). Tolerance and empathy for all points of view must be maintained throughout the process. Tolerance requires parties to appreciate that perspectives other than their own exist, even if they are viewed as objectionable and the general approach should be one where the ideas are debated, rather than demonising those who hold them, thereby reducing the potential for aggressive and confrontational behaviour (Neenan & Dryden, 2020). Aggressive behaviour is characterised by highly critical and vicious responses to the ideas of others, blaming, displaying hostility and anger, or denigrating others (Malone, 2017). Under such circumstances, a mediator will make it clear that such behaviour is unacceptable in a calm and neutral manner and at the same time note the strong feelings before eliciting constructive responses from others (Malone, 2017). Each party is provided an opportunity to speak to the mediator privately and confidentially to raise any uncomfortable or sensitive issues that are difficult to discuss when the other party is present. The goal of the mediation is to ensure that both parties are left feeling they have benefited from both the process and the outcome and that their own constructive solutions to the conflict are incorporated into the solution (Mayer, 2020).

Persuasion, information sharing and clarifying misunderstandings are important forms of communication used in mediation (Miller, 2015). Given the communication skills required in this role, Jameson (2019) has expressed concern that organisational communication scholars have paid little attention to mediation. The rise of interest in wellbeing has generated interest in exploring alternative approaches to many organisational practices and approaches including mediation. Baber and Fletcher-Chen (2020), for example, have explored Buddhist approaches to mediation including the use of mindfulness (being aware of self, facts available, positions and opinions as objects of the mind that are separable from the situation or self).

Power and hierarchical position are highly relevant to negotiation and other conflict situations (Cordell, 2018; Miller, 2015). The seminal work of French and Raven (1959) identified different kinds of power vested in individuals. Those with position or formal power ultimately rely upon the belief of subordinates that someone with formal power can rightfully prescribe and control the behaviour of organisational members. Some researchers clearly take the view that exerting power is an undesirable approach to resolving conflicts. Malone (2017), for example, researching in medical contexts, suggests that conflict resolution principles should rest upon a leader's capacity to influence rather than resorting to the power of authority. Someone with information power has access to highly relevant information and can make decisions about with whom that information can be shared or not. Some individuals can lay claim to personal qualities that inspire others to oblige them and this third form of power is thus known as person power or informal power because it does not operate through a formal hierarchy. Finally, those with reference power are credited with something akin to charisma, so much so, that others wish to emulate and please them. Understanding these forms of power is essential for the mediator who needs to address any power imbalances that arise in conflicts (Mayer, 2020) that may be impeding a successful resolution.

Like the mediator, a conciliator does not make a ruling on an outcome but counsels parties about potential solutions or legal and other matters (De Janasz et al., 2014). An arbitrator is also a neutral third party but unlike the mediator or conciliator, has the legal power to bind both parties to an agreement determined by the arbitrator. Arbitration is similar to a formal court process in that parties are expected to prepare and submit documents and summaries of their positions and although relatively expensive, is less so than a legal court proceeding but should agreements not be honoured, legal action can ensue (Baber & Fletcher-Chen, 2020).

Information communication technology (ICT) and negotiation

As with many aspects of organisational and interpersonal communication, technological advances have made a considerable impact upon negotiation. A case in point is artificial intelligence and innovative applications that are able to negotiate. Algorithms developed originally by behavioural science researchers now have the capacity to simulate the human cognitive processes that shape negotiations and can even detect the common errors of neophyte negotiators (Gratch, 2021). For those who lack confidence or expertise and have an aversion to negotiation, using AI options on their behalf may seem particularly attractive, especially since when employees do negotiate salaries, for example, they tend to achieve higher rates of pay than those who do not (Gratch, 2021). Another advantage of this kind of technology is that some nonverbal cues, capable of negatively influencing counterpart perceptions, can be altered using real-time video communication when someone's identity can be altered through a 3D representation interactively and in live communication (Baten & Hoque, 2021). Call centre agents globally who are potentially judged based on their accents and perceived race can have their voices altered in real time to ones resembling the preferences of targets and those who suffer from diseases like Parkinson's will be able to negotiate in real time without feeling at a disadvantage, thereby boosting confidence because tremors that can be addressed technologically, for example, may be judged by counterparts (Baten & Hoque, 2021). Quite obviously there are ethical risks and some benefits in these kinds of situations and especially so when accompanied by a lack of transparency and guidance that comes through appropriate development of guidelines and policies with respect to the use of this kind of technology that will certainly form the basis of a new future in negotiation (Baten & Hoque, 2021).

Intercultural negotiation

Many of the concepts about intercultural communication discussed in Part II of this book are applicable in this chapter but obviously the discussion here focuses upon the context of negotiation. Intercultural negotiation as a study takes a somewhat distinct form from international negotiations. The field of international negotiation pertains to the institutional impact of varied international legal, economic, and political considerations whereas intercultural negotiations are concerned with the dynamic interaction of parties who come from different cultural groups (Kumar & Bulow, 2011). Intercultural negotiation invites one to consider the space co-created by negotiators from different cultures and within which both parties agree to operate. Cross-cultural negotiation tends to be concerned with the cultural similarities and differences between parties and the likely implications for communication. The concepts, or more specifically the studies in international, intercultural, and cross-cultural perspectives, do however inform one another, though according to Liu (2019) far less work has been undertaken on intercultural than cross-cultural negotiation.

The more informed negotiators are about relevant cultural norms (their own and others), the more effective they will be in providing practical advice to practitioners in planning and executing a successful negotiation (see Chan, 2020; Liu, 2019; Pely & Shimoni, 2019). Being open to other ways of seeing things broadens the range of possibilities and solutions beyond one's own cultural perspective (Marsella, 2005). Not doing so is a major factor in the failure of intercultural negotiations and why they are generally considered to yield poorer outcomes than intracultural negotiations (negotiations amongst those of the same culture) (Lewicki et al., 2007; Liu, 2019). Certainly, the traditional view has been that the more similar negotiating parties are culturally (and in other ways too), the greater the chance of successful communication and the opposite is also true (see Beamer, 1995; Ghauri, 1986).

However, although scholars assume that negotiators would benefit from being able to predict to some extent, how parties from other cultures may approach the process (Kumar & Bulow, 2011), very little empirical work is available (Imai & Gelfand, 2010). Some scholars even question the extent to which a particular cultural norm can be isolated as a valid cultural consensus in large organisations with multicultural and international staff (Kumar & Bulow, 2011) and this is relevant to internal negotiations and in terms of each negotiating party being composed of culturally diverse teams, in representing their organisations with others. Another limitation in achieving positive outcomes in intercultural negotiations is that scholars continue to bemoan inadequate opportunities for training in this area (Ting-Toomey, 2007; Woo & Liu, 2001) despite the increasing research attention being brought to intercultural negotiation communication as a result of globalisation and free trade (Gardani, 2017).

The literature provides multiple examples of how culture influences just about all aspects of negotiation (Chung, Eichenseher, & Taniguchi, 2008; Fisher, Doughty, & Mussayeva, 2008; Hofstede, 2001; Jian, Pettey, Rudd, & Lawson, 2007; Lewicki et al., 2007; Low, 2020; Macduff, 2006; Rivers & Lytle, 2007; Ting-Toomey & Oetzel, 2001). They include how parties plan for, prioritise, or approach problem solving and task completion, parties' propensity for risk (see uncertainty avoidance in Part II), what strategies are considered ethical (or not), how emotions are expressed, how interpersonal relationships are conducted and who can be trusted with what kinds of information. Intercultural contexts add additional layers of complexity with respect to the meaning, functions, and dynamics of a negotiation (Kong & Yao, 2019). An illustration in this latter case of trust is provided in one study exploring how Japanese and Australian employees construct trust and trustworthiness in rather different ways (Crossman & Noma, 2012). Communication in intercultural negotiation, in terms of procedures and outcomes, will also be influenced by disparate verbal and written language (Gardani, 2017) that Goodwin (2019) maintains is left largely unaddressed in research about negotiating in a second or third language, unless an expert interpreter is used.

Negotiation and cultural dimensions

Much of the literature on intercultural communication in negotiation contexts has explored the implications of Hofstede's cultural dimensions. The dimension of individualism and collectivism is probably one of the most common lines of enquiry with respect to potential miscommunication in negotiations arising from the literature (Dubrin, Dalglish, & Miller, 2006; Hofstede & Bond1984; Ting-Toomey & Oetzel, 2001). Earlier in the twenty-first century, scholarly studies tended to address this dimension from a somewhat generalised, cross-cultural, bipolar examination of differences between East and West. Part of the motivation for doing so may lie in the intensification of international trade and political relationships since the 1980s (Crossman et al., 2011; Zhu, McKenna, & Sun, 2007) though more recently, such relationships have been tested. Asian countries and perhaps the PRC, particularly so, has, in somewhat blanket terms, been described as characteristically collectivist, though much diversity exists within the PRC itself, if one considers the cultural variations that exist to one extent or another amongst Taoist, Buddhist, Maoist, anti-Confucian, and regional variances (Chung et al., 2008; Dragga, 1999).

Despite the usefulness of cultural dimensions in being applied to negotiation, it is essential to be highly sensitive to the potential for stereotyping that in the view of Lin (2010) has damaged the quality of intercultural research. Cultural dimensions should be set against the knowledge that many Asian collectivists may behave in individualist ways depending upon the situation (Fang, 2010). For example, someone may behave more like an individualist at work and a collectivist at home (Triandis, 1995). In comparing Finland, Turkey, Mexico, and the US, Metcalf, Bird, Peterson, Shankarmahesh, and Lituchy (2007) also questioned polarised approaches to cultural constructs because cultures in their study exhibited a range of negotiation strategies across dimensions.

Collectivists value harmony and the avoidance of conflict highly in communication. To illustrate, the Japanese even compared to other Asian cultures such as China and Korea tend to say, 'we'll think it over' as a euphemism for 'no' in order to maintain harmony (*wa*). To put this into perspective, Japanese negotiators will say, 'no', less than two times per hour compared to Americans who, on average, say it five times an hour, Koreans seven times and Brazilian executives 42 times (see Triandis, 1995; Hodgson, Sano, & Graham, 2008). For this reason, individualist negotiators in negotiation with a Japanese team may wrongly assume that agreement has been established because they have not heard an unequivocal 'no' during a discussion. In Japanese culture, 'no' may mean that someone is thinking, wants to hear more or simply mean that your proposal has been heard rather than constituting unqualified agreement (Low, 2020). Nodding may also be interpreted in rather different ways culturally in the context of agreement such that an American may interpret a nod as agreement whereas for a Japanese negotiator, it may simply convey an acknowledgement that a message has been received (Eaves & Leathers, 2018).x

The tendency for collectivist cultures to maintain harmony is also evident in a broad avoidance of conveying bad news and when it is necessary, to do so indirectly, though reportedly, Asians have become more accustomed to the comparative directness of western cultures (Low, 2020). With reference to Indonesians, Low (2020) explains how in stressful situations, the culturally appropriate response may be to smile in a non-assertive way and the more angry someone else becomes, when faced with a conflict, the more calm an Indonesian counterpart is likely to become.

In a similar vein, the cultural dimension of masculinity and femininity may also have implications for the preservation of harmony. One study found that highly masculine cultures appear to be far more likely to adopt anti-social negotiation tactics (Jian et al., 2007) and another, that in moderately feminine Malaysia, conflicts are often addressed in indirect, conciliatory, and polite ways (Paramasivam, 2007). The dimension of masculinity and femininity is also relevant to the gender of negotiators and their approach to the process. Reif, Kugler, and Brodbeck (2020) challenged the social role theory that assumed women were less likely to initiate negotiation and had lower expectations of success because the negotiator role is inconsistent with the feminine gender role. Reif et al. (2020) maintained that such assumptions would be moderated in feminine cultures where there is a greater consistency between the negotiator role and the feminine role than in masculine cultures where the feminine role and the role of the negotiator are more likely to be inconsistent. Mayer (2020) also supports the view that culture influences the part gender plays in negotiation and conflict on the basis that each culture has its own expectations about the opportunities, roles, rights, and responsibilities associated with gender.

Also, for some time, negotiation scholars have acknowledged that collectivist and individualist cultures approach social relations rather differently in that collectivist negotiators may place a higher premium on developing long-term relationships. In Low's (2020) text, largely directed towards westerners who wish to negotiate in Asia, he maintains that Asian (e.g. he specifies Chinese, Cambodians, Japanese, and those from Kazakhstan) business people tend to prefer dealing with those with whom they are familiar, creating relationships based on developing trust, mutual obligation, and reciprocity that command at least as much attention as profits (Low, 2020). The concept of *win-win* or integrative negotiation has strong associations with the Japanese construct of Gojo-Gojo that pertains to mutual cooperation and compromise, lauded as a virtue in reaching decisions by showing goodwill and making fine adjustments (*Kaizen*) to that end (Low, 2020).

One of the advantages of longstanding relationships is that they are less likely to engage in unethical behaviour (Sobral & Islam, 2013). Negotiators from collectivist cultures (e.g. China, the Middle East and Mexico) will tend to ask individualist counterparts about personal information such as age, family, and marital status that may be met with some discomfort by western individualists (Zhang, 2013) who would prefer to quickly move to task-focused matters (Thomas & Inkson, 2004). However, some evidence suggests that Asian Generation Y negotiators may spend less time on relationship building in ways similar to western, individualist negotiators (Vieregge & Quick, 2011). The emphasis upon relationship development may also be reflected in the observation that individualists tend to change negotiators more regularly than collectivist organisations who view each negotiation not as an end in itself, but as an episode in what may become a long-lasting partnership (Koeszegi, 2004; Lewicki et al., 2007) where the same negotiators are more likely to be in place over time. The relational focus is not limited to collectivist and individualist cultural dimensions however. One might also consider how negotiators from universalist cultures in ideal conditions prepare thoroughly and aim to have an agreed strategy, and attendant drafted contracts ready, in contrast to negotiators from particularist cultures who also prepare to some extent for a negotiation, but will remain flexible until they meet their counterparts in person, and have spent some time developing the relationship, prior to making any decisions or drafting contracts (Velo, 2012).

Face and facework in intercultural contexts

Goffman (1955, p. 213) is believed to have first coined the term 'face' as a metaphor, that he defined, 'as the positive social value a person effectively claims for himself [sic] by the line others assume he [sic] has taken during a particular contact'. His reference to a positive social value essentially meant that individuals who generally wish to be liked, are indeed viewed favourably by others. Goffman (1955), a sociologist, thus saw face as an image of oneself that is presented to others that aligns with approved or highly regarded social attributes. So, when someone conforms to the social expectations of a profession or religion, for example, both these groups and the person concerned, attract a favourable impression (Goffman, 1955). Thus, facework is understood to be socially constructed (Kwek, Wang, & Weaver, 2019).

Cupach and Metts (1994) later drew attention to the implications for identity that continues to be a salient concept in face studies today:

> The conception of self that each person displays in particular interactions with others is called face. When a person interacts with another, he or she tacitly presents a conception of who he or she is in that encounter and seeks confirmation for that conception. In other words, the individual offers an identity that he or she wants to assume and wants others to accept.
>
> *(Cupach & Metts, 1994, p. 3)*

Contemporaneously, a study conducted in the PRC (Kwek et al., 2019, p. 396) defined face as a form of 'self-reflection through another's gaze facilitated by face strategies ("facework") to regulate social dignity'. Face is culturally determined and has implications when people raised in different cultures interact, not least because behaviour is interpreted as being polite or impolite, depending upon culture, in such a way that face-threatening impoliteness may result in face-loss, misunderstanding, or even a complete breakdown of communication (Lu, 2018).

The strategies adopted for facework or face-saving practices will vary depending upon individuals and their membership in subcultural and cultural groups (see Goffman, 2003). This is likely to be why facework and its functions has commanded significant attention and attracted empirical work about intercultural communication in negotiation contexts (Jwa, 2017) and is now widely understood to be an essential element in avoiding embarrassment, dealing with difficult emotions, and building trust amongst individuals, groups, and organisations (Jabs, 2005; Lin & Yamaguchi, 2011; Ting-Toomey, 2007; Ting-Toomey & Oetzel, 2001).

Since the notion of face appears to have originated from Confucianism and is manifested widely in Chinese (Kwek et al., 2019) behaviour and values, it is not surprising to find that face is often associated with Asian negotiators (see Pely & Shimoni, 2019). Face in the PRC or *mianzi* is an important, albeit, fragile commodity about which the Chinese are acutely sensitive to the extent that loss of face, taken to extremes, has led to a loss of life (Low, 2020). Its seriousness is one reason, no doubt, why causing someone to lose face attracts condemnation from both targets and Asian bystanders (see Low, 2020). However, negotiators from individualist cultures also care about face though they may work to protect self-face rather than the face of a counterpart (Lin & Yamaguchi, 2011; Ting-Toomey, 2007). Foreign guests are able to enhance face in another party in the PRC by extending compliments about employees or acknowledging efforts (Low, 2020). Providing recognition even in these rather simple ways carry weight and are appreciated (Low, 2020).

Pely and Shimoni (2019) maintain that face is one of three cultural syndromes; face, honour, and dignity that have been brought to the study of negotiation and conflict resolution by theorists in order to describe and indeed predict how individuals and groups will behave in negotiation contexts. Each of these three syndromes have been associated with particular cultures and dignity, according to Pely and Shimoni (2019), has been inappropriately assumed to be a significant western syndrome. Dignity has been associated with face over many decades (Goffman, 1955; Woo & Prud'homme, 1999) and more recently by Kwek et al. (2019) in an Asian context, suggesting that dignity is not a value limited to western culture by any means and also that these three syndromes are far from being distinct concepts but, rather, are interrelated.

To conclude, face, as a form of public self-image, does seem to be culturally determined and plays a crucial role in intercultural negotiations (Lin & Yamaguchi, 2011; Jabs, 2005). It encompasses notions of status, dignity, and prestige at individual and organisational levels (Woo & Prud'homme, 1999) that, when compromised, place a successful negotiation in doubt.

Decision making and empowerment in intercultural negotiation

Power is highly useful to negotiators, principally because it can be brought to apply pressure, persuade others to concede, and ultimately to bring about the achievement of objectives (Lewicki et al., 2016). How power is used and approached will, however, be moderated by ethical standards and whether a distributive or integrative approach characterises the negotiation.

The literature suggests that culture has a bearing on who has the power to negotiate and ultimately make decisions. Some of the work on power distance, discussed in Part II, is also relevant in that in high power distance cultures (Malaysia, Japan, Spain, Brazil, and Indonesia) the negotiator is almost always controlled by those more senior in an organisation and in low power distance cultures (Australia, Germany, Ireland, Israel, the Netherlands, and America), where power is more highly distributed, it is acceptable for negotiators to operate with far more autonomy. Similarly, Hodgson et al. (2008) have noted how Japanese negotiators are invariably directed regarding any actions or decisions by those in senior positions, prior to the negotiation. In intercultural contexts, who has power in negotiating teams may be inscrutable to the outsider and gender may complicate any assessments further. As Woo and Liu (2001) observed of Chinese corporate negotiations, although women play an increasing part in them, they may nevertheless outwardly display great deference towards male subordinates on their team. Doing so may lead cultural outsiders to make completely mistaken assumptions about who has power in the room.

Time, negotiation, and culture

Perceptions of time and timing are also culturally determined and can influence interpersonal relationships in negotiations. Positive or negative impressions are created through nonverbal messages about punctuality or how much time is allocated to meetings. In Indonesia, Cambodia, and in other parts of Asia, people tend to take more time in meetings early on in the negotiation process in order to observe social courtesies and establish rapport (Low, 2020). Doing so can make the discussion of difficult issues subsequently much easier though it is important to stay away from sensitive topics such as military or political matters that may embarrass Asian counterparts or sex, politics, and religion when a negotiating party is western (Low, 2020).

How quickly negotiators are likely to come to a decision is also linked to culture. Greenberg (2005) illustrates this point in contrasting how Americans respect quick decisions as a sign of decisiveness as opposed to those negotiators from the Middle East who tend to take longer periods to make decisions in order to avoid hasty and ill-advised responses. Similarly, an apparent preference for haste in drawing up legal contracts on the part of western negotiators, believing it will avoid later misunderstanding, may convey a lack of trust to collectivist counterparts (see Hynes, 2008; Koeszegi, 2004; Velo, 2012; Volkema & Fleck, 2012) and impede progress in discussions.

Offers and concessions

The tactic of beginning by asking for more than a counterpart is likely to concede on the basis that concessions will later become necessary is a common amongst skilled negotiators (Dorochoff, 2016). However, culture influences initial offers and concessions (Hodgson et al., 2008; Thomas & Inkson, 2004) in terms of how high a first offer is likely to be and how prepared negotiators may be to revise their initial positions. For example, even though both Arabs and Russians tend to submit high offers initially, Russians are likely to resist altering original offers or accepting concessions, believing that doing so would be a sign of weakness. Arabs, however, are more open to revising initial high offers. In Japanese culture, the approach of asking outrageous prices that are quickly lowered when objections are raised is known colloquially as *banana no tataki uri* because the tactic was historically (if not notoriously) used by Japanese street vendors selling bananas.

Nonverbal communication in negotiations

Being able to interpret nonverbal communication accurately is an important aspect of negotiation (Lewicki et al., 2016) in wide-ranging ways. Competent negotiators observe the nonverbal cues of their counterparts to guide active listening and empathy in their interactions, understanding that in essence, negotiators depend upon one another (Baten & Hoque, 2021; Schoop, 2021). Improving communication has relational benefits. Nonverbal cues influence how a negotiator is perceived by a counterpart and may well have an effect upon the outcome of a negotiation (Baten & Hoque, 2021).

A host of examples of how nonverbal behaviours are culturally bound are accessible in published works concerned with negotiation. For example, the fast-talking western negotiator may feel uncomfortable with periods of silence in discussions with Japanese counterparts and Pacific Islanders who regard silence as a period of respectful listening (Macduff, 2006). Similarly, a smile in one cultural context may indicate nervousness, embarrassment, or that a request is perceived as inconvenient rather than simply the communication of warmth and friendship. Pointing upturned soles towards a Chinese negotiator may be interpreted as an insult (Woo & Liu, 2001). Headshaking conventions in India may also create misunderstandings for western negotiators. In that national culture, the shaking of the head from side to side often expresses thoughtfulness or a positive response but may be interpreted by westerners as conveying opposition (Low, 2020).

Culture to one extent or another also influences how negotiating partners view certain numbers and suspicions surrounding them. For example, in Monaco, the number 3 connotates prosperity. In Hong Kong, the number 4 may suggest promotion. In Asia and parts of the West, 13 is associated with death but Jews see it as a lucky number. In Hong Kong and the PRC, 8 and 6 indicate prosperity and luck, but one airline discovered people were not booking on flights numbered 858 and 859 because 58 means not rich and 59 means rich, but not for long (Huang,

TABLE 9.1 Nonverbal behaviour and interpretations in negotiation contexts

Behaviour	Possible interpretations and notations
Looking left and nose stroking.	Deception (or an itch?)
Rapid eye blinking.	Feeling uncomfortable, tense or alert, being untruthful, exaggeration
Rubbing eyes.	Non-acceptance of ideas and may need more explanation or persuasion.
Face touching/covering with hands.	Non-acceptance or a reaction to perceived aggression.
Changing behaviour.	When consistent behaviours are suddenly changed, it could be a ploy. For example, if someone has not engaged in direct eye contact and suddenly does so.
Crossed arms, furrowed brows, clenched fists and teeth, stiff posture, perspiring, averted gaze, yelling, swearing, sarcasm.	Anger and anxiety. ★ Stiff posture may be moderated by culture in that Canadians have a more relaxed culture which may send different messages depending who the other party is and how they would interpret it.
Leaning in.	Positive response. Leaning in excessively can feel intrusive and aggressive however.
Continual checking of clothes.	Not listening.
Spreading files and possessions on a table.	Suggests dominance through space but will be influenced by culture. Chinese parties will tend to use more space at a negotiation table.
A bright light behind someone who is seated on a higher chair than a counterpart.	A possible tactic to create the impression of power or to accentuate it in order to diminish confidence in the counterpart.
Use the right hand in presenting a business card in Moslem countries such as Indonesia.	The left hand is used for cleaning and toiletry cleansing habits and would be perceived as disrespectful or unhygienic.

2010; Low, 2020). It is not difficult to see how numbers can affect a multitude of nonverbal perceptions and decisions.

Although examples of how nonverbal cues may be interpreted interculturally are broadly useful, the process is complex and mastering the skill takes time and study. Table 9.1 nevertheless provides direction to guide negotiators, based on the literature (see Cahn & Abigail, 2007; Hynes, 2008; Lewicki et al., 2007; Low, 2020). Some of these examples are more pertinent to intracultural negotiations and others are more relevant in intercultural negotiation.

Gift giving

Gift giving in some cultures is a common way of building negotiation relationships (Baber & Fletcher-Chen, 2020). It can be a genuine indication of good faith but in intercultural negotiation, conventions are by no means straightforward and ignorance of them can create unwanted impressions. To illustrate, gifts tend to be viewed with suspicion in the UK, Germany, and Belgium but are used extensively in China where recipients may say 'thank you, but no' before eventually accepting (Cahn & Abigail, 2007; Hynes, 2008; Lewicki et al., 2007). One reason for a degree of reluctance to accept a gift lies in the fear that doing so may later compromise the decisions that a negotiator makes, feeling indebted, in some way, to the gift-giver. Gift giving may include not only tangible items that afford individuals with personal pleasure. The concept also extends to the idea of granting favours, including concessions, or may apply to the sharing of information in such a way that it comes with an expectation to respond in a similar way (Baber & Fletcher-Chen, 2020). As Baber and Fletcher-Chen (2020) maintain, the giving of gifts and favours is integral to the Chinese notion of *guanxi* and resonates with other similar cultural expectations in Japan and South-East Asia.

In intercultural negotiations, it is essential for parties to familiarise themselves with those gifts most likely to be pleasing, conveying genuine respect and goodwill and indeed to ensure that a gift does not in some way cause embarrassment, distress, and relational negativity. To that end, a wealth of literature exists that advises negotiators on appropriate gifts and will not be extensively discussed in this section of the chapter. In China, appreciation for a gift will depend upon both the effort and thought communicated and the expense involved (Crossman et al., 2011; Qian & Keng, 2007). Gifts of brandy, whisky, liqueurs, and mandarins are often well received in Hong Kong and the PRC (Low, 2020). The colour of the gift or its wrapping may also be relevant in any choice made, in that red is considered auspicious in China, for example, whereas in Kazakhstan, gifts in blue and gold are associated with wealth (Low, 2020).

Persuasion

Persuasion (as distinct from coercion, manipulation, and deceit) is a powerful option in the arsenal of negotiators and merits careful attention in planning and remaining flexible as new and unexpected information arises (De Janasz et al., 2014). Effective persuaders are able to establish credibility, reinforce their position, and connect emotionally with their audience (Conger, 1998). Drawing on passion, emotions, and facts in unison is powerful. So is simple, clear communication, put forth with confidence rather than aggression, especially in Asian contexts (Low, 2020). In addition, on an interpersonal level, creating an impression of intimacy and commonality is another effective way to persuade people and gain trust. This assumption is based on the theory of cognitive dissonance purported by Festinger (1957), suggesting that individuals are more likely to be persuaded when ideas are highly similar to the values they already hold. Thus, cognitive dissonance and the allied concept of homophily explain why it is so necessary in diverse workforces for negotiators to become informed and sensitised with respect to the perspectives of others.

Managing conflict

Negotiation is a form of addressing conflict and both negotiation and conflict are essentially communication issues (Bowman & Mulvenon, 2020; Cahn & Abigail, 2007; Croucher, 2011). For more than 60 years, conflict studies have pursued ways to minimise, if not resolve, any deleterious effects in the interests of psychological wellbeing and maintaining workplace efficiency and performance (Pondy, 1967).

Conflict occurs *intra*-personally, *inter*-personally, and between and amongst groups, departments, and organisations (Malone, 2017; Miller, 2015). It manifests in a variety of behaviours such as verbal and nonverbal behaviours, like yelling, focusing on differences in perspectives, crying, cold silences (Turner & West, 2018), and venting. Venting is a behaviour where strong emotions are expressed in an uninhibited way. Pondy (1967) suggested that venting to others helps people to maintain a level of internal equilibrium. However, more recent work maintains that far from assuaging feelings of anger, the opposite is the case and, indeed, venting may well exacerbate a problem (Maravelas, 2020). Presumably, one reason why venting is less than useful is that if punching a pillow or yelling at someone represents a re-direction of anger, engaging in those activities does not actually address the felt emotion. The other consideration is that if another person is on the receiving end of venting, he or she becomes subjected to unwarranted aggressive behaviour that may prove psychologically damaging.

Whether organisational conflict is evident or hidden (Zoller & Ban, 2019), appropriate management is crucial. However, one of the complexities of conflict is that although it is often framed as a phenomenon to be managed, it is nevertheless inevitable and, indeed, a normal part of life and human relationships (Malone, 2017; Tsia, 2020). Although associated with negative events, it can also be positive. Paradoxically, conflict is constructed as functional or dysfunctional, constructive or destructive, productive or unproductive, a threat or an opportunity for useful feedback (see Miller, 2015; Pondy, 1967). Indeed, a conflict may be captured somewhere along a continuum between these respective endpoints.

Constructive approaches to conflict have been associated with many benefits. They include improved decision making, enhanced curiosity, creativity, innovation, the airing of problems and tensions, the clarification of key issues, the facilitation of self-evaluation and change, increased engagement, social cohesion and positive personal growth (De Janasz et al., 2014). On the other hand, unmanaged conflict gives rise to negativity, poor productivity, stress, tension, hostility, and anxiety (Malone, 2017; Pondy, 1967) when left unmanaged or inappropriately so. In such circumstances, individuals and organisations are held hostage to unresolved anger, personality clashes, poor self-esteem, and a loss of self-confidence that unravels productivity, morale, retention, and trust (De Janasz et al., 2014). These outcomes are obviously not conducive to communication, working relationships, or team work, especially where conflicts arise from 'turf wars' (see Malone, 2017, p. 215). Conflict can also serve to diminish the effectiveness of leadership and impede the necessary inspiration and innovation to initiate and lead change (Malone, 2017), crucial to organisational success.

Since employees invest so much of who they are into what happens at work, the consequences of workplace conflicts and clashes can be highly distressing. Maravelas (2020) provides a sobering account of how anger and hostility amongst employees can have a huge impact on personal health. The author explains how researchers often refer to anger as 'flooding', because the body is literally flooded with biochemicals and hormones that can take more than two hours to leave the bloodstream. Centuries ago, hunters in the community who were typically male needed to fend off physical danger and subdue prey. The flooding mechanism was useful because it served to thicken the blood so that if threatened and wounded, a hunter would not bleed as much. Nowadays, in workplaces, although most conflicts are less dramatic than being confronted by a wild animal, the body still responds in similar ways such that, over time, flooding can contribute to arteriosclerosis or hardening of the arteries that can significantly increase the risk of heart disease (Maravelas, 2020). Unfortunately, the human body is highly alert when faced with any threat because people respond to negative influences far more than positive ones (Maravelas, 2020). Apart from the physical impact of anger there are implications for how people think. Flooding also impairs the ability to solve problems and analyse because of its effects on the human brain (Maravelas, 2020). Thus, as conflict and fear escalate, our reactions become more counterproductive and more destructive (Maravelas, 2020).

Organisations have a responsibility to proactively manage conflict both at the macro and micro level, and in response to conflicts as they arise. Crucial in this endeavour is gathering and framing employee feedback positively, rather than as the voices of complaint that need to be silenced, particularly because such actions only diminish trust in organisational justice (Jameson, 2019). Building trust takes patience and collaboration and management can assist the process by making suggestions rather than issuing directives (Goodwin, 2019) and editing out employee criticism as a matter of course. When the ideas of others are indiscriminately disregarded, it is likely to damage creative processes or lead to withdrawal and indifference (Malone, 2017).

Fostering the regular, free, and open exchange of information and ideas, honest communication, trusted grievance procedures, and processes for resolving conflicts are crucial in guiding conflict situations and particularly those most sensitive such as discrimination and sexual harassment (De Janasz et al., 2014; Goodwin, 2019; Jameson, 2019; Proksch, 2016).

Another organisational strategy is the increasingly popular promotion of conflict coaching where an employee is connected with a well-experienced expert in a relevant area who can assist in understanding a conflict and suggest a way to proceed and any necessary communication skills that need to be developed (Jameson, 2019). From an organisational perspective, such approaches or strategies can be brought to prevent conflict through managing communication structurally and addressing them early helps to ease tensions before they escalate (see Proksch, 2016).

On a personal level, conflicts can escalate quickly and leave people feeling anxious, hurt, and/or angry but taking some time to assess a situation and one's own contribution to it, rather than acting impulsively (De Janasz et al., 2014), although challenging, is highly productive. Accepting personal mistakes and faults as well as those of others however is not the same thing as taking or attributing blame but, rather, a process of reflection that hopefully deepens insights into how things got to be where they now are. In moving a conflict towards resolution, it is well to remember that trying to change others is much less likely to succeed than addressing one's own behaviour (De Janasz et al., 2014).

Types of conflict

Over the years, scholars have provided typologies of conflict, directing us to consider 1. amongst whom such conflicts arise, 2. about what, and 3. how they are addressed. How they are addressed often relates to the nature of communication brought to situations. Pondy's (1967) work relates most closely to the first category. He identified three different types of conflict in organisational contexts: 1. negotiation relating to conflict among parties, usually in competition for scarce resources, 2. bureaucratic conflict between parties in a vertical, superior-subordinate relationship, especially when organisations exert high levels of control, and 3. conflict among parties in lateral working relationships. Four decades later, Turner and West (2018) distinguished between conflicts arising from: 1. Content, specifically focusing on any facts or opinions, 2. Image, where a self-image conflicts with the image others have 3. Relational issues such as when parties disagree about how they define a relationship, 4. Meta-conflicts (conflicts about conflicts) and how they are conducted such as listening/not listening and engaging in habits such as 'talking over'. Although some conflicts are related to single, defined issues and incidents it is not uncommon for parties to engage in serial or repeated conflicts (Turner & West, 2018).

Other references in the literature add greater specificity about the kinds of issues that can trigger workplace conflicts or in other words, are examples of the 'about what' variety (see Malone, 2017; Maravelas, 2020; Mayer, 2020; Miller, 2015; Pondy, 1967). They include;

- Incompatible goals, objectives, interests, values, ways of approaching problems.
- Poorly designed processes.
- Negative reciprocity.
- Performance measures that intensify competition amongst employees.

- Personality and working style clashes.
- Role/responsibility/conflict/ambiguity.
- Pressure and stress from heavy workloads.
- Unclear expectations.
- Interpersonal styles.
- Organisational change.

- Remuneration.
- Conflicts about facts based on conflicting or misinterpreted information.

- Different ideas about the distribution of resources, attitudes, perceptions, processes or procedures.
- Threatened autonomy.
- Ambiguous and poor communication.
- Cultural differences.
- Fuzzy boundaries.
- Conflicts of interest.

As Maravelas (2020) has pointed out, conflicts can also be caused by pressures or constraints that are not immediately apparent and urges those involved to explore what may lie beneath a behaviour. Negative reciprocity as a causal factor in workplace conflict is a concept that has been well embedded in anthropological studies for close to a century. It refers to a human drive to match the behaviours of others. In conflict situations, what is known as negative reciprocity is illustrated by the returning of an insult received from a colleague or where an employer is perceived to have behaved unfairly or badly, destroying property or sabotaging systems (Maravelas, 2020).

Stages of conflict

Historically, Pondy's (1967) early, seminal work is largely responsible for the enduring view that conflict progresses through a series of stages (see Miller, 2015). Simply put, Pondy (1967) identified five stages of conflict but acknowledged that not all conflicts pass through every stage. The first stage is one of latency and participants may not even be aware of the conflict, beyond a level of feeling uncomfortable in someone's company. The second stage is referred to as perceived conflict. The third stage is felt conflict. The fourth stage is manifest conflict when it becomes apparent to everyone through observable behaviour such as verbal and physical aggression that a conflict exists. However, since aggressive behaviour is generally discouraged, in most workplaces how the conflict manifests may be somewhat subdued (Pondy, 1967). The final stage is concerned with the aftermath of the conflict. If a conflict is genuinely resolved to everyone's satisfaction, a more cooperative relationship is likely to ensue with participants feeling more confident about being able to address any other issues should they arise (Pondy, 1967). Obviously, some relationships will end badly and irrevocably.

Conflict styles

How people behave in conflict situations is influenced by a variety of factors. Early, formative childhood observations and experiences arising in family socialisation, personality, communities, and cultural factors all contribute to the way that someone learns to address conflict (Malone, 2017; Mayer, 2020). It is also important to recognise that *feeling* and *perceiving* conflict are not the same thing and it is possible for some (but not others) to recognise a conflict with another but remain fond of them nevertheless (Pondy, 1967).

The concept of individual conflict styles was identified early on in research work (Jameson, 2019) and has been associated with scholarship about communication styles (Mayer, 2020). A conflict style pertains to personal, preferred responses or natural inclinations when faced with conflict, though individuals may well respond to different kinds of conflict situations in different ways (Malone, 2017). Understanding the various available strategies for dealing with conflict assists in developing the ability to modify behaviours to their best effect (Malone, 2017).

Salient in the literature (see De Janasz et al., 2014; Jameson, 2019; Malone, 2017; Miller, 2015) are the conflict styles of avoiding, compromising, accommodating, collaborating, and competing/forcing. An avoiding conflict style is one where someone is unassertive, consistently fails to deal with issues or take sides, ignores what they hear, retreats, and hopes matters will resolve themselves without personal intervention. As a strategy, it is rarely useful because often, conflicts will reappear and/or intensify if they are not addressed. A compromising style is adopted when someone agrees to relinquish at least part of a personal goal in order to reach an agreement. Compromising can be useful on a temporary basis when time pressures exist and other conflict styles for whatever reason are not practicable. An individual with a collaborating/integrating style is committed to a win–win and problem-solving strategy. Collaboration is often viewed as a preferred and more effective conflict style whereby someone is clearly highly assertive and simultaneously cooperative, and is able to define a problem and its solution. Integrity, active listening, and honesty are the mantras of those who adopt this approach.

A compromising style is characterised by a somewhat assertive and cooperative approach but only meets some of the needs of parties concerned. Those with a competing or forcing style score high on assertiveness scales and low on cooperativeness and are intent upon achieving personal goals and take a 'I win, you lose' approach without much concern if a relationship is sacrificed. Intercultural literature suggests that collectivists tend to adopt avoiding, obliging, and compromising conflict styles that assist in preserving the face of others (Lin & Yamaguchi, 2011; Ting-Toomey, 2007) rather than competitive styles. Historically and culturally, the influence of the Buddhist faith may be at play here, in its advocation of conflict resolution through compromise rather than exercising power in a coercive manner (Mayer, 2020).

These conflict styles of avoiding, compromising, collaborating, and competing resonate with the following five styles, described by Mayer (2020). They are:

1. Attacking style. Someone who adopts this style is an active participant in the conflict and voices their own opinion, often in an offensive and intimidating manner. Such a person tends to believe that attack is the best means of personal protection.
2. Defensive style. A person with this style adopts a defensive posture in conflict situations and attempts to explain and justify his or her position. These individuals may present as unsettled, insecure, and often appear to have a weak self-image and low self-esteem.
3. Escape/Flight style. Someone with a flight style prefers to avoid conflicts, is evasive, withdraws early on, and, thus, his or her personal position is difficult to establish.
4. Immobile/Freeze style. In the face of conflict, a person with this style becomes paralysed and may be silent, fearful, isolated, and withdrawn.
5. Distraction style. Typical of this conflict style is the tendency to raise unrelated matters during a conflict, perhaps by bringing others into the discussion even when they do not seem to have any involvement suggesting the behaviour is motivated by a desire to create distraction.

Related to the idea of conflict styles is the distinction between 'hot' and 'cold' conflicts because they are also concerned with how people approach conflict. Mayer (2020) provides a useful account, distinguishing between the two. He maintains that hot conflicts are associated with intense emotions and strongly-held ideas and convictions, linked to self-image and where at least one party is unwilling to forego them and is intent on convincing others of their unquestion-able truth. Cold conflicts are as potentially destructive as hot conflicts. They arise from deep internal frustrations and disappointments that are not directly com-municated but are characterised instead through sarcasm, cynicism, and thinly veiled hurtful insults. Conflict parties involved in cold conflicts tend to have low self-esteem and may not be highly concerned about the ethical implications of communicating in the conflict as they do. According to Mayer (2020), feelings of coldness and emptiness come hand in hand with the negative projections on others involved in the conflict and, as a result, direct communication may break down completely.

Intercultural conflict

Culture not only influences how people view conflict but also how it should be managed (Ting-Toomey & Oetzel, 2001). It is not uncommon for conflict to occur because of frustrations over apparently incompatible values, norms, behaviours, language and culture, and the rise of global, virtual teams adds another level of communication complexity because it can act as a limitation to developing trust and effective conflict management (Jameson, 2019; Ting-Toomey & Oetzel, 2001). One of the reasons for this may be that human beings resist anything that creates unacceptable levels of uncertainty and doubt and since cultural beliefs are embedded very deeply within cognitions and per-ceptions, when they are challenged by other cultural frames, they are often resisted (Marsella, 2005; Nicholson & Wong, 2001). However, there are merits in keeping an open mind about conflicts in intercultural contexts. As Marsella (2005) implies, an opportunity to broaden possibilities for resolving conflicts that extend beyond the narrow limits of those to be found through one's own cultural frame, is hugely beneficial. An open mindset is also likely to diminish ethnocentrism, the evaluation of behaviours based on personal cultural standards that so often proves a barrier to communication in intercultural conflict (Ting-Toomey & Oetzel, 2001).

Culture is also intimately intertwined with language, and participants and medi-ators involved in conflict resolution processes are best advised to be conscious of its influence in sensitive discussions. Being aware of how native language affiliation can impact perceptions and have the potential to include some and not others, provides a powerful rationale for investing in the services of a highly experienced translator, capable of ensuring that contextual, linguistic, and conceptual aspects of the communication serve the process well (see Mayer, 2020).

Addressing conflict

Conflict situations often involve participants taking responsibility for their part in how things got to be the way they are (see Malone, 2017). Addressing conflict and facilitating its de-escalation is served by bringing certain tools and strategies to the process. The following suggestions are illustrative (see Mayer, 2020; Proksch, 2016).

- Identify an overarching or superordinate goal that is common to both parties and serves as a motivation in transcending value-based conflicts.
- Establish those things parties do agree upon in order to inspire confidence in progress.
- Bring attention to value differences that may influence the perspective of parties. Owning, naming, and reflecting upon these differences can help to provide insights into how the conflict began or became exacerbated.
- Cultivate empathy (which should not be confused with agreeing).
- Establish facts that can be lost through misinformation.
- Adopt a neutral tone to convey that no blame or judgement is attributed to anyone's feelings or point of view.

Third parties are often called upon to provide advice in managing conflict and, in a sense, advice is a useful tool in managing conflict. Advice is a culturally supportive form of persuasive communication where others can be influenced to voluntarily change their attitudes or behaviour in assertive ways (Bo Feng, Wenjing Pan, & Quan, 2019). Advice tends to be most effective and more favourably received in both American and Chinese cultural groups where it is accompanied by some kind of rationale and sensitivity towards a recipient's face needs (Bo Feng et al., 2019).

Some other techniques arising from scholarly work are elucidated in more detail and include reflective and active listening, role-reversal techniques, using I-statements, framing, and filtering.

One of the main reasons why conflict occurs is that one or both parties do not pay careful attention to what is communicated or is not understood (Malone, 2017). Active listening has been recognised as an important communication tool in counselling (Lewicki et al., 2016; Malone, 2017) and it is highly effective in enabling conflict parties (including negotiation parties) to work through issues (see Macnamara, 2015) and ensure that communication is effective and focused, but it does not come naturally and requires practice (Malone, 2017). Active listening lessens the possibility of a conflict escalating, helps both parties to think things through and communicate in difficult situations, and makes it possible for participants to vent their feelings and concerns without interruption or contradiction (Gill, 2019). It is vital to listen to another party because conflict resolution is rarely about what one party wants but rather an interactive process.

Active listening is characterised, amongst other techniques, through paraphrasing or checking understanding by repeating what has been heard using one's own words. Known as 'mirroring', this concise echoing of statements lets someone know they have been heard. However, westerners should be cautious since in some parts of Asia, summarising or echoing what has been said may be considered extremely rude behaviour if it is assumed that the technique is motivated by the desire to draw attention to some ambiguity in the original statement or to suggest that a correction is warranted (Mayer, 2020).

Effective and active listening can be powerful in conflict and negotiation and is facilitated by asking relevant questions that can 'break the ice' and foster a sense of ease in obtaining and exchanging information (Low, 2020, p. 83). Sometimes questions arise out of a capacity for empathy and thinking about an issue from the perspective of other stakeholders (Cahn & Abigail, 2007; Hynes, 2008; Lewicki et al., 2007). Open-ended questions show attention and interest, elicit more information and ideas, or enable clarification, for example, by asking, 'how did I understand you correctly and/or incorrectly?' (Cahn & Abigail, 2007; Hynes, 2008; Lewicki et al., 2007).

Active listening involves the following behaviour but is mediated by cultural differences (Baber & Fletcher-Chen, 2020; Malone, 2017):

TABLE 9.2 Active listening behaviour

Concentration	Focus on the speaker	Listening to the who message
Suspended judgement	Observation	Making eye contact
Reflection	Checking understandings	Paraphrasing and summarising what has been heard
Separating fact from feeling	Eliminating distractions	Allowing silences
Provide feedback on feelings and content	Using nonverbal behaviour such as leaning forward, extending eye contact, nodding	

Various kinds of noise (see Part I) are likely to impede active listening (Malone, 2017):

- poor hearing
- not understanding the topic
- feeling confused
- a noisy, distracting environment, perhaps using other devices simultaneously
- not liking what is said
- boredom.

It is useful to check that these kinds of noise are not intruding on active listening and ultimately reducing the likelihood of resolving conflicts. Also, by being aware of how we have been taught to think, through experience, it is possible to make changes in the interests of effective communication by becoming more sensitive to faulty thinking, exaggeration, over-generalisation, catastrophising, self-blaming, and misperception about being treated unfairly because these responses tend to exacerbate negative thinking and miscommunication that are both linked to conflict (Malone, 2017).

Role reversal

A powerful technique that can help those in conflict to appreciate the perspective of another is to invite them to participate in a role-reversal exercise whereby each party has to argue the position of the other party or simply ask questions like, 'what would you do in my position?' until some kind of greater understanding and empathy can be achieved (Lewicki et al., 2016). Although empathy will be discussed in greater depth in the chapter about emotions, suffice it to say, in this context, using devices like role reversal to develop empathy is an important means of understanding the values of others, augmenting and ameliorating mutual gains and satisfaction and avoiding unethical practices (Baber & Fletcher-Chen, 2020).

Filtering and framing

Framing is an important skill in communication, persuasion, and conflict management (Lewicki et al., 2016). A frame basically describes a subjective mechanism that people use to make sense of situations through the lens of their own assumptions, values, attitudes, and beliefs (Dwyer, 2020; Lewicki et al., 2016). Framing means that issues are presented positively or negatively, as urgent or non-urgent, important or less important, so a problem may be presented as a major difficulty in moving forward or, more positively, as a challenging opportunity to collaborate on solutions (Baber & Fletcher-Chen, 2020).

Reframing or filtering is a communication strategy adopted as a conscious manipulation of information to make it more acceptable to others but may run the risk of appearing inauthentic from the perspective of either sender or receiver (De Janasz et al., 2014). Nevertheless, it is generally regarded as a constructive technique, often used in intercultural contexts when it involves the positive rewording of expressions in order to manage any feelings of anger or disgust, for example, of another party who may have interpreted a statement as offensive (Mayer, 2020). The technique of stepping back from a situation and recasting someone's words is useful as a way to appreciate someone else's point of view and to facilitate the creation of new perspectives in consequence (Dwyer, 2020). Rather than saying, for example,

'I don't want to work with you because I will wind up doing all the work'.

Consider, reframing the statement to;

> 'I just want to make sure that you will be available to collaborate with me on the project as your input is important to me'.

The reframed statement is able to probe the same issue but it is less confrontational and judgemental and therefore less likely to result in a conflict deteriorating further.

Forgiveness

Finding forgiveness is not easy but plays an important part in moving forwards from distress and conflict. It involves accepting that few people are perfect, least of all ourselves. Forgiveness plays an important part in interpersonal communications but is not always expressed in the same way. Males tend to communicate forgiveness by minimising preceding events that caused a problem in the relationship whereas women favour discussion and conditional forgiveness (Sheldon & Sheldon, 2019).

I-messages and meta-dialogue

The use of I-messages in communication is a technique usefully adopted in conflict management (see Malone, 2017). People tend to send 'you-messages' (ideas about the values and behaviour of other parties) that can be hurtful, rather than 'I-messages' that convey thoughts by expressing personal perspectives (Mayer, 2020; Proksch, 2016). I-messages or I-statements are regarded as an assertive form of communication but nevertheless one that conveys meaning in a non-threatening way without necessarily ascribing judgement or blame (Dwyer, 2020; Mayer, 2020). The value of 'I' statements lies in the fact that how one feels is difficult to challenge (Cahn & Abigail, 2007; Hynes, 2008; Lewicki et al., 2007). I-messages can also help to improve self-confidence in empowering ways because it involves standing up for and taking responsibility for oneself and personal feelings in direct ways (Mayer, 2020).

An example of an 'I' statement might be,

> I feel frustrated/upset/angry/exasperated [express appropriate feelings] when you don't let me know you will be late [name unwanted behaviour] because I am unable to reschedule easily [state the effect of the unwanted behaviour], so I would like you to let me know if you are likely to be late [state desired behaviour].
>
> *(see Dwyer, 2020; Malone, 2017)*

The techniques that can be brought to conflict resolution are not hard to learn but with practice they become increasingly effective and will appear less contrived. The choice of how to approach a conflict, however, will also need to take context into consideration.

Conclusion

Negotiation is a form of conflict and both managing conflict and effective negotiation are largely communication driven. As such, these two disciplines are intertwined and have thus been included in the same chapter. Negotiation is an everyday occurrence personally and professionally. After reading this chapter, readers should be familiar with key concepts associated with negotiation and have an understanding of it as a process and the necessary preparation and planning that needs to be brought to each of its stages. Third party input in negotiations in the form of mediation, conciliation, and arbitration can be highly beneficial in bringing about an acceptable outcome for all parties. The way in which negotiations are conducted are changing as a result of technological innovation that may bring accommodations to those who would otherwise attract various forms of bias. Building on the chapter dedicated to intercultural communication in Part II, this chapter focused upon the context of intercultural negotiations. Topics such as face, decision making, power, time, offers and concessions, gift giving, as well as cultural suspicions, have been explored, amongst others, through the lens of intercultural negotiation.

Managing conflict also attracts significant attention in this chapter. Its causes, defining characteristics, and strategies brought to its resolution have been discussed in some detail, in ways that draw together both theory and practical applications.

References

Altschul, C. (2007). Internal coordination in complex trade negotiations. *International Negotiation*, *12*(3), 315–331.

Baber, W., & Fletcher-Chen, C. (2020). *Practical business negotiation*. London: Routledge.

Baten, R., & Hoque, E. (2021). Technology-driven alteration of nonverbal cues and its effects on negotiation. *Negotiation Journal*, *37*(1), 35–47.

Beamer, L. (1995). A schemata model for intercultural encounters and case study: The emperor and the envoy. *Journal of Business Communication*, *32*(2), 141–161.

Bo Feng, J., Wenjing Pan, S., & Quan, W. (2019). Comparing the effects of argumentation and facework on Americans and Chinese responses to advice in supportive interactions. *Asian Journal of Communication*, *29*(1), 1–17.

Bowles, H., Thomason, B., & Bear, J. (2019). Reconceptualizing for career advancement. *Academy of Management Journal*, *62*(6), 1645–1671.

Bowman, S., & Mulvenon, S. (2020). Effective management of generational dynamics in the workplace. In *Management association, information resources editor: Five generations and only one workforce: How successful businesses are managing a multigenerational workforce* (pp. 76–92). Hershey, PA: IGI Global. doi:10.40181978-1-7998-0437-6

Brett, J., & Thompson, L. (2016). Negotiation. *Organizational Behaviour and Human Decision Processes*, *1136*, 68–79.

Broome, B., Derk, I., Razzante, R., Steiner, E., Taylor, J., & Zamora, A. (2019). Building an inclusive climate for intercultural dialogue: A participant generated framework. *Negotiation and Conflict Management Research*, *12*(3), 234–255.

Cahn, D., & Abigail, R. (2007). *Managing conflict through communication*. New York: Pearson.

Chan, M. (2020). *English for business communication*. London: Routledge.

Chung, K., Eichenseher, J., & Taniguchi, T. (2008). Ethical perceptions of business students: Differences between East Asia and the USA and among 'Confucian' cultures. *Journal of Business Ethics, 79*(1–2), 121–132.

Conger, J. (1998). The necessary art of persuasion. *Harvard Business Review, 76*(3), 84–98.

Cordell, A. (2018). *The negotiation handbook.* London: Routledge.

Crossman, J., Bordia, S., & Mills, C. (2011). *Business communication for the global age.* Sydney: McGraw-Hill.

Crossman, J., & Noma, H. (2012). Sunao as character: Its implications for trust and intercultural communication within subsidiaries of Japanese multinationals in Australia. *Journal of Business Ethics, 113*(3), 543–555.

Croucher, S. (2011). Muslim and Christian conflict styles in Western Europe. *International Journal of Conflict Management, 22*(1), 60–74.

Cupach, W., & Metts, S. (1994). Face management in interpersonal relationships. In *Facework* (Vol. 7, pp. 1–16). Thousand Oaks: Sage. doi:10.4135/97814833269.n1

De Janasz, S., Crossman, J., Campbell, N., & Power, M. (2014). *Interpersonal skills in organisations.* Sydney: McGraw-Hill Education.

Dorochoff, N. (2016). *Negotiation basics for cultural resource managers.* London: Routledge.

Dragga, S. (1999). Ethical intercultural technical communication: Looking through the lens of Confucian ethics. *Technical Communication* Quarterly, *8*(4), 365–381.

Dubrin, A, Dalglish, C., & Miller, P. (2006). *Leadership.* New York: John Wiley & Sons Ltd.

Dwyer, J. (2020). *Communication for business and the professions: Strategies and skills.* Melbourne: Pearson.

Eaves, M., & Leathers, D. (2018). *Successful nonverbal communication: Principles and applications.* Florence: Routledge.

Eunson, B. (2007). *Conflict management.* Milton: John Wiley & Sons Ltd.

Fang, T. (2010). Asian management research needs more self-confidence: Reflection on Hofstede (2007) and beyond. *Asia Pacific Journal of Management, 27*(1), 155–170.

Festinger, I. (1957). *A theory of cognitive dissonance.* Stanford, CA: Stanford University Press.

Fisher, C., Doughty, D., & Mussayeva, S. (2008). Learning and tensions in managerial intercultural encounters: A dialectical interpretation. *Management Learning, 39*(3), 311–327.

Fisher, R., Ury, W., & Patton, B. (1988). *Getting to yes: Negotiating an agreement without giving in.* London: Century Business.

Fisher, R., Ury, W., & Patton, B. (1991). *Getting to yes: Negotiating without giving in.* New York: Penguin Books.

Fisher, R., Ury, W., & Patton, B. (2011). *Getting to yes: Negotiating agreement without giving in.* New York: Penguin.

French, J., & Raven, B. (1959). The bases of social power. In D. Cartwright (Ed.), *Studies in social power* (pp. 151–163). Ann Arbor, MI: University of Michigan Institute for Social Research.

Gardani, F. (2017). Business negotiations. In G. Mautner & F. Rainer (Eds.), *Handbook of business communication: Linguistic approaches* (pp. 91–110). Retrieved February 4, 2020, from https://ebookcentral.proquest.com

Ghauri, P. (1986). International business negotiations: A turn-key project. *Service Industries Journal, 6*(1), 74–89.

Gill, H. (2019). *Communication: How to connect with anyone.* Chichester: Capstone John Wiley & Sons.

Goffman, E. (1955). On face-work. *Psychiatry,* 18(3), 213–231.

Goffman, E. (2003). On face-work: An analysis of ritual elements in social interaction. *Reflections, 4*(3), 7–13.

Goodwin, J. (2019). Communication accommodation theory: Finding the right approach. In M. Brown & L. Hersey (Eds.), *Returning to the interpersonal dialogue and understanding human communication in the digital age* (pp. 168–185). Hershey, PA: IGI Global.

Gratch, J. (2021). The promise and peril of automated negotiators. *Negotiation Journal, 37*(1), 13–34.

Greenberg, J. (2005). *Managing behaviour in organisations.* Upper Saddle River, NJ: Pearson.

Hodgson, J., Sano, Y., & Graham, J. (2008). *Doing business with the new Japan: Succeeding in America's richest international market.* New York: Rowman & Littlefield Publishers, Inc.

Hofstede, G. (2001). *Culture's consequences.* Thousand Oaks: Sage.

Hofstede, G., & Bond, M. (1984). The need for synergy among cross-cultural studies. *Journal of Cross-Cultural Psychology, 15*(4), 417–433.

Huang, H. (2010). Cross-cultural communication in business negotiations. *International Journal of Economics and Finance, 2*(2), 196–199.

Hynes, G. (2008). *Managerial communication strategies and application.* New York: McGraw-Hill Irwin.

Imai, L., & Gelfand, M. (2010). The culturally intelligent negotiator: The impact of cultural intelligence (CQ) on negotiation sequences and outcomes. *Organizational Behaviour and Human Decision Processes, 112*(2), 83–98.

Jabs, L. (2005). Collectivism and conflict; conflict response styles in Karamoja, Uganda. *International Journal of Conflict Management, 16*(4), 354–378.

Jameson, J. (2019). Conflict. In A. Nicotera (Ed.), *Origins and traditions of organizational communication to the field* (pp. 307–326). New York: Routledge.

Jian, G., Pettey, G., Rudd, J., & Lawson, D. (2007). Masculinity/femininity and compliance-gaining in business negotiations: A cross-cultural comparison. *Journal of the Northwest Communication Association, 36*, 93–110.

Jwa, S. (2017). Facework among L2 speakers, a close look at intercultural communication, *Journal of Multilingual and Multicultural Development, 38*(6), 517–529.

Koeszegi, S. (2004). Trust-building strategies in inter-organizational negotiations. *Journal of Managerial Psychology, 19*(6), 640–660.

Kong, D., Dirks, K., & Ferrin, D. (2014). Interpersonal trust within negotiations: Meta-analytic evidence, critical contingencies, and directions for future research. *Academy of Management Journal, 57*(5), 1235–1255.

Kong, D., & Yao, J. (2019). Advancing the scientific understanding of trust and culture in negotiations. *Negotiation and Conflict Management Research, 12*(2), 117–130.

Kulik, C., Sinha, R., & Olekalns, M. (2020). Women-focussed negotiation training: A gendered problem. In M. Olekains & J. Kennedy (Eds.), *Research handbook in gender and negotiation.* Cheltenham: Edward Elgar Publishing.

Kumar, R., & Bulow, A. (2011). Culture and negotiation. *International Negotiation, 16*(3), 349–359.

Kwek, A., Wang, Y., & Weaver, D. (2019). Face and facework in ethnic Chinese shopping-intensive package tours: Dynamics and outcomes. *Tourism Management, 74*, 396–407.

Lewicki, R., Barry, B., & Saunders, D. (2007). *Essentials of negotiation.* Sydney: McGraw-Hill.

Lewicki, R., Barry, B., & Saunders, D. (2016). *Essentials of negotiation.* New York: McGraw-Hill.

Lin, C. (2010). Studying Chinese culture and conflict: A research agenda. *International Journal of Conflict Management, 21*(1), 70–93.

Lin, C., & Yamaguchi, S. (2011). Under what conditions do people feel face-loss? Effects of the presence of others and social roles on the perception of losing face in Japanese culture. *Journal of Cross-Cultural Psychology, 42*(1), 120–124.

Liu, M. (2019). How power distance interacts with culture and status to explain intra- and intercultural negotiation behaviours: A multilevel analysis. *Negotiation and Conflict Management, 12*(3), 192–212.

Low, K. (2020). *Successfully negotiating in Asia.* Cham, Switzerland: Springer.

Lu, P. (2018). When different 'codes' meet: Communication styles and conflict in intercultural academic meetings. *Language and Communication, 61,* 1–14.

Maaravi, Y., Ganzach, Y., & Pazy, A. (2011). Negotiations as a form of persuasion: Arguments in first offers. *Journal of Personality and Social Psychology, 10*(2), 245–255.

Macduff, I. (2006). Your pace or mine? Culture, time, and negotiation. *Negotiation Journal, 22*(1), 31–45.

Macnamara, J. (2015). *Organizational listening: The missing essential in public communication.* Bern, Switzerland: Peter Lang Books.

Malone, L. (2017). Dealing with conflict. In D. Stanley (Ed.), *Clinical leadership in nursing and healthcare: Values into action* (pp. 215–233). Chichester: John Wiley & Sons Ltd.

Maravelas, A. (2020). *Creating a drama-free workplace: The insider's guide to managing conflict, incivility and mistrust.* Newbury Port, MA: Career Press.

Marsella, A. (2005). Culture and conflict: Understanding, negotiating, and reconciling conflicting constructions of reality. *International Journal of Intercultural Relations, 29*(6), 651–673.

Mayer, C. (2020). *Intercultural mediation and conflict management training: A guide for professionals and academics.* Cham, Switzerland: Springer.

Mayer, R., Davis, J., & Schooman, F. (1995). An integrative model of organizational trust. *Academy of Management Review, 20,* 709–734.

Metcalf, L., Bird, A., Peterson, M., Shankarmesh, M., & Lituchy, T. (2007). Cultural influences in negotiations: A four country comparative analysis. *International Journal of Cross-Cultural Management, 7*(2), 147–168.

Miller, K. (2015). *Organizational communication: Approaches & processes.* Stamford, CT: Cengage Learning.

Neenan, M., & Dryden, W. (2020). *Cognitive behavioural coaching: A guide to problem-solving and personal development.* Oxford: Taylor & Francis Group.

Nicholson, J., & Wong, Y. (2001). Culturally based differences in work beliefs. *Management Research News, 24*(5), 1–10.

Paramasivam, S. (2007). Managing disagreement while managing not to disagree: Polite disagreement in negotiation discourse. *Journal of Interpersonal Communication Research, 36*(2), 91–116.

Pely, D., & Shimoni, D. (2019). The culture of interest: A proposed addition and revision of the three-culture model. *Negotiation Journal, 35*(2), 247–268.

Pondy, L. (1967). Organizational conflict: Concepts and models. *Administrative Science Quarterly, 12*(2), 296–320.

Proksch, S. (2016). *Conflict management.* Cham, Switzerland: Springer.

Qian, W., & Keng, K. (2007). Chinese cultural values and gift-giving behaviour. *Journal of Consumer Behaviour, 24*(4), 214–228.

Raj, R. (2008). Business negotiations: A 'soft' perspective'. ICFAI *Journal of Soft Skills, 2*(1), 7–22.

Reif, J., Kugler, K., & Broadbeck, F. (2020). Why are women less likely to negotiate? The influence of expectancy consideration and contextual framing on gender differences in the initiation of negotiation, *Negotiation and Conflict Management Research, 13*(4), 287–303.

Rivers, C., & Lytle, A. (2007). Lying, cheating foreigners!!! Negotiation ethics across cultures. *International Negotiation, 12*(1), 1–28.

Royce, T. (2005). Case analysis. The negotiator and the bomber: Analysing the critical role of active listening in crisis negotiations. *Negotiation Journal, 21*(1), 5–27.

Samina, A., & Vinita, M. (2010). The art of negotiating. *Advances in Management, 3*(9), 26–30.

Schoop, M. (2021). Negotiation communication revisited. *Central European Journal of Operations Research, 29*(1), 163–176.

Schoop, M., Kohne, F., & Ostertag, K. (2010). Communication quality in business negotiations. *Group Decision Negotiation, 19*(2), 193–209.

Sheldon, M., & Sheldon, P. (2019). Is friendship worth keeping?: Gender differences in communicating forgiveness in friendships. *Communication Quarterly, 67*(3), 291–311.

Simosi, M., Rousseau, D., & Weingart, L. (2021). Opening the black box of I-deals negotiation: Integrating I-deals and negotiation research. *Group and Organisation Management, 46*(2), 186–122.

Sobral, F., & Islam, G. (2013). Ethically questionable negotiating: The integrative effects of trust, competitiveness, and situation favourability on ethical decision making. *Journal of Business Ethics, 117*, 281–296.

Thomas, D., & Inkson, K. (2004). *Cultural intelligence: People skills for global business*. San Francisco: Berrett-Koehler Publishers Inc.

Thompson, L. (2009). *The mind and heart of the negotiator*. Hoboken, NJ: Pearson International.

Ting-Toomey, S. (2007). Intercultural conflict training: Theory-practice approaches and research challenges. *Journal of Intercultural Research, 36*(3), 255–271.

Ting-Toomey, S., & Oetzel, J. (2001). *Managing intercultural conflict effectively*. Thousand Oaks: Sage.

Triandis, H. (1995). *Individualism and collectivism*. Oxford: Westview Press.

Tsia, M. (2020). The important issues for millennial workers. In *Management association, information resources editor: Five generations and only one workforce: How successful businesses are managing a multigenerational workforce* (pp. 203–232). Hershey, PA: IGI Global. doi:10.40181978-1-7998-0437-6

Turner, L., & West, R. (2018). *An introduction to communication*. Cambridge: Cambridge University Press.

Velo, V. (2012). *Cross-cultural management*. New York: Businessexpert Press.

Vieregge, M., & Quick, S. (2011). Cross-cultural negotiations revisited. *Cross Cultural Management, 18*(3), 313–326.

Volkema, R., & Fleck, D. (2012). Understanding propensity to initiate negotiations. *International Journal of Conflict Management, 23*(3), 266–289.

Wach, P. (2012). Negotiation without confrontation. *Workplace Health & Safety, 60*(6), 255–256.

Weiss, J., & Ury, W. (2020). *The book of real-world negotiations*. Newark: John Wiley & Sons Ltd.

Woo, H., & Liu, J. (2001). Gender impact on Chinese negotiation: Some key issues for western negotiators. *Women in Management Review, 16*(7), 349–359.

Woo, H., & Prud'homme, C. (1999). Cultural characteristics prevalent in the Chinese negotiation process. *European Business Review, 99*(5), 313–322.

Zhang, Y. (2013). The politeness principles in business negotiation. *Cross-Cultural Communication, 9*(4), 50–56.

Zhu, Y., McKenna, B., & Sun, Z. (2007). Negotiating with Chinese: Success of initial meetings is the key. *Cross Cultural Management, 14*(4), 354–364.

Zoller, H., & Ban, Z. (2019). Chapter 12, power and resistance. In A. Nicotera (Ed.), *Origins and traditions of organizational communication: A comprehensive introduction to the field* (pp. 228–249). New York: Routledge.

10

WORKING IN GROUPS

Defining and differentiating between teams and groups

Scholars have been studying teams and groups for decades (McComb & Kennedy, 2020). The attention is understandable given that intergroup (and indeed intragroup) communication occurs continuously in day-to-day organisational interaction (Rakic & Maass, 2019). The terms 'team' and 'group' are often used interchangeably probably because many findings from empirical communication studies tend to overlap, or in other words, are relevant to both teams and groups (Costello, 2020). In this section, some of the distinctions between teams and groups are highlighted but for the remainder of the chapter, the discussion will focus upon those elements relevant to both, unless otherwise specified.

Some authors have defined teams and groups in terms of the number of people involved. For example, Berger (2016) defines teams as small, interactive groups of between three and 12 people. Linarby and Castro (2021) refer to small groups as those with three or more people connected through a shared purpose and identity. Turner and West (2018) define a small group as greater in number than a dyad but having fewer than 15 members, but at the same time, acknowledge that it is probably more useful to frame groups in terms of their characteristics rather than focusing upon their size. Such advice is useful, especially if one notes that in differentiating teams from groups, size is clearly not a criterion that distinguishes one from another particularly well.

It is hardly surprising that researchers have been interested in teams for some time. They are 'ubiquitous in organizations' (McComb & Kennedy, 2020, p. 1) and most work is carried out by them so their performance accounts in no small measure for organisational success (Hartley & Chatterton, 2015). Teams are also widely credited with a gamut of other workplace benefits when operating optimally. They reportedly facilitate creativity (Grijalva, Maynes, Badura & Whiting,

DOI: 10.4324/9780429318948-13

2020), improve commitment, raise morale, build a sense of fellowship, lower stress, and improve problem solving (De Janasz, Crossman, Campbell, & Power, 2014). Over time, studies about teams have shifted from being concerned with how they are formed, their composition, leadership, and roles but focus has shifted more recently to larger, less stable teams such as supply chains, partnerships, and alliances (Pasmore & Woodman, 2017).

Team members may have individual roles but share an ultimate purpose and are collectively responsible for the performance of the team as a whole (De Janasz et al., 2014). They are generally formed for a specified period and their membership is often flat, in that each member is expected to contribute to a similar degree (Bowman & Mulvenon, 2020). They may be formal or informal. Formal teams are those formed by managers to undertake and report upon the achievement of specified goals whereas informal ones arise through regular employee interaction, when personal needs may be relinquished in some way in the best interests of the team (De Janasz et al., 2014).

Teams are formed for different purposes. De Janasz et al. (2014) differentiate between three kinds of teams:

1. Task-based teams are commonly set up to function in a temporary, low cost, ad hoc capacity, perhaps to develop a product, service, or system, or to address a particular problem.
2. Purpose or mission-based teams are focused upon using organisational resources to produce effective results.
3. Cross-functional teams describe those where members are specialists drawn from multiple departments to collaborate on addressing some kind of organisational issue.

However, another example of an overlap in conceptualising groups and teams is that Turner and West (2018) also refer to groups as being formal or informal, task based, and formed to address long- or short-term problems. When Costello (2020) describes a group as a collection of people who collaborate in a unifying activity or interest, it is difficult to imagine how one might distinguish such a definition from others available with respect to teams. Also, the description of team goals being essentially 'directed towards changing the current state [of an organisation] to some future, more profitable'(McComb & Kennedy, 2020, p. 1) might be equally apt when applied to groups. What these examples illustrate is that considerable ambiguity surrounds differentiating how teams and groups are defined and the ways in which they function.

Lines of enquiry and paradigms in the study of group communication

Much research about groups is generated by communication experts. Those academics who specialise in the study of organisational communication processes may also work with others from multiple disciplines. Enquiry over the years in this area has commonly explored how groups make decisions (Ballard & Mandhana, 2019; Salem & Timmerman, 2018). Early research into teamwork and group decision making, mostly from a psychological perspective, was based upon the work of the Tavistock Institute that focused on training groups (Ballard & Mandhana, 2019).

Costello (2020) observes that groups are a microcosm of the society that creates them. In other words, the culture, values, and norms that exist in wider society will broadly influence intragroup and intergroup communication. Diverse societies are more likely to be reflected in diverse organisational group memberships. Organisations are increasingly recruiting diverse teams in order to capitalise upon their capacity to inform decision making. Diverse teams reflect the perspectives of a wide range of potential consumers and clients in multicultural societies and go some way to offset the potential for cultural biases in the decision making of homogenous groups (Pasmore & Woodman, 2017), though homogenous groups tend to come to decisions more quickly than diverse ones (De Janasz et al., 2014). One area of group diversity research has explored how different generations communicate and work together. Bowman and Mulvenon (2020) point out, for example, that older generations tend to take the view that members should be present while a project is being undertaken, whereas younger generations appear to prefer completing tasks independently before reporting back to the group. That said, the authors note that Generation Ys perform well and enjoy working in groups because they provide opportunities for developing experience in making decisions and solving problems. Because of observable differences in how generations prefer to work and communicate in groups, Bowman and Mulvenon (2020) suggest that care needs to be taken in forming groups to ensure that the respective strengths, values, and motivations of members are taken into account during planning stages and recommend forms of professional development that pair younger and more experienced members in order to facilitate reciprocal mentoring, not least because doing so can improve retention rates and raise morale, and, ultimately, profits.

Globalisation has meant the proliferation of dispersed work teams and much scholarship is concerned with the relationship between technology, virtual collaboration, and decision making (Jameson, 2019) and how they transcend time, space, and organisational boundaries in a shared purpose (De Janasz et al., 2014). Typically, virtual groups are facilitated by Skype, Zoom, and Google hangouts, but a variety of platforms are available and changing rapidly.

Future research in group communication will probably focus on these technological mediums as they evolve. Some innovations in technology and its implications for communication are addressed in Part I of this book.

Much of the communication that occurs within groups is concerned with ensuring that members are engaged and progressing towards their goals. This may involve briefing sessions, setting agendas, and sending and receiving updates (Turner & West, 2018) that are shared, in turn, at the organisational level (Ballard & Mandhana, 2019). Face to face and/or online meetings commonly provide the appropriate fora for performing these functions. As social and goal-orientated activities, meetings, from a communication perspective, involve complex, linguistic activities (Menz, 2017) and formal structures to guide progress. Some of the disadvantages of meetings are that they involve rituals and formalities that can take some time and experience to understand and they are commonly time consuming, inefficient, and tedious (Menz, 2017) unless they are tightly monitored by an efficient chair and members who are able to understand priorities, concisely communicate ideas, and ensure the ideas communicated are relevant to the issue in hand.

Other lines of enquiry in group communication include resilience (how groups recover from adversity) as a critical element in organisational survival, especially during turbulent times globally (Stovernick, Kirkman, & Benson, 2020). How groups evolve over time and any implications for communication in developing relationships, including any conflicts that arise (Jameson, 2019), is another area of interest, though McComb and Kennedy (2020, p. 2) suggest that this is an area where much more work needs to be undertaken. With respect to group conflicts, they are widely considered to be inevitable on some level, and are even desirable, as a necessary condition of change, but engaging in transparent and positive communication, being welcoming, and exchanging feedback respectfully makes it more likely that the conflict will be directed towards constructive outcomes.

The study of group communication and decision making has been influenced by a variety of perspectives or paradigms, three of which are outlined by Ballard and Mandhana (2019) as follows:

1. Functionalism focusses upon the communication of messages. It is assumed that groups are goal orientated and that their performance is directly related to a combination of internal and external influences.
2. A symbolic-interpretive perspective emphasises meaning creation, rooted in the traditions of hermeneutics and the concept of *verstehen* or understanding, and phenomenology that addresses knowledge based on consciousness and experience. The symbolic-interpretive perspective assumes that groups are socially constructed and are defined by or exist solely as a result of member interaction
3. The network perspective considers the ties between individuals and groups with particular attention being paid to the notion of self and collective interests and the obvious implications for social exchange, dependency, and homophily. Theories along these lines date from the 1930s but by the 1990s, network studies became influenced by the rise of network software and emerging ideas about social capital, cliques, and connections among people, known as nodes. These connections are often explored in terms of how culture, trust, expertise, or collaboration, for example, affect team and group interactions. Elsewhere, studies from a network perspective may be directed towards formal groups with designated boundaries, such as political party networks that compare communication patterns from within or beyond them.

ACTIVITY: CRITICALLY IDENTIFYING PARADIGMS IN GROUP COMMUNICATION STUDIES

Select one or two empirical journal papers from whatever resources you have available. Review them carefully and identify any paradigms that appear to influence the approach that is taken by the researchers. Make notes based on evidence for your rationale in coming to conclusions, and share your perspectives and analysis with a wider group.

Group roles

Within groups, members play particular roles that may be productive or unproductive. Such roles are to be distinguished from any title a member otherwise holds and are fluid in nature (Omilion-Hodges & Ptacek, 2021). They may be assigned, or assumed by virtue of a number of factors depending upon their natural inclinations, experience, or personality, for example. The literature provides a variety of descriptions of role behaviours/functions, many of which overlap and titles similar descriptions of role behaviours in slightly different ways. Dwyer (2020) suggests that group role functions can be described as being task related, maintenance related, defensive or dysfunctional. She explains that task-related roles serve to ensure that the group continues to focus on its goals. Maintenance-related roles are attentive to people and relationships, defensive roles function to relieve a group from anxiety, and dysfunctional roles, as the title suggests, impede group functioning.

Table 10.1 illustrates in an attenuated form, some common descriptions of roles (see Dwyer, 2020; Omilion-Hodges & Ptacek, 2021):

TABLE 10.1 Group roles

Role descriptor	Explanatory note
Expediter.	Maintains the group's focus on goals and deadlines.
Information Seeker/Clarifier.	Asks questions, seeks opinions and clarification in discussions in ways that help to reduce the risk of groupthink.
Gatekeeper.	Ensures no one dominates the discussion and that everyone's view is heard.
Recorder.	Serves to capture discussions, often in the form of taking minutes.
Supporter.	Develops interpersonal relationships and tends to demonstrate other-orientated communication. May also provide emotional support to other members.
Tension Releaser/reliever.	Alleviates tensions and encourages fellowship by using wit/jokes, filling awkward silences with chatter, or suggesting breaks. This person displays careful reading of group dynamics but can sometimes deflect a group from its tasks and goals.
Harmoniser.	Assists members in the navigation of any interpersonal conflict.

Role descriptor	Explanatory note
Interpreter.	Mediates and facilitates intercultural communication that may otherwise cause conflict.
Scapegoat.	The scapegoat protects the group from anxiety when it does not function well. The scapegoat deflects attention from feelings of failure or incompetence by other group members.
The Blocker.	Makes irrelevant remarks, spends undue time arguing a point.
Pessimist.	Dwells upon the weaknesses and or failure of the group or its capacity to succeed.
Rebel.	Rebels against group norms and questions those in authority.
Lobbyist.	Seeks to achieve personal goals that may not be consistent with the best interests of the group.
Recognition seeker.	Regularly calls attention to personal accomplishments.
Summariser.	Identifies and summarises key points, ideas, and plans of action.

ACTIVITY: REFLECTION

Reflect upon a group in which you are a member. Consider if any of the roles listed are applicable to your own in the group. Are other roles observable in the members of the group? Can you identify any particular instances where a group member seemed to be playing one of these roles?

ACTIVITY: CRITICAL DISCUSSION

Of the examples provided in Table 10.1, discuss with others those roles which seem to be either; task related, maintenance related, defensive, or dysfunctional.

Social elements and groups

The social aspect of groups is integral to many lines of enquiry and indeed the paradigms brought to their examination. One of the core functions of groups is to fulfil certain employee social needs (Grijalva, Maynes, Badura, & Whiting, 2020). As Linarby and Castro (2021, p. 17) point out, 'Across individuals, societies and even eras, humans consistently seek inclusion over exclusion, membership over isolation and acceptance over rejection.' The theory of social worth affirmation relates to the need that people have to feel valued socially, and positive team and group memberships can do much to alleviate concerns about social acceptance by encouraging members to share useful perspectives (Cunningham, Gino, Cable, & Staats, 2020) in ways that cultivate a sense of belonging. Social acceptance strengthens confidence in personal identity that has a follow-on effect when individuals join other new groups because they have developed confidence in expressing their own unique perspectives in previous interactions that can be transferred to other situations (Cunningham et al., 2020). Favouritism has also been found to influence feelings of acceptance and belonging in intragroup and intergroup relationships and communications. Yadong and Bates (2020) identified how relationships with outgroups are often conceptualised as intercultural because during cross-group communication, members tend to compare their identity group with others. Sometimes, group members may express favouritism for other groups to which they do not belong, perceiving them to have a higher status than their own group or others (Yadong & Bates, 2020). So, group identity and perceptions of status will affect communication amongst groups and how willing one group might be to engage in some sort of relationship with another.

Evolving stages of groups

Tuckman (1965) identified five stages in the development of groups: forming, storming, norming, performing, and adjourning but these stages are to be understood as flexible such that a particular team may skip or revisit a stage. The following table conveys information about each group development stage, drawing upon Tuckman's (1965) work and other sources (Costello, 2020; De Janasz et al., 2014; Dwyer, 2020).

TABLE 10.2 Developmental stages of teams/groups

Forming.	A group is established to undertake a particular task and goals will be defined. Team members may experience a level of uncertainty because relationships are not yet established but, with time, members will inevitably begin to self-disclose as they become more comfortable and commit to the group purpose. Initial discussions may involve deciding how tasks are divided and the resources available.
Storming.	Conflicts arise as group performance is critiqued with reference to the leadership style, alternative viewpoints, workload, roles, the nature of feedback, responsibilities, and some doubts may be expressed about the group's ability to meet its objectives. Open communication helps to keep conflict healthy but if a conflict cannot be resolved then a consultant facilitator may help. Conflicts may lead to feelings of fear and shame.
Norming and Performing.	Teams work through differences and membership stabilises. As the task becomes clear, the team become motivated, working closely together and beginning to recognise member strengths and weaknesses. The group begins to feel comfortable and establishes ground rules and defines boundaries. Norming cannot occur until any anxiety about how members are ranked is resolved. Resistance is overcome as cohesion develops and the group becomes more effective in solving problems and accepting the delegation of tasks. The group takes on greater significance than individual memberships. Work commences, and some conflicts are overlooked in the interests of harmony and the greater good.

Forming.	A group is established to undertake a particular task and goals will be defined. Team members may experience a level of uncertainty because relationships are not yet established but, with time, members will inevitably begin to self-disclose as they become more comfortable and commit to the group purpose. Initial discussions may involve deciding how tasks are divided and the resources available.
Adjourning.	Feelings of disappointment or gratitude for a positive experience. Tying up loose ends as the group prepares to disband. Debriefing on the project and discussing any lessons learned. Commitment no longer required, relationships fade.
Mourning.	Mourning was added by Tuckman and Jensen in 1977 and describes the fear and anxiety that arise as a group recognises that its job is completed and members move into finalising decisions, disengaging, and ultimately separating.

Factors that inhibit group effectiveness

Group performance may be inhibited by a wide variety of factors that managers need to be aware of and anticipate. Some research findings are shared in this section but no attempt is made to rank them in terms of their potential to damage group performance.

Probably one of the best known and documented impediments to group effectiveness is homophily and group think. Homophily is a common pattern of human relationships whereby people tend to associate with others who are similar to themselves and have enjoyed similar experiences (Lawrence & Shah, 2020). As a result, shared ideas tend to take on a highly consistent quality and new ways of seeing problems and solutions are overlooked. This phenomenon is known as group think. Group think was first coined by Irving Janis (1982), and focused on the way that individuals with similar backgrounds and values tend to reach agreement quickly when making group decisions. Although scholars largely agree on the meaning of homophily, less agreement exists about how it can be measured (Lawrence & Shah, 2020). Research suggests that groupthink inhibits innovation, creativity, critical thinking, and seeking out alternative points of view (Chewing, 2019). The most obvious response to groupthink is to recruit diverse teams so that decision making and problem solving can be optimised (see Linarby & Castro, 2021).

Teams and groups perform less well when social loafing is tolerated. *Social loafing* is a term that describes dissimilar ethical perspectives and workstyles, leaving some members working harder than others to make up for the shortfall (De Janasz et al., 2014; Linarby & Castro, 2021). It is generally managed by transparently and methodically dividing responsibilities and embedding checks to ensure that each group member is making an appropriate contribution (De Janasz et al., 2014).

The social aspects of membership in teams and groups cannot be understated. So, when individual social needs are not fulfilled, it can affect the performance of members. Teams can fail when members do not feel they are accepted, valued, or trusted socially and may well respond by being overly cautious and unconfident in expressing personal perspectives (Cunningham et al., 2020). Obviously, when members are reluctant to contribute, the performance of a group is diminished so managers and leaders need to understand how to optimise performance by developing its members as social beings, in order to capitalise upon the knowledge and expertise of individuals (Cunningham et al., 2020).

The personalities of group members and leaders also have an impact upon how well a team functions. One recent study undertaken by Grijalva et al. (2020) explored narcissism, a personality disorder characterised by a sense of entitlement, arrogance, an inflated sense of self-importance, and a lack of empathy for others. These researchers found that when groups have a high mean level of narcissism and individuals in influential positions also have high levels of narcissism, those teams are less well coordinated and perform less effectively than teams with lower levels of narcissism (Grijalva et al., 2020). O'Reilly, Chatman, and Doerr (2020) in their paper on exploring leader narcissism and its potential for contributing to organisational dark sides also revealed that narcissists are less likely to collaborate or demonstrate integrity. Although managers planning group composition are generally not psychologists, many organisations do seek the assistance of psychologists in the final phases of recruitment, who are qualified to make assessments based on test data. Human resource managers may well be able to advise managers confidentially, in selecting group members for critical tasks based on this data.

Leadership in groups

Such is the attention given to leadership that Ruben and Gigliotti (2019, p. 10) refer to it as an 'obsession' but there is little denying that groups invariably have leaders, whether they are formally appointed or emerge by virtue of certain qualities. This section begins with a concise account of salient theories about leadership to the extent that it is useful to do so in the context of groups, whilst also acknowledging that leadership is culturally contingent, as the GLOBE project (see Part II) for example, made clear (Brown, Paz-Aparicio, & Revilla, 2018).

Although leadership is highly debated (Crossman & Crossman, 2011), it is a significant line of enquiry in the discipline of organisational behaviour (Turner & West, 2018). Many scholars agree that leaders have an important role in groups because they guide the actions of others (Dwyer, 2020) horizontally and vertically, and influence what people feel and think (Costello, 2020). Although the concepts of leadership and management have some common features, managers are often described as being involved in planning and coordinating routine work activities and managing order and consistency, whereas leader behaviours include the rather more glamorous activities of inspiring others, risk management in rapidly changing circumstances, building trust, encouraging innovation, and creating and articulating a vision for the future (Dwyer, 2020; Ruben & Gigliotti, 2019).

Traditionally, leadership research assumed that it lay with individuals who demonstrated certain traits (Burns, 1978; Turner & West, 2018), actions, and competencies and often characterised leaders as heroic and privileged in some way (Barge, 2019). Typically, trait-based leadership theories also paid attention to underlying communicative, social, physical, and cognitive factors that distinguish leaders from others and contribute to their effectiveness (Barge, 2019). The trait theory began to be questioned however because successful leaders did not appear to share the same traits (Turner & West, 2018). Certainly, no one universal trait could be identified and no leadership style can be deemed more or less effective without a detailed appreciation of context (Linarby & Castro, 2021).

Situational leadership (Hersey & Blanchard, 1969) emerged as an approach that acknowledged how followers influence leaders. The term 'followers' may sometimes be used interchangeably with colleagues/stakeholder or group members (Ruben & Gigliotti, 2019). The situational approach to leadership assumes that the situation determines what kind of leader would be successful so, for example, start-ups may require one kind of leader and an established organisation may require another (Turner & West, 2018). It is important to note, however, that individualistic or trait leadership theories also acknowledge that individuals can be a leader or a follower but the distinction with situational leadership is in the belief that one cannot be a leader or a follower, concurrently (Barge, 2019). Another leadership theory in a suite allied to situational leadership is known as the path-goal theory. Path-goal leadership is so called because it concentrates on the importance of leaders providing members with a clear path towards a particular goal (Linarby & Castro, 2021). Phillips and Phillips (2016) maintain that this theory is robust, cognitively grounded and a well-established framework, incorporating elements of the leader-follower perspectives embedded in situational leadership. Others have criticised the theory as being unduly complex with inconclusive research findings and an inadequate recognition of the abilities and contribution of followers (see Ruben & Gigliotti, 2019). Nevertheless, path-goal theory is also associated with initiatives that focus on motivating followers and encouraging them to feel they are able to perform their work and that their efforts will result in success (Ruben & Gigliotti, 2019). Leaders who embrace this approach tend to encourage a supportive, participative, and achievement-orientated experience, mindful of the need to respond quickly to the needs and wants of subordinate/followers (Farhan, 2018, p. 17). Both trait and situational theories are described by Ruben and Gigliotti (2019, p. 22) as 'classical' approaches to leadership.

The study of transformational leadership was introduced by Burns (1978). Transformational leadership also assumed that leaders and followers interact interdependently, such that leadership depends upon the perceptions and support of followers and vice versa (Turner & West, 2018). That support or compliance depends upon much more than authority, as followers expect leaders to demonstrate many other qualities, including having respect for those they lead and displaying authenticity (Pasmore & Woodman, 2017). Some have even referred to authentic leadership in its own right, although allied to both transformational and servant leadership. Authentic leadership pays particular attention to the role of self-awareness, a sense of moral perspective, relational transparency, and being true to oneself in ways that promote an aura of trustworthiness (Ruben & Gigliotti, 2019). Transformational leadership, however, is credited with a high level of idealisation that can be highly motivating (Barge, 2019) for group members in inspiring them to transcend self-interest for the good of a group and, ultimately, the organisation (Huhn, Meyer, &

Racelis, 2018). However, a level of complexity exists in distinguishing leadership from followership. As Crossman and Crossman (2011) noted, within the literature, the concepts of leadership and followership tends to be represented or defined in very similar ways.

Historical and cultural factors have also contributed to some overlapping in the conceptual development of transformational, environmental, and spiritual leadership, that appear to promote and demonstrate some common values, gathering up allied constructs such as the notion of the social good, stewardship, sustainability, calling, meaning, connectedness, and servanthood or servant leadership (Crossman, 2011). Spiritual leadership is a line of enquiry within workplace spirituality discussed in Part II. Similarly, moral leadership is concerned with taking a moral stance on issues and convincing others to do likewise (Solinger, Jansen, & Cornelissen, 2020). Servant leadership emerged from the seminal work of Robert Greenleaf in the 1970s (Greenleaf, 1991). Like transformational leadership, servant leadership is characterised by prioritising follower wellbeing over self-interest but has been criticised for its lack of a consistent theoretical framework and an overly idealistic and moralising tone (Ruben & Gigliotti, 2019). Ruben and Gigliotti (2019) label these forms of leadership, including authentic leadership, as contemporary approaches.

Transactional leadership also considers the interaction between leaders and followers but constructs the relationship between them as one based on social exchange, such that leaders are able to achieve follower compliance through the granting of contingent and noncontingent rewards (Barge, 2019; Linarby & Castro, 2021). Transactional leaders also tend to be adept at guiding followers towards the achievement of goals by assiduously clarifying requirements (Huhn et al., 2018). In similar ways, leader-member exchange (LMX) theory also acknowledges that leadership depends upon, is complemented by and shared or distributed amongst group members (Barge, 2019). Leader-member exchange theory marked a significant shift away from leadership traits, characteristics, and behaviours and is considered to be one of the first relational and people-centred approaches to leadership (Omilion-Hodges & Ptacek, 2021).

ACTIVITY: RESEARCH, EXPERIENTIAL, AND REFLECTION

Identify someone in your own experience of an organisation or a group who you believed displayed the qualities of a leader. It may be sensitive to keep this person's identity anonymous in your discussions with others. Reflect upon their actions and approaches as a leader and drawing upon supporting literature from sources available to you, consider the kind of leader they appear to be, based on the theories presented in this chapter and your own experience. Were there any behavioural factors that you feel distracted from this person's success as a leader, and may have had a negative impact upon group performance? Discuss with others, the conclusions you came to.

Leadership and communication

One of the most widely explored areas of group communication lies in leadership (Linarby & Castro, 2021). Leadership communication tends to focus upon how language and discourse create meaning about what is happening in organisations (Barge, 2019). Other lines of enquiry are explored in the context of leadership and communication in areas that hone in on situations where negotiation, culture, reflexivity, ethics, and how social influence and leadership work together dynamically (Ruben & Gigliotti, 2019). Leaders communicate with others, taking into consideration their roles, tasks and goals in order to fulfil a particular vision. They use communication to motivate others and to encourage productive and healthy relationships (Brown et al., 2018) and largely through communication, leaders become powerful 'agents of social influence' (Ruben & Gigliotti, 2019, p. 15).

However, leader communication styles will mean their influence on organisational groups will vary, suggesting that not all leadership is inherently 'good' or necessarily focused on the wellbeing of their members. For example, in their study of leader communication styles in Peru, Brown et al. (2018) distinguished between leaders with an aggressive communication style and those who had what they referred to as a questioning communication style. The former display anger and displeasure, rely on authoritarianism, and such individuals may well make derogatory remarks with little respect for the opinions and feelings of subordinates whereas the latter invite open discussion and debate in ways that improve commitment. The personalities of leaders thus influence groups and more broadly, organisational culture, positively or negatively (Brown et al., 2018; O'Reilly et al., 2020; Dwyer, 2020). However, although considerations about the interplay of personality and leadership have been debated for some time, most scholars agree that whatever part personality does play in effective leadership, it is not the only determinant because leadership can be learned and developed, experientially and otherwise (Ruben & Gigliotti, 2019).

Some communication research has considered the ways in which gender is relevant to leadership. More than a decade ago, Kelan and Dunkley Jones (2010) observed that leadership communication tends to be constructed in masculine speech that highlights assertion, independence, competitiveness, and confidence. These findings were not surprising given the dominance of males in organisational leadership positions. They did raise questions about whether other genders need to replicate similar means of communication in order to be accepted as leaders. The dangers of females adopting male communication patterns have been noted in Part II of this book but it now seems clear that females can and do bring positive benefits to the groups they lead. For example, women in leadership positions use humour more often and in more inclusive ways than males (Menz, 2017) and it has been known for some time that staff retention is also improved when females are recruited to leadership positions (Kreitner & Kinicki, 1998; Perriton, 2009). More attention, however, needs to be brought to studying the implications of a wider range of genders in leadership positions.

Conclusion

This chapter has provided a brief account of group communication and the role of leadership. It began with some clarification of the concepts of teams and groups and described some of the paradigms brought to lines of enquiry in group communication. The relevance of social needs to communication and the experience of group members was also highlighted. How groups evolve and what factors impede their success is a critical aspect of forming and leading them towards realising their goals. The chapter concludes with a section that provides an attenuated presentation of leadership theories and some of the implications of leader communication.

References

Ballard, D., & Mandhana, D. (2019). Groups, teams & decision making. In A. Nicotera (Ed.), *Origins and traditions of organizational communication to the field* (pp. 288–306). New York: Routledge.

Barge, J. (2019). A communicative approach to leadership. In A. Nicotera (Ed.), *Origins and traditions of organizational communication to the field* (pp. 326–347). New York: Routledge.

Berger, A. (2016). *Messages: An introduction to communication.* Retrieved from https://ebook-central.proquest.com

Bowman, S., & Mulvenon, S. (2020). Effective management of generational dynamics in the workplace. In *Management association, information resources editor: Five generations and only one workforce: How successful Businesses are managing a multigenerational workforce* (pp. 76–92). Hershey, PA: IGI Global. doi:10.40181978-1-7998-0437-6

Brown, O., Paz-Aparicio, C., & Revilla, A. (2018). Leader's communication style, LMX and organizational commitment: A study of employee perceptions in Peru. *Leadership & Organization Development Journal, 40*(2), 230–258.

Burns, J. (1978). *Leadership.* New York: Harper & Row Publishers.

Chewing, L. (2019). Communications networks. In A. Nicotera (Ed.), *Origins and traditions of organizational communication to the field* (pp. 168–186). London: Routledge.

Costello, J. (2020). *Workplace wellbeing: A relational approach.* London: Routledge.

Crossman, J. (2011). Environmental and spiritual leadership: Tracing the synergies from an organizational perspective. *Journal of Business Ethics, 103*(4), 553–565.

Crossman, B., & Crossman, J. (2011). Conceptualising followership – a review of the literature. *Leadership, 7*(4), 481–497.

Cunningham, J., Gino, F., Cable, D., & Staats, B. (2020). Seeing oneself as a valued contributor: Social worth affirmation improves team information sharing. *Academy of Management Journal.* doi:10.5465/amj.20180790

De Janasz, S., Crossman, J., Campbell, N., & Power, M. (2014). *Interpersonal skills in organisations,* Sydney: McGraw-Hill Education.

Dwyer, J. (2020). *Communication for business and the professions: Strategies and skills.* Melbourne: Pearson.

Farhan, B. (2018). Application of path-goal leadership theory and learning theory in a learning organisation. *The Journal of Applied Business Research, 34*(1), 13–22.

Greenleaf, R. (1991). *Servant leadership: A journey into the nature of legitimate power and greatness.* New York: Paulist Press.

Grijalva, E., Maynes, T., Badura, K., & Whiting, S. (2020). Examining the 'I' in team: A longitudinal investigation of the influence of team narcissism composition on team outcomes in the NBA. *Academy of Management Journal, 63*(1), 7–33.

Hartley, P., & Chatterton, P. (2015). *Business communication: Rethinking your professional practice for the post digital age* (2nd ed.). London and New York: Routledge.

Hersey, P., & Blanchard, K. (1969). Management of organizational behavior. *Academy of Management Journal, 12*(4), 526–526.

Huhn, M., Meyer, M., & Racelis, A. (2018). Virtues and the common good in leadership. In A. J. Sison, I. Ferraro, & G. Guitian (Eds.), *Business ethics: A virtue ethics and common good approach* (pp. 24–50). London: Taylor & Francis Group.

Jameson, J. (2019). Conflict. In A. Nicotera (Ed.), *Origins and traditions of organizational communication to the field* (pp. 307–326). New York: Routledge.

Janis, I. (1982). *Groupthink*. Boston: Houghton-Miltlin.

Kelan, E., & Dunkley Jones, R. (2010). Gender and the MBA. *Academy of Management Learning & Education, 9*(1), 26–43.

Kreitner, R., & Kinicki, A. (1998). *Organizational behaviour*. New York: McGraw-Hill.

Lawrence, B., & Shah, N. (2020). Homophily: Measures and meaning. *Academy of Management Annals, 14*(2), 513–592.

Linarby, J., & Castro, M. (2021). *Small group communication: Forming and sustaining teams*. Small Group Publication.

McComb, S., & Kennedy, D. (2020). *Computational methods to examine team communication*. Cham, Switzerland: Springer.

Menz, F. (2017). Business meetings. In G. Mautner & F. Rainer (Eds.), *Handbook of business communication: Linguistic approaches* (pp. 111–131). Boston: De Gruyter. doi:10.1515/9781614514862

Omilion-Hodges, L., & Ptacek, J. (2021). *Leader-member exchange and organizational communication: Facilitating a healthy work environment*. Cham, Switzerland: Springer.

O'Reilly, C., Chatman, J., & Doerr, B. (2020). When 'Me' Trumps 'We': Narcissistic leaders and the cultures they create. *Academy of Management Discoveries*. doi:10.5465/amd.2019.0163

Pasmore, W., & Woodman, R. (2017). The future of research and practice in organizational change and development. In *Research in organizational change and development* (Vol. 25, pp. 1–32). Bingley: Emerald Publishing Limited. doi:10.1108/50897-3016201

Perriton, L. (2009). 'We don't want complaining women!' A critical analysis of the business case for diversity. *Management Communication Quarterly, 23*(2), 218–243.

Phillips, A., & Phillips, C. (2016). Behavioural styles of path-goal theory: An exercise for developing leadership skills. *Management Teaching Review, 1*(13), 148–158.

Rakic, T., & Maass, A. (2019). Communicating between groups, communicating about groups. In H. Giles, J. Harwood, J. Gasiorek, H. Pierson, J. Nussbaum, & C. Gallois (Eds.), *Language, communication and intergroup relations: A celebration of the scholarship of Howard Giles* (pp. 66–97). New York: Routledge.

Ruben, B., & Gigliotti, A. (2019). *Leadership, communications and social influence: A theory of resonance, activation and cultivation*. Bingley: Emerald Publishing.

Salem, P. J., & Timmerman, C. E. (2018). Forty years of organizational communication. In P. Salem & E. Timmerman (Eds.), *Transformative practice and research in organizational communication* (pp. 1–28). Hershey, PA: IGI Global. doi:10.4018/978-1-5225-2823-4.ch001

Solinger, O., Jansen, P., & Cornelissen, J. (2020). The emergence of moral leadership. *Academy of Management Review, 45*(3), 504–527.

Stovernick., A., Kirkman, S., &Benson, R. (2020). Bouncing back together: Toward a theoretical model of work team resilience. *Academy of Management Review, 45*(2), 395–422.

Tuckman, B. (1965). Developmental sequences in small groups. *Psychological Bulletin, 63*(6), 384–399.

Tuckman, B., & Jensen, M. (1977). Stages of small-group development revisited. *Group and Organization* Studies, *2*(4), 419–427.

Turner, L., & West, R. (2018). *An introduction to communication.* Cambridge: Cambridge University Press.

Yadong, J., & Bates, B. (2020). Measuring intercultural/international outgroup favouritism: Comparing two measures of cultural cringe. *Asian Journal of Communication, 30*(2), 141–154.

11

DEVELOPING OTHERS FOR GROWTH

Developing employees for organisational growth

Employees and organisations need to grow in order to maximise capability in periods of continuous change. Some of the basic principles of change have already been addressed in Part I of this book and will serve well to create a sense of context for discussing personal and organisational growth and development largely from a communication and relational perspective. Growing means having the resources to be flexible, often in a state of 'not knowing' (Crossman & Doshi, 2014) when crises or, simply, the pace of change demand it. Taking the perspective of the mentee, Axelrod (2019) describes growth as the means to enjoy increased engagement, more confidence, better performance and career development. It is no accident that mentoring has gained momentum from the 1980s in a climate of competition and fast-changing markets where those who are innovative, creative, and flexible are able to quickly adapt and learn in change environments (Gray, Garvey, & Lane, 2016). To grow, organisations and employees need to be attuned to these changing demands and circumstances and to be ready for them, having the skill sets, insights, and capacity to deal with them.

Much of the literature on mentoring and coaching has directed attention to western and, particularly, North American contexts. It is clear that scholars and publishers would profit from broadening the range of publications to accommodate other cultural settings, particularly in Asia. Countries like India and China, for example, are significant economic, political, and military hubs of innovation and many western companies are owned by individual business entrepreneurs and organisations from the East (Gray et al., 2016). Indeed, the demand for coaching and mentoring programmes in the East is on the rise and opportunities for experts in the field exist but what is needed is a departure from Anglo-American psychological mindsets and a drastic shift towards thinking and leading programmes

DOI: 10.4324/9780429318948-14

that are more representative of Eastern perspectives and transpersonal philosophies (Gray et al., 2016).

Developing concepts and approaches for mentoring

Mentoring has traditionally been defined as an interpersonal, dyadic relationship between a mentor, as a senior employee, and a mentee within the same organisation (Chandler, Murphy, Kram, & Higgins, 2016; De Janasz, Crossman, Campbell, & Power, 2014). This construction likely emanates from Kram's early work in the 1980s that many scholars still appear to accept today (see for example, Lim & Parker, 2020). That said, this chapter will explore other ideas or constructions of the mentoring relationship.

The term 'mentor' is derived from a king in Greek mythology who appointed his trusted friend, named Mentor, to educate his son (Lim & Parker, 2020). Historically, mentoring practices in one form or another, dates back centuries. Indirect references were made to relationships that appeared to involve some kind of mentoring between knights and squires in England (Gray et al., 2016) and it is likely similar relationships, particularly in religious and military contexts, were occurring in other parts of the world too. It was not until the eighteenth century however, that the word 'mentoring' was recorded in the English language in a letter from Lord Chesterfield to his son (Gray et al., 2016).

Gray et al. (2016) maintain that both coaching and mentoring are contested and diversified fields. Some of this debate surrounds how coaching and mentoring are defined and differentiated. Kram (1983) viewed coaching as an alternative form of mentoring. More recently, Lim and Parker (2020) suggest that mentoring is concerned with nurturing the whole person – a process that takes some time because it entails getting to know someone quite well. However, coaching, they suggest, is far less time consuming since it is usually limited to assisting someone to improve in the performance of a specific skill. Discussion amongst scholars is also evident in distinguishing formal and informal forms of mentoring, both of which make an important contribution to the enculturation of individuals into organisations (Chandler et al., 2016). Some view formal mentoring arrangements as those that are assigned for a specific period to address particular goals, generally on a top-down basis between a supervisor/senior/manager and a mentee (who does not always have much say or choice on matter), while informal mentoring is thought to occur organically (Atay, 2021; De Janasz, et al., 2014). Lim and Parker (2020) account for the contested distinctions between formal and informal mentoring as a consequence of the growing number of alternative constructions for the mentor and the mentee. One perspective, these authors relate, is that if a mentor engages voluntarily in the process, then the relationship is considered informal but if the mentor is coerced in some way or reluctant, then the mentoring is determined as formal. Others, according to Lim and Parker (2020), simply (or simplistically) take the view that if the mentoring process takes some time, then it is regarded as formal and that if it doesn't, it must be informal. So, even basic concepts associated with mentoring are somewhat inconsistent. Added to the criticism that mentoring lacks robust empirical research and is too dependent upon small-scale case studies (Gray et al., 2016) it would seem that the field is ripe for further investigation.

A prime rationale for research about mentoring lies in the benefits that studies reveal in their findings across a wide range of industries (e.g., healthcare, education and the military in the US and Singapore) (Chandler et al., 2016; Lim & Parker, 2020). These benefits extend to both the individuals involved and the organisations that employ them. From an organisational perspective, mentoring is valued as a means of developing human resources that can facilitate the process of socialising and assimilating new recruits into a particular culture (Lim & Parker, 2020). Other benefits arising from the literature also include; greater preparedness for responsibility, leadership/career advancement/promotion, higher levels of performance, and morale that contribute towards enculturation (Chandler et al., 2016; De Janasz et al., 2014; Lim & Parker, 2020; Peno, Silva, & Kenahan, 2016). Additionally, individuals may enjoy a strengthened self-esteem, self-efficacy, and a sense of identity, improved communication skills, and entry to networks and relationships not otherwise available (Chandler et al., 2016; De Janasz et al., 2014).

However, any gains that come with mentoring can be diminished in certain circumstances. In the best of circumstances, a mentor can experience a great deal of personal satisfaction in helping others (De Janasz et al., 2014) but that satisfaction is less likely to occur in situations where a mentor feels obligated rather than enthusiastic about undertaking a responsibility, perhaps because it holds no intrinsic attraction or where it adds to an already taxing workload. Similarly, mentees may also have reservations, especially when there is lack of transparency about why the mentoring relationship has been suggested. Given the power implications in allocating a mentor to mentee, the notion of mentoring being a voluntary process as suggested by Axelrod (2019) is debatable. The consequences of coercion, subtle or otherwise, can backfire and result in few positive outcomes for either party. There are also occasions when the kind of support an employee needs at a particular point in time might be a trusted friend or therapist rather than an organisational mentor (Fournier, 2018). Finally, mentoring may not succeed at the wrong time or when other related issues in the organisation are left unaddressed. For example, when employees are experiencing high levels of emotional labour or demanding workloads (see Denker et al., 2021), there may be little appetite from the perspective of mentor or mentee in undertaking another time-consuming obligation and forcing the issue may well be counterproductive. As Fournier (2018) observed, sometimes it is in the interests of all concerned to decline the opportunity.

Declining an opportunity for mentoring when time is short is understandable given the exacting responsibilities that come with the role. Axelrod (2019) suggests that the role for a mentor is to provide a safe conversational space in order to:

- support career ambitions and aspirations
- boost confidence
- broaden perspectives

- raise awareness
- overcome obstacles
- encourage experimentation
- increase a mentee's influence
- sustain a momentum for growth
- assist in expanding a mentee's influence
- provide a clear structure and ground rules, focusing on a mentee's professional growth.

The demanding nature of the role of mentor, however, is not without limitations and does not extend to being responsible for the work duties of a mentee or fulfilling performance requirements (Axelrod, 2019). This is why it is so important to clarify expectations with respect to the roles of mentor and mentee from the outset.

Scoping mentoring research

A burgeoning literature is devoted to mentoring that has focused almost exclusively upon organisational contexts and career development (Chandler et al., 2016; Trebing & Atay, 2021). Kram's (1983) early, seminal work was based upon a qualitative study of mentoring relationships with data collected from interviews in one corporate setting and she found that the process facilitates both career and psychosocial development. For Kram (1983) the relational element of mentoring was a defining issue, its exact nature determined by individual needs and organisational circumstances. Psycho-social forms of mentoring have typically emphasised counselling, role-modelling, and friendship (Chandler et al., 2016; Kram, 1983). Friendship and the associated ethical implications in such relationships continues to be acknowledged as a key element in mentoring relationships co-constructed by mentor and mentee (see Petre, Giorgia, Petre, & Harshbarger, 2021).

It is now generally considered unlikely that an individual will have all their career needs met by a single source of support so mentoring strategies are more likely to encompass both formal and informal approaches with applications across varied contexts (Chandler et al., 2016). This recognition has also largely given rise to the growth of interest in developmental networks. A developmental networks approach is a departure from the traditional form of mentoring as a single, dyadic relationship between senior mentee and subordinate in a top-down approach towards a network of developers (Chandler et al., 2016; Chang, Baek, & Kim, 2021). The approach has been adopted in a variety of industries including sport (see Lefabvre, Bloom, & Duncan, 2021).

Simply put, a developmental network is a group of people from varied social spheres including those formally assigned or informally cultivated relationships that work to enhance someone's personal and professional growth (Chandler et al., 2016). Developmental networks explain how individuals in 'real life' access multiple mentoring experiences and scholars are keen to clarify what factors contribute to their effectiveness (Chandler et al., 2016). One study undertaken in Korea explored female experiences of developmental networks, motivated by the perspective that 'women's success at work matters' (Chang et al., 2021, p. 733). The results were encouraging such that developmental networks were found to have a positive effect on career development, career satisfaction and psycho-social support with the potential to address the problem of female under-participation at senior levels of organisations.

Although power enters into all mentoring relationships in one form or another (Denker et al., 2021), developmental networks and peer mentoring have found favour in the literature as alternatives to the top-down, formal approach to mentoring. Another advantage of peer mentoring is that it facilitates higher levels of reciprocity in the process, in contrast to top-down mentoring relationships, where a mentor is unlikely to openly express ideas given the power imbalance and lack of confidentiality (Axelrod, 2019). A peer who has been through a recent, similar experience in an organisation (such as onboarding) may also relate most closely to it (Fournier, 2018). Greater trust, too, may be exhibited for peers than for managers though without any contract in place, informal collegial support may end, sometimes abruptly when workloads intensify and relationships turn sour (Axelrod, 2019). Alternatives to top-down, traditional approaches to mentoring are now also being explored in creative ways to facilitate diversity and provide support for otherwise marginalised employees. Over time, some research has attended to the role that factors like personality, age, race, and gender play in the mentoring process (Chandler et al., 2016) though Trebing and Atay (2021) suggest that few of these studies appear to reflect feminist perspectives or offer a counter to perpetuating power structures that privilege white males.

Understanding these factors is crucial because mentoring programmes can do much to empower those employees who are not well represented in an organisation from a socio-economic, cultural, gendered, or generational perspective, for example. Communication scholars and those researchers working in other disciplines recognise that diversity issues need to be addressed in the mentoring process to enable those from marginalised communities to gain access to mentors and to form productive and meaningful, deep relationships (Atay, 2021; Petre et al., 2021; Trebing & Atay, 2021). In the context of academia, at least, those from international or LGTBQ+ profiles are underrepresented in senior roles so it is difficult for mentees from these communities to find mentors with whom they can relate in terms of shared identities (Atay, 2021). However, this argument does not seem to take into account that individuals are able to relate to one another on multiple levels beyond race or gender and that all relationships are in some way intercultural. One approach that would be helpful in countering homophily amongst senior managers and any bias that may exist would be to develop a mentoring process where junior employees from marginalised identities in organisations participate in a reciprocal mentoring process where the senior individual is mentored in co-cultural experiences in organisational life and the subordinate is mentored by the senior employee in ways to enhance opportunities for career and personal development. Lim and Parker (2020) have also referred to a similar process, known as reverse mentoring, where junior executives are assigned to work with senior executives who would benefit from extending their knowledge or deepening their perspectives in areas where their juniors have a level of expertise or some insight, for example in social media marketing.

Principles and phases of mentoring

Most processes are driven by underlying principles to guide and inform all phases. Although many models of mentoring phases exist, principles represent the criteria that need to be addressed throughout every stage of the mentoring process and at each meeting unless otherwise specified. The following principles of effective mentoring are based on the work of Axelrod (2019) but informed by other sources as cited.

1. Start where the mentee is

Starting where a mentee is, means focusing on a mentee at a particular point in time and not where a mentor believes that person should be. Mentees often have different ideas about their current and future status that may well differ from those of a mentor. Mentors should ask questions to understand mentee aspirations and interests, and to explore what is required to realise the future they see for themselves.

2. Create a space for conversational safety

The essence of this principle is focusing on the quality of the relationship between mentor and mentee. A place of conversational safety is usually confidential and one where a mentee feels understood, trusted, and respected and therefore confident about personal expression and candour without judgement. Creating spaces of conversational safety is a hallmark of successful mentoring and requires mentors to be self-aware, disciplined, and engaging in active listening in order to appreciate the attitudes and feelings of mentees. Without a sense of safety, mentees are likely to restrict communications to those remarks they believe will be well received. When this happens, it can be self-defeating because a mentor learns little from such a limited response and is constrained in identifying ways to assist a mentee best. A mentor's best leadership strategy is to model these qualities expected in professional leadership. Doing so can provide the inspiration needed for a mentee to flourish.

3. Cultivate a positive and resilient relationship

The purpose of both coaching and mentoring is to address relational and supportive needs (Gray et al., 2016). Being positive is entwined with establishing resilience and vitality in a mentee and helps to establish the mentor/mentee relationship. Resilience involves acknowledging that negative emotions arise in the workplace and drawing upon productive actions to overcome challenges that can be achieved through mindfulness, for example (see Tracy & Redden, 2019). In individuals, however, resilience is not a fixed state and may vary depending upon the circumstances (see Neenan & Dryden, 2020). A positive relationship is strong even when ideas are not totally aligned but, crucially, new ideas, creativity, and insight nevertheless flourish. The unexpected is welcomed and any anger or frustration is viewed as a catalyst for exploring possibilities and constructive outcomes.

4. Be goal orientated but flexible

Well-crafted goals help to avoid a sense of drifting and unfulfilled desires. They are best formulated based on discussions between mentor and mentee. Meetings between mentor and mentee should address progress in terms of accomplishing goals. However, a focus upon goals should not obstruct discussions about other possibilities or unexpected circumstances that may also suggest some modification of the goal.

5. Encourage risk taking for new mindsets and behaviours

A paradox in the mentor relationship is to maintain a balance between a sense of safety whilst also encouraging risk taking in ways that empower a mentee. In driving risk taking to achieve new mindsets and behaviours, a mentee becomes able to not only tolerate but also to thrive upon situations that may initially appear to be uncomfortable. This principle enables mistakes to become a key element of learning and development.

6. Explore the internal world of mentees as a driver for external actions

Mentee effectiveness is a greatly shaped by self-awareness. How well personal preferences, strengths, and weaknesses are attuned and consciously connected to motives will contribute to the quality of interactions with others. An effective mentor uses productive questioning to help a mentee uncover motivations, assumptions, and other internal drivers of behaviour that help to create reflection.

7. Bring your best self

Axelrod (2019) encouraged mentors to be fully present and prepared for each meeting in order to achieve the best possible outcomes. Doing so enables the personal development and growth of both mentor and mentee.

In Kram's (1983) seminal work, she noted that mentoring relationships varied in length and changed over time, reflected in four predictable but not necessarily distinct stages in the mentoring process. The relationship begins with an initiation phase followed by a cultivation phase when the range of functions may expand.

The third stage she refers to as a separation stage during which time the relationship is significantly changed because of psychological shifts in one or both parties or because of some alteration to organisational structures. The final redefinition phase marks the formulation of a new perspective that is quite different from the one held previously and at this point the mentoring relationship may end.

Axelrod (2019) identified five phases of mentoring, providing practical details outlining how a mentor is advised to manage the process. As Fournier (2018) observed, both mentor and mentee are best advised to prepare for the process, so with this in mind, a pre-phase has been embedded into Table 11.1 that also draws on ideas expressed in Axelrod's (2019) and De Janasz et al. (2014).

TABLE 11.1 Phases of the mentoring process

Pre–Phase	Preparing for the process.	Prior to the first meeting: • Exchange resumés, bios, links to social media. • Review applications for the process and statements about any motivations to participate as a basis for later discussions about expectations. • Examine and reflect upon any possible assumptions and biases that may exist.	
Phase 1	Establishing the relationship.	Addressed during the first two meetings: • Get to know one another. • Find common ground. • Set the tone for future conversations. • Discuss respective roles and expectations. • Agree on preferred means of communication between meetings. • Agree on the length & frequency of meetings. • Discuss how long the process will be and how the parties will decide that it is coming to an end. • Identify any topics that will not be discussed. • Establish shared understandings about confidentiality.	E.g.; email, phone, text, video calls? E.g., personal issues

		• How will any obstacles or difficulties in the relationship or process be addressed? • Consider using the issues discussed as a basis of a formal, signed and dated agreement.	
Phase 2	Setting the direction.	Addressed during the first three or four meetings: • Explore mentee aspirations. • Work with mentee to prioritise meaningful and realistic developmental goals in the time available. • Determine criteria for establishing if/when goals have been achieved. • Establish a method for your meetings. • Explore how a mentee learns best.	Identify any skills/ knowledge/behaviours necessary to achieve goals. Research learning styles relevant to this discussion.
Phase 3	Exploring mentee work experiences and applying revised mindsets and behaviours.	Addressed in ongoing meetings: • Consider agenda setting to stay on track. • Explore mentee daily experiences as opportunities for development. • Maintain a healthy relationship. • Address any obstacles. • Monitor goal accomplishment, making any necessary adjustments. • Use insightful questioning to raise insights. • Inspire confidence and hope. • Build mentee self-awareness and broaden perspectives.	Examples of new behaviours for development. • Keeping a reflective journal of workplace activities and any trialling of new behaviours and outcomes. • Shadow experts to learn a new skill. • Observe others, assessing what works or not for them. • Invite a role model for coffee. • Use volunteer work as an opportunity to learn new skills. • Trade feedback with peers and others. • Mentor suggests articles, books, case studies or TED Talks that may help to develop insights.

(*Continued*)

TABLE 11.1 (Continued)

		• Encourage mentee to experiment with new behaviours between meetings and to report back. • Track progress. • Mentors to draw on other experienced mentors to develop this skill set further.	
Phase 4	Perfecting your mentees' new capabilities.	Last third of meetings: • Vary approaches to mentee development. • Encourage mentee risk taking by applying new skillsets. • Enhance mentee influence by providing a larger platform to display new skills. • Urge mentee to consider settings where new skills can be applied.	
Phase 5	Anticipating closure	Last 2–3 meetings: • Raise any remaining priority issues. • Establish an end date. • Prepare the mentee for the value and content of the final meeting. • Facilitate a meaningful and positive final conversation. • Reflect upon and consolidate your learning and experience as a mentor with other mentors as part of a personal de-brief.	Closure is signposted by: • agreement that goals set have been achieved. • evidence of mentee growth (e.g., greater confidence, self-awareness, increased capacity for independence). • patterns of postponing, shortening, or cancelling meetings may emerge.

Source: Axelrod, 2019; De Janasz et al., 2014

Coaching

Defined as a one-to-one developmental intervention aimed at achieving professional/career outcomes, coaching is characterised as a collaborative, reflective, goal-orientated process that is conducted face to face or through e-coaching using available technologies (see Jones, Woods, & Guilliame, 2016; Kram, 1983; St.

John-Brooks, 2014). Drawing on a practical methodology, coaching is an increasingly popular form of training in the workplace to improve an individual's behaviour, broadly or in some specified area, to assist them in adjusting to a new responsibility or a changing set of circumstances at work (Zuniga-Collazos, Castillo-Palacio, Montana-Narvadez, & Castillo-Arevalo, 2020). Indeed, coaching is particularly helpful in periods of organisational change (Kowalski, 2020) and can lead to positive transformations within both coach and coachee (Atad & Grant, 2021).

In the last decade, both mentoring and coaching, as lines of enquiry, have decisively departed from being perceived as esoteric practices on the fringes of mainstream scholarship to become a powerful form of workplace learning across a wide range of organisational contexts and disciplines such as sporting education, education more broadly, business (including family business) management (Gray et al., 2016; Kowalski, 2020), nursing, and leadership. As observed in other themes and chapters in this text, organisations are no longer limited to a focus upon profitability but also to the creation of value in human terms that are associated with wellbeing and holistic and qualitative perspectives. Zuniga-Collazos et al. (2020) see coaching as an empowering developmental, supportive process that assists in balancing these two organisational responsibilities. Operating at its best, it is the glue organisations need between their goals and ensuring that employees are in the best place possible to achieve them.

Within the literature, coaching has been credited with a wide range of benefits that build capacity for both individuals and organisations (see; Atad & Grant, 2021; Jansen & Terblanche, 2021; Neenan & Dryden, 2020; Proksch, 2016; Zuniga-Collazos et al., 2020). The development of skills and insights are acknowledged in the following areas:

- Life satisfaction	- The broadening of perspectives	- Solution focused thinking/decision making
- Reflection to generate insights	- Self-esteem	- Confidence
- Conflict management skills	- Mindfulness	- Communication
- Interpersonal relationships	- Collaborative skills	- Leadership

Coaching can assist individuals in leadership development (St. John-Brooks, 2014) so that they become better at inspiring and encouraging others to achieve desired results and when a coachee is in a management position, the benefits can have a flow-on effect because those improved skills are brought to influence the commitment of individuals and teams (Zuniga-Collazos et al., 2020). Since an earlier call for more empirical studies to strengthen evidence of both the organisational benefits of coaching as well as any correlations with specific outcomes (Jones et al., 2016), some progress in this area has been noted (Zuniga-Collazos et al., 2020).

Despite assertions that mentoring and coaching are different (see St. John-Brooks, 2014), coaching and mentoring are terms that are often used interchangeably in publications, seemingly regardless of whether a work is titled as one focusing on mentoring or coaching (Axelrod, 2019). Coaches and mentors do draw on many of the same skills however, sufficiently so for some coaches who are appropriately experienced to move between coaching and mentoring as required (St. John-Brooks, 2014). The emphasis placed on certain aspects of these processes respectively may not be the same however.

Both mentoring and coaching are goal orientated (see De Janasz et al., 2014; Kowalski, 2020; Proksch, 2016) but coaching is more likely to be concerned with short-term goal setting (De Janasz et al., 2014) and focused on the present and near future (Kowalski, 2020). Also, to one extent or another, both processes aim to develop career and personal development and improve performance (see Axelrod, 2019; Gray et al., 2016; St. John-Brooks, 2014; Zuniga-Collazos et al., 2020). Although performance has been assessed in quantitative terms in the past, coaching literature tends to suggest that both academics and practitioners counter this view and acknowledge qualitative aspects of performance are at least as important (see Zuniga-Collazos et al., 2020). Additionally, mentoring and coaching also share a respect for establishing safe zones for in-depth communications where an employee can feel comfortable about discussing their feelings, for example, when reporting on what happened after testing new behaviours (see Axelrod, 2019).

Mentoring and coaching differ however in that a mentor is more likely to be older and certainly more senior (Kram, 1983) and experienced than a mentee and imparts what they have learned to a mentee. It is not necessarily so in the case of coaching where a high level of equality exists in the relationship (Proksch, 2016; St. John-Brooks, 2014). Older coaches may even need to discourage a coachee from moving into pupil mode, even unconsciously, and expecting to be told what to do, especially if there is an age difference (St. John-Brooks, 2014). The more equal relationship characterising coach and coachee, however, may be compromised in what is known as *managerial coaching* whereby a manager-as-coach works with a subordinate as a coachee, in order to address behaviours that may be impacting on professional performance (Zuniga-Collazos et al., 2020). As Jones et al. (2016) remark, it is not the role of the coach to supervise a coachee though some line managers do loosely adopt a coaching approach.

In addition, mentoring is more often undertaken without payment (Gray et al., 2016) whereas external coaches are remunerated. There is also a sense of greater equality in a coaching relationship than in a mentoring one. This equality may arise because neither party is necessarily an expert in all areas under discussion. For example, as Proksch (2016) points out, a coachee is often experienced in the issues and problems of a particular department or function in the organisation with which the coach may not necessarily be familiar. What the coach does have to offer, however, is expertise in the coaching process. In not knowing about a particular aspect of a coachee's workplace environment, genuine questions are generated on the part of the coach in ways that may feel more meaningful or genuine.

The role of an internal coach or a mentor can involve up to ten hours a month and it can be challenging to undertake the task and simultaneously meet the requirements of a substantive position (St. John-Brooks, 2014). As demanding as this commitment is, the self-reported rewards by coaches include feeling that they are making a contribution, satisfaction when a coachee gains valuable insights, learning more about the organisation in which they are employed, and enhancing personal learning and growth that may make coaches and mentors better managers and leaders, capable of fostering organisational cultures that value high performance (St. John-Brooks, 2014).

External and internal coaches

By the twenty-first century, most organisations had become aware of the services of external coaches, mostly procured to work with senior managers (St. John-Brooks, 2014). These external and professional coaches are usually highly skilled, trained, certified, and paid by organisations for a specified time, often during periods of organisational change (Atad & Grant, 2021; Axelrod, 2019; De Janasz et al., 2014). However, the appointment of in-house/internal coaches is becoming popular, largely as a cost-cutting measure (St. John-Brooks, 2014). The transition has not been entirely straightforward where systematic weaknesses compromise the process. Managers may receive inadequate guidance on how to undertake a coaching role, are not necessarily motivated to carry it out, or appear to have little aptitude for it (St. John-Brooks, 2014). In well-organised, mature, internal programmes, coaches are supported by being assigned to a buddy with more experience, as part of a community of others who have the same role and supervised by a lead coach (St. John-Brooks, 2014).

According to St. John-Brooks (2014), internal coaching is defined by some features with the caveat that roles may vary depending upon organisational requirements. First, it is a learning and developmental process facilitated by one person in an organisation for another and where no chain of command relationship exists. Human Resource managers may seem a useful appointment as coaches because they generally sidestep line management relationships but it is quite possible, given their role, that a conflict of interest may emerge subsequently in dealing with grievance investigations or promotion. Other defining aspects of internal coaching may well also be applied to external coaches in that they refer to the aim of facilitating personal, professional/career growth, leadership, improved effectiveness, transitions support, and skills development. Finally, despite the obvious differences between internal and external coaches, they are both expected to have been trained to conform to standards of professional and ethical behaviour.

Ethical issues in coaching

Ethical dilemmas are ubiquitous in organisations and ethical behaviour is essential for all employees regardless of their role. However, the intimate nature of many coaching relationships may have a particular bearing on the kinds of ethical issues that arise (St. John-Brooks, 2014). For example, a coachee may arrive at a morning meeting smelling of alcohol, may self-disclose a cocaine habit, or wishes to raise the issue of a difficult relationship with whom a coach shares a meaningful friendship (St. John-Brooks, 2014). Confidentiality is often a consideration in ethical issues like these and coaches are generally trained to facilitate confidential discussions (De Janasz et al., 2014). Indeed, without the assurance of confidentiality it would be difficult to create an environment that is safe (St. John-Brooks, 2014) or to claim that coaching emphasises the value of building trust in the coaching relationship (Gray et al., 2016). As St. John-Brooks (2014) points out, the flipside of confidentiality is whistle blowing where the choices available are for a coach to share information and evidence with a manager, accompany a coachee who shares sensitive information with a manager, or where a coachee is encouraged to take responsibility by raising a sensitive issue with a line manager personally (St. John-Brooks, 2014).

Psychology in coaching

For two decades, debate has ensued about the role of psychologists and therapists in coaching (Gray et al., 2016) and, by extension, the psychological discourse about mentoring (Kram, 1983). The growing numbers of coaches with therapeutic backgrounds is welcomed at least by Atad and Grant (2021) who nevertheless suggest that qualifications in psychology do not obviate the need for training in coaching. As De Janasz et al. (2014) suggested, coaches focus on human needs as well as organisational requirements and so it is hardly surprising that many coaches are often psychologists (Axelrod, 2019). Psychology also lends itself well as a discipline to aspects of the coaching role such as self-disclosure, the generation of alternative perspectives (De Janasz et al., 2014; Proksch, 2016), visualisation techniques, and trust building (Gray et al., 2016). However, unlike therapeutic processes, coaching assumes that a coachee is generally in good health mentally (Zuniga-Collazos et al., 2020).

Both mentoring and coaching are informed by a range of fields in psychology, including Gestalt and neurolinguistic programming NLP, rational pragmatic discourse (concerned with practical applications) as well as behavioural, cognitive, psychoanalytic, therapeutic, critical, and humanistic discourses (Gray et al., 2016). One of the salient techniques that qualified therapists and psychologists are able to bring to coaching is borrowed from CBT that can help coachees to revise some of the ways they think about events (Neenan & Dryden, 2020) when certain thoughts become barriers to development. How people think about events affects how they react to them and CBT is a powerful tool in the difficult task of changing thinking and embracing balanced and realistic appraisals of aspects of their lives (Neenan & Dryden, 2020). Neenan and Dryden (2020) have explored the notion of bringing CBT to coaching and have coined the term cognitive behavioural coaching (CBC). They describe CBC as a therapeutic process that helps individuals to work on goal-focused capabilities in ways that focus upon thoughts, feelings, and behaviours.

Communication in mentoring and coaching

Communication plays a critical role in mentoring and coaching from a number of perspectives. For example, the effectiveness of these processes depends upon the quality of the communication between participants, and second, coaching and mentoring, in turn, tend to foster the development of communication skills (De Janasz et al., 2014; Fournier, 2018; Zuniga-Collazos et al., 2020). Coaching and mentoring are thus explored by scholars working in the relevant fields of organisational communication, communication education, and instructional communication often using a critical lens (Atay, 2021; Kahl, 2021; Trebing & Atay, 2021). Communication in coaching, however, tends to be more casual/informal than in mentoring relationships and emphasises transparency, mutual respect, and empathy (Kowalski, 2020) but these imperatives are generally also upheld in mentoring relationships too.

Active listening (see Part I) is an essential skill for mentors and coaches in order to meet the needs of participants in the process in ways conducive to enabling personal and professional growth (Axelrod, 2019; Gray et al., 2016; St. John-Brooks, 2014). Indeed, the need for continual active listening may be one reason why Jansen and Terblanche (2021) suggest that the process itself provides opportunities for developing listening competence. Listening to one another carefully is one aspect of creating a trust-filled relationship in contexts of both mentoring and coaching. Both these developmental strategies prioritise safe environments for in-depth communication where employees are able to be comfortable about discussing their feelings after testing new behaviours (see Axelrod, 2019).

When things go wrong

When things go awry in a mentoring relationship, it can feel akin to a breakup in a long-term, personal relationship (Lim & Parker, 2020) – and indeed, sometimes it is just that. Relationships and communication are interrelated, and mentoring and coaching are not immune from interpersonal challenges that may arise for a variety of complex reasons. Not all mentoring relationships end well and sometimes become destructive, ambivalent, resentful, and fuelled by anger (Kram, 1983). If there are obstacles in developmental relationships, it is important to address them (Axelrod, 2019) because relational issues matter.

Where ethical misalignment exists between expectations of mentor and mentee, some tensions may arise. Axelrod (2019) considers situations where a mentor may perceive dishonesty in the form of lying on the part of a mentee and advises a patient approach, maintaining that people lie when they believe the truth will be found unacceptable. Rather than issuing swift condemnation, the author recommends assessing and deepening trust levels in the relationship, in the hope that a dishonest mentee will eventually find the confidence to correct an initial lie, or at least recognise the value of not repeating the behaviour and, better still, transferring their newly acquired authenticity to other work situations. As trust develops in the relationship, a mentor may explore other areas where a mentee may not feel acceptable (Axelrod, 2019).

Axelrod (2019) also considers defensive behaviour in the mentoring relationship as a potential impediment to success. Although defensiveness is a common human response in some situations, he maintains that it becomes problematic when it forms the basis of someone's communication style. Defensiveness is characterised by self-protective and often unconscious mechanisms, exhibiting behaviours such as an unwillingness to accept feedback, a failure to acknowledge personal mistakes, blaming others, and rationalising errors rather than taking responsibility (Axelrod, 2019). Defensiveness may be a way to hide feelings of shame and personal insecurity that emanate from childhood and a heightened sensitivity to being regarded negatively by others and, for this reason, the author advocates a supportive approach and communicating to a mentee that they are appreciated and valued.

While patience in observing and assessing the behaviour of others has some merit, the direction taken will largely depend upon the nature and seriousness of any unethical behaviour and it cannot be assumed that all individuals necessarily become more ethical as trust deepens. Neither is a mentor necessarily a psychologist or therapist but rather an advisor or guide (see De Janasz et al., 2014; Proksch, 2016). So, probing areas where someone feels inadequate may prove to be a highly sensitive terrain to explore. These concerns aside, encouraging self-disclosure in safe environments can be helpful in personal development and in supporting others at work.

Providing feedback

When criticism is constructive and genuine, feedback presents an opportunity for self-acceptance and making the necessary changes to advance personal and professional development (Neenan & Dryden, 2020). Professional development relies upon effective feedback, but for it to be beneficial, it should (see De Janasz et al., 2014; Proksch, 2016):

- be interactive, taking into consideration the needs of giver and receiver
- refer to concrete rather than generalised issues
- be helpful in that it relates to those things a recipient is able to influence
- be provided promptly when memories are fresh
- be delivered with the development of insights and confidence in mind
- be positive/constructive
- provide encouragement about performance and necessary adjustments to realise success
- be given having established that the receiver is in a position to and prepared to receive it.

Asking open questions to facilitate discussion and communication

Effective coaching entails asking powerful questions (Jansen & Terblanche, 2021) as it does in mentoring. Asking open questions reveals and facilitates transparency in communication, especially when accompanied by active listening. The following probing questions are inspired and informed by some suggestions from Axelrod (2019) and are particularly useful early on in the process when mentor and mentee are establishing a relationship and getting to know one another. Although Axelrod (2019) differentiated between those questions that might be addressed to a mentor and those to a mentee, many may actually be productively posed by either party and are indicated by an asterisk.

Questions for a mentee

Why have you decided to participate in a mentoring programme? ★
What have been the most significant highlights in your career to date? ★
Describe your work currently. ★
What aspirations do you have? ★
What do you hope will be different for you at the conclusion of this process?
How do you generally cope with/manage obstacles/stress/conflict? ★
How would you self-assess your level of resilience when unexpected events arise?

Questions for a mentor

Are there any particular events you feel have defined your career? ★
Is there an area in your current role that you find particularly engaging and
   enjoyable? ★
What aspects of your previous mentoring experiences do you believe will inform
   the current one most usefully?
Is there anything you would particularly like to get out of this mentoring process? ★

Other questions that may come earlier or later in the process

What role do you think values play, especially in stressful situations at work?
Are you able to provide examples of how ethics and values have played a part in
   your decisions at work?
In making decisions with an ethical element, how do you think others were affected
   by them from their perspective?

Conclusion

This chapter commenced with a brief discussion of how 'growth' as a concept is interpreted in organisational literature. The historical development of mentoring and its complex, conceptual relation to coaching has been explored throughout, taking careful note of similarities and differences. The benefits of mentoring and coaching were discussed, with some attention to the kinds of contexts and factors that tend to distract and diminish from them. Whilst much attention has been afforded to mentor/mentee relationships, assigned in a top-down process, the growth of interest in peer-to-peer, reciprocal mentoring relationships and other alternatives to traditional conceptions have also been examined in organisations wishing to enhance equity, release the potential of diversity, and promote marginalised groups. The chapter provided some direction on principles guiding the mentoring process, some of which are relevant to mentee wellbeing and managing the phases that provide a structure to the process. The latter part of the chapter was devoted to coaching as a means of developing employees and drawing attention to some communication strategies relevant to successful mentoring and coaching relationships.

References

Atad, O., & Grant, A. (2021). How does coach training change coaches-in-training? Differential effects for novice vs. experienced 'skilled helpers'. *Coaching: An International Journal of Theory, Research and Practice, 14*(1), 3–19.

Atay, A. (2021). Collaborative cultural mentoring: An academic compass. In D. Trebing & A. Atay (Eds.), *Mentoring and communication theories and practices* (pp. 91–110). Bern, Switzerland: Peter Lang.

Axelrod, W. (2019). *10 steps to successful mentoring*. Alexandria, VA: Association for Talent Development.

Chandler, D., Murphy, W., Kram, W., & Higgins, M. (2016). Bridging formal and informal mentoring: A developmental network perspective. In K. Peno, E. Managiante, & R. Kenahan (Eds.), *Mentoring in formal and informal contexts* (pp. 1–20). Charlotte, NC: Information Age Publishing Inc.

Chang, J., Baek, P., & Kim, T. (2021). Women's developmental networks and career satisfaction: Developmental functions as a mediator. *Journal of Career Development, 48*(5), 733–750.

Crossman, J., & Doshi, V. (2014). When not knowing is a virtue: A business ethics perspective. *Journal of Business Ethics, 131*(1), 1–8.

De Janasz, S., Crossman, J., Campbell, N., & Power, M. (2014). *Interpersonal skills in organisations*. Sydney: McGraw-Hill Education.

Denker, K., Duty, K., Will, M., Escobio, I., Gibbs, A., & Fox, J. (2021). Mentoring, emotional labour and risk in academia: Exploring what we really learn through research through a lens of critical communication pedagogy. In D. Trebing & A. Atay (Eds.), *Mentoring and communication theories and practices* (pp. 185–201). Bern, Switzerland: Peter Lang.

Fournier, C. (2018). *Mentoring*. Beijing: O'Reilly Media, Inc.

Gray, D., Garvey, B., & Lane, D. (2016). *A critical introduction to coaching and mentoring*. London: Sage.

Jansen, G., & Terblanche, N. (2021). The spill-over effects of postgraduate coaching studies in the resilience of women on triple roles. *Coaching: An International Journal of Theory, Research and Practice, 14*(1), 78–91.

Jones, R., Woods, S., & Guilliame, Y. (2016). The effectiveness of workplace coaching: A meta-analysis of learning and performance outcomes from coaching. *Journal of Occupational and Organizational Psychology, 89*(2), 249–277.

Kahl, D. (2021). Dwelling in revolutionary intimacies: Performing mentoring and/as reflexivity. In D. Trebing & A. Atay (Eds.), *Mentoring and communication theories and practices* (pp. 35–50). Bern, Switzerland: Peter Lang.

Kowalski, K. (2020). Coaching. *The Journal of Continuing Education in Nursing, 51*(1), 12–14.

Kram, K. (1983). Phases of the mentor relationships. *Academy of Management Journal, 26*(4), 608–625.

Lefabvre, J., Bloom, G., & Duncan, L. (2021). A qualitative examination of the developmental networks of elite sport coaches. *Sport Exercise & Performance Psychology, 10*(2), 310–326.

Lim, P., & Parker, A. (2020). *Mentoring millennials in an Asian context: Talent management insights from Singapore.* Bingley: Emerald Publishing Limited.

Neenan, M., & Dryden, W. (2020). *Cognitive behavioural coaching: A guide to problem-solving and personal development.* Oxford: Taylor & Francis Group.

Peno, K., Silva, M., & Kenahan, R. (Eds.). (2016). *Mentoring in formal and informal contexts.* Charlotte, NC: Information Age Publishing Inc.

Petre, E., Giorgia, G., Petre, J., & Harshbarger, J. (2021). One class can make a difference: The intersecting paths of mentoring friendship. In D. Trebing & A. Atay (Eds.), *Mentoring and communication theories and practices* (pp. 73–90). Bern, Switzerland: Peter Lang.

Proksch, S. (2016). *Conflict management.* Cham, Switzerland: Springer.

St. John-Brooks, K. (2014). *Internal coaching: Inside story.* London: Taylor & Francis Group.

Tracy, S., & Redden, S. (2019). The structuration of emotion. In A. Nicotera (Ed.), *Origins and traditions of organizational communication: A comprehensive introduction to the field* (pp. 348–369). New York: Routledge.

Trebing, D., & Atay, A. (Eds.). (2021). *Mentoring and communication theories and practices.* Bern, Switzerland: Peter Lang.

Zuniga-Collazos, A., Castillo-Palacio, M., Montana-Narvadez, E., & Castillo-Arevalo, G., (2020). Influence of managerial coaching on organizational performance. *Coaching: An International Journal of Theory, Research and Practice, 13*(1), 30–44.

12

ETHICAL APPROACHES TO ORGANISATIONAL ISSUES, COMMUNICATION, AND RELATIONSHIPS

A brief account of the study of business ethics

It is apparent from the content of textbooks, journals, and courses that the field of behavioural business ethics began to gain ground as a study from the1980s (Kish-Gephart, Trevino, Chen, & Tilton, 2019). Business ethics attracted the attention of practitioners and scholars in an environment of growing concerns about the ethical practices of organisations. It was also apparent, and continues to be so, that employees and managers routinely face ethical and moral dilemmas and when there is a high level of organisational pressure, the potential for misconduct can rise (Schwartz, 2017). In a study of 902 managers across organisations, Huntala, Feldt, Lamsa, Mauno, and Kinnunen (2011) found that managers are routinely called upon to address complex ethical issues largely and broadly concerned with occupational wellbeing, globalisation, economic recession, and competition.

How ethical and moral misconduct is manifested

Ethical misconduct in organisational settings is manifested in many ways (see Dwyer, 2020; Meyer-Galow, 2018; Schwartz, 2017):

- abusive behaviour fuelling hostile work environments
- conflicts of interest where personal interests are placed over company interests
- violating company policies about Internet use
- illegal price fixing
- discriminating against employees
- violating health and safety regulations
- lying to employees, customers, vendors, or the public
- retaliation against someone who has reported misconduct

DOI: 10.4324/9780429318948-15

- falsifying time reports or hours worked
- falsifying balance sheets and account manipulation
- inventory falsification
- bribery
- breaches of confidentiality
- misuse of organisational property
- the misuse of big data in ways that compromise the privacy of individuals by passing on personal information without seeking consent to third parties.

ACTIVITY: RESEARCH

Research organisational ethical breaches, using case studies, business ethics publications, or newspaper reports to identify any forms of unethical behaviour that can be added to the preceding list.

Deception

Deception is another form of unethical behaviour. It has been defined, 'as the intentional misinterpretation of information or emotions' (Gasper & Schweitzel, 2019, p. 40). Obviously, many of the items included in the list of unethical behaviours involve one form of deception or another. Deceitful behaviour is learned from early childhood and by adulthood the average person reportedly lies up to three times in about ten minutes (Schwartz, 2017) so deceit is common. Deceit is a concept that includes a variety of behaviours such as breaking promises, cheating, and lying (Schwartz, 2017). Some individual characteristics have been identified as antecedents of unethical behaviour. Notably, a recent study (Gasper & Schweitzel, 2019) undertaken in the context of deceit amongst negotiators found that those high in self-confidence and self-efficacy were more likely to engage in deceitful, unethical behaviour.

Employees may adopt strategic decisions about how they utilise one form of communication over another to deceive most effectively but such decisions can be risky. For example, when someone thinks a problematic truth will be easier to detect when conveyed via one medium of communication, they may well select an alternative. To illustrate, someone who considers himself or herself to be a poor liar in a face-to-face medium may choose to engage in deceit using a telephone or email (see Swol & Paik, 2017). However, face-to-face communication is perceived as less suspicious than other mediums, so when someone chooses an alternative when face-to-face communication is easier and logical, they are likely to invite reservations about the validity of the message (Swol & Paik, 2017). Thus, the risks of deceit can be counter-intuitive and not least because it may actually be harmful to one's health. Deceivers suffer from psychological symptoms (distress, guilt, fear and discomfort) as well as co-related and damaging physical symptoms (Burgoon, Hamel, Blair, & Twyman, 2020).

Ethical concepts and principles

Ethical principles can be brought to address complex issues that arise in the workplace and serve as a lens for making decisions and developing strategies. To this end, a brief explanation of some salient ethical concepts and perspectives is appropriate. Virtue ethics, utilitarianism, and Kant's deontology are three major schools informing the field of business ethics (Sison, Ferrero, & Guitian, 2018).

Virtue ethics

Virtue ethics is considered a major study in moral philosophy and an influential normative theory in business ethics (Alzola, Hennig, & Romar, 2020). This statement requires some explanation of basic terminology. The term 'normative' pertains to a behavioural standard or norm derived from a community, society, or culture. Also, although ethics and 'moral' philosophy are often used interchangeably, more precisely, morals refer to personal beliefs about what is considered right or wrong, whereas ethics relates to assumptions about collective social standards (Lewicki, Barry, & Saunders, 2016). It is from parents, the wider family, friends, neighbourhoods, and national culture that individuals develop a sense of right and wrong (St. John-Brooks, 2014). Since the virtue ethics tradition pays particular attention to individual decisions, it is generally regarded as being 'agent-centred' (Sison et al., 2018, p. 1).

Virtue ethics is historically rooted in the works of Aristotle and Plato in ancient Greece. Aristotle's virtue ethics was strongly teleological (Snow, 2020; St. John-Brooks, 2014), meaning that it was focused on the purpose that virtues serve. Aristotle referred to virtues as rational excellences (Snow, 2020), likely because the term 'virtue' is a translation of the Latin word 'virtus', which basically meant 'human excellence' (Sison et al., 2018, p. 2). Aristotle concluded that a good life is achieved through eudaimonia (or flourishing) and achieved by both possessing and exercising virtue informed by practical wisdom or phronesis (Alzola et al., 2020; Sison et al., 2018; Snow, 2020). Today, however, flourishing is more generally understood to be an agentic activity emphasising prosocial emotions to enable employees to overcome emotional suffering to become more resilient (Tracy & Redden, 2019). To flourish, Aristotle maintained, people need to live in accordance with such virtues as honesty, courage, and generosity (Snow, 2020). Honesty has gained much attention in virtue ethics literature and has been largely constructed as a form of transparency (Crossman & Doshi, 2014; Crossman & Noma, 2013). Virtues are also intertwined with the concepts of both character and integrity in complex ways. To illustrate, character has been described as the performance of habitual virtuous actions in personal behaviour (Huhn, Meyer, & Racelis, 2018; Sison et al., 2018), and the literature suggests that integrity is associated with character, high moral standards, virtues, and consistency between words and actions (Crossman & Perera, 2017).

Despite its rich pedigree in both western and Eastern philosophy contemporaneously, published work has been dominated by a focus on virtue ethics as part of the western tradition (Alzola et al., 2020). This is unfortunate because an informed approach to business ethics can only come with a global and open perspective. It is also somewhat curious that more comparative work has not been undertaken, given some of the obvious synergies in how virtue ethics is constructed in both East and West. Literature concerned with Eastern ethics has been influenced by the philosophers, Confucius and Mencius, and is generally described as a non-consequentialist, normative form of virtue ethics whereby moral and ethical consideration can be fluidly applied to business practice (Kim, Mondejar, Roque, & Cuervo, 2018). Confucian ethics, as it is known, focuses on the cultivation of specific character traits necessary for both acting and living well, most particularly expressed in the prioritisation of the common good, virtue rather than material desires, or a thirst for power (Kim et al., 2018). Clearly, much more work needs to be undertaken in the area of cross- and inter- cultural virtue ethics before any universal theories of virtue ethics can be confidently formulated (Alzola et al., 2020).

As Chapter 10 explained, much scholarship has been invested into identifying the characteristics of effective leaders but the idea of innate characteristics has now largely been rejected in favour of regarding leadership as a learned pattern of behaviour (Huhn et al., 2018). The capacity to function as an ethical leader is no exception. Ethical leaders have a crucial role in influencing organisational environments and exercising corporate social responsibility in modelling their beliefs, values, and behaviours and demonstrating that they are at least as important in rational decision making as intellectual prowess and task performance alone (Huhn et al., 2018). The emphasis upon rationality emanated from the rise of science and the enlightenment during the late seventeenth and early eighteenth centuries and led to a philosophical disengagement from teleology (Snow, 2020) such that virtue ethics had almost disappeared completely from the work of western academics until the late 1950s when a marked revival of interest took place in Anglo-American philosophy (Alzola et al., 2020; Sison et al., 2018).

Kantianism and the categorical imperative

Kantianism is based on the ideas of an eighteenth-century German philosopher, Immanuel Kant (1724–1804). Kant maintained that the moral worth of an action is dependent upon the rationale or motive for acting. Ideally, the motivation for action should emanate from a sense of moral duty or principal rather than self-interest (Bobbit, 2020; Schwartz, 2017). Kant's thesis is referred to as deontology, or deontological ethics. He maintained that actions are inherently right or wrong. If an activity is wrong, it is always wrong irrespective of the consequences (Jonson, McGuire, & O'Neill, 2015; St. John-Brooks, 2014).

Kant developed a particular principle to determine moral duty which he referred to as the 'categorical imperative' (Schwartz, 2017). The categorical imperative assumes that being ethical requires conformance to moral absolutes, rules, or principles based on criteria such as logical soundness, in contrast to pragmatic approaches that acknowledge the value of appraising the merit of a situation in hand (Bobbit, 2020; Turner & West, 2018). Such a perspective also differs from the ideas of Emile Durkheim (1858–1917), a French sociologist who promoted the philosophical concept of relativism, suggesting that ideas cannot be considered universally right or wrong because what may be considered wrong from one person's perspective may seem ethically acceptable to another (Bobbit, 2020). Cultural relativism also has implications for how those from different cultures may vary in their perspectives of ethical/unethical actions.

Schwartz (2017) suggests three criteria to inform ethical decision making: universalisability, reversibility, and respect. The criteria of universalisability suggests that it is ethical to act when such action is available to all and when it would be self-defeating not to conform. So, for example, if someone breaches a 'lockdown' implemented as a result of increased cases of COVID, and secretly interacts with a large group of friends, it defeats the object of limiting the spread of COVID in the community. It is an action that places the individuals concerned at risk and all others in the community. In a business context, a universalist approach would assume that principled/ethical actions and standards are always applicable and should always be adopted (Akbar & Vujic, 2014, p. 192; Deresky & Christopher, 2008). Reversibility invites one to consider a decision that affects another or others. It begs the question that if positions were reversed, would the decision be accepted with the same enthusiasm? Contemporaneously, the wellbeing literature concerned with mindfulness appears to be sympathetically aligned with this particular criterion. Meyer-Galow (2018), for example, maintains that mindfulness is one means of gaining personal insight that overcomes ego, self-interested behaviours and ill-advised notions – all in an overarching encouragement of empathetic behaviour. Third, the criterion of respect demands that ethical decision makers treat others as having intrinsic worth rather than simply serving as a means to the personally desired end of a decision maker.

Moral rights

The notion of moral rights, like Kantianism, is considered to be deontological or duty-based and determines that a decision is only morally sound if it extends respect to the rights of any individual(s) affected by an action (Schwartz, 2017). Schwartz (2017) illustrates this point as it applies to organisational settings and management. Managers, he maintains, should disclose potential dangers or risks to employees or customers in any action. They should also keep in the forefront of their minds, fairness and justice. For example, any benefits such as wages or responsibilities such as taxes (known as distributive justice) should be fairly distributed. Managers also have a role in ensuring that the moral right of employees to be compensated when injured in an unsafe working environment, for example (compensatory justice), and insisting upon fairness being applied to any decision-making process (procedural justice). Finally, adherence to the principles of moral rights includes striving to make sure that the least advantaged in society benefit most from an action (societal justice). Those cultures influenced by Confucian teachings are likely to consider moral and ethical individual, organisational, and professional behaviour in terms of how demonstrates virtue, loyalty, and obedience (Tan & Snell, 2002).

Utilitarianism

Utilitarianism is a theory put forth by the nineteenth century by philosopher John Stuart Mill (1806–1873) who stated that ethical decisions should be governed by what brings the greatest good for the greatest number of people (Turner & West, 2018). Mill's work on utilitarianism was also influenced by Jeremy Bentham (1748–1832), another English philosopher, born in the mid-eighteenth century (Snow, 2020). Mill is largely remembered as a reformer and social activist who wished to improve the condition of workers in nineteenth-century Britain (Bobbit, 2020). As a teleological or consequentialist theory, in contrast to Kant's ideas, it focuses upon the consequences of actions rather than any moral principles that motivate them (Alzola et al., 2020; Schwartz, 2017; Turner & West, 2018). Therefore, making utilitarian decisions involves carefully weighing any potential benefits or harm for anyone concerned and acting on the decision that achieves the greatest good/utility/benefit/happiness or least harm in a particular situation (Jonson et al., 2015; Schwartz, 2017; Turner & West, 2018). Like Kantianism, utilitarianism is considered to be 'action-centred' though it makes assessments of actions or outcomes based on prioritising those where benefits outweigh costs in contrast to Kantianism that advocates actions that are consistent with laws or rules (Sison et al., 2018). Utilitarianism, however, has been criticised for its potential to be unethical in that it does not consider those who do not benefit from the decision and, further, that it is hard to measure the value placed on happiness, life, and health and, finally, utilitarianism fails to address the issue of moral rights in the context of justice (Schwartz, 2017).

Organisations and ethics

Early approaches to business ethics tended to focus upon damage control and reputational crisis related to ethical breaches (Meyer-Galow, 2018). More recently, profit-orientated organisations and businesses are increasingly called into account with respect to ethical practices. It is no longer acceptable to frame issues in exclusively economic or legal terms in ways that serve as an impediment to ethical behaviour (see Schwartz, 2017). One motivation for the strategic development of ethical decisions and actions is that it has now become a competitive asset that organisations communicate internally and externally via value statements, reporting, declarations, and ethical codes though it would be a mistake to assume that such communications are always reflected in actual behaviours (Huntala et al., 2011).

Business ethics is making an impact on organisational cultures that would otherwise and hitherto have made decisions based on a 'profit at any cost' mindset in exchange for one that has the potential to operate efficiently, economically, and profitably, whilst simultaneously espousing ethical practices (see Meyer-Galow, 2018). Cultivating an ethical organisational culture is essential because it clearly communicates to all employees what is expected and what kinds of behaviour would be considered acceptable or not. An ethical organisational culture determines the conditions necessary to be able to predict and explain unethical behaviour at any level and highlights where ethical strain (tension between individual and organisational ethical values) appears to be misaligned (Huntala et al., 2011).

Organisations would be well served by taking an inclusive and holistic approach to embedding ethical practices at all levels. If indeed managers tend to express a more positive view of the ethical quality of organisations than non-managers (Huntala et al., 2011), what story does this tell? Is it one of managers massaging appearances to avoid unpleasant consequences from a quality assurance or public relations perspective? A delusion or a mismatch between reality and lukewarm managerial intent? Such mismatches tend to invite a deeper, revealing investigation that would not arise if a strong inclusive ethical culture existed and was embedded and reinforced at every stage of enculturation, starting with thorough research into the background of applicants, onboarding, ongoing workplace professional development, performance measures, and managers patently and authentically modelling sound ethical practices. Obviously, the development of organisational policy will serve to clarify expectations of ethical behaviour (Cowan & Horan, 2014) to accompany other strategies as stated, but will almost certainly be insufficient on its own. Such steps will assist in taking a pre-emptive approach to avoid organisational identity breaches. An organisational breach refers to a perception that beliefs closely tied to an organisation's identity have been violated by one or more of its members (Jacobs, Kreutzer, & Vaara, 2020). As Kundro and Nurmohamed (2020) have observed, cover-ups of unethical actions not only have the potential to be expensive, they fail to address any ethical wrongdoing that will, as a result, likely continue. It also sends mixed message to other employees about the organisational culture with respect to expectations about ethical behaviour and decision making. Doing so impedes effective organisational communication and creates confusion, likely giving rise to subsequent breaches.

In an interconnected world where global partnerships are common, the question of mismatches in what constitutes ethical practice sometimes arises. Ethical decisions are influenced by cultural context so what is perceived as the norm in one culture in terms of values, decisions and attitudes, may not be acceptable universally in all others (Fok, Payne, & Corey, 2016; Turner & West, 2018). The implications of cross-cultural ethics for organisations has given rise to increasing research in this area (Fok et al., 2016). One response to the knowledge that people have different ideas about what is right or wrong is known as cultural relativism. Cultural relativism assumes that one should not judge another culture by the standards or worldviews of one's own culture. In a business/organisational context, a cultural relativist approach would be to adapt policies to whatever is adopted in the local context in which an organisation is operating in the world (Akbar & Vujic, 2014; Deresky & Christopher, 2008).

ACTIVITY: APPLYING THEORY TO CONTEXT

The following case has been adapted from the work of Rachels (1995).

Darius the king of Persia was known for his interest in cultural differences. He discovered that a tribe of people known as Callatians honoured a long tradition of eating the bodies of their dead fathers. Darius also knew that the Greeks cremated their fathers. He summoned some Greeks and asked them if they would consider eating their dead fathers. The Greeks were deeply shocked! He then summoned the Callatians, and asked them if they would burn their dead fathers' bodies and they were equally appalled at the prospect. The Callatians thought eating their fathers was a sign of respect, wishing their spirit to remain within individuals, whereas burning the dead, to them, was seen as a rejection. The Greeks, in contrast, were horrified that anyone would dishonour a father by eating him.

In small groups, discuss which culture has taken the most ethical approach in dealing with the death of a parent. The Callatians or the Greeks? Or neither, or both? Identify whether any of your responses take a universalist/relativist/consequentialist/deontological approach. Consider how each of these ethical approaches might be brought to the case.

A culturally relativist approach in an organisational context is fraught with problems. For example, failure to acknowledge and address any breaches of human rights, such as forced child labour, breaches of health and safety practices, and human trafficking on an international level in organisational partnerships is now widely considered to be tantamount to condoning and supporting unethical behaviour. Many companies have been widely criticised for adopting a relativist approach to cultural ethics. For example, Volkswagen, Hyundai, and the Australian Wheat Board were lambasted and condemned for bribery internationally because they felt this was the only way to get things done on a local basis (Deresky & Christopher, 2008; Martin, Cullen, Johnson, & Parboteeah, 2007). The lessons learned as a result of brand damage cost them dearly. The blindness some organisations have demonstrated towards human rights abuses in the pursuit of profit, whatever the consequences for others, may also be linked to Bazerman's (2014) observation that when organisations are several steps away from an ethical breach, they may not readily grasp their own responsibility in the process. This may represent an explanation but does not constitute an excuse. Ethical training for expatriates and international leaders and the promotion of transparency and accountability in organisations is essential (Akbar & Vujic, 2014), though demonstrating a knowledge of local sensitivities is wise. As Gift, Gift, and QinQin (2013) advise, due diligence on the ethical practices of overseas organisations is essential before decisions are taken to work with them or avoid them.

As a virtue ethics scenario, Murase (1982) explored the nature of *Sunao* in Japanese culture. Sunao is a highly revered value of character, relating to the concepts of concern and empathy for others with a focus on trust development and harmony in interpersonal relationships rather than more easily measurable outcomes. Later work (Crossman & Noma, 2013) also considered how Sunao, as a form of character, influenced intercultural communication and trust relationships in multinational organisations. They found that poor cultural understandings in this regard came to cause tensions amongst Japanese managers and Australian workers and called for a variety of developmental strategies to address tensions with respect to personal values, including the distinctions made culturally between what was perceived as providing an explanation as opposed to an excuse.

Workplace scenarios as illustrative sites for ethical reflection and discussion

In this section, certain aspects of organisational life, specifically in terms of interpersonal relationships and communication, will be addressed in order to stimulate discussion about any potential ethical implications. They include relational issues at work, theft, and corruption.

Professional and personal relationships at work

Early studies of organisational communication focused upon workplace relationships, particularly supervisor-subordinate relationships, but by the 1990s increasing attention began to be paid to friendship and romances (Sias & Shin, 2019). Specifically, this shift in focus was one from vertical to horizontal, non-hierarchical, peer relationships and from formal to informal relationships. Organisational communication is a useful disciplinary lens for studying informal relationships at work because it is communication that structures, enables, and constrains these relationships that so clearly matter (Sias & Shin, 2019). Friendships and romantic relationships patently arise in the workplace and may be perceived differently from an ethical perspective depending upon the organisational and, indeed, societal cultural context. That said, despite globalisation and multinational businesses becoming commonplace, little work has explored personal and informal workplace relationships in varied cultural settings or, indeed, interculturally (Cowan & Horan, 2014; Sias & Shin, 2019).

Workplace friendships

Friendships naturally occur when employees spend periods of time working alongside one another but unlike friendships that develop in other social circumstances, the literature has regarded these relationships as blended in that they combine the roles of both co-worker and friend (Sias & Shin, 2019). Unlike formal working relationships, workplace friendships are voluntary. They appear to be based primarily on providing support and exchanging information (Sias & Shin, 2019) and tend to be accompanied by affectionate communication (Turner & West, 2018). Friendships are based on trust and as with non-workplace relationships any betrayal of trust presents a threat to their continuation (Sias & Shin, 2019). A test, if not a threat to workplace friendship may arise if one party is promoted to a position of direct authority or supervision over the other when, previously, the relationship may have occurred between peers (Sias & Sin, 2019).

Romantic workplace relationships/nonplatonic workplace romances (WR)

People experience powerful emotions at work that may and commonly do (at least in contemporary western organisations) become romantic (Costello, 2020; Cowan & Horan, 2014). Cowan and Horan (2014) cited western literature suggesting that early in the twenty-first century, somewhere between 40–47 per cent of employees were actively involved in WR or had been in the past. More recently, a 2013 study using surveys conducted by the Society for Human Research Management (SHRM) in the United States found that over 40 per cent of HR professionals reported that about a quarter of employees were involved in a workplace relationship at that time or had been so previously (Sias & Shin, 2019).

Infatuation, dependence, sexual attraction, and a desire to be physically close and relationally exclusive are other feelings associated with new romances (Larson, 2018). These kinds of relationships involving mutual affection and that are not confined to expectations around professional roles are often referred to as nonplatonic workplace relationships or WR (Cowan & Horan, 2014). However, little is yet known about how communication functions in initiating, developing, and possibly the deterioration of romantic relationships (Sias & Shin, 2019). As with friendships, society and culture (including organisational culture) influence the norms governing romantic and sexual expression but co-worker responses to WR may vary depending upon the status of those involved in terms of whether parties are married or have children, for example, and individual perspectives of fellow employees (Cowan & Horan, 2014; Larson, 2018). Females engaged in WR appear to bear a greater burden than males in terms of being judged harshly by colleagues and those judgements matter because when they are negative they have the potential to harm health, mutual respect, and the productivity of organisational members (Cowan & Horan, 2014). Co-workers who are also friends tend to view WR more empathetically even if they don't entirely approve, and will also shield a friend from office gossip, but others who learn of the issue by observation of kissing, suggestive glances, gestures, and through gossip are much less supportive (Cowan & Horan, 2014).

ACTIVITY: DISCUSSION, APPLICATION, CREATIVITY

Ask and answer the following questions:

1. Should people engage in romantic relationships at work? Why? Why not?
2. Should married couples work together? Why? Why not?
3. Discuss how the theories of Kantianism and utilitarianism and virtue ethics may be relevant to the ethical implications of intimate relationships at work.
4. Explore potential risks in engaging in nonplatonic workplace relationships for those employees immediately concerned and for co-workers.
5. In your experience (if you have had such an experience) how have nonplatonic workplace relationships been managed? Did you think the strategy of management was effective and ethically appropriate?
6. Much of the literature cited in this chapter has been based on studies undertaken in the West and particularly the US. If you do not come from the West, comment on how and why you believe the results might be different in the culture with which you are most familiar?
7. Work with one or two others to write a brief policy statement to be inserted into a staff handbook on nonplatonic relationships. Explain how the organisation's position on the issue and its culture may have a bearing on the way such relationships should be disclosed and managed. Share your statements of no more than 200–300 words with the wider group and consider how statements differed.

Theft

Reportedly, about two-thirds of employees engage in workplace theft, mostly entailing petty theft and the personal use of stationary (Schwartz, 2017). From an ethical perspective, some people differentiate between minor instances like this and those where large sums are embezzled from companies, for example. Time theft is another issue under discussion and pertains to using work time for personal activities in ways regarded as unsanctioned/unauthorised and unethical (see Brock, Martin, & Buckley, 2013). Hollinger and Clark (1983) appear to be the first authors to refer to the concept of time theft. At that time, and today, much less work has been dedicated to time theft compared to petty theft (Crossman & Perera, 2017). Time theft incorporates behaviours such as arriving late and leaving work early, working slower, time wasting, taking more and longer breaks, engaging in online personal interests during work hours, taking sick leave without being genuinely sick, and addressing personal issues via the phone, email, or other mediums of communication (Crossman & Perera, 2017). Institutions should be concerned about time theft, not least because its widespread occurrence significantly impacts upon profitability, productivity, morale, and workplace relationships (Crossman & Perera, 2017). According to Atkinson (2006), at the time of publication, US data suggested that approximately five weeks paid time per employee a year is lost to organisations as a result of time theft. On a national scale, it is estimated that in financial terms, the practice amounts to hundreds of billions of lost dollars annually to companies (Martin, Brock, Buckley, & Ketchen, 2010). Although few organisations appear to approach time theft in a strategic way, some evidence suggests that about one hour a day is factored in by human resource departments to compensate for employee time theft (Crossman & Perera, 2017).

A number of factors are likely associated with the rise of time theft. Even before the emergence of Covid-19 that necessitated many workers to operate in isolation at home or in quarantine facilities, other forces were beginning to make an impact on the prevalence of time theft or, at least, its potential to damage organisations unsure about how it might be managed. Flexible work practices may also have led to some ambiguity about the boundaries between personal and work time (Crossman & Perera, 2017). Where unpaid overtime occurs, employees may feel taking some time of their own to address personal affairs is a justifiable way to derive some compensation.

The complexity of time theft makes it difficult to address as an ethical matter as much as a management issue. Where time theft arises because of boredom, ambiguity about company expectations, or an ineffective and inconsistent approach to breaches of rules (Crossman & Perera, 2017) the problem is not simply confined to the unethical behaviour of individual employees. Although organisations do not appear to have consistently addressed time theft well from a strategic perspective, some have implemented processes to screen applicants using honesty tests or using various surveillance methods including peer reporting and electronic monitoring devices to accompany policies and guidelines (Crossman & Perera, 2017). An additional tool in the recruitment process available to organisations in the twenty-first century is, of course, the Internet. What it now means is that any historical reputational issues are much more likely to be detected and, indeed, the MeToo movement has demonstrated the power of global networks in enabling virtual strangers build social coalitions and collective intelligence, especially in contexts of unethical behaviours (Frank & Solby, 2020).

However, strategies to combat time theft can come with their own disadvantages. Surveillance serves to hamper empowerment and autonomy and has the potential to create a high level of stress, depression, anxiety, sleep disturbance, and nervousness – even about going to the toilet (Moore, 2000; Snider, 2001;

Stevens & Lanvin, 2007). Indeed, Frank and Solby (2020) argued that there is less need for employee surveillance where organisational members work together in a social environment that requires interdependence and is generally characterised by honest and open communication. The need for constant surveillance is also less necessary where such close social interaction occurs and where breaches will likely cause censure and gossip (Frank & Solby, 2020).

ACTIVITY: REFLECTION, DISCUSSION, APPLICATION, AND CREATIVITY

1.   Share experiences with others of time theft in any organisations with which you are familiar. Take care not to disclose the names of the company or any individuals involved, as this information could be sensitive. Explain your own assessment of the time theft behaviour and how it was managed.

2.   Where time theft occurs in highly collaborative teams and where interdependence is essential, how might the principle of self-defeating behaviour, as an aspect of universalisability in the Kantian categorical imperative, apply to time theft?

3.   In small groups, prepare for and engage in a debate representing agreement or refutational response to the following statement: *Time theft is an unethical practice exercised by employees of poor character and can claim no mitigating circumstances to justify it.*

4.   By pooling your ideas and reading about time theft, co-author a definition in pairs or very small groups.

5.   As a manager, what arguments might you accept for time theft by an employee and how would you manage the situation? It may help to determine specific forms of time theft (e.g., tardiness, too frequent breaks, paying personal bills on line in company time, spending time on Facetime, Twitter, or LinkedIn or other social platforms).

6.   What concepts in your reading about ethics might be brought to help explain and manage time theft (such as but not limited to: virtue ethics, Kantianism, moral rights).

7.   Collaborate with others to write a case study based on a perceived breach of company ethics through time theft and how employees and managers behaved. Compile a few questions about how the manager and the employee should proceed. Exchange case studies and questions with other groups, answering questions posed and making recommendations for improving the case study.

8.   Discuss with others the perspective of petty theft as less serious (morally and economically) than other forms of theft where the objects purloined are more expensive or valuable. Would you agree with this perspective? Why? Why not?

Corruption

From the perspective of Castro, Phillips, and Ansari (2020), corporate corruption or corruption at work is considered as a moral failing pertaining to the improper use of formal power by an organisational representative and is most commonly associated with bribery. Cross-cultural scholarship over decades has continued to inform understandings on corruption through a business ethics lens. Some of this work has considered linkages between corruption and cultural dimensions. Akbar and Vujic (2014) reported correlations between corruption and high power distance, masculinity, uncertainty avoidance, and those cultures with a strong sense of fatalism. Martin et al. (2007) maintained that bribery (a form of corruption) is linked to cultures that emphasise humane values less. These associations contrast with those countries with less apparent corruption and that are considered egalitarian, with robust whistle-blower processes in place (Akbar & Vujic, 2014).

To some extent, what constitutes corruption, however, is culturally constructed (Castro et al., 2020), and is likely to stimulate discussion, with some espousing relativist constructions of ethical perspectives. Costello (2020) bemoans the conceptual limitation of corruption to bribery, fraud, embezzlement, and extortion and maintains that it should be expanded to include other behaviour rooted in self-interest such as depriving individuals from information they need by obfuscation and deflecting questions and ignoring communications until long after the information ceases to be relevant. The manager who manipulates work schedules, for example, to strategically disrupt subordinate leave applications with the intention of harming others and increasing anxiety in the process, damages worker wellbeing in ways that constitute unethical behaviour (Costello, 2020).

ACTIVITY: EXPERIENTIAL CASE STUDY ABOUT CARLOS GHOSN: APPLICATION AND CREATIVITY

The following case study has primarily been drawn and adapted from one source at the time of writing (see Kostov & Maremont, 2020).

> *Nissan ex-head, Carlos Ghosn, holds French, Brazilian, and Lebanese citizenship. Born in Brazil to Lebanese parents, he was educated in France as an engineer. Ghosn had been one of the world's most acclaimed executives until he reportedly jeopardised the alliance between Nissan and top shareholder, Renault.*
>
> *He was arrested and sacked as Nissan Chairperson in late 2018 for understating his income and directing in excess of $7 million of Nissan money to projects that were personally beneficial and imprisoned for four months before being released on bail. After weeks of planning and assisted by supporters in Japan, he was able to secretly flee to the Lebanon on a private jet via Istanbul using a Lebanese ID and French passport and since*

> *Beirut officials maintained he had entered the country legally, no action was taken and he was allowed to stay in a family residence under surveillance but nevertheless in fear of being abducted and returned to Japan. Mr Ghosn is regarded as a hero in Lebanon where he insists he would be able to clear his name and be tried fairly for any financial wrongdoing.*
>
> *These events surprised even his own Japanese lawyer and took place even when assurances from prosecutors that he would receive a fair trial were provided. Ghosn maintained his innocence and explained away his actions as a way to escape alleged discrimination, injustice, a lack of conformance to human rights, and political persecution. Japan has extradition treaties with only the US and South Korea so it could be difficult to force Mr Ghosn to return to stand trial from the Lebanon but Tokyo officials have provided assurances that he would be treated like any other suspect.*

This case study is informed by information available at the time of writing. Search online for further information, taking careful note of sources. What new information and insights did you discover? Based on the sources you are able to access, re-write and update the case study.

Discuss aspects of this case with others from an ethical perspective, supporting your observations with sources drawn from business ethics literature and the concepts presented in this chapter.

Conclusion

This chapter has highlighted how ethical perspectives are relevant to a number of practical scenarios in business and organisations. It begins with an exposition about the study of business ethics and the relatively recent attention brought to it. Some examples of the varied behaviours associated with ethical misconduct in the workplace were provided. Ethical concepts and principles such as virtue ethics, Kantianism and the categorical imperative, and moral rights and utilitarianism were introduced so that they could later be brought in critical ways to activities for analysis, discussion, reflection, application, and research subsequently in the chapter. Certain topics and illustrations of ethical scenarios in the workplace are provided, namely concerning worker relationships, theft, and corruption.

References

Akbar, Y., & Vujic, V. (2014). Explaining corruption: The role of national culture and its implications for international management. *Cross Cultural Management, 21*(2), 191–218.

Alzola, M., Hennig, A., & Romar, E. (2020). Thematic symposium editorial: Virtue ethics between East and West. *Journal of Business Ethics, 165*(2), 177–189.

Atkinson, W. (2006). Stealing time. *Risk Management Magazine, 53*(11), 48–52.

Bazerman, M. (2014). Becoming a first-class noticer. *Harvard Business Review, 92*(7–8), 116–119.

Bobbit, R. (2020). *Exploring communication ethics: A Socratic approach*. Oxford: Routledge.

Brock, M., Martin, L., & Buckley, M. (2013). Time theft in organizations: The development of the time banditry questionnaire. *International Journal of Selection and Assessment, 21*(3), 309–321.

Burgoon, G., Hamel, L., Blair, P., & Twyman, N. (2020). Factors that facilitative or impair kinesic and vocalic nonvernal behaviours during interpersonal deception. In R. Sternberg & A. Kostic (Eds.), *Social intelligence and nonverbal communication* (pp. 79–117). Cham, Switzerland: Palgrave Macmillan.

Castro, A., Phillips, N., & Ansari, S. (2020). Corporate corruption: A review and an agenda for future research. *Academy of Management Annals*. doi:10.5465/annals.2018.0156

Costello, J. (2020). *Workplace wellbeing: A relational approach*. London: Routledge.

Cowan, R., & Horan, S. (2014). Love at the office? Understanding workplace romance disclosures and reactions from the co-worker perspective. *Western Journal of Communication, 78*(2), 238–253.

Crossman, J., & Doshi, V. (2014). When not knowing is a virtue: A business ethics perspective. *Journal of Business Ethics, 131*(1), 1–8.

Crossman, J., & Noma, H. (2013). Sunao as character: Its implications for trust and intercultural communication within subsidiaries of Japanese multinationals in Australia. *Journal of Business Ethics, 131*(1), 1–8.

Crossman, J., & Perera, S. (2017). Time theft: An integrity based approach to its management. In M. Orlitzky & M. Monga (Eds.), *Integrity in business & management* (pp. 40–66). New York: Routledge.

Deresky, H., & Christopher, E. (2008). *International management: Managing across borders and cultures*. Frenchs Forest, NSW: Pearson, Education Australian.

Dwyer, J. (2020). *Communication for business and the professions: Strategies and skills*. Retrieved from http://ebookcentral.proquest.com

Fok, L., Payne, D., & Corey, C. (2016). Cultural values, utilitarian orientation and ethical decision making: A comparison of US and Puerto Rican professionals. *Journal of Business Ethics, 134*(2), 263–279.

Frank, M., & Solby, A. (2020). Nonverbal communication: Evolution and today. In R. Sternberg & A. Kostic (Eds.), *Social intelligence and nonverbal communication* (pp. 119–162). Cham, Switzerland: Palgrave Macmillan.

Gasper, J., & Schweitzel, M. (2019). Confident and cunning: Negotiator self-efficacy promotes deception in negotiations. *Journal of Business Ethics, 171*(1), 139–156.

Gift, M., Gift, P., & QinQin, Z. (2013). Cross-cultural perception of business ethics: Evidence from the United States and China. *Journal of Business Ethics, 114*(4), 633–642.

Gonzalez-Araujo, V., Alvarez-Delgado, R., & Sancho-Rodriguez, A. (Eds.). (2020). *Ethics in business: New challenges in the digital world communication*. Bern, Switzerland: Peter Lang. Retrieved February 21, 2021, from https://ww.peterlang.com/new/tit.e/71387

Hollinger, R., & Clark, J. (1983). *Theft by employees*. Boston, MA: Lexington Books.

Huhn, M., Meyer, M., & Racelis, A. (2018). Virtues and the common good in leadership. In A. Sison, I. Ferraro, & G. Guitian (Eds.), *Business ethics: A virtue ethics and common good approach* (pp. 24–50). London: Taylor & Francis Group.

Huntala, M., Feldt, T., Lamsa, A., Mauno, S., & Kinnunen, U. (2011). Does the ethical culture of organisations promote managers' occupational well-being? Investing indirect links via ethical strain. *Journal of Business Ethics, 101*(2), 231–247.

Jacobs, C., Kreutzer, K., & Vaara, E. (2020, April 13). Political dynamics in organizational identity breach and reconstruction: Findings from the crisis in UNICEF Germany. *Academy of Management Journal*, 1–67. doi:10.5465/amj.2018.0821

Jonson, E., McGuire, L., & O'Neill, D. (2015). Teaching ethics to undergraduate business students in Australia: Comparison of integrated and stand-alone approaches. *Journal of Business Ethics, 132*(2), 477–491.

Kim, R., Mondejar, R., Roque, R., & Cuervo, J. (2018). Confucian traditions in virtue ethics. In A. Sison, I. Ferraro, & G. Guitian (Eds.), *Business ethics: A virtue ethics and common good approach* (pp. 187–22). London: Taylor Francis Group.

Kish-Gephart, J., Trevino, L., Chen, A., & Tilton, J. (2019). Behavioural business ethics: The journey from foundations to futures. In D. Wasieleski & J. Weber (Eds.), *Business ethics* (pp. 3–34). Retrieved from https://ebookcentral.Proquest.com

Kostov, N., & Maremont, M. (2020). *Ghosn escape weeks in the planning.* Retrieved from theaustralian.com.au/wsj

Kundro, T., & Nurmohamed, S. (2020, April 13). Understanding when and why cover-ups are punished less severely. *Academy of Management Journal,* 1–16. doi:10.5465/amj.2018.1396

Larson, K. (2018). *Adaption and well-being.* London: Routledge.

Lewicki, R., Barry, B., & Saunders, D. (2016). *Essentials of negotiation.* New York: McGraw-Hill.

Martin, K., Cullen, J., Johnson, J., & Parboteeah, K. (2007). Deciding to bribe: A cross level analysis of firm and home country influences on bribery activity. *Academy of Management Journal, 50*(6), 1401–1422.

Martin, L., Brock, M., Buckley, R., & Ketchen, D. (2010). Time banditry: Examining the purloining of time in organizations. *Human Resource Management Review, 20*(1), 26–34.

Meyer-Galow, E. (2018). *Business ethics 3.0: The integral ethics from the perspective of a CEO.* Boston: De Gruyter.

Moore, A. (2000). Employee mentoring and computer technology: Evaluation surveillance v privacy. *Business Ethics Quarterly, 10*(3), 697–709.

Murase, T. (1982). Sunao: A central value in Japanese psychotherapy. In A. J. Marcella & G. M. White (Eds.), *Cultural conception of mental health and therapy* (pp. 317–329). Boston and Dordrecht: Springer.

Pasmore, W., & Woodman, R. (2017). The future of research and practice in organizational change and development. In *Research in organizational change and development* (Vol. 25, pp. 1–32). Bingley: Emerald Publishing Limited. doi:10.1108/50897-3016201

Rachels, J. (1995). *The elements of moral philosophy.* New York: McGraw-Hill.

Radosavac, A., Sretic, M., Mircetic, V., & Vukcevic, M. (2019). Business ethics in marketing communication. *Quaestus, 15,* 188–196.

Schwartz, M. (2017). *Business ethics: An ethical decision – making approach.* Retrieved from https://ebookcentral-proqest-com.virtual.anu.edu.au

Sias, P., & Shin, Y. (2019). Workplace relationships. In A. Nicotera (Ed.), *Origins and traditions of organizational communication: A comprehensive introduction to the field* (pp. 187–206). New York: Routledge.

Sison, A., Ferraro, I., & Guitian, G. (2018). *Business ethics: A virtue ethics and common good approach.* London: Taylor & Francis Group.

Snider, L. (2001). Crimes against capital: Discovering theft of time. *Social Justice, 28*(3), 105–120.

Snow, N. (2020). *Contemporary virtue ethics.* Cambridge: Cambridge University Press. doi:10.101719781108580496

St. John-Brooks, K. (2014). *Internal coaching: Inside story.* London: Taylor & Francis Group.

Stevens, A., & Lanvin, D. (2007). Stealing time: The temporal regulation of labour in neo-liberal and post-Fordist work regime. *Democratic Communique, 21*(2), 40–61.

Swol, L., & Paik, J. (2017). Deciding how to deceive: Differences in communication and detection between good and bad liars. *Communication Quarterly*, *65*(5), 503–522.

Tan, D., & Snell, R. (2002). The third eye: Exploring Guanxi and relational morality in the workplace. *Journal of Business Ethics*, *41*(4), 361–384.

Tracy, S., & Redden, S. (2019). The structuration of emotion. In A. Nicotera (Ed.), *Origins and traditions of organizational communication: A comprehensive introduction to the field* (pp. 348–369). New York: Routledge.

Turner, L., & West, R. (2018). *An introduction to communication*. Cambridge: Cambridge University Press.

Vitrano, C. (2014). *The nature and value of happiness*. New York: Routledge.

13

DARK ISSUES

The metaphor of the 'dark side' and its relation to organisational communication

The metaphor of 'the dark side' of organisations has attracted scholarly attention in the twenty-first century, but nevertheless remains poorly theorised since Mills (2011) first made this observation a decade or more ago. In general terms, the negative impact of dark practices in organisations, as various as they are, has been associated with illness, stress, poor morale, absenteeism, low staff retention, interpersonal and intergroup conflict, poor productivity, risky practices, unethical behaviours (such as fraud, misconduct, deviance and internal terrorism), and a wealth of mistakes, disasters, and scandals (Mills, 2011). Many of these unwanted outcomes are associated with the specific contexts discussed in this chapter and carry significant human and financial costs as a shared responsibility for all organisational members and wider societies.

In her journal paper, Mills (2011) also draws together the strands of communication and the dark side of organisations. She remarks that communication as an integral part of organising determines what is deemed as dark or not. It is through the collective constructions of actors that over time can become institutionalised and sanctioned, when unchallenged, and attract a level of symbolic power in prevailing values and beliefs. Destabilising entrenched, harmful ways of working requires courage, certainly, in speaking out. Macro processes committed to acknowledging wrongs, identifying discourse that supports them and embedding unheard, often marginalised voices have the potential to inform strategic new ways of thinking and operating. Striking out at some of the unsavoury practices illustrated in this chapter may cause its own kind of pain where routine assumptions and norms come into question and where seats of power become threatened. The process is not one that can be hastily undertaken if it is to achieve more than the most basic of cosmetic adjustments. The concerted efforts and communication

DOI: 10.4324/9780429318948-16

of not only individual organisations but also of governments, international bodies, and global networks will be required.

Workplace bullying

Workplace bullying is common in organisations internationally and apart from documented studies in the US, Australia, and the UK, some reports reveal alarming rates in previously underrepresented countries in the literature, such as South America, the Asia-Pacific, and the Middle Asia regions (Farley, Casamunt, & Crossman, 2016; Leon-Perez, Escartin, & Giorgi, 2021). It has also been explored across a variety of professions and disciplines such as higher education (Hollis, 2021), policing (Farr-Wharton, Shacklock, Brunetto, Teo, & Farr-Wharton, 2017), and nursing (see Leong & Crossman, 2016), a context that dominates many of the bullying studies conducted in Asia (Leon-Perez et al., 2021.

The term 'workplace bullying' emerged in the 1990s although 'mobbing' was more commonly adopted in Scandanavia where early research was conducted. Leymann (1996) suggested that mobbing referred to a less direct form of aggression than the concept of bullying but others have concluded that cultural differences rather than conceptual ones lie at the heart of any distinctions (see Einarsen, Hoel, & Zapf, 2020). With the development of research over time, some other terminological and conceptual shifts have occurred in workplace bullying discourse. For example, the terms harassment and bullying are often used interchangeably (Costello, 2020), no doubt because, as Einarsen et al. (2020) observed, few differences between the two concepts are evident. Nevertheless, harassment tends to focus on a particular feature of a target's identity that is difficult to change, such as, race, age, religion, and gender (Brandon & Robertson, 2007). Terminology with respect to workplace bullying has also altered over time to become more neutral so 'target' has generally replaced emotive terms such as 'victim', and 'perpetrator' is now more frequently used than 'bully'.

Clear definitions of bullying are surprisingly elusive (Costello, 2020) but a recent contribution published by three seminal authors working in this field gathers up the essential features of this behaviour:

> Bullying at work is about repeated actions and practices that are directed against one or more workers that are unwanted by the target and may be carried out deliberately or unconsciously, but clearly cause humiliation, offense and distress.
>
> *(Einarsen et al., 2020, p. 10)*

Some work has suggested that a defining aspect of systematic bullying also pins it to a particular time period, usually for more than half a year (Hassan, Al Bir, & Hashim, 2015; Einarsen, Hoel, Zapf, & Cooper, 2011; Farley et al., 2016; Leymann, 1996; Proksch, 2016). Tying the period of abuse to six months, however, may be less relevant to *how many* weeks or months the behaviour persists and more a matter of emphasising that bullying is not a 'one off' or brief circumstance. Like perpetrators, targets of bullying can be at any stage of someone's career, regardless of who they are. That is, bullying may be initiated by subordinate, peer, or supervisor (Farley et al., 2016) so although an unbalanced power relationship is common in a bullying dynamic, this is not always the case (Costello, 2020).

Bullying behaviour channelled through technology, known as cyberbullying, has recently attracted interest amongst scholars and generated empirical research (Farley, Coyne, & D'Cruz, 2021). The phenomenon has no doubt arisen from the now ubiquitous use of the Internet in contemporary organisations coupled with personal consumption, presenting opportunities for some to engage in online forms of abuse. Cyberbullying may occur via online text mediums of communication such as emails and texts, online visuals communication such as photos and videos, or verbally through voice mails and telephone calls (Farley et al., 2021). With little evidence of remorse and the ease of anonymity for the perpetrator, cyberbullies who target individuals often go unpunished (Turner & West, 2018) though laws in Australia at least have now been tightened in order to ensure that cyber bullying is captured. A pernicious aspect of cyberbullying is that target anxiety and humiliation is intensified because the accusations are made public (Turner & West, 2018).

Bullying behaviours

Workplace bullying can be physical but as Tracy and Redden (2019) observed, it is primarily a form of emotional abuse. Over time, it can give rise to severe social, psychological, and psychosomatic problems that can be more debilitating for the target than all other forms of work-related stress put together (Einarsen et al., 2020). Persistent behaviours associated with bullying include, but are not limited to (Christensen & Evans-Murray, 2021; Costello, 2020; Mills, 2011; Proksch, 2016; Tracy & Redden, 2019):

TABLE 13.1 Bullying behaviours

• ridiculing and shaming	• insulting, derogatory, abusive language
• undermining someone's authority	• setting the target up to fail, sometimes by overloading competent workers
• spreading rumours and malicious gossip	• ostracising (denying eye contact, using a cool tone, excluding)
• making unfounded threats about job security	• blocking promotion or training opportunities
• labelling targets as trouble makers	• engaging in unwanted sexual behaviours and banter
• humiliating publicly	• constantly criticising
• yelling and screaming	• intimidating and making threats
• social withdrawal and not speaking to a target	• making reputational attacks
• making physical attacks	• gaslighting

Gaslighting

One of the behaviours in Table 13.1, gaslighting, deserves some greater explanation given its complexity psychologically. Gaslighting is a term that refers to occasions when individuals are persuaded that they are not able to make logical judgements about what is happening or who is at fault and begin to mistrust their own emotions (Costello, 2020). It is associated with narcissism, lies, and disingenuous complaints, praise and positive reinforcement designed to create confusion, chaos, and doubt on the part of the gaslightee giving rise to target hyper-vigilance, anxiety, addiction, and suicidal ideations, as well as the physical symptoms also associated with stress (Christensen & Evans-Murray, 2021). Gaslighting as a pernicious form of bullying is gaining attention in such fields as nursing and academia, but it is difficult to grasp because of the subtleties surrounding the behaviours that accompany it (Christensen & Evans-Murray, 2021).

Those who suspect they are targets of gaslighting should speak to a trusted colleague, a union representative, an HR specialist, or all three because their multiple perspectives will be illuminating and also provide support to counter the isolation that a target in these circumstances often experiences (Costello, 2020). As is the case in other forms of abuse, gaslighters themselves often suffer from anxiety and depression and become aggressive as a way to protect themselves from feelings of inadequacy (Christensen & Evans-Murray, 2021).

ACTIVITY: REFLECTION AND EXPERIENTIAL LEARNING

Review the bullying behaviours in Table 13.1. In any experience you have of organisations, note behaviours that you have personally witnessed/experienced that you believe characterise bullying but have not been included in the table. Consider your rationale for including these additional behaviours as examples of bullying. You may like to re-read the definition of workplace bullying provided and what characterises it. Discuss your thoughts with others.

Taking responsibility for the dire consequences of bullying

In reviewing the literature, Farley et al. (2016) noted that targets and bystanders often choose not to report workplace bullying because of a multitude of often justifiable risks. Gender may have a moderating role, however, in that some work suggests that men are less likely to report than women (see Costello, 2020). Rationales for not reporting include (see; Costello, 2020; Farley et al., 2016; Samnani, 2013):

TABLE 13.2 Rationales for not reporting workplace bullying

feeling disinclined to become personally involved in a painful, protracted process following a report.	fearing that reporting will escalate the bullying.
fearing retaliation in the form of downgrading roles, engineering poor performance evaluations, threats of job loss, social isolation, reprimands, and even violence.	lack of faith in the support of unbiased Human Resource managers who may be peers of line managers as perpetrators.
difficulty in proving bullying.	feeling ashamed of being a target of abuse and not being able to cope.

ACTIVITY: REFLECTION AND DISCUSSION

Reflect upon the following questions and make a note of your responses before discussing them with others.

1. If you were bullied, would you report it to a manager? Why?/Why not?
2. If you were a bystander of bullying behaviour, would you report it to a manager? Why?/Why not?

Managers, supervisors, and team leaders have a responsibility to provide a safe workplace environment, free from bullying (Dwyer, 2020). At the same time, so do all employees, if one subscribes to the view that organisations are the embodiment of its members. Although much attention is focused upon individuals in cases of bullying, workplace cultures can be complicit directly or indirectly. For example, aggressive supervisor behaviours towards underperforming subordinates with the intention of goading them into resigning in some organisational cultures may conveniently pass unsanctioned (Farley et al., 2016). Sometimes, targets of supervisor abuse may blame themselves and paradoxically try to work even harder for an abusive supervisor to atone in some way for perceived shortfalls (Troester & Van Quaquebeke, 2020). It is incumbent upon organisations to investigate any known cases of bullying in a fair manner and to develop policies and procedures that are well informed by empirical research to guide all those who are involved.

Bullying harms individuals and organisations. It damages team relationships, diminishes morale and commitment, and increases the chances of distraction, absenteeism (directly or via related health issues), intentions to leave, and high turnover (Dwyer, 2020; Farley et al., 2016). Employees who are targets of supervisor abuse also become less likely to cooperate (Troester & Van Quaquebeke, 2020). Reputational damage as targets share their story in the community is another potential problem. Organisations can pay a high price for inaction with respect to workplace bullying in the form of legal costs, compensation claims, or losing experienced staff who seek other employment or who retire early unnecessarily (Giga, Hoel, & Lewis, 2008). It is not only the targets of bullying who can be harmed by this toxic behaviour since the effects flow on to others in the organisation. Bystanders can be affected by bullying (Costello, 2020) and may also suffer from stress, insomnia, exhaustion, and headaches (Farley et al., 2016) just as targets do. These outcomes all negatively impact work, both qualitatively and quantitatively.

ACTIVITY: RESEARCH

Use the research resources available to you to identify laws in your own country that are applicable to workplace bullying and the responsibility that organisations have. Share your findings and sources with others.

What can be done?

As individuals, targets of bullying will need to consider the risks and benefits of the actions they take. Early on in the experience of bullying, according to Gilmore (2018), it can be powerful and effective to speak directly to a perpetrator using 'I' statements. For example, one might say, 'I find the comments you have made hurtful and unfair. Please do not speak to me again in this manner'. It is important to document a perpetrator's behaviour, explaining the nature of incidents including any relevant dates and times. If others witnessed the incident, make this clear. Sign your report. In some countries, documented target reports constitute evidence. Descriptions of incidents should be clear and factual but they can also include mental and physical consequences of ongoing abuse, particularly if supported by medical health practitioners and therapists (Catanzariti & Egan, 2015).

A surprising amount of evidence to support claims of bullying is available via email, text, and social media communications that organisations may well have the right to access, especially if they have made ownership clear in policies about online communication (Catanzariti & Egan, 2015). Farley et al. (2021) also emphasise how companies vary with respect to rules about how employee private social media accounts are used. Trade union representatives may also be able to provide advice and support to their members.

At the organisational level, Human Resource departments may have systems in place to ensure that when a supervisor or line manager is the perpetrator, someone neutral and with authority is recruited to manage the issue in conjunction with the Human Resource department. Many large, reputable organisations have guidelines in place that explain processes and policies that should be easily accessible and available to all employees and routinely addressed in onboarding and professional development. A commitment at CEO and other levels of senior management that bullying will not be tolerated communicates a strong message throughout the organisation, especially if it becomes clear through allied guidelines, practices, policies, and actions that such commitment represents more than tokenism. Confidentiality when investigating bullying is essential (Catanzariti & Egan, 2015). Some options to address bullying may include counselling and mediation but both these possibilities for resolving the issue have their own advantages and disadvantages.

The future of empirical work in workplace bullying, as Leon-Perez et al. (2021) suggest, calls for more cross-cultural work. Considering similarities and differences amongst global cultures, prevalence rates (the number/percentage of workers exposed to bullying), and the nature of bullying behaviour would assist in establishing some global solutions. Given the pace of globalisation from an organisational perspective, such information should inform partnerships and networks on an international scale.

Extreme/long work hours

Many employees find that from time to time, they are called upon to put in extra hours at work in order to fulfil a personal or organisational goal (the two are generally reciprocal). However, working consistently for long hours is unacceptable on many levels, not least of which is the effect that it can have upon the health of workers.

In western countries, public debate and concern about the number of hours people worked was evident from eighteenth century (Lu & Chou, 2017) as the industrial revolution changed workplaces dramatically. Such concern was arguably less observable from the latter part of the nineteenth century when the early social-democratic and labour movements in Europe worked hard to instate the eight-hour working day (Burger, 2020). Unionisation in the first half of the twentieth century meant that many employees were better protected in terms of working conditions than they had been at any other point in history. However, with the rise of labour market policies, collective bargaining institutions, new labour market structures, and the diminishing power of unions (Burger, 2020), many felt that hard won protections were beginning to be seriously eroded. Thus, from the second half of the twentieth century, social scientists began to raise the alarm with respect to increasing working hours of employees (Burger, 2020). At about the same time, during the 1970s in Japan, disturbing reports about the phenomenon of *Karoshi*, a term used to describe death from overwork, were beginning to emerge (Lu & Chou, 2017).

Based on their research (Blagoev & Schreyögg, 2019) maintained that working 60 to 120 hours per week is generally considered to be extreme, though other accounts refer to a 55-hour week to fall within this category (Pega et al., 2021). Internationally, common agreements about what constitutes long working hours is hard to establish or, consequently, regulate because legal working hours vary from one country to another (Lu & Chou, 2017). Inconsistencies can be ethically problematic for multinational organisations operating globally.

ACTIVITY: RESEARCH

Using the research tools available to you, establish what laws in your country are in place with respect to the number of hours an employee can be expected to work per week.

Why employees work long hours is less a matter of personal choice and more likely to be influenced by the complex interaction of factors such as institutional regulations, working conditions, cultural values, incentive schemes, the macroeconomic climate, workplace constraints (Lu & Chou, 2017), and indeed, organisational culture. Whatever the rationales for working extreme hours, the many millions of people who do face an early death or disability. By 2016, an estimated 745,194 deaths and 23.3 million disability adjusted life years from heart disease and stroke directly related to working excessive hours were substantiated in a global study conducted by Pega et al. (2021). Incidences of heart disease and stroke were found to be disproportionally high in South-East Asia and the West Pacific regions (Pega et al., 2021). Other work reports that extreme work hours are associated internationally with burnout, poor sleep patterns, diminished safety at work, fractured families, and lower fertility rates (Burger, 2020; Yamauchi et al., 2019).

Despite a body of knowledge indicating the detrimental effects of long working hours for employees, organisations, and society as a whole, many organisations continue to require them (Blagoev & Schreyögg, 2019) overtly or more subtly. Extreme work hours are not simply an issue in 'sweat shops' in countries struggling with poverty. Blagoev and Schreyögg (2019), for example, focused their historical case study of an elite consulting firm and traced the genesis, reinforcement, and maintenance of extreme working hours over a period of four decades. Indeed, within the US, extreme working hours have increased since the 1970s (Burger, 2020). So, the abuse of workers can be endemic, protracted, and recurrent where historically many imagined it to be a practice of the past. Long working hours are not only the preserve of the US however. Asian scholars, too, are calling for change in Confucian cultures such as Taiwan, China, Hong Kong, Japan, Korea, and Singapore where long hours seem to be most salient (see Lu & Chou, 2017).

Human trafficking

Much of this chapter, and indeed this book, is largely focused upon mainstream workplaces and organisations where workers are afforded protection by laws and internal initiatives that protect their rights and wellbeing to one degree or another. This brief section on human trafficking is a reminder of how many people are suffering around the world, trying to survive in unpaid working conditions not of their choice and from which they cannot escape. Trafficking human beings (THB) is a serious crime that violates the most basic of human rights (Jagers & Rijken, 2014). From a human rights perspective, trafficked individuals are regarded as victims of abuse rather than as criminals who breach immigration laws (Eriksson, 2013).

The California Department of Education suggests that labour trafficking is the fastest growing enterprise in the world as an estimated $150 billion-a-year industry from which even young children are not immune (cited in Salas & Didier, 2020). Reliable statistical evidence is not freely available, and sources vary, but the International Labor Organisation (ILO) claimed that in the second decade of the twenty-first century, nearly 21 million people globally had been trafficked (Jagers & Rijken, 2014). As a global phenomenon, THB arises wherever opportunists interact with the vulnerable, most notably women and children (Eriksson, 2013; Salas & Didier, 2020). According to the ILO, more than half of trafficked people are female and in terms of sex trafficking that figure is not far short of 100 per cent (Jagers & Rijken, 2014).

People are trafficked largely from Asia, the Pacific regions, and increasingly from Africa (Jagers & Rijken, 2014). Those taken from Myanmar and Cambodia are handed over to captains of Thai fishing ships for a price and made to work for months or years, receiving little or no payment for their labour of up to 20 hours a day in deprived conditions (Jagers & Rijken, 2014). Slavery is not an abomination consigned to history or applicable only to poor nations, however. Indeed, within the UK, human trafficking has been exposed in agri-/aqua-cultural industries, nail bars, car washing companies, and construction. Into these enterprises, disempowered, illegal immigrants, with little command of the language, are recruited and forced to repay debts they are told they have incurred simply for grasping perceived opportunities that will take them from lives of poverty and danger in the hope of a better future (Amis, Mair, & Munir, 2020).

In a world where global networks and supply chains have become the norm, it is incumbent upon organisations to learn as much as they can about how services are supplied and products are made, by whom, under what circumstances, and from which those organisations benefit. Undertaking extensive due diligence may be costly and time consuming but is essential not only to lay bare human trafficking, but other practices such as using child labour or paying people who live in desperately poor conditions below subsistence levels to produce designer label clothing for western retailers or provide vegetables to major European supermarkets (Jagers & Rijken, 2014).

Communication scholars in the twenty-first century are beginning to explore lines of enquiry such as online communication and rhetorical patterns in the context of human trafficking (Gagnon, 2017; Kamler, 2013; Pop, 2013; Raets & Janssens, 2017; Rusnac, 2019). On a practical level, online communication is used to recruit targets, organise logistical matters internationally in the movement of people around the world, and indeed to advertise and provide some of the services offered (see Raets & Janssens, 2017). Online communication has thus facilitated the expansion of human trafficking operations. At the same time, advancements in online, digital forensics have proven one tool in exposing and combatting those communication networks (Raets & Janssens, 2017).

Some scholars specialising in rhetoric have criticised non-government organisations (NGOs) for the way they have communicated the issue of human trafficking and their own role in combatting it. Gagnon (2017) refers to dominant narratives that cast NGOs in rescue and liberating roles and offering up a simplistic account via commodifying stories. Kamler (2013), too bemoans the cultural soundbites of NGO discourse that do little to convey the complexity of human trafficking. The voices of those who are trafficked are reportedly unheard and 'written out' of the text (Gagnon, 2017). Apart from the obvious disempowerment involved in muting communication, the intelligence value of these lived experiences is largely lost and any responsive strategies fail to take into account the input that those who have been trafficked could usefully have. Listening to these stories, acknowledging and actioning them would make a vital contribution to how NGOs approach the issue. As Gagnon (2017) points out, doing so will enable the construction of collective meanings and a new language capturing a multiplicity of voices and values in a way that could be far more responsive to the fluidity and complexity of human trafficking.

From a cultural perspective, Kamler (2013), like Gagnon (2017), raises concerns about the colonial mindset and narratives of NGOs that serve to privilege their own perceptions and insights in benevolent characterisations in order to attract greater funding (not least to ensure the retention of employee jobs). Based on a study in the context of Thailand, Kamler (2013, p. 78) interrogated those narratives and the embedded stereotypes that run through them and identified five main themes:

TABLE 13.3 NGO narratives

1.	Thailand as backwards	Civilising narrative
2.	Thai values are not modern	Moralising narrative
3.	An expectation of gratitude	Saviour narrative
4.	Thailand is unintelligible to the West	Othering narrative
5.	Sex workers lack agency	Victim narrative

Source: Kamler, 2013

Such narratives provide a framework to assist those who work for NGOs to explain, categorise, and manage the daily complexities of their work (Kamler, 2013). The criticisms of dominant narratives, however, should not serve to demonise those who seek to end the brutal practice of human trafficking, often under difficult conditions and with personal costs and sacrifices. The literature serves to draw attention to the way that communication in organisations becomes limited and thus less effective, when the voices of key stakeholders are uninvited or at least underrepresented. Paradoxically, underrepresentation constitutes one form of discrimination and harm in order to address another.

Conclusion

All of the contexts presented in this chapter suggest some difficult questions about how people organise themselves to achieve certain goals. Sometimes the price paid for achieving those goals is catastrophically high, superseding the value placed on human experience and, indeed, human life itself. Entrenched myopia, too often goes unchecked, and is even actively protected and sustained. Whistle blowers are marginalised and regarded as troublesome individuals, and even silence is not neutral but rather another form of, albeit, passive endorsement (see Mills, 2011).

So much depends on responsible leaders and their followers in organisations (see Crossman & Crossman, 2011), who in defining organisational goals and communicating them, should also set simultaneous standards and protocols that constrain achieving those goals at any cost. The wellbeing movement and mechanisms to protect health and safety has done much to advance safe and compassionate organisations but based on the literature cited in this chapter, much is left to be done if societies are to temper dark and rapacious organisational practices.

ACTIVITY: BRAINSTORMING

The abstract of this chapter has listed areas where workforces can exhibit 'dark' (unethical, exploitative, and harmful) practices. Brainstorm in small groups about other potential forms of dark behaviour that might have been included in this chapter but were not.

References

Amis, J., Mair, J., & Munir, K. (2020). The organizational reproduction of inequality. *Academy of Management Annals, 14*(1), 195–230.

Blagoev, B., & Schreyögg, G. (2019). Why do extreme work hours persist? Temporal uncoupling as a new way of seeing. *Academy of Management Journal, 62*(6), 1818–1847.

Brandon, M., & Robertson, L. (2007). *Conflict and dispute resolution: A guide for practice.* Melbourne: Oxford University Press.

Burger, A. (2020). Extreme work hours in Western Europe and North America: Diverging trends since the 1970s. *Socio-Economic Review, 18*(4), 1065–1087.

Catanzariti, J., & Egan, K. (2015). *Workplace bullying.* Chatswood, NSW: LexisNexis Butterworths.

Christensen, M., & Evans-Murray, A. (2021). Gaslighting in nursing academia: A new or established covert form of bullying. *Nursing Forum, 56*(3), 640–647.

Costello, J. (2020). *Workplace wellbeing: A relational approach.* London: Routledge.

Crossman, B., & Crossman, J. (2011). Conceptualising followership – a review of the literature. *Leadership, 7*(4), 481–497.

Dwyer, J. (2020). *Communication for business and the professions: Strategies and skills.* Melbourne: Pearson.

Einarsen, S., Hoel, H., & Zapf, D. (2020). Bullying and workplace harassment in the workplace. In *Theory, research & practice* (3rd ed.). New York: Taylor & Francis Group.

Einarsen, S., Hoel, H., Zapf, D., & Cooper, C. (2011). *Bullying and harassment in the workplace: Developments in theory, research and practice* (2nd ed.). Boca Raton: CRC Press.

Eriksson, M. (2013). The prevention of human trafficking – regulating domestic criminal legislation through the European convention on human rights. *Nordic Journal of International Law, 82*(3), 339–368.

Farley, S., Casamunt, A., & Crossman, J. (2016, September 7). *To report or not to report? Factors influencing failure to report workplace bullying.* British Academy of Management Conference, Newcastle University, Newcastle upon Tyne.

Farley, S., Coyne, I., & D'Cruz, P. (2021). Cyberbullying at work: Understanding the influence of technology. In P. D'Cruz, E. Noronha, G. Notelaers, & C. Rayner (Eds.), *Handbooks of workplace bullying, emotional abuse and harassment: Concepts, Approaches And Methods* (pp. 234–252). Singapore: Springer.

Farr-Wharton, B., Shacklock, K., Brunetto, Y., Teo, S., & Farr-Wharton, R. (2017). Workplace bullying, workplace relationships and job outcomes for police officers in Australia. *Public Money and Management, 37*(5), 325–332.

Gagnon, J. (2017). How cultural rhetorics can change the conversation: Towards new communication spaces to address human trafficking. *An Interdisciplinary Journal of Rhetorical Analysis and Invention, 12*(2), 1–21.

Giga, S., Hoel, H., & Lewis, D. (2008). *The costs of workplace bullying.* Manchester: University of Bradford.

Gilmore, C. (2018). Tackling bullying. *Kai Tiaki: Nursing New Zealand, 24*(1), 33–33.

Hassan, A., Al Bir, A., & Hashim, J. (2015). Workplace bullying in Malaysia: Incidence, Consequences and role of organisational support. In *Innovation finance and the economy* (pp. 23–35). Cham, Switzerland: Springer.

Hollis, L. (2021). *Human resource perspectives in workplace bullying in higher education: Understanding vulnerable employees.* London: Routledge.

Jagers, N., & Rijken, C. (2014). Prevention of human trafficking for labor exploitation: The role of corporations. *Northwestern University Journal of Human Rights, 12*(1), 47–73.

Kamler, E. (2013). Negotiating narratives of human trafficking: NGOs, communication and the power of culture. *Journal of Intercultural Communication Research, 42*(1), 73–90.

Leon-Perez, J., Escartin, J., & Giorgi, G. (2021). The presence of workplace bullying harassment worldwide. In P. D'Cruz, E. Noronha, G. Notelaers, & C. Rayner (Eds.), *Handbooks of workplace bullying, emotional abuse and harassment: Concepts, approaches and methods* (pp. 55–87). Singapore: Springer.

Leong, L., & Crossman, J. (2016). Tough love or bullying: New nurse transitional experiences. *Journal of Clinical Nursing, 25*(9–10), 1356–1366.

Leymann, H. (1996). The content and development of mobbing at work. *European Journal of Work and Organizational Psychology, 5*(2), 165–184.

Lu, L., & Chou, C. (2017). Long working hours and presenteeism in Asia: A cultural psychological analysis. In C. Cooper & M. Leiter (Eds.), *The Routledge companion to wellbeing at work* (pp. 135–149). New York: Routledge.

Mills, C. (2011). Grappling with the dark side of organisations. *Australian Journal of Communication, 38*(1), 1–19.

Pega, F., Nafradi, B., Momen, N., Ujita, Y., Streicher, K., Pruss-Ustun, A., . . . Woodruff, T. (2021). Global, regional, and national burdens of heart disease and stroke attributable to exposure to long working hours for 194 countries, 2000–2016: A systematic analysis from the WHO/ILO joint estimates of the work-related burden of disease and injury. *Environment International, 154*, 1–15.

Pop, I. (2013). Communicating in fighting the trafficking of human beings. *Journal of Identity and Migration Studies, 7*(2), 64–89.

Proksch, S. (2016). *Conflict management*. Cham, Switzerland: Springer.

Raets, S., & Janssens, J. (2017). Trafficking and technology: Exploring in the role of digital communication technologies in the Belgian human trafficking business. *European Journal on Criminal Policy and Research, 27*(2), 215–238.

Rusnac, L. (2019). Human trafficking as a social phenomenon and media event: Contectualization and speech. *Sociology of Communication, 9*(2), 136–140.

Salas, R., & Didier, K. (2020). California adds human trafficking prevention training to its 7–12 grade curriculum: Should other states follow? *The Clearing House, 93*(1), 12–18.

Samnani, A. (2013). The early stages of workplace bullying and how it becomes prolonged: The role of culture in predicting target responses. *Journal of Business Ethics, 113*(1), 119–132.

Tracy, S., & Redden, S. (2019). The structuration of emotion. In A. Nicotera (Ed.), *Origins and traditions of organizational communication: A comprehensive introduction to the field* (pp. 348–369). New York: Routledge.

Troester, C., & Van Quaquebeke, N. (2020). When victims help their abusive supervisors: The role of LMX, self-blame and guilt. *Academy of Management Journal*. doi:10.5465/amj.2019.0559

Turner, L., & West, R. (2018). *An introduction to communication*. Cambridge: Cambridge University Press.

Yamauchi, T., Sasaki, T., Takahashi, K., Umezaki, S., Takahashi, M., & Yoshikawa, H. (2019). Long working hours, sleep-related problems, and near-misses/injuries in industrial settings using a nationally representative sample of workers in Japan. *PLoS One, 14*(7). doi:10.1371/journal.pone.0219657

14

EMOTIONS AT WORK

Introduction

Emotionality is genetically hardwired in humans (Larson, 2018) so we are all predisposed to experiencing emotion as a temporary, complex, psychological, and physiological state (Eaves & Leathers, 2018). Emotions differ from moods, primarily because emotions tend to focus on a specific target and can be intense and ephemeral but moods are felt more generally and globally (Bowen, 2014).

From the 1990s, scholars have become increasingly interested in how the subjective nature of emotions impact upon the day-to-day life of organisations (Crossman, Bordia, & Mills, 2011; Miller, 2015). Emotional nuances in workplace contexts such as organisational policies and how individuals address one another have the potential to constrain or encourage emotional expression (Miller, 2015; Tracy & Redden, 2019). Sometimes emotions can become highly problematic at work as they do in other contexts. They demand attention because complex, unresolved emotional issues intrude on life and work in undesirable ways and may need the expertise of a therapist (Neenan & Dryden, 2020). Where an underlying emotional disorder exists, complexity can intensify unless a plan for managing a particular condition that includes the intervention of therapeutic experts and a recognition of diversity amongst employees in a particular organisation is in place. Roseman (2018) notes that emotional disorders include bipolar disorder where emotions are felt intensively or psychopathy, where emotions are not expressed or expressed inappropriately. Therapeutic support, however, does not obviate the need for understanding and tolerance of mental ill-health in the workplace. The parameters of this chapter, however, are primarily confined to situations where no serious emotional disorder exists or is otherwise appropriately managed.

DOI: 10.4324/9780429318948-17

Historical roots and the development of ideas about emotions

Charles Darwin (1809–1882) was one of the first scholars to explore the emotions of humans and animals from a scientific perspective. His assessment that emotions were the preserve of women, children, and animals (Ashforth & Humphrey, 1993) resonates with ideas about emotions in the context of the workplace in the twentieth century. During this period,

> organisational literature focused upon rationality and did little to acknowledge or encourage emotions (see Tracy & Redden, 2019). Workplace discourse emphasised masculinity, meritocracy and individuality reflecting prevailing norms (Tracy & Redden, 2019). For some time, the notion that emotions were irrational and a source of 'trouble' with the potential to give rise to harm persisted (Lench & Carpenter, 2018). Conventions about how one expresses emotions both publicly and privately, are known as emotion rules. Such rules are powerful and governed by society (including organisations) (Hochschild, 1979). The fact that emotions were not encouraged in the workplace for much of the last century may indicate something about how resistant to change emotion rules may be. However, by the 21st century, scholars such as Kallas and Reino (2014) were observing how the study of emotions was developing rapidly as a research focus in the discipline of organisational behaviour.

Today, research about emotion is approached from a variety of perspectives (Mayer, 2020), including a functionalist one that assumes individuals are attuned to environmental changes relevant to their wellbeing or personal goals (Karnaze & Levine, 2018). In other words, emotions function as a set of strategies to influence others in a social context (Roseman, 2018). Some work takes an evolutionary perspective. Sociolinguists, for example, have considered the role emotions have played throughout human history in facing danger, loss, or persisting to achieve goals despite any obstacles (Goleman, 2020). Evolution has thus dictated how people respond to everyday situations such that their function is viewed as an impulse to act (Goleman, 2020). In essence, emotions help us to make instantaneous decisions about whether to attack, defend, flee, or care for others (Matsumoto & Hwang, 2012).

The nature of emotions

Hundreds of emotions are captured in languages around the world and some scholars have grouped them into families of related concepts that gather up nuances/blends/mutations of primary emotions (Goleman, 2020). Although some debate exists about which emotions might be regarded as primary, Goleman (2020) is disposed to acknowledge that anger, sadness, fear, enjoyment, love, disgust, and shame rank amongst them. Table 14.1 displays these emotions as primary with the suggestions that Goleman (2020) makes for others that are related to each of them.

TABLE 14.1 Primary and associated emotions

Primary emotion	Associated emotions
Anger	Fury, hostility, annoyance, violence.
Sadness	Grief, sorrow, loneliness, despair, depression.
Fear	Anxiety, terror, panic, phobia.
Enjoyment	Happiness, joy, bliss, euphoria, mania.
Love	Acceptance, friendliness, trust, devotion, kindness.
Disgust	Contempt, aversion, revulsion.
Shame	Guilt, embarrassment, regret, mortification.

ACTIVITY: BRAINSTORMING FOR SYNTHESIS

Brainstorm other emotions not listed in Table 14.1 and add them to one of the existing families associated with a primary emotion. Feel free to use examples from your first language if that does not happen to be English. As you undertake the task, discuss whether these primary emotions are acceptable. Should others be added? Does using another language suggest to you that the primary emotions might be different?

Researchers have undertaken studies to try to learn more about human emotions such as anger, happiness, sadness, fear, and jealousy, and all of them are in evidence in workplace settings and embedded in relationships and communication.

Fear, anxiety, anger, and shame

Emotions such as fear and anxiety serve to motivate people to avoid harm, contamination, or danger in overcoming obstacles (Karnaze & Levine, 2018; Lench & Carpenter, 2018). Human fears are infinitely varied. They can include the fear of rejection, being run over by a car, losing face, or failing in some way (Larson, 2018). Anxiety is tied to future-orientated thinking that entails a level of danger or a threat that exposes personal vulnerabilities (Neenan & Dryden, 2020), and a general apprehension rather than focusing on a specific situation (Larson, 2018). Some anxieties are to be expected. One might be nervous about delivering a presentation for example or negotiating a raise. However, when an inappropriate level of anxiety occurs in response to a given situation, the outcome can disrupt and disable someone's life, leading to an unwarranted focus upon negative rather than positive suppositions (Larson, 2018). Developing a capacity for reflection may be one helpful way to disentangle tangible and rational perceptions of threat and irrational and neurotic fears (Larson, 2018). Most people, however, at some time or another, involuntarily experience anxiety-based automatic negative thoughts

(ANTs) or images/day dreams/fantasies that enter into one's mind without much rational thinking to support them (Neenan & Dryden, 2020).

Like fear and shame, anger is addressed comprehensively in workplace literature and felt at varied levels of intensity and in different forms (Costello, 2020). Anger is often associated with aggressive behaviour, characterised by intimidation designed to demean or manipulate (Neenan & Dryden, 2020). Aggression is to be distinguished from assertion, a more prudent response that may avoid some of the unpleasant consequences of aggression by taking a less demonstrative approach or indeed remaining silent or calm, on occasion (Neenan & Dryden, 2020).

It is possible that anger is more likely to occur where those involved have a low tolerance for frustration. Low frustration tolerance (LFT) refers to the inability of certain individuals to accept frustration or discomfort of some kind and, apart from anger, may result in procrastination (Neenan & Dryden, 2020). Frustration when needs and wants are thwarted, resentment, feelings of injustice, and perceived transgressions are common causes of verbally or physically expressed anger (Larson, 2018; Matsumoto & Hwang, 2012; Neenan & Dryden, 2020). Some evidence suggests that in many Asian societies, loss of face, social humiliation, image issues, ideas about status, and feelings of being discounted and disempowered are more common triggers (Larson, 2018; Neenan & Dryden, 2020). Hurt may be felt for similar reasons but in behavioural terms is more often associated with reactions such as closing off communication, aloofness, and what is sometimes referred to as sulking (Neenan & Dryden, 2020).

Anger is an emotion that essentially functions to change the behaviour of targets and is constructed by some scholars as a strategy for interpersonal coercion or finding an alternative way to achieve a goal that may have otherwise been blocked (Roseman, 2018). Anger has been associated with animus, specific behaviours, and consequences that prove challenging on many levels (Roseman, 2018). It may manifest as other emotions such as despair, jealousy, sadness, contempt, and regret and, in turn, invite retaliation and distancing (Costello, 2020). Angry individuals make threats verbally and physically and work to generate experiences of guilt and other forms of psychological and physical pain (Roseman, 2018). Anger and hostility are hard to disguise because authentic feelings are conveyed nonverbally (Larson, 2018) through facial expressions or foot tapping, for example (Hartley & Chatterton, 2015). Since expressing anger openly at work is uncommon, it may otherwise be communicated through passive aggressive behaviours such as spreading rumours, tardiness, not responding to emails, arriving late to meetings, or failing to engage in them (Costello, 2020; Neenan & Dryden, 2020). Making decisions about how to express anger at work can be a calculated process. Deciding whether to direct anger by yelling or giving someone the silent treatment in order to make a target feel contrite will depend upon how many people are involved, their identity, and target sensitivities and goals (Roseman, 2018). Although the silent treatment (e.g., refusing to communicate verbally with another person and acting as though they do not exist) is a passive form of anger and highly distressing from the perspective of the target.

Another workplace scenario that sometimes occurs is the displacement of anger so that it is misdirected to someone who is not involved in events that originally gave rise to the emotion. For example, when an individual is experiencing some kind of a conflict with a superior, they may feel that it would be circumspect not to show anger but, instead, direct it to peers and co-workers, subordinates, or even family (see Larson, 2018). Displaced anger provides an alternative, similar to venting, but not necessarily a healthy one. The target of the displaced anger is likely to be understandably confused and disaffected in receiving apparently undeserved anger, feel aggrieved, and may withdraw and communicate less (see Larson, 2018). When colleagues begin to restrict communication, performance and wellbeing invariably suffer.

Although anger has unwanted consequences, suppression is not always the best course of action, because doing so may serve to intensify repressive and unhealthy practices and cultures of resentment and cynicism that supervisors would not otherwise be aware of, such as discrimination or unethical events (Geddes, Roberts Callister, & Gibson, 2020). Knowing about wrongdoings that cause anger may in the long term lead to potential improvements to the wellbeing of those working in an organisation (Geddes et al., 2020). A similar perspective is expressed by Larson (2018) who also acknowledges the relationship between public emotion and wellbeing. Listening to an angry person for a short period, however, should not be confused with accepting violent, abusive, or disrespectful behaviour that would obviously not be conducive to the benefits of getting to the bottom of where a problem lies.

Shame arises when someone publicly reveals a negative personal/self – evaluation of an inadequacy of some sort, likely to be shared by the community (Neenan & Dryden, 2020). Some work suggests that it is associated with an individual's heightened desire for perfection so when that perfection is not achieved and shortcomings are laid bare, the result is personally devastating (April & Soomar, 2013). The emotion is often accompanied by feelings of embarrassment and a deep sense of self-contempt (April & Soomar, 2013; Boudewyns, Turner, & Paquin, 2013). Such is the acuteness of the embarrassment that someone ashamed feels to desire to hide, withdraw socially, disappear, and in some cases, die (April & Soomar, 2013; Neenan & Dryden, 2020).

Lay people and some communication researchers often use the terms shame and guilt synonymously (Boudewyns et al., 2013) but there are differences between the two concepts. April and Soomar (2013) maintain that guilt is a psychological mechanism socialised through culture. Shame shares these features. Guilt refers to 'a moral violation or lapse' (Neenan & Dryden, 2020, p. 19) in the context of personally held beliefs and values (April & Soomar, 2013) and arises when someone recognises they have done something wrong that violates those beliefs and values. Guilt and shame differ in that guilt tends to be linked to a specific event but shame is a sense that something is deeply and fundamentally wrong with one's whole self (April & Soomar, 2013). Someone suffering from guilt will be conscious of it and feel a sense of remorse and responsibility for thoughts, feelings, or actions (Boudewyns et al., 2013) that may have hurt or harmed another. Sometimes, a genuine acknowledgement of an error and an apology is all that colleagues and the individual concerned need in order to forgive and move on.

Unlike the experience of guilt, shame is somewhat more complex and difficult to address (Boudewyns et al., 2013). The emotion can be a painful, debilitating negative scrutiny of self (April & Soomar, 2013) so efforts personally and professionally to improve the distress might be regarded as an investment in wellbeing. Acknowledging shame can lead to some positive outcomes such as learning to accept oneself as a vulnerable human being without focusing too much on the potential for criticism by others. Neenan and Dryden (2020) suggest that feelings of shame can be assuaged by separating the behaviour from self, illustrated by them in the observation that one may act foolishly sometimes without necessarily being a fool.

Happiness and sadness

Most theorists agree that happiness is a psychological state (Vitrano, 2014) and a positive emotion that ranges from contentment to elation and expressed prototypically through face, voice and body in ways that may vary depending upon factors such as culture or gender (Messinger et al., 2019). It is hard to describe happiness in simple terms because it is a concept that gathers up so many others. Anand (2018), for example, define it with reference to peace, tranquillity, a zest for life, a sense of meaning, connectedness, clarity, the capacity to be realistic, practical, sensible, and positively anticipating the future. The other perspective Anand (2018) brings to understanding happiness, is that it has no limits in that someone happy can become even happier and in so doing, a normal life can be made extraordinary.

As an emotion, happiness ameliorates cognition, physiology, behaviour, and health and provides individuals with a distraction from everyday concerns (Storbeck & Wylie, 2018). Tandler, Krauss, and Proyer (2020) identified connections between happiness/wellbeing and performance, creativity, engagement, and lower rates of absenteeism. On the other hand, where an employee feels employers have not fulfilled their promises or met expectations and the psychological contract has been breached, the capacity for happiness and thriving in the workplace is diminished. So, given the benefits of being happy, the rationale for reflecting deeply on what makes one happy constitutes a great deal more than simply self-indulgence. Wealth and the comforts of the twenty-first century has not necessarily made people much happier but the quality of personal relationships such as friendships do seem to play a key role (Vitrano, 2014). Similarly, Qaiser, Abid, Arya, and Farooqi (2020) found that in workplace environments, supportive colleagues boost happiness and thriving at work. Karnaze and Levine (2018) suggest that achieving one's goals also contributes to happiness.

ACTIVITY: REFLECTION AND DISCUSSION

Reflect for a few moments on those things that make you feel happy at work (or in some other organisational setting such as a university or an organisation where you volunteer, for example). Make a list of some of those things that come to mind. Compare your list with others, discussing any similarities and differences that you note.

Some of the ideas we have today about happiness are rooted in the works of Greek philosophers such as Plato (428–347 BC), Aristotle (384–322 BC), and Epicurus (341–270 BC). The idea that happiness is achieved by avoiding pain and pursuing pleasure is known as hedonism (Storbeck & Wylie, 2018). Epicurus questioned the idea of hedonism, advising instead that moderation is the pursuit of pleasure and avoidance of painful experiences in order to secure a level of tranquillity (Vitrano, 2014). A eudaimonic perspective on happiness assumes that it is achieved by living virtuously and resisting temptation (Storbeck & Wylie, 2018; Vitrano, 2014). Stoicism is a philosophic school of thought founded by Zeno of Citrium in Athens early in the third century BC that espoused the idea of happiness resulting from virtue (see Anand, 2018). Stoics also maintained that to be happy, humans need to distinguish between what is within and what is beyond one's personal control such that happiness is achieved by remaining apathetic or emotionally unaffected by those unpleasant things that happen beyond our own sphere of influence (Vitrano, 2014). By the nineteenth century, the philosophers Jeremy Bentham (1748–1832) and John Stuart Mill (1806–1873), proponents of utilitarianism (see Chapter 16 on ethics), framed moral actions as those that maximised the happiness or pleasure of everyone influenced by the consequence of the action (Vitrano, 2014). Utilitarianism clearly resonated with the notion of happiness as living virtuously, after the Greek tradition. These ideas, rooted in historical philosophy, are reflected in the work of Segman who maintained early in the twenty-first century that authentic happiness at work was to be found in three orientations: the life of pleasure (via hedonism), engagement (task absorption), and meaning (via eudaimonia); a way of feeling part of something larger than ourselves (cited in Tandler et al., 2020). Much of the workplace wellbeing literature has also been informed by both hedonistic and eudaimonic lenses (Costello, 2020; Scaria, Brandt, Kim, & Lindeman, 2020).

A common antonym of happiness is unhappiness or sadness, caused by painful experiences such as grief, depression, or despair but according to Epicurus, the most common source of unhappiness is fear of some sort (Vitrano, 2014).

Triggers of sadness include (Huron, 2018):

TABLE 14.2 Common causes of sadness

• bereavement	• the end of a relationship	• parenting difficulties	• loneliness
• financial problems	• poor health	• loss of social status	• feeling powerless
• frustrated goals	• insecurity	• injury	• a sense of failure

Whether sadness emanates from personal or professional situations, emotional issues in one area of life almost inevitably spill over to others. Sadness powerfully affects how someone feels and is evident in a gamut of physical, psychological, and behavioural symptoms such as withdrawal, restricted speech, cognitive changes, excessive rumination, anergia and consequent reduced activity, changes in appetite, poor sleep patterns, slumped posture, slow movements, and shallower respiration (Huron, 2018; Karnaze & Levine, 2018). Sadness affects how people approach their work and their workplace relationships in ways that matter. Many organisations know this and provide free access to counselling when feelings of sadness for any of the reasons cited become prolonged and debilitating.

What Huron's (2018) identification of triggers of sadness reveals is that the sources of unhappiness are multifarious. How individuals make a journey back from sadness towards equilibrium, contentment, peace, and happiness will depend on the circumstances specific to each person's situation. For this reason, it is probably unwise to offer generalised prescriptions on how to move from sadness to happiness. Sometimes, time, reflection, and self-awareness will facilitate the journey and sometimes what is required is much more messy and requires help from professional and personal supports in our networks. The other thing to consider is that sadness as an emotion, is not necessarily a bad thing but a normal response to some kinds of experiences.

In many ways, this section ends with a version of how it began. That is, by providing an idea of what it means in practical terms to be happy. If one can envision happiness, it can provide a map for moving forward and appreciating our progress towards it. Anand (2018) provides a clear account of what constitutes a state of happiness and his work is the basis of and inspiration for the remarks that follow.

1. Self-acceptance

Self-acceptance means that we accept those aspects of ourselves that we would find very hard to change. Rather than suppressing them, one might observe those behaviours with a lighter perspective and self-awareness in ways that allow for a little more humour in our self-assessments and understanding why we are the way we are.

2. Proportional reactions

Proportional reactions are those that appear to respond in an appropriate manner to the nature of events as they are presented. Responses appear reasonable and are neither perceived as excessive or insensitive to what has occurred.

3. Ability to 'switch off'

Being able to think about and worry less about work during weekends, evenings and holidays.

4. Decisive calls on controllable factors

If the matter is under your control and you can do something about it, you will think and act decisively and even if the decision proves unwise in some way, you will learn the lesson and move on. If the issue is uncontrollable, you will not spend undue time on what others might have done and you did not do.

5. Accurate decision making

Invest in exploring rational explanations of the circumstances that are based on empirical evidence.

6. Bounce back from setbacks

With some forward planning and reflection setbacks have less of a negative impact because preparing for them will reconstruct them as anticipated events.

7. Easy and confident body language

Confident, warm, and expansive body language connotes a relaxed and peace-loving impression. Attentiveness is displayed through active listening. It is useful to notice and reflect upon personal body language. Folded arms and clenched fists (closed postures) can appear defensive and aggressive to others. Sometimes opening up the palms not only helps someone to feel more relaxed but can also put others at their ease.

8. A happy person sleeps deeply and wakes up rejuvenated and ready for the day to unfold

9. Lucid dreams

Lucid dreams are those when you are aware of the fact that you are dreaming and have a sense of being able to direct dreams in a way that you wish. However, letting them unfold without intervention can bring insights into one's personal subconscious.

10. Feeling connected

Feeling connected is tied to the notion of accepting others for who they are, both their faults and more attractive characteristics. It relates to the recognition that others, like ourselves, are made up of complexities and that no one is perfect.

11. Feeling secure and grateful

Even when suffering at times when things are not working out well, it is still possible to be happy by acknowledging and feeling grateful for those things in life that remain and are personally valued.

12. Efforts are focused and also relaxed

Efforts in achieving goals are focused but counterbalanced by the attitude that in doing one's best, there is no need to be regretful about not having tried hard enough.

13. Mindfulness

Even when busy, listen to your body. (See Part I on mindfulness.)

14. A zest for life

A sense of youthful engagement towards all that you encounter

15. Neither excited nor bored

A sense of calm prevails even in times when life is somewhat predictable

16. Seeing the world as it is

Having a sense of clarity about the world as it is and separating that from any unhelpful thoughts about oneself that may cloud perceptions and judgements. Your ego no longer drives what you do.

17. Heroic and humble

Balancing feelings of confidence and bravery that come through a mind filtered by rationality and at the same time recognising that our personal place in the universe and the great scheme of things gives rise to humility.

ACTIVITY: REFLECTION

Reflect upon each of these 17 conditions of happiness. Consider those that resonate with your experience now and those that do not. It may help to compose a personal journal entry of your thoughts to evaluate your own level of happiness. Which of the 17 conditions helped you to identify ways in which you can foster your own sense of happiness at work more proactively?

Jealousy

Jealousy is usually explored in the context of romantic relationships and constructed as an actual or imagined threat to a relationship posed by another (Neenan & Dryden, 2020). It is characterised by Yong and Li (2018) as a form of hyper-vigilance in the protection of a valuable relationship. Romantic relationships do occur at work but there are other triggers of jealousy such as those caused by seeing others as a competitive threat on a regular basis (Yong & Li, 2018). Some workplace cultures that cultivate highly competitive environments can be harmful and encourage jealousy directly or indirectly. In the worst of cases, jealousy has been known to create great distress, paranoid stalking, or violent aggression (Yong & Li, 2018).

Envy as an emotion is often confused with jealousy but is best described as a coveted desire to possess the advantages or good fortune of another (Neenan & Dryden, 2020). An employee may envy the perks enjoyed by a senior staff member (company car, business class tickets, an entertainment budget) or the success enjoyed by others in reaching personal goals. Self-acceptance can help to lessen the impact of unpleasant emotions like jealousy and envy but where self-esteem/self-worth is compromised by the desire for things one does not have, the result can be personally damaging and may flag the need for therapeutic assistance (Neenan & Dryden, 2020).

Emotional labour (EL)

Arlie Hochschild (1979, 1983) produced seminal work on emotional labour experienced by Delta flight attendants and another study concerned with debt collection. Her contribution to the field has informed studies in the decades that have followed in a variety of sectors and disciplines.

Organisations are able to control and manage the expression of emotions both formally and informally and can have both functional and dysfunctional implications for wellbeing (Hatzinikolakis & Crossman, 2021). The concept of EL explains how the public display of emotions in organisational contexts is managed and sold by employees for a wage as an exchange value (Hatzinikolakis & Crossman, 2010). In simple terms, EL involves concealing genuine emotions or indeed manufacturing emotions to comply with organisational expectations. Hochschild (1983) distinguished between surface and deep acting whereby surface acting pertained to a conscious strategy to influence others and deep acting where an actor genuinely begins to feel an emotion, thereby unconsciously aligning personal emotions with organisational expectations. Emotional labour does not generally lend itself well to employee wellbeing, however. Expressing inauthentic or false selves at odds with personal identities can cause suffering at work (Tracy & Redden, 2019) and appears to extend to national cultures around the world (Jia, Cheng, & Hale, 2017). It can contribute to burnout (Miller, 2015), stress, frustration, loss of autonomy, and consequent feelings of disempowerment (Hatzinikolakis & Crossman, 2021).

Like leadership, it is influenced by culture and one recent study undertaken in China exploring the relationship between teacher commitment, leadership and emotional labour illustrates the value of research studies being conducted in a variety of cultural contexts (Zheng, Shi, & Liu, 2021). This study revealed how paternalistic leadership, rooted in Confucianism, is a leadership style common in East Asia and the Middle East that entails both fatherly benevolence and strong authority. Zheng et al. (2021) concluded that school leaders may be able to adopt benevolent leadership practices to facilitate commitment through managing teacher emotions. What this study suggests, more broadly, is the complexity of emotional labour and how culture will affect a variety of factors that impact on emotional labour.

Communication and emotions

Part of communicating effectively is appreciating the experience, expression, management, regulation and influence of emotions (Goodwin, 2019). Some literature suggests not all emotions are expressed as felt in the workplace in that some are more likely to be displayed and others concealed. For example, happiness is expressed as felt or with less intensity, sadness/anger is generally not displayed or de-emphasised, disgust, and fear are rarely displayed and fear/anxiety/frustration may manifest as aggression/withdrawal (see Amanatullah, Morris, & Curhan, 2008; Diefendorff & Greguras, 2009; Druckman & Olekalns, 2008; Lieberman, 2006). Working out what someone is actually feeling is no easy matter and thus paying attention to verbal and nonverbal signals as well as context and adopting active listening (see Part I) is essential (De Janasz, Crossman, Campbell, & Power, 2014). The attention to how emotions are communicated is warranted because employee emotions arising from daily communication are a powerful means of building and maintaining relationships for the betterment of the employee experience (Jia et al., 2017) and, thus, wellbeing.

Emotions are more readily communicated nonverbally than verbally. Tone of voice, gestures, facial expressions, and posture are all clues to felt emotions. Eaves and Leathers (2018) suggest that posture is an important nonverbal way of communicating emotions such as anxiety, fear, and contempt through head tilting and stiffness, for example. Dislike, they suggest, is expressed in postures such as limited gestures, visual inattentiveness, closed posture, and bodily tension. Positive emotions, they maintain, may be detected in cues such as leaning forward, adopting an open body posture, adopting affirmative head nods, close interpersonal distances, relaxed posture, touching, smiling, and postural mirroring (exhibiting similar or congruent postures). Emotion Recognition Ability (ERA) is generally considered to be a positive aspect of emotional intelligence, and conducive to empathy (see Buck, Graham, Ryan, & Hancock, 2020; Schlegel, 2020). It is a skill that contributes to social and professional success and refers to individuals who are able to recognise and label emotions such as sadness, happiness, anger, and disgust that are communicated nonverbally (Schlegel, 2020).

Culture and emotions

Part of the discussion in the literature of emotional expression in cultural contexts over recent decades has been devoted to the consideration of whether universal meanings can be identified in human emotions (see Jack, 2013; Sauter, Eisner, Ekman, & Scott, 2015). Some consensus has been reached based on studies about emotions across cultures that all humans experience emotions but cultural norms influence how emotions are displayed or regulated in the presence of others (Davis et al., 2012; Sadeh & Ziber, 2019). As an illustration, Goleman (2020) explains that while sadness through grief is felt regardless of culture, how they are displayed or withheld for private moments depends upon one's cultural upbringing. Paul Ekman uses the term 'display rules' to describe social conventions about which feelings can be shared or not (Goleman, 2020). Display rules may minimise or exaggerate the expression of emotion from a relative perspective.

In the latest edition of their book, entitled, *Riding the waves of culture: Understanding diversity in global business*, Trompenaars and Hampden-Turner (2020) discuss how cultures tend to be more or less neutral or affective. They argue that those who come from cultures that encourage neutral displays of emotions tend to control and subdue their expression and be somewhat self-possessed in their conduct. Those people who live in affective cultures tend to express their feelings with fewer inhibitions by smiling, laughing, gesturing or scowling, for example. National cultures such as Finland and Norway are highly neutral but Singapore, Hong Kong, Japan, Australia, Canada, South Korea, and China when ranked on a continuum are also considered to be neutral cultures (Trompenaars & Hampden-Turner, 2020). Although people from neutral cultures tend to repress emotions, this does not mean that they never express anger or explode, especially under pressure (Trompenaars & Hampden-Turner, 2020). Everyone has their limits! Described as affective cultures, Kuwait, Egypt, Spain, Saudi Arabia, Venezuela, the Philippines, Russia, and France are those where animated expressions tend to be admired both verbally and nonverbally (Trompenaars & Hampden-Turner, 2020).

China as an emotionally neutral culture, has a long tradition of moderating emotions, cooling hot emotions and calming agitations in order to maintain homeostasis (Krone & Morgan, 2000). One illustrative study (Davis et al., 2012) involved showing participants pictures to arouse certain emotions, and found that Chinese people regulated their emotions more than those in the US. Specifically, Chinese men regulated their emotions more than men in the US, Chinese females regulated emotions slightly less that Chinese males and US women regulated emotions less than US men. Finally, ethnic Chinese Americans regulate less than non-US Chinese participants, suggesting that enculturation moderates emotional display.

Trompenaars and Hampden-Turner (2020) also suggest that people from affective cultures interacting with neutrals may find it useful to ask for time out if emotions become hard to deal with and those from affective cultures should be aware that an apparent lack of emotional expression should not be interpreted as boredom or disinterest. At the same time, the authors argue that people from neutral cultures should not assume that those from affective ones have made up their minds in a negotiation, for example, even if they appear to be vehemently emotional in expressing some concerns. These observations aside, in negotiation an offer is more likely to be accepted when emotions displayed by both parties are consistent with cultural expectations (Trompenaars & Hampden-Turner, 2020). As Kopelman and Rosette (2008) observed, inconsistent emotional and cultural norms can damage relationships and prospects so learning something about the conventions of parties and the degree to which they regulate emotions is wise.

Although Hall (1973), an eminent and seminal scholar in cultural theory, asserted all emotions were saturated in culture, culture is not, however, the only influence on emotional display. Children learn emotion rules from feedback provided by families and communities in ways that vary within cultures (Buck, Graham et al., 2020; Larson, 2018). Individual personalities will also make a difference to emotional display. This is why generalisations about culture and its influence upon emotional expression may need to be modified as relationships deepen.

Emotional intelligence (EI)

For some decades, theorists and practitioners have become aware of the importance of interpersonal ability and specifically what has now become known as emotional intelligence (Hartley & Chatterton, 2015). Following a period where emotional intelligence (like care and empathy) was far from rewarded and underrated in organisations (Tracy & Redden, 2019), this is, in many quarters, a welcomed development. EI is a significant line of enquiry in the study of emotions and their communication. Peter Salovey and John Mayer (see Mayer, DiPaolo, & Salovey, 1990) and Daniel Goleman (1997, 2000, 2020) are arguably the most influential scholars of EI, contributing seminal works that have informed the field for decades. Salovey, a professor at Yale, first proposed the idea of emotional intelligence and his graduate student, John Mayer, later published in the same area (Goleman, 2020). IQ only accounts for about 20 percent of the factors that contribute to success in life with EI/EQ (emotional quotient), social class and luck contributing to the other 80 per cent (Goleman, 2020) so addressing our own EI will have a considerable impact upon our personal and working lives.

Salovey and Mayer (1990) defined EI as a set of skills that enable people to express, appraise, and regulate their own emotions and those of others to motivate, plan for, and achieve in life. In the decades since Salovey's and Mayer's (1990) work, few have veered far from this original conception. Owens and Daul-Elhindi (2020) and Mullins (2010) described it as an ability to perceive, process, understand, and manage emotions in self and others. Dwyer (2020) refers to EI as an ability to recognise, regulate, and respond to personal emotions and those of others in productive ways. Goleman (2020) also draws on how emotions motivate individuals and suggests that, in addition, they help in encouraging persistence in achieving goals, dealing with frustration, managing any delays of gratification, regulating mood, ensuring distress doesn't cloud thinking, developing empathy, and feeling hope. Emotional intelligence, however, like other forms of intelligence, varies from one individual to another. Some findings suggest that gender-based emotional miscommunications, for example, are related to women being able to express higher levels of positive emotions and emotional intelligence than men (Larson, 2018).

EI is a critical aspect of developing meaningful, rewarding, interpersonal relationships and communication across a range of situations and professions including business, education, and nursing, with implications for wellbeing. For example, a recent study of nurses in one Chinese hospital found positive correlations among emotional intelligence, communication, and job wellbeing (Li, Feng, Wang, Geng, & Chang, 2021). High levels of EI can also reduce many barriers to communication and address conflict in workplaces (Goodwin, 2019; Malone, 2017). The emotional intelligence of leaders may also influence employer turnover intention (Mohammad, Chai, Aun, & Migin, 2014) so recruiting managers with emotional intelligence should represent a priority.

Emotional intelligence is a concept based on a composite of communication skills and behaviours defined in the literature (see Buck, Graham et al., 2020; Crossman et al., 2011; Goleman, 2020; Goodwin, 2019; Pradarelli, Shimizu, & Smink, 2020; Proksch, 2016). Empathy as a form of sensitivity that enables people to appreciate the feelings of others (Crossman et al., 2011; Proksch, 2016) is an essential element of communicating interpersonally and an aspect of EI. Learned experientially from infancy through touch and other interactions, emotional empathy is a shared signal system involving displays by a sender with a pre-attuned notion that gives attention to the needs of a receiver (see Buck, Stifano, Graham, & Allred, 2020). Those with a high level of EI also demonstrate a level of self-awareness, that is, an ability to be realistically aware of personal feelings and what drives them (Proksch, 2016). They also have a capacity for self-regulation relating to expertise in dealing with emotions in order to accomplish certain tasks, delaying gratification as necessary, and demonstrating a level of resilience in being able to bounce back from emotional strain (see Goodwin, 2019; Proksch, 2016). EI is associated with being able to deal with emotions in order to accomplish certain tasks, delay gratification as necessary, and command sufficient resilience to bounce back from emotional strain (see Goodwin, 2019; Proksch, 2016). EI also appears to encompass social skills and interacting with others that in turn depend upon comprehending social situations and relational networks (Proksch, 2016). Other capacities associated with EI include active listening and knowing how to ask the right questions (Pradarelli et al., 2020), transparency, authenticity, and engagement (Goodwin, 2019). These aspects of EI collectively encompass sophisticated communication skills necessary to persuade, lead, negotiate, and mediate (see Proksch, 2016).

It is possible to learn how to improve emotional intelligence (Gilar-Corbi, Pozo-Rico, Sanchez, & Castejon, 2018; Goleman, 2020; Larson, 2018; Li et al., 2021) and specifically to understand and change personal emotional responses to events at work. Doing so has advantages for both employees and organisations in that EI is associated with communication effectiveness, improved teamwork, relationship building (Hendon, Powell, & Wimmer, 2017), productivity, satisfaction, market share, and fewer resignations (Goleman, 2020).

One useful technique is known as the ABC model, used in CBT. The ABC model is a mnemonic, originally developed by Albert Ellis who formed a structure to illustrate a theory about how human behaviour acts upon events, thoughts, and beliefs with emotional consequences (Neenan & Dryden, 2020), illustrated as follows:

- ACTIVATING event: A colleague is promoted faster than Ms Wong (A)
- BELIEFS & thoughts: Ms Wong experiences beliefs and thoughts about her efforts not being appreciated at work (B)
- Emotional CONSEQUENCES: In consequence, emotional and behavioural issues become prominent in the form of depression and disengagement from work (C).

Neenan and Dryden (2020) explain the ABC model in detail. They claim that A-C thinking, (the assumption that A causes C) is, however, often misguided because the decision to promote Ms Wong's peer may be entirely unrelated to how her own performance is perceived. When feelings are inappropriate or problematic, they can be altered by adding D (disrupting, discussing, or questioning self-defeating beliefs) and E (effect or consequence of challenging the self-defeating beliefs or feelings) to the model. When upsetting self-defeating beliefs are questioned or disrupted, it serves to help people to view them more objectively, regarding them as hypotheses, beliefs, or assumptions rather than facts and considering other explanations for events and behaviours. Useful questions for individuals to pose, as part of the process of disruption, might be (see Neenan & Dryden, 2020);

1. If this thought is true, how would I cope with the situation?
2. If others were forming such negative judgements and assumptions about themselves, how would I respond to them? Why might I judge myself more harshly than I would another in the same situation? What advice would I offer that I may not be heeding for myself at this time?
3. What evidence is available to refute or support the thoughts and feelings I have?

It is also helpful to reflect upon possible distortions of events and personal patterns of thinking that can create upsetting emotions. Some examples of these are: exaggerating negative thoughts and minimising positive ones, attributing too much personal blame for events for which one is not wholly responsible, believing something is true because personal feelings are so strong, or attaching a negative global label to oneself in response to a singular or specific behaviour (Neenan & Dryden, 2020).

Conclusion

This chapter has explored the history of studying emotions in organisational contexts, the nature of emotions, and how they influence behaviour and relationships in the workplace, influenced as they are by a variety of factors including culture. Employers are now actively seeking recruits with skills in communication and emotional intelligence (Goleman, 2020; Hendon et al., 2017) so it behoves applicants to build their skills in these areas to improve their opportunities for employment.

Workplaces and educational institutions can also play an important role in introducing studies in EI into the curriculum and providing training courses in the workplace because, as the studies cited suggest, they work (assuming they are well designed and based on empirical evidence by experts). Some literature suggests that by investing in the development of employee EI training, organisations can make a return on their investments by 400 per cent (Goleman, 2020). At the very minimum, they should build in processes to include feedback on emotional intelligence (Goleman, 2020) and integrate clear linkages to EI through performance management.

References

Amanatullah, E., Morris, M., & Curhan, J. (2008). Negotiators who gave too much: Unmitigated communion, relational anxieties, and economic costs in distributive and integrative bargaining. *Journal of Personality and Social Psychology, 95*(3), 723–738.

Anand, R. (2018). *Happiness at work: Mindfulness, analysis and well-being.* Thousand Oaks: Sage.

April, K., & Soomar, Z. (2013). Female breadwinners: Resultant feelings of guilt and shame. *Effective Executive, 16*(4), 32–47.

Ashforth, B., & Humphrey, R. (1993). Emotional labor in service roles: The influence of identity. *Academy of Management Review, 18*(1), 86–115.

Boudewyns, V., Turner, M., & Paquin, R. (2013). Shame-free guilt appeals: Testing the emotional and cognitive effects of shame and guilt free appeals. *Psychology and Marketing, 30*(9), 811–825.

Bowen, J. (2014). Emotion in organizations: Resources for business educators. *Journal of Management Education, 38*(1), 114–142.

Buck, R., Graham, B., Ryan, A., & Hancock, R. (2020). Nonverbal receiving ability as emotional and cognitive empathy: Conceptualization and measurement. In R. Sternberg & A. Kostic (Eds.), *Social intelligence and nonverbal communication* (pp. 21–49). Cham, Switzerland: Springer.

Buck, R., Stifano, S., Graham, B., & Allred, R. (2020). Empathy as spontaneous communication. At the intersection of the traditional social and behavioural sciences and the new affective and communication sciences. In R. Sternberg & A. Kostic (Eds.), *Social intelligence and nonverbal communication* (pp. 51–77). Cham, Switzerland: Springer.

Costello, J. (2020). *Workplace wellbeing: A relational approach.* London: Routledge.

Crossman, J., Bordia, S., & Mills, C. (2011). *Business communication for the global age.* Sydney: McGraw-Hill.

Davis, E., Greenberger, E, Charles, S., Chen, C., Zhao, L., & Dong, Q. (2012). Emotion experience and regulation in China and the United States: How do culture and gender shape emotion responding? *International Journal of Psychology, 47*(3), 230–239.

De Janasz, S., Crossman, J., Campbell, N., & Power, M. (2014). *Interpersonal skills in organisations*. Sydney: McGraw-Hill Education.

Diefendorff, J., & Greguras, G. (2009). Contextualizing emotional display rules: Examining the roles of targets and discrete emotions in shaping display rule perceptions. *Journal of Management, 35*(4), 880–898.

Druckman, D., & Olekalns, M. (2008). Emotions in negotiation. *Group Decision Negotiation, 17*(1), 1–11.

Dwyer, J. (2020). *Communication for business and the professions: Strategies and skills*. Retrieved from http://ebookcentral.proquest.com

Eaves, M., & Leathers, D. (2018). *Successful nonverbal communication: Principles and applications* (5th ed.). New York: Routledge. doi:10.4324/9781315542317

Geddes, D., Roberts Callister, R., & Gibson, D. (2020). A message in the madness: Functions of workplace anger in organizational life. *Academy of Management Perspectives, 34*(1), 28–47.

Gilar-Corbi, R., Pozo-Rico, T., Sanchez, T., & Castejon, J. (2018). Can emotional competence be taught in higher education? A randomized experimental study of an emotional intelligence training program using a multimethodological approach. *Frontiers in Psychology, 9*, 1–11.

Goleman, D. (1997). *Emotional intelligence: Why it can matter more than IQ*. New York: Bantham Books.

Goleman, D. (2000). *Working with emotional intelligence*. New York: Bantham Books.

Goleman, D. (2020). *Emotional intelligence: Why it can matter more than IQ*. London: Bloomsbury Publishing.

Goodwin, J. (2019). *Communication accommodation theory: Finding the right approach. Returning to the interpersonal dialogue and understanding human communication in the digital age* (pp. 168–185). Hershey, PA: IGI Global. doi:10.4018/98-1-5225-4168-4.ch008

Hall, E. (1973). *The silent language*. New York: Doubleday Anchor Press.

Hartley, P., & Chatterton, P. (2015). *Business communication: Rethinking your professional practice for the post digital age* (2nd ed.). London: Routledge.

Hatzinikolakis, J., & Crossman, J. (2010). Are business academics in Australia experiencing emotional labour? A call for empirical research. *Journal of Management and Organization, 16*(3), 425–435.

Hatzinikolakis, J., & Crossman, J. (2021). The management of emotional labour in the work of Australian university business school academics and the implications for well-being. In S. Dhiman (Ed.), *The Palgrave handbook of workplace well-being* (pp. 1165–1185). Cham, Switzerland: Springer. doi:10.1007/978-3-030_30025-8_43

Hendon, M., Powell, L., & Wimmer, H. (2017). Emotional intelligence and communication levels in information technology professionals. *Computers in Human Behaviour, 71*, 165–171.

Hochschild, A. (1983). *The managed heart*. Berkeley: The University of California Press.

Hochschild, A. (1979). Emotion work, feeling rules, and social structure. *American Journal of Sociology, 85*(2), 551–575.

Huron, D. (2018). On the functions of sadness and grief. In H. Lench (Ed.), *The functions of emotions* (pp. 59–91). Cham, Switzerland: Springer.

Jack, R. (2013). Culture and facial expressions of emotions. *Visual Cognition, 21*(9–10), 1248–1286.

Jia, M., Cheng, J., & Hale, C. (2017). Workplace emotion and communication supervision nonverbal immediacy: Employees' emotion experience and communication motives. *Management Communication Quarterly, 31*(1), 69–87.

Kallas, E., & Reino, A. (2014). Interactions between emotion-evoking events and organisational culture: An example of Estonian service companies. *Journal of Management and Change, 32–33*(1–2), 56–76.

Karnaze, M., & Levine, L. (2018). Sadness, the architect of cognitive change. In H. Lench (Ed.), *The functions of emotion* (pp. 45–58). Cham, Switzerland: Springer.

Kopelman, S., & Rosette, A. (2008). Cultural variation in response to strategic emotions. *Group Decision Negotiation, 17*(1), 65–77.

Krone, K., & Morgan, J. (2000). Emotion metaphors in management: The Chinese experience. In S. Fineman (Ed.), *Emotion in organizations* (pp. 83–101). London: Sage.

Larson, K. (2018). *Adaption and well-being.* London: Routledge.

Lench, H., & Carpenter, Z. (2018). What do emotions do for us? In H. Lench (Eds.), *The functions of emotions.* Cham, Switzerland: Springer. doi:10.1007/978-3-319-77619-4_1

Li, X., Feng, X., Wang, L., Geng, X., & Chang, H. (2021). Relationship between emotional intelligence and job well-being in Chinese registered nurses: Mediating effect of communicating satisfaction. *Nursing Open, 8*(4), 1778–1787.

Lieberman, A. (2006). The A list of emotions in mediation from anxiety to agreement. *Dispute Resolution Journal, 61*(1), 46–50.

Malone, L. (2017). Dealing with conflict. In D. Stanley (Ed.), *Clinical leadership in nursing and healthcare: Values into action* (pp. 215–233). Chichester: John Wiley & Sons Ltd.

Matsumoto, D., & Hwang, H. (2012). Culture and emotion: The integration of biological and cultural contribution. *Journal of Cross-Cultural Psychology, 43*(1), 91–118.

Mayer, C. (2020). *Intercultural mediation and conflict management training: A guide for professionals and academics.* Cham, Switzerland: Springer.

Mayer, J., DiPaolo, M., & Salovey, P. (1990). Perceiving affective content in ambiguous visual stimuli: A component of emotional intelligence. *Journal of Personal Assessment, 54*(3/4), 772–781.

Messinger, D., Mitsven, S., Ahn, Y., Prince, E., Sun, L., & Rivero-Fernandez, C. (2019). Happiness and joy. In V. LoBue, K. Perez-Edgar, & K. Buss (Eds.), *Handbook of emotional development* (pp. 171–198). Cham, Switzerland: Springer.

Miller, K. (2015). *Organizational communication: Approaches and processes* (7th ed.) Stamford, CT: Cengage.

Mohammad, F., Chai, L., Aun, L., & Migin., M., (2014). Emotional intelligence and turnover intention. *International Journal of Academic Research, 6*(4), 211–220.

Mullins, L. (2010). *Management and organisational behaviour* (9th ed.). Hoboken, NJ: Prentice Hall, Financial Times.

Neenan, M., & Dryden, W. (2020). *Cognitive behavioural coaching: A guide to problem-solving and personal development.* Oxford: Taylor & Francis Group.

Owens, T., & Daul-Elhindi, C. (2020). *The 360 librarian: A framework for integrating mindfulness, emotional intelligence, and critical reflection in the workplace.* Chicago: Association of College and Research Libraries.

Pradarelli, J., Shimizu, N., & Smink, D. (2020). Important terms in wellbeing. In E. Kim & B. Lindeman (Eds.), *Wellbeing* (pp. 23–30). Cham, Switzerland: Springer.

Proksch, S. (2016). *Conflict management.* Cham, Switzerland: Springer.

Qaiser, S., Abid, G., Arya, B., & Farooqi, S. (2020). Nourishing the bliss: Antecedents and mechanisms of happiness at work. *Total Quality Management, 31*(15), 1669–1683.

Roseman, I. (2018). Functions of anger in the emotion system. In H. Lench (Ed.), *The functions of emotions* (pp. 141–173). Cham, Switzerland: Springer.

Sadeh, L., & Ziber, T. (2019). Bringing together: Emotions and power in organizational responses to institutional complexity. *Academy of Management Journal, 62*(5), 1413–1443.

Salovey, P., & Mayer, J. (1990). Emotional intelligence. *Imagination, Cognition and Personality, 9*(3), 185–211.

Sauter, D., Eisner, F., Ekman, P., & Scott, S. (2015). Emotional vocalizations are recognized across cultures regardless of the valance of distractors. *Psychological Science, 26*(3), 354–356.

Scaria, D., Brandt, M., Kim, E., & Lindeman, B. (2020). What is wellbeing? In E. Kim & B. Lindeman (Eds.), *Wellbeing* (pp. 3–11). Cham, Switzerland: Springer.

Schlegel, K. (2020). Inter- and intrapersonal downsides of accurately perceiving others' emotions. In R. Sternberg & A. Kostic (Eds.), *Social intelligence and nonverbal communication* (pp. 359–395). Cham, Switzerland: Palgrave Macmillan.

Storbeck, J., & Wylie, J. (2018). The functional and dysfunctional aspects of happiness: Cognitive, physiological, behavioural and health considerations. In H. Lench (Ed.), *The functions of emotions* (pp. 195–220). Cham, Switzerland: Springer.

Tandler, N., Krausss, A., & Proyer, R. (2020). Authentic happiness at work: Self-and peer-rated orientations to happiness, work satisfaction and stress coping. *Frontiers in Psychology, 11*, 1–16.

Tracy, S., & Redden, S. (2019). The structuration of emotion. In A. Nicotera (Ed.), *Origins and traditions of organizational communication: A comprehensive introduction to the field* (pp. 348–369). New York: Routledge.

Trompenaars, F., & Hampden-Turner, C. (2020). *Riding the waves of culture: Understanding diversity in global business* (4th ed.). New York: McGraw-Hill.

Vitrano, C. (2014). *The nature and value of happiness*. New York: Routledge.

Yong, J., & Li, N. (2018). The adaptive functions of jealousy. In H. Lench (Ed.), *The functions of emotions* (pp. 121–140). Cham, Switzerland: Springer.

Zheng, X., Shi, X., & Liu, Y. (2021). Leading teachers' emotions like parents: Relationships between paternalistic leadership, emotional labour and teacher commitment in China. *Frontiers in Psychology, 11*, 1–9. doi:10.3389/fpsyg.2020.00519

INDEX

Page numbers in **bold** indicate a table on the corresponding page.